D. M. SHAPIRO

3 September 1990

The Grants Economy and Collective Consumption

Most of economics is written on the implicit assumption that goods and services are produced by enterprises that sell them in a market and thus recover the costs of their production, expanding if demand requires it, contracting if demand is lacking, always under the guidance of the market. But in reality a large proportion of all goods and services are produced and consumed outside the market system. At least until very recently this proportion has constantly increased. Sometimes these goods and services are provided free. Sometimes a charge is made. Sometimes it is expected that charges will come near to covering costs and sometimes it is recognised that a service must be considerably subsidised. In addition a large number of educational and cultural activities depend wholly or very largely on grants from a variety of grant-giving institutions.

The International Economic Association Conference that is recorded in this book was in large measure breaking new ground. It aimed to establish, for a variety of countries, the extent to which collective consumption prevails, the criteria they use to determine what shall be in the market sector and what in the collective sector, how to hold the balance between collective and personal consumption and yet provide incentives, the principles that should determine whether in a particular case services should be provided free or a charge made, and more generally the defects and difficulties of operating a system of collective consumption.

The countries whose problems, experiences and thinking are analysed range from the USA and Switzerland as predominantly private enterprise countries with, nevertheless, a considerable grants economy, through West Germany, the United Kingdom, the Netherlands, Norway and Japan as mixed economies, to Yugoslavia, Poland, Hungary and the USSR, where in predominantly socialist economies many of the same problems of the financing and pricing of collective consumption and the division between collective and individual consumption equally arise. And apart from these countries, some of the relevant experience of a number of others has been contributed by participants in the course of the discussions, recorded by G. B. Stafford, which as in all IEA volumes are almost as interesting as the papers.

The authors include K. Boulding (the first to explore this subject), M. A. H. Dempster, H. Leibenstein (USA), B. Frey (Switzerland), A. Boltho (FRG), L. Pliatsky (UK), A. J. Meys (Netherlands), A. Sandmo (Norway), H. Uzawa (Japan), E. I. Kapustin (USSR), M. Pohorille (Poland), R. Hoch (Hungary).

R. C. O. Matthews, who as chairman of the Programme Committee had planned the conference, contributes an overview of the issues, written beforehand and discussed in the final session of the Conference. He and G. B. Stafford, in the introduction to the book, sum up the work of the Conference in retrospect.

The Grants Economy and Collective Consumption

Proceedings of a Conference held by the International Economic Association at Cambridge, England

Edited by

R. C. O. MATTHEWS

and

G. B. STAFFORD

First published 1982 by
THE MACMILLAN PRESS LTD
London and Basingstoke
Companies and representatives throughout the world

ISBN 0 333 28600 6

Printed in Hong Kong

Contents

Acknowledgements

The holding of the Conference recorded in this volume was made possible by generous grants made for the purpose by the Nuffield Foundation, the British Academy, the Bank of England and the Royal Economic Society. To all these we express our most grateful thanks. The continuing work of the International Economic Association has been made possible by the support of UNESCO and the Ford Foundation. To both of them we also wish to express our gratitude.

The Conference was held in Sidney Sussex College, Cambridge. To the Master and Fellows of the College and to our other hosts in Cambridge University we owe the pleasure of meeting in a most congenial academic setting.

Programme Committee

R. C. O. Matthews (Chairman)
S. Tsuru (President of IEA)
K. Boulding
B. Csikós-Nagy
L. Johansen
P. Maillet
E. I. Kapustin

List of Participants

Professor Tamacs Bacskai, National Bank of Hungary, Budapest, Hungary

Mr Andrea Boltho, Magdalen College, Oxford, England

Professor Dieter Bös, Institute für Gesellschafts und Wirtschaftswissenschaften der Universität Bonn, West Germany

Professor Kenneth Boulding, Institute of Behavioural Science, University of Colorado at Boulder, USA

Dr Michael Dempster, International Institute for Applied Systems Analysis, Laxenburg, Austria

Professor Luc Fauvel, Secretary General, International Economics Association, Paris, France

Professor Bruno Frey, Institute for Empirical Economic Research, University of Zurich, Switzerland

Professor Horst Hanusch, Lehrstuhl für Volkswirtschaftslehre V, Augsburg, FRG

Dr Robert Hoch, MTA Közgazdasgtudomanyi Intézet, Budapest, Hungary

Dr Zoran Jašić, Ekonomski Institut, Zagreb, Yugoslavia

Dr Pero Jurković, Ekonomski Institut, Zagreb, Yugoslavia

Professor E. I. Kapustin, Institute of Economy of the Academy of Science of the USSR, Moscow, USSR

Mr Michael Kaser, St Antony's College, Oxford, England

Professor T. S. Khachaturov, Association of Soviet Economic Scientific Institutions, Moscow, USSR

Professor Rudolf Klein, University of Bath, Bath, England

Professor Harvey Leibenstein, Harvard University, Cambridge, Massachusetts, USA

Professor Pierre Maillet, Centre Interuniversitaire de Recherches en Science Humaines, Lille, France

Professor Gunter Manz, Hochschule für Okonomie Bruno Leuschner Berlin, GDR

Mr Robin Matthews, Clare College, Cambridge, England

Mr Th. A. J. Meys, Director General of the Budget, Ministry of Finance, The Hague, Netherlands

Professor Franco Modigliani, Alfred P. Sloan School of Management, Massachusetts Institute of Technology, Cambridge, Massachusetts, USA

Professor H. M. A. Onitiri, Nigerian Institute of Social and Economic Research, University of Ibadan, Nigeria

Professor J. J. Paunio, Institute of Economics, University of Helsinki, Finland

Sir Leo Pliatzky, Department of Trade, London, England

Professor Maksymilian Pohorille, Central School of Planning and Statistics, Warsaw, Poland

Professor Sir Austin Robinson, Cambridge University, England

Professor Agnar Sandmo, The Norwegian School of Economics and Business Administration, Bergen, Norway

Dr Bernard Stafford, University of York, England

Professor Shigeto Tsuru, The Asahi Shimbun, Tokyo, Japan

Professor Victor Urquidi, El Colegio de Mexico, Mexico

Professor Hirofumi Uzawa, University of Tokyo, Japan

Mr H. Verwayen, Commission for the Development of Policy Analysis, The Hague, Netherlands

List of Observers

Professor Dong Fu Reng, Institute of the Chinese Social Science Academy

Mr Peter Lengyel, UNESCO, Paris

Introduction

R. C. O. Matthews and G. B. Stafford

The economic analysis of collective consumption, whether in theoretical, empirical or practical terms, has not kept pace with the growth in collective consumption's importance in national economies. Public macroeconomics offers an analysis of the effects on the economy of public expenditure for collective consumption without any consideration of why collective consumption has grown as it has; whereas much of public microeconomics aims to identify optimal reallocations of resources devoted to collective consumption without asking whether existing political and bureaucratic procedures will result in outcomes consistent with prescribed plans.

With such discrepancies in mind the International Economic Association chose collective consumption as the topic for its 1979 Round-table Conference. Many, though not all, of the problems involved are common to capitalist economies and to socialist ones, and the topic thus seemed a particularly appropriate one for the International Economic Association, whose gatherings are among the chief forums for serious discussion between economists of East and West. The aim set out at the planning stage of the conference was to analyse the positive and normative aspects of the long-run development of collective consumption, taking into account the political and bureaucratic methods by which its amount and composition are determined. The committee was pleased to secure papers from two very senior civil servants, Director-General Meys and Sir Leo Pliatzky, thus following a precedent in some earlier IEA Round-table Conferences of bringing economists and practitioners together.

Collective consumption can be defined in various ways, each appropriate for different purposes. The central concept used in the conference was goods or services provided free of charge, or nearly free of charge, to the beneficiary (a much wider concept than public goods in the strict Samuelsonian sense). In most of the papers and discussion sessions reported in this volume, the measure of collective consumption turned out to be not much different from public authorities' current expenditure on goods and services, although there were some divergences of view: thus some argued that public transfers on income maintenance should be regarded as collective consumption on the grounds that they provide the benefit of security, and Boltho argued that defence expenditures should be excluded.

However, as is shown in Boulding's concept of the grants economy and in Hoch's and Kapustin's references to personal collective consumption, the issue of definition is really a broader one. Supply without charge by the state is not the only alternative to a market arrangement for individual purchases and private consumption, nor is it the only way in which what might reasonably be called collective consumption is organised in real life. Charitable organisations and clubs are important in capitalist countries, and in one socialist country, Yugoslavia, the 'communities of interest' that are the chosen vehicle of collective consumption are actually seen as a way of moving towards the Marxian goal of the withering away of the state. Moreover, in capitalist countries, a considerable amount of provision that could be made by the state is made also or instead by employers to their employees, both in the form of provision in kind, such as canteen facilities and sports grounds, and in the form of income-maintenance, especially pensions. Provision by employers (enterprises) is a still more important feature of arrangements in socialist countries. The fact that enterprises in socialist countries are themselves organs of the state makes for difficulties in defining and measuring the extent of state provision there.

This raises some important questions about the positive and normative relationship between governmental and non-governmental collective consumption in capitalist and socialist economies. That relationship is touched on at various points in this book, but it is not a central theme and requires further exploration. It is not difficult to see a direction such an initiative might take, for there is an obvious relationship between the theory of clubs developed by western economists and the concept of personal collective consumption developed in the papers of Hoch and Kapustin.

It is, however, the great rise in governmental collective consumption that has brought the subject into prominence. This rise has been a long-run trend, apparent already before the Second World War, but more rapid in the post-war period than it had been before. Trends in western countries are well documented in Boltho's paper. The conference papers unfortunately do not include any equally comprehensive data on socialist countries, but relevant material is provided by Hoch and Kapustin and in the comment by Kaser on pp. 328–9. These data leave it rather unclear whether socialist countries have experienced a trend rise in collective consumption's share in national income comparable to that in the West. The historical circumstances in the socialist countries were rather different from those in capitalist countries. The period of rationing and shortages lasted much longer after the Second World War than in capitalist countries, and the transition from that period provided one force making for some actual reduction in collective consumption's share.

A major theme in the conference discussions was the normative rationale of collective consumption. A difference of view emerged between eastern and western participants that had little to do with the difference between capitalist and socialist methods of *production*. Participants from capitalist countries all tended to see the rationale as the maximisation of the sum of individual utilities in circumstances where the market, for one reason or another (including income distribution), failed to bring that result about. The socialist economists were not in complete agreement among themselves on the question, but they were unanimous that the welfare of the people is inadequately represented by preferences revealed in the market. Some of them, moreover, while firmly disclaiming paternalism, were unwilling to agree that the welfare of the people is identical to the sum of the welfare of individuals. Thus eastern participants argued that individual preferences in capitalist economies are distorted by business interests and the media (p. 106) and more generally, and in any case, that individual preferences must be assessed in terms of their consistency with well-defined goals relating to the development of the whole society (pp. 72–3). As a consequence they insisted that a variety of political as well as economic channels are needed in order to make known what it is that welfare consists of. These differences reflect in part the differing philosophical origins of the two systems of thought. Western economics is deeply rooted in Benthamite individualism. Socialist economics goes back, through Marx, to Hegel.

The honours in this debate were not all on one side. Participants from western countries expressed suspicion of anything providing a pretext for despotism, however paternalistic. But they were conscious that utility-maximisation is a jejune psychological postulate. At one point a western participant said that he tended to adopt the axiom of utility-maximisation mainly out of deference to the wishes of American journal editors. His East European neighbour at the table was then heard to say 'Oh, so you have trouble with orthodoxy too'. Boulding came nearest to the concerns of the socialist economists when he remarked that one of the reasons for struggling to avoid the manifest potential pathologies of the grants economy is that, if the grants economy itself becomes discredited, the legitimacy of the whole social system comes under threat. The issues here stretch far beyond the realm of collective consumption as normally defined, and an easy resolution is not to be expected.

The extent of common ground between eastern and western participants was much greater on the issue of the practical difficulties encountered in implementing programmes of collective consumption. Well-recognised in capitalist economies are the problems of the choice between grants in kind and grants in cash, of the effects of grants of all kinds on incentives, and of unequal access to and overprovision of services provided free. The papers by Hoch, Pohorille and Kapustin and the comments by Bacskai (p. 136) gave valuable insights into how such problems manifest themselves in socialist economies, and show that agreed solutions are no more available in the East than in the West.

None of the western papers at the conference was primarily concerned with the effects of the growth of collective consumption, as opposed to its causes. Nor did the conference include any representatives of the extreme school of thought that sees collective consumption itself as a pathological phenomenon, rather than as a phenomenon susceptible of pathological disorders. Dempster and Wildavsky perhaps came nearest to that position, but not on ideological grounds – rather on the grounds that the collective organisation of consumption is not well adapted to respond to economic change.

Be that as it may, all sensible people must agree that collective consumption is a major constituent of national income and is likely to remain so. Hence theoretical analysis of how it is and ought to be determined is a major item on the agenda of economists. Two quite different approaches exist, both represented in this volume. One is optimisation theory, well represented by Sandmo's contribution. This approach is normative and is in the mainstream of welfare economics. The other is the theories of public choice (Frey, Dempster and Wildavsky) and of bureaucracy (Leibenstein), which in principle are positive. It is to be expected that positive and normative economics should be different. But in this case they appear to inhabit universes of discourse that differ to an excessive extent. Moreover both, in their different ways, have proved rather unsatisfactory for their stated purposes. Optimisation theory has had a disappointingly small impact on policy-making, except at the strictly OR level (the best way of shunting railway wagons). The theories of public choice and of bureaucracy are interesting but they are short on specific testable propositions.

The question naturally arises whether these deficiencies are related to each other. Optimisation theory as a rule does not take account of the processes by which political and bureaucratic decisions are arrived at, by whom, and with what motives. It therefore runs the risk of posing questions, ostensibly about policy, in a form that is non-operational. Some interesting observations on this subject were made in the course of the discussion (pp. 263–4) of the paper by Meys, a paper which described the attempts made in the Netherlands to integrate formal analysis in the decision-making process. But while it is easy to criticise optimisation theory for neglecting the processes of non-market choice, theories of non-market behaviour have proved difficult to construct.

It was the original intention of the programme committee that a good deal of the attention of the conference should be given to decision-making processes affecting collective consumption. This intention was formed in the belief that economics needs to develop a way of analysing non-market economic phenomena to match its existing way of analysing market phenomena. It was felt that, in current public discussion about decision-making and the administrative and political aspects of collective consumption, preoccupation with the *control* of expenditure, however necessary, tended to produce a one-sided emphasis, such as might be produced if one thought of the price mechanism merely as a device for keeping *down* consumption. Valuable contributions in this area were made in the papers by Frey, Leibenstein, Pliatzky, Meys, and Dempster and Wildavsky. None the less, it was noticeable throughout the discussion sessions that participants, eastern and western alike, showed a reluctance to come to grips with these questions and tended to veer off into the philosopher-king assumption and talk about questions about optimisation more familiar to most economists.

Does this reflect an inherent difficulty of producing general propositions about non-market decision-making that do not depend over much on the institutions of a single country? Do the price-mechanism and central planning under full information constitute economic systems more susceptible to intellectual analysis than systems where the market does not operate and power is diffused? The theory certainly has a long way still to go. Public choice theory offers the apparently attractive prospect of a single model embracing the economic and political behaviour of the individual; but it is far from giving generally usable conclusions. Much the same can be said about the theory of bureaucracy, though it too has provided useful insights. Both seem to be more successful in analysing the proximate factors bearing on programmes of collective consumption than in explaining major changes in direction within and between programmes; and neither of them is very successful in analysing the forces responsible for shifts in the frontier between collective and individual consumption. The conference pointed to the need for continuing efforts by economists in this area. This effort is needed both in order to understand how 'endogenous governments' behave and in order to bring the expertise of economics more effectively to bear on an area of decision-making where the scope for oscillating dogmas and wasteful fudges is so great.

Part One
Theoretical Principles

1 Pathologies of the Public Grants Economy

Kenneth E. Boulding

UNIVERSITY OF COLORADO

I THE FEATURES OF THE GRANTS ECONOMY

There are two basic economic relationships between economic parties: exchange, in which there is a mutual transfer of economic goods from each party to the other; and the grant or transfer which is a one-way transfer of economic goods from one party to another, without equivalent economic goods passing in exchange, although there may be non-economic goods passing. Neither of these are clear concepts, nor should they be. They lie toward opposite ends of a continuum of possible relationships, with a penumbra of related concepts around them. There are, for instance, accounting concepts which revolve around the transfer of net worth. In a simple accounting exchange, the things exchanged are assumed to have equal values, so that assets are rearranged among owners by the exchange, but the net worth of neither party changes. The decline in asset value of the thing given up is equal to the increase in asset value of the thing received for both parties. The pure grant transaction, from the accounting point of view, is one in which net worth is redistributed, the net worth of the grantor declining and that of the recipient increasing by an equal number.

Exchange values and accounting values, of course, are not the only ones to be considered. There are non-economic goods which participate even in exchange. The parties to an exchange of economic goods also exchange trust, courtesies, communications, changes in images of each other and so on, which do not usually get into accounting systems. Non-economic goods are important in the concept of reciprocity, which differs from exchange in that it is informal and non-contractual. In exchange, A gives B something only if B gives A something, and the terms are usually arranged in advance of the actual transfer. In reciprocity, A gives B something unconditionally, B gives A something unconditionally. The relations of husband and wife, the exchange of Christmas presents, the enormous gift-giving that takes place in Japan, are all examples of reciprocity. Just as in exchange there are terms of trade, the exchange ratio – how much of *x* one gets for giving up a unit of *y* – so there are terms of reciprocity in experience, even though these may be informal and understood rather than contractual. If the terms either of exchange or of reciprocity are believed to be unsatisfactory by either party, the relationship is threatened, for both exchange and reciprocity are relationships that can be vetoed by either party, though the extent and the power of the veto may vary. A person who feels that the terms of trade are too unfavourable, that not enough is being received per unit of what is being given up, may refuse to continue the relationship. Similarly, a person who feels that the terms of reciprocity are unfavourable, and a great deal is being given up and not very much received, also may threaten to end the relationship. This explains divorce, the breaking of a friendship, treason, migration and many related phenomena.

The public grants economy consists of those one-way transfers in which at least one of the parties is a public authority vested with some kind of coercive power. In the accounting sense, it would be defined as any transaction in which one party is a public authority, in which there is a transfer of net worth from one party to the other. Thus, when I pay my income tax, my net worth goes down and that of the government goes up. When the government pays me a pension or unemployment benefits, my net worth goes up and that of the government goes down. When the central government pays out a grant to a local government, the net worth of the central government goes down and that of the local government goes up, all in the moment of the transaction. All taxes and subsidies, therefore, clearly belong to the public grants economy, but government purchases and sales of goods and services usually do not, though the different accounting standards applied to public bodies and private parties complicate the matter, especially as government capital accounting is apt to be rather primitive. If we were to apply the same standards, however, it is clear that when government purchases a building or furniture, its assets should go up in the moment of the transaction equal to the money paid. Similarly, when the government hires somebody, the value of what the employee does in accounting terms should be equal to the wage or salary, though government accounting does not always recognise this.

The situation is complicated by the fact that there are two kinds of grants – direct, in which there is an easily identifiable transfer from one party to the other; and indirect or implicit. Indirect grants are often very hard to trace but are important. An indirect grant is a redistribution of net worth among parties, perhaps among many parties, which is the result of some activity that does not involve direct transfer from the parties whose net worth declines to those whose net worth increases. The problem of the incidence of taxation is a classic example. A tax on a commodity that is collected, let us say from the wholesaler, represents a direct transfer from the wholesaler to the government. The wholesaler passes this on in increased prices to the retailer, who passes it on in increased prices to the customer, so that ultimately after the effects have rolled all around the system, some persons have lower net worth and the government has a higher one, but the persons having a lower worth may not be the ones who made the direct transfer. Even income taxes may have indirect effects, in so far as they discourage activity or produce migration.

The problem of incidence, therefore, is to be seen as a very large problem, far beyond the usual limits of the incidence of taxation, involving the overall redistribution of net worth which takes place as a result of the total activity of society. These redistributions are often unexpected, and even unnoticed and unattributed, but they can be quite large. I have argued indeed that if we could do distributional impact statements showing who is favourably affected, who is unfavourably affected, and who is unaffected by any particular law or regulation, transaction or even personal act, these would turn out to be very surprising. In all aspects of the public grants economy, therefore, we have to look not only at the direct transfers but also at the indirect consequences.

Regulatory law and the administrative regulations which accompany it also create a large indirect grants structure. Regulatory law implies setting up an elaborate structure of taboos, with penalties for violations. These involve such things as building standards, safety standards, clean air, water and emission standards, standards for the disadvantaged, equal opportunity regulations, child labour laws, anti-monopoly laws, regulation of monopoly laws, zoning, restrictions on vehicles, rationing – the list is very long. The distributional impacts of regulatory law may be quite large, though very hard to discover. There is a certain illusion, perhaps, among the virtuous liberal-minded that regulation is costless; in fact, it always involves a public grants economy. It may involve redistribution either from the poor or from the rich. Most of the public grants economy implied in regulation is indirect, although there are a few direct grants in such things as licence fees and so on.

It is a tricky question in public accounting as to the extent to which the services of government should be regarded only as an intermediate good, so that the impact of government should be reflected wholly in private accounts. Unfortunately, there is no simple answer to this question. Sometimes government produces genuinely public goods which are widely enjoyed. The most obvious ones are fine public buildings, the layout of streets and squares; more subtle ones involve pride or a sense of identity which comes from belonging to a significant and meaningful nation. Still further down the level of imponderability are things like law and order and the whole framework within which the private economy operates. It is not unreasonable to suppose that somewhere between per capita GNP and per capita net personal income is the real measure of economic welfare, but where it comes in this gap is very hard to say. The public grants economy, besides providing public goods, also provides the framework within which private goods can be more efficiently produced, and this should be counted as a product of government even though it is very hard to assess.

II THE PURPOSES OF THE PUBLIC GRANTS ECONOMY: REDISTRIBUTION

Before we can assess the public grants economy, we must look at the purposes for which it is set up, though even these may be divided into direct and ostensible as against the indirect and perhaps covert. Three general purposes can be distinguished easily. It is tempting to call them the 'three R's' – redistribution, reallocation and regulation. Redistribution involves changing the overall distribution of riches, real income, and ultimately some measure of quality of life or human welfare away from what it would have been in the absence of a public grants economy to what it is in the presence of it. The public grants economy often arises because of a political value which can be expressed in legislation and regulation, that the distribution of human welfare in the absence of a public grants economy is too unequal, or at least goes to some of the wrong people. Equality is not the only possible criterion of redistribution, for justice also demands that some people should get what they deserve, so that we try to redistribute welfare away from criminals and perhaps even fools. There is an almost universal feeling today, however, that the redistribution of welfare that results from a pure market economy in the absence of any public grants economy would result in too great inequality from the point of view of the widely perceived quality of a society, or even from the point of view of its potential instability.

The dynamics of distribution over time is a very subtle system and it is by no means easy to comprehend in its entirety. There are certainly random elements in it involving good and bad luck, the choice of occupations and investments, spouses, the personal incidence of the costs and benefits from the high-cost or high-benefit individuals and so on. There are also important non-random biases, which suggests that, if left to itself, distribution might become too unequal. One is the famous 'Matthew principle', mentioned three times in that Gospel, expressed as 'to him that hath shall be given'. It is easy to see why perfect equality might be unstable. There would be random variations disturbing this equality, making some people better off than others, and those who were better off would find it easier to save and become still better off, while those who were worse off would find it more difficult and might even find their welfare declining.

Inheritance complicates the problem. Inheritance still goes largely through the family, in spite of the efforts of many societies to provide a social inheritance for each individual born, so that if the rich marry each other and have few children, and the poor also marry each other and have many children, the rich will get richer and the poor poorer. There are, of course, diminishing returns to the Matthew principle as to all others. The rich become careless and lose their riches, especially in the third and fourth generations. The aristocracy, as Galton pointed out, often marry heiresses. These tend to come from infertile stock (otherwise they would not be heiresses) and hence old families tend to die out and their capital is scattered among foundations or large numbers of remote kin. There is much ancient evidence, however, going back at least to Biblical times, that rich landowners accumulate more land, poor landowners tend to lose it, and society, if the process is unchecked by years of jubilee, revolutions or offsetting taxation, ends up with a relatively small class of property owners and a large class of propertyless.

One factor that offsets the drift to inequality is the increasing value of the human person in a technologically developing society, where the capital value of the worker often becomes much greater than that of the physical capital with which he works. A rise in the value of human capital, therefore, tends towards equality rather than inequality. Distribution is also a function of the product mix itself. As Adam Smith pointed out, the highland chieftain who may own all the food of the clan has to distribute it fairly equally among the members, simply because of the limited capacity of the human stomach. This indeed is the first mention of the 'invisible hand' in *The Theory of Moral Sentiments*. The same principle applies to machine-made clothing, automobiles, washing machines, television sets and so on. When the productivity of the society is such that the total stock of these things is approximately equal to the number of families, or even the number of persons, every family or person will tend to have one. There is no point in the rich man owning 50 automobiles or 100 television sets, though he may be able to have large houses and servants if these are major components of the total product.

Redistribution may also be direct or indirect. It may take the form of simple payments in welfare, unemployment, health payments (in extreme form, of course, negative income tax), or it may take the form of an indirect grants structure through things like the minimum wage that will tend to redistribute income away from the young, the uneducated, and perhaps recent immigrants, into the lower middle-income groups, thus almost certainly increasing inequality. A very difficult and still largely unresolved question is the causes and impacts of the distribution of national income as between labour income and non-labour income, which may be affected by certain aspects of the public grants economy, though one suspects not very much. The Great Depression, however, certainly resulted in a large shift towards labour income and away from non-labour income, and this may have made for somewhat greater equality.

A very tricky question is the redistributive effects of the tax system, particularly in regard to progressivity or regressivity. Virtually all countries have an ostensibly progressive tax system. In the United States, however, this is so eroded by a great variety of tax offsets that in fact it seems as if the middle 85 to 90 per cent of American families pay about the same proportion of their income in taxes and that the total tax-subsidy structure only becomes progressive at the top 5 or bottom 5 to 10 per cent. This is probably less true of the other advanced capitalist societies, and it is difficult to evaluate what this means in the socialist societies, where it is hard to distinguish taxes from profit.

Inflation, which, as we shall see later, may be regarded as a failure of the public grants economy, also produces certain redistributions, though its overall impact is somewhat obscure. It certainly acts as a tax on the foolish who store money in mattresses, and perhaps this is one reason why it is rather popular. It also perhaps widens the gap between the successfully speculative and the more ordinary citizen.

III REALLOCATION OF RESOURCES

The second important purpose of the public grants economy is reallocation of the resources of a society as between occupations and industries. Thus, the public grants economy undoubtedly expands education, research, police, fire protection, conservation activities and the military far beyond what these segments of the labour force or economy would be in its absence. Here again, there is a political feeling that just as the exchange economy will not produce proper redistribution if left to itself, so it will not produce a proper allocation of resources. The free market left to itself would allocate too much to luxury, vice and private goods and not enough to necessities, virtue and public goods. If this represents a certain lack of confidence in the value of individual choice, so be it. Here again, the impact of the public grants economy on allocation may be either direct or indirect. It is very direct when we get public grants for education, research, medical services and so on. There is also a very powerful indirect reallocation through such things, for instance, as discriminatory commodity taxation. We tax vice in the shape of liquor and tobacco, we subsidise virtue in cheapening education, perhaps even the arts.

The allocational effects of the public grants economy may also include an offset to the short views and near-time horizons of individuals, or even of private organisations, by contrast with the supposedly long views of the public authority. If we have something, for instance, which is cheap and plentiful now, and which threatens to be scarce and expensive, say, in 50 years, there is a great deal to be said for making it expensive now, simply because this will encourage private behaviour towards both conservation and the finding of alternative sources of supply and means of satisfying demand. A good example of this might be water in California, and certainly oil and natural gas on a world scale. Unfortunately, the public grants economy is often concerned with making these things cheap rather than expensive, which could be quite disastrous.

Economists are familiar with the use of the public grants economy to offset externalities and market failure, especially for public goods, and public goods which cannot be allocated to individuals on the basis of private property. This is presumably why we have stoplights at intersections and would have, if economists had their way, taxes on vice, noxious effluents, loud noises and irresponsible parents, and subsidies to virtue, clean air and fine private gardens.

IV REGULATION AND CONTROL OF CHANGE

The third purpose of the public grants economy, which I have called regulation, involves the control of undesirable changes in the general framework of the society. The solution of the inflation/unemployment dilemma might well require a subtle and discriminating public grants economy, for instance, to subsidise the wages of otherwise inframarginal workers and to tax the sort of behaviour which leads to inflationary rises in prices or wages.

The primary source of continuing inflation in all modern societies is the public cash deficit. This may be modified upward or downward by what is happening in the banking and financial system. If, however, government takes in $100 from taxes and the sale of securities and pays out $110, it is clear that there is $10 more somewhere in the pockets or bank accounts in the private sector. If the bonds that it sells become reserves for the banks, this will also increase the money stock in the hands of the private sector, and without a continual increase in this money stock, it is very hard to have a continuing inflation. A government deficit does involve the public grants economy, but it is, however, very hard to estimate. There is an increase in net worth to the people who are not paying taxes they would otherwise have to pay if government expenditures remained unchanged. The redistributive effects on the expenditure side are more complicated. There are certainly something like implicit adjustment taxes, diminutions in net worth of the people who would be fired from government employment and have to find employment elsewhere. There are tricky questions of accounting involved here. Inflation increases the dollar value of the net worth of the whole society, but not necessarily the real value. If we did our accounting in 'real dollars', the distributions would look rather different than if we were dealing in current dollars. This is a problem about which there is not very much information.

The relation between unemployment and the public grants economy is a very tricky question to which no simple answer can be given. Unemployment is partly the result of the inability of the relative wage and price structure to clear the market for labour. If this sounds rather neoclassical, it is still a place to begin. This failure to clear the market may be a result of the difficulty of adjusting the relative wage structure. This is, also, as Keynes pointed out, a result of the difficulty of adjusting the real wage structure, that is, wages relative to the prices of wage goods. A fall in money wages in response to unemployment may produce a further fall in the price of wage goods and may not result in much change in real wages. There are problems here from which regulation shrinks. Those that would regulate the labour movement, for instance, play with considerable political fire and consequently we have devised a public grants economy in the form of budget deficit and inflation which actually takes advantage of the failure of the price structure to adjust, and adapts to it in other ways, providing offsets to this adjustment.

Unemployment also has to be regarded not only as a failure in the labour market, but also as failure in markets both for real capital and for financial instruments. Unemployment is the easiest reaction of employers when they are faced with unwanted accumulations of goods in the form of unsold inventories or unused plant and equipment. This is the classical Keynesian theory of unwanted rise in stocks as a result of consumption falling too much below production, resulting in a decline in production to try to bridge the gap, a further decline in consumption, failure to close the gap, until the system moves down to intolerably low levels of employment, output and income.

There is another factor that has been much neglected in the last 40 years, which is the failure of financial markets to adjust the relation between interest and profit. When an employer hires someone, interest is sacrificed for the hope of profit. It is only rational, as profit is uncertain, that the profit hoped for should be sufficiently larger than what can be clearly and easily gained from putting out the money at interest. In the Great Depression in the United States, profits became negative in 1932 and 1933, being completely gobbled up by a rise in interest as a result of deflation and the rise in the proportion of national income going to labour, so that anyone who hired a worker was either a philanthropist, a fool or a long-run optimist. We face a serious dilemma today in that the financial markets have now adjusted to the inflation, nominal interest rates are on the order of 12 per cent and, if we stopped the inflation tomorrow, we would almost certainly have a catastrophic depression unless we could bring down the nominal interest rate. The financial market, unfortunately, cannot really do this quickly because its contracts are of such diverse periods. The price of stopping the inflation, therefore, would almost certainly be drastic intervention into financial markets on the order, for instance, of declaring all existing contracts invalid unless the rate of interest in them is halved. It is strange how little attention has been given in economic writing or political discussions to the problem of the regulation of interest rates. This may not only be the most important problem but even the most tractable, by contrast to the enormous amount of attention that has been given to the control of money wages and prices, which is extraordinarily difficult and almost certain to be ineffective.

V EVALUATION OF THE GRANTS ECONOMY

We now come to the problem of the evaluation of the public grants economy. This involves two rather different kinds of critiques. First of all, there is the critique of the ostensible purposes of the public grants economy, as to whether these purposes are in fact valid and desirable. And secondly, there has to be an evaluation and appraisal of the extent to which the public grants economy in fact achieves these purposes. If, of course, it fails to achieve undesirable purposes, this is presumably a point in its favour. These evaluations are not something purely academic. They go on all the time and play an important role in the ongoing dynamic of any society. If there is a widespread evaluation that the existing structure is a failure, there will be strong pressures to change it.

These evaluations are found in a number of different, though interacting levels. The most obvious in the short-run – perhaps the most significant – level is that of political evaluation. In democratic societies, politicians frequently want to be re-elected and aspiring politicians want to be elected. Even in the most arbitrary dictatorship, the values of the dictator can change under perceptions of failure, though a dictator is much more insulated from these perceptions than are democratic politicians. There is interesting evidence from the United States and its regular cycle of elections that the public grants economy (part of the larger picture of government action) is related to the election cycle and that in particular it is likely to be expanded the year before an election.[1] There are also long-run changes in political climate and evaluation. Certainly the change in England, from William Ewart Gladstone and his desire to have money 'fructify in the pockets of the people' to his successors of 100 years later who had little hesitation in creating an 18 per cent per annum inflation, is a substantial change. Certainly we have

[1] Edward R. Tufte, *Political Control of the Economy* (Princeton, New Jersey: Princeton University Press, 1978).

seen in the last 100 years a great expansion of the public grants economy in terms of redistributions, for instance, from less than 1 per cent to more than 10 per cent of the gross national product, and this has happened under the impact of cumulating political evaluations, especially a rise in the feeling that the inadequacy of the public grants economy produced either distributional, allocational or regulatory structures that needed correction.

These long-run political changes are very closely related to changes in the structure of moral evaluations of a society. The very idea that the social institutions were not given by nature or God, but could be changed to improve the human lot, may perhaps have distant roots in Plato's Republic, but it only really begins to penetrate the thinking of politically active and concerned people after Adam Smith. It has to be chalked up as one of the important contributions of Marx and Engels that however Ptolemaic their view of society, and however unrealistic their image of the future, they did at least let loose the idea on the world that there could be a 'leap from necessity into freedom', that social institutions did not have to be merely accepted but could be changed, presumably for the good, though what change is for the good may remain a subject of dispute.

We can trace a continuing moral change from the eighteenth century which is just as significant and indeed has a great deal to do with the accelerated pace of both technical and political change. This moral change has many dimensions – a search for greater participation and equality, a push for something that the nineteenth century at least was not ashamed to call progress, a feeling also that the circle of concern must expand from the individual and the family to the larger society, not only to the nation but to the whole human race. These changes are significant in the ongoing, changing evaluation of the public grants economy. The development, for instance, of foreign aid programmes, feeble as they now are, is a profound qualitative change in the evaluation of the public grants economy, which suggests that governments have responsibilities beyond their own borders and their own citizens. This comes out of a moral change which is then often imperfectly and belatedly translated into political action, which in turn feeds back to moral change.

Whether we can identify a separate economic evaluation is a tricky question. The great contribution of economics to social evaluation was the concept of the Paretian optimum. In its negative form this is the idea that it is unequivocally good if somebody can become better off without anybody else getting worse off. This abstracts, for instance, from the deplorable human propensity towards malevolence, and the optimum is a very large plateau in which it is often hard to find our way around. Still the idea is an important contribution to the moral imperative, precisely in its implicit denial of the value of malevolence, even if it also denies the value of benevolence. Economic man neither loves nor hates. It is not surprising that economists have been resistant to the idea of grants economics, which is in the last analysis an economy of love and fear.[2]

A distant cousin of the Paretian optimum is the concept of social cost-benefit analysis, which also owes a lot to economics. This, again, is an important moral principle. It is one of the great fallacies of moralists and political activists of all stripes to believe that if you have proved that something is bad that is sufficient argument against it, whether this is liquor in the case of prohibitionists, Jews and Blacks in the case of the Klu Klux Klan, or nuclear power in the case of the anti-nuclear movement. The economist tends to come along and ask: Granted that this is bad – practically everything is rather bad – is there anything that is either better or worse? What are the alternatives? This is an important moral principle which applies also to the evaluations of the public grants economy.

VI WHAT ARE THE PATHOLOGIES OF THE GRANT SYSTEM?

The danger for the economist is, however, that it is so hard to find anything that is better than almost any existing situation, no matter how bad, that there is a tendency to fall into the Panglossian fallacy that this is the best of all possible worlds, and so to deny even the possibility of the Engels' leap from necessity into freedom and from helplessness into positive action for human betterment. It may be that the answer to this dilemma is to look for pathologies rather than for perfection, so to be able to correct what is clearly wrong once it is perceived, and to leave open what is ultimately right. Health is merely the absence of disease, and even the most scoundrelly, abject, tyrannical and disgusting person may be healthy. The same might be said of societies. We may be able to identify social sicknesses and disorders; it is very hard to know what is the ideal. To put the matter in another way: What I am mainly concerned with is human betterment. I want to know which way is up rather than down; I do not pretend to know what there is at the top.

[2] K. E. Boulding, *The Economy of Love and Fear: A Preface to Grants Economics* (Belmont, California: Wadsworth, 1973).

We can then identify certain pathologies, both of the grants economy in general and especially of the public grants economy. There are pathologies, also, of the exchange economy – those we know very well – unemployment, monopoly, externalities, ignorance, deception and so on. We seem to be curiously insensitive to the pathologies of the grants economy, a carryover perhaps from the days of Lady Bountiful, the feeling that anybody who makes a grant must be very virtuous and unselfish, so that consequently grants should not be inquired into too closely. Now, however, the grants economy is too large to be accepted uncritically. It is particularly foolish to suppose that all grants are good and that all exchange is bad, as our radical friends sometimes tend to think. I shall outline, therefore, at least four possible pathologies of the public grants economy, for all of which many examples could be given.

The first pathological feature of the public grants economy is its tendency towards inadequate feedback, particularly by comparison with a reasonably active competitive market. I have sometimes called this 'Edsel's law', from the reflection that when the Ford Motor Company produced an Edsel, a car for which apparently the public demand fell far below expectations, it soon found that it had made a mistake and corrected it, even though there are some who argue that it should have persevered! If the Ford Foundation produces an Edsel, however, and still more if the government produces an Edsel, it may never find out at all; it may not even want to find out, and even when there is a feedback, it is likely to be long delayed. Intervention in Vietnam, for instance, was a prize Edsel of the American government; it took 20 years or more to provide adequate feedback.

Unfortunately, there are no very easy and obvious correctives for this problem. In a democracy there may be certain political feedbacks. But when the public grants economy becomes so enormously complex with so many subdivisions, as it is today, failure in any particular division of it is rarely reflected in any large-scale political agitation or pressure. Even the people who experience the failure may have a strong temptation to keep quiet about it, if their jobs are dependent on it. It often rests on what have come to be called 'whistle blowers', unusually conscientious and public-spirited individuals who are perhaps prepared even to sacrifice their own advantage, their own chances of promotion, by calling attention publicly to gross defects in the public grants structure of which they are aware. On the other hand, even whistle-blowing can be abused, as we see perhaps in the case of Senator Proxmire, whose 'Golden Fleece Award' for what he or his staff regards as politically unacceptable research projects, has done real damage to the research community, if only because an unfortunate title often masks a significant contribution. A number of professional societies, including the American Association for the Advancement of Science, have now associated themselves in a legal challenge to Senator Proxmire's sour note whistles. There seems to be no answer to this question, but the awkward one of encouraging both the whistle blowers and the people who blow the whistle on the whistle blowers, in the hope that better feedback will emerge and that it will have some effect.

A second source of pathology in the public grants economy is common to virtually all decision-making systems and is particularly acute in the public grants economy because of the failures of feedback. This is the failure of decision-makers, and even more perhaps of those who influence them, to understand the larger, and especially the long-run dynamics of the systems in which they are operating. In ecological and social systems, where everything depends on everything else, and there is a very complex web of interaction and feedback, simple cause and effect systems are rare. What we have is mutual determination and mutual interaction, which often produces what Jay Forrester calls 'counterintuitive systems', which may even have the opposite dynamic properties from what ordinary intuition leads us to expect.

These surprises seem to be particularly common in distributional systems, so much so that I have formulated what I call the 'law of political irony' – that everything that we do to help people hurts them and everything that we do to hurt people helps them. There are some happy exceptions to this principle, but the number of cases where it applies is large enough to be disturbing. To give an example already mentioned, a minimum wage may easily hurt the very people it is intended to help and result in more unemployment rather than an increase in their wages, though this is not always true. A famous historical case in the United States was the period of the New Deal, from 1932 to 1940, when a great amount of pro-labour legislation was passed, such as the Wagner Act, the labour movement rose from a little over 3 million to nearly 15 million, and collective bargaining became very widespread in American industry, especially in the North. In that same period, the proportion of national income going to labour fell sharply, from about 72 per cent to about 62 per cent, because of the recovery of profits, among other things. The naïve idea that collective bargaining redistributes income from profits to wages and that what the workers gain the employers lose is hopelessly unrealistic because of the capacity of employers to pass on wage increases in higher prices to consumers.

Another classic example in the New Deal era was the tobacco quota in

1934, which resulted in at least a six-fold eventual increase in the value of farms that happened to be producing tobacco in that year, as compared with identical farms that were not. This was a grant from society to the owners of land that happened to be producing tobacco in a single year, which is surely hard to justify on any grounds of social justice. American agricultural policy in general benefited the rich farmer much more than the poor, and indeed has driven millions of poor farmers out of agriculture. This itself might not be a bad thing in the long run, but it certainly was not what was intended. Similarly, defence expenditures lead to insecurity, a great upsurge of medical research (government-sponsored after 1955) coincided with the virtual cessation of the improvement in the expectation of life, and the story of foreign aid is full of situations in which the people who were not aided did better than those who were. The grants economy is often associated in the public mind with 'doing good', but skill in doing good is by no means easy to come by.

Other by-products of the public grants economy may be corruption of the recipients, the creation of dependency, and the creation of vested interests in continuing grants, which postpone adjustments which are necessary until they sometimes become almost impossible to make. These pathological conditions of the public grants, it must be emphasised again, are an argument for doing it better rather than for not doing it, but, if it is not done better, the case for not doing it at all becomes much stronger.

The third source of pathology of the public grants economy arises out of certain pathologies which are highly characteristic of public life and the political order. I have argued that political science has a dismal theorem, like the Malthusian dismal theorem in economics (a good example, incidentally, of a system dynamics pathology). The dismal theory of political science is that the skills which lead to the rise of power all too frequently unfit people to exercise it. We see this most strikingly in the hereditary monarchy, where royal genes are no guarantee whatever of royalability, and where the good king has a strong tendency to have a bad son. We see it dramatically in leaders who rise to power by war, external or internal – Napoleon, Stalin, Sukarno: the list is very long – with catastrophic uses of power because they transferred the skills for the rise to power into its exercise. Even in democratic societies, the skills which lead to election sometimes lead to catastrophe in office. It may well be that the only answer to this problem is an optimum degree of randomness in the selection of the occupants of powerful roles, for this at least would offset the perverse bias that the political system so often exhibits, even though it would be no guarantee that the powerful would always be good and competent.

Another aspect of the pathologies of power that applies to private as well as to public power, is the high payoffs for short-run solutions which may actually aggravate the long-run problems. People achieve power only in later life and at that age the 'après moi le déluge' of Louis XV may be a strong subconscious refuge, especially in the face of extremely difficult decision-making problems. In democracies, of course, people are elected for relatively brief terms, and it is not surprising that their horizon rarely extends beyond the next election. This means that the public grants economy easily gets turned toward temporary solutions of short-run problems to the neglect of the long-run. There is no easy answer to this, short of the generation of a widespread long horizon in society. There is a strong case for Fred Polak's contention that the nature of the image of the future which is prevalent in a society has a strong influence on its success or failure. A society with widely shared long-run views and a sense of reasonable optimism is more likely to make the decisions which will justify that optimism than if its views are short and despairing.

VII ARE THERE CURES?

It is easier to identify the pathologies of the public grants economy than it is to cure them. Recognition of them, however, is at least the prelude to cure and students of society should feel a strong obligation to work on these problems. Ineffectiveness in the public grants economy is no light matter, because it could lead to a withdrawal from it which could be the most pathological thing of all. A public grants economy is necessary in any society and as society becomes more complex, it probably becomes more necessary. It is a fundamental principle of grants economics, however, that the willingness to make grants depends to a very large extent on the perception of their efficiency. If by sacrificing a dollar I can save your life, I am very likely to do so; if by sacrificing a dollar I will only benefit you 10 cents, I will be most unlikely to do so. An increasing sense of the inefficiency of public grants is a great danger to any society, for it is destructive to its morale, its self-confidence, its image of the future and its ability to manage its affairs.

Ultimately, I have argued that the 'integry', that network of relationships in society which establishes legitimacy, community, mutual respect and love, dominates all the other systems. If that collapses, neither the economy nor the polity can function. Grants, I have argued, are a very important part of the dynamics of the integrative systems. They can either build it up or tear it down. This is particularly true of the public grants economy. If it becomes discredited, there is real danger that society can disintegrate into anomie, where all legitimacy is lost.

Discussion of 'Pathologies of the Public Grants Economy' by Professor K. E. Boulding

Professor Urquidi expressed some regret at the imbalance in the representation at the Conference in favour of developed economies. He suggested that the three purposes of the grants economy identified in Professor Boulding's paper (redistribution, reallocation and regulation) be supplemented by a fourth, development of developing economies. He pointed to the structural, long-term and partly non-economic nature of the policy changes required for development, and insisted on the inadequacy of market mechanisms and on the importance of public intervention for this purpose. Grants may therefore have a special role, even if they appear to be aberrations from market norms. Professor Urquidi cited the Mexican experience of agricultural, railway, industrial, health and educational development as evidence of the substantial contribution that public grants can make to development in an economy whose citizens are prepared to adopt a long-term view. However he also pointed to the difficulty involved in operating a policy of public grants in a developing economy. He referred specifically to the difficulty of explicitly assessing the cost of subsidy programmes and to the redistributions towards the rich involved in public projects such as land irrigation. *Professor Onitiri* likewise stressed the danger of focusing the discussion of grants on marginal issues and changes in a situation in which problems of development and wealth distribution in the world economy were structural in nature. He suggested that the concept of the grants economy should be defined so as to include foreign aid. Discussion should be extended to include an analysis of relationships between developed and developing economies in which transfers of profits from developing to developed economies should be explicitly considered. Grants could be considered a necessary precondition for the exchanges that were the central topic of traditional economics.

Professor Tsuru wondered whether the notion of 'grants' and the 'grants economy' added anything to the analysis of the problems of development provided by an application of more conventional tools. *Mr Boltho* argued that development should be viewed as a purpose of the grants economy only if subsidies to firms were included in the definition of grants; the experience of Japan in this regard showed how much difference would be made by a broader or narrower definition of grants. *Mr Matthews* suggested that the problems of developing economies were sufficiently different to those of developed economies to make a separate discussion of them the most sensible strategy.

Professor Hoch did not see a clear distinction between the grants economy and the economy as a whole in view of the very extensive involvement of public institutions in the functioning of both socialist and capitalist economies. *Professor Pajestka* doubted the explanatory power of a theory of the grants economy based on neo-classical concepts to the extent that Professor Boudling's implicitly was. In his view an historical analysis of specific social functions would be more useful in promoting an understanding of major acts of collective consumption in the past (for example, the construction of pyramids and the foundation of Cambridge colleges); and the same applied to the current crisis of collective consumption in economies such as the United Kingdom.

Professor Maillet thought that the distinctions market-grants and private-public were too simple. The question was, who decided about the allocation of GNP? In practice the answer was not straightforward; there were complex interactions between decision-makers in the public and private sectors. For example, an anti-trust policy could be seen as a grant to consumers at the expense of monopoly profits. On this, Professor Boulding suggested that the existence of monopoly profits could itself be regarded as a grant, by comparison with the norm of perfect competition.

Mr Kaser suggested that the critical question was where to draw the distinction in the range between the accounted exchange and the 'pure' grant. He wondered whether Boulding needed to have taken the special case as his extremum, *viz.* that a pure grant was one in which the net worth of the donor was reduced in an equal amount as the net worth of the recipient increased. This was the complete Kaldor compensation principles but Boulding's extreme of a 'pure grant' was satisfied by the absence of a gain by the donor when the net worth of the recipient rose.

Mr Boltho questioned Professor Boulding's conclusion about the danger of instability in the development of grants economies. He argued that in western economies increases in the ratio of grants to national income had been associated with greater stability and social cohesion. LDCs had a lower ratio of collective consumption to GNP than developed countries and they also had less social cohesion.

Professor Khachaturov cited the development of education in the USSR as evidence of the social and economic efficiency of a grants economy, notwithstanding Professor Boulding's pathologies. *Professor Pohorille* argued that the pathologies of the grants economy identified by Professor Boulding constituted an important problem for both socialist and capitalist economies, but insisted that market mechanisms were equally vulnerable to the problems of inefficient feedback and decision-making. The important task was to devise means of overcoming the pathologies and improving the efficiency of collective consumption as a method of economic organisation. *Professor Klein* drew attention to the informational bias in grants economies arising from the acitivities of organised groups of beneficiaries – farmers, pensioners and so on. Regulation of private agents by law was an alternative instrument to the provision of grants.

In reply to the discussion, *Professor Boulding* insisted that the analysis of the grants economy was not confined to marginal changes within developed economies and did not observe a sharp distinction between public and private institutions. The important phenomenon of granting behaviour within the family was cited in support of the latter point: in the US grants within the family had been reckoned to comprise 30 per cent of GNP, in contrast to the 10 per cent of GNP redistributed through government. He agreed in principle that it was important to try to find ways of avoiding pathologies in collective consumption, but this was not an easy task. He was less optimistic than Mr Boltho about the stability of grants economies which in his view were afflicted by the massive pathology of large military expenditures: the ultimate advent of the Third World War was no less certain, on present courses, then the next San Francisco earthquake – and no less consigned away from people's consciousness. He expressed a preference for the visibility of direct grants as against the often concealed operation of legal regulation.

Professor Boulding drew attention to a conflict in grants economy not made explicit in his paper: that between redistributions in the interests of equality and redistributions in favour of the economically competent. He also had some doubts, or second thoughts about whether regulation should be considered an aim of the grants economy, on a par with redistribution and reallocation; perhaps it was better regarded as a means.

Finally, on the question of optimality and possible divergences from it, Professor Boulding expressed himself as less concerned than many people. Decisions matter less than you might think. You could have married a different girl or taken up a different career, and very likely the outcome would not have been much better or much worse. The world of decisions is made up of plateaus, not Matterhorns.

2 Social Stability and Collective Public Consumption

Hirofumi Uzawa

UNIVERSITY OF TOKYO

I INTRODUCTION

It is one of the most fundamental propositions in the neo-classical theory of welfare economics that the allocative mechanism in a purely competitive market economy necessarily results in an efficient allocation of scarce resources. As is well known, this proposition presupposes that all the scarce resources limitational to the economic activities engaged in by the members of the society are privately appropriated, without involving significant costs either in the administration of such a private ownership or in the organisational efficiency of economic agents involved. However, in many contemporary capitalist economies, a significant portion of scarce means of production is not privately appropriated but socially administered, as typically illustrated by the existence of a large class of means of production usually termed as social overhead capital or common property resources. Those scarce resources that are classified as social overhead capital are either produced collectively by the society, as in the case of social capital such as highways, harbours, bridges, etc., or simply endowed within the society, as in the case of natural capital such as air, water, soil, forests, etc. The services produced from social overhead capital are provided to the members of the society, either free of charge or with nominal fees, and the provisions of such social overhead capital are distributed among the members of the society according to their need, not based upon the principles underlying the market mechanism.

In an economy where social overhead capital plays a significant role, the nature of the working of the market mechanism is sufficiently different from that of a purely competitive market economy that some of the more fundamental propositions in welfare economics are no longer valid, and it becomes necessary to re-examine both the stability properties of the market mechanism and the optimum properties of the resulting allocation of scarce resources. In a number of previous contributions, I have formulated the concept of social overhead capital in such a manner that it may capture certain aspects of social overhead capital which are characteristic of contemporary capitalistic societies, and examined the nature of modifications in the basic propositions of the neo-classical theory of welfare economics that are required to obtain social optimum allocations of scarce resources where such a concept of social overhead capital plays a central role (Uzawa [3], [4], [5]).

The concept of social overhead capital formulated in these articles is an extension of the concept of pure public goods, introduced in Samuelson [1, 2]; however, it differs from the Samuelsonian concept of pure public goods in two aspects. The first aspect is that the services obtained from social overhead capital are not passively provided to the members of the society as is the case with the Samuelsonian public goods, but each member of the society determines how much of such services are to be used, according to individual needs and the prices to be paid for such services. The second aspect is concerned with the phenomenon of what might be called congestion, resulting from the use of the identical social overhead capital by the members of the society. When the quantity of social overhead capital of a particular kind which exists in the society at a given moment of time is scarce relative to the magnitude of economic activities, the benefit each member of the society may obtain from the use of a certain amount of social overhead capital depends upon the extent to which other members of the society are using the services of the same social overhead capital, thus resulting in the phenomenon of congestion. Again, the Samuelsonian concept of pure public goods necessarily excludes the possibility of congestion arising out of the use of social overhead capital which is scarce from the society's point of view.

As is to be expected, the allocative mechanism of a purely competitive economy does not necessarily result in an efficient allocation of scarce resources, either from the static or from the dynamic point of view. It has been shown that the criteria under which the intertemporal allocation of scarce resources including both private capital and social overhead capital is optimum differ significantly from the criteria applicable to a purely competitive market economy. In particular, it has been shown that the public corporation in charge of a particular social overhead capital has to follow a set of administrative criteria which are significantly different from that of a private corporation. Only when the effect of social overhead capital is neutral in the sense defined in Uzawa [3], the criteria to be imposed upon the social institution in charge of the management and construction of such overhead capital are essentially identical with those for the private institutions in a purely competitive market economy.

In the previous discussion on the theoretical analysis of social overhead capital, as was the case with the Samuelsonian theory of public goods, I have not examined the circumstances under which certain scarce resources are classified as private capital, while others are classified as social overhead capital. The classification of scarce resources between private capital and social overhead capital is not solely based upon the economic-technical characteristics of the scarce resources in question, but it also crucially depends upon the historical, political and cultural aspects of the society itself. Thus it is often the case that a certain type of social overhead capital is classified as a private capital in one society, while it may be classified as a social overhead capital in another society. Or, it is entirely possible and is often the case that the same type of scarce resources may be classified as private capital at one time, and as social at another time, within the identical society.

It is the purpose of the present paper to investigate the circumstances under which certain scarce resources are classified as social and to relate it to what is temporarily termed as the social instability of the allocative mechanism of a purely competitive market economy. It will be shown that, in a situation where the general price level is increasing, the prices of those commodities for which the price elasticities of demand and supply are small tend to increase at rates higher than those for which either the demand elasticity or the supply elasticity is larger. Thus, in a situation where the price level in terms of wage-units is increasing, the prices of those goods and services which are necessary and indispensable in the processes of economic activity tend to increase at rates higher than the average rate of inflation. Hence, the level of the minimum income, to be defined as the minimum level of income required to maintain a socially acceptable minimum standard of living, increases at a rate higher than the average income. In such a situation, if one tries to solve the problem of the redistribution of incomes through an income transfer scheme, then the amount of income transfer needed to guarantee the socially acceptable living standard steadily increases relative to the level of the per capita income, increasing at the same time the rate of increase in the level of the minimum income.

Such a phenomenon of social instability inherent to the competitive market mechanism may be resolved by classifying as social those scarce resources which are indispensable to the maintenance of the minimum standard of living, and by distributing the services obtained from such social overhead capital according to a certain criterion which is desirable from a social point of view, differing from the criteria for a competitive market economy in general. Indeed, one may argue that a significant part of social overhead capital common to most of the contemporary capitalist economy has been classified as social because of its implications upon the social stability of the allocative and distributive mechanism in a market economy.

II A MODEL OF PRICE DETERMINATION

The problems discussed in the Introduction may be analysed in terms of a simple model of price determination where the rates of price increase differ according to the nature of commodities in question. To make the exposition simpler, we consider an economy which is composed of two commodities, to be denoted by 1 and 2. As will be more explicitly spelled out, commodity 1 represents those items which are indispensable in order to maintain the minimum level of living standard, while commodity 2 represents selectives or luxuries.

Income and prices will be measured in terms of wage-units; let y and p_1, p_2 be respectively the per capita income and the prices of commodities 1 and 2, all measured in wage-units. Demand functions for commodities 1 and 2 are denoted by the following:

$$x_1 = x_1(p_1, p_2, y), \quad x_2 = x_2(p_1, p_2, y), \tag{1}$$

where x_1, x_2 respectively denote the amounts of commodities 1 and 2 to be demanded by a representative unit. These demand functions satisfy the following budget equation:

$$p_1 x_1(p_1, p_2, y) + p_2 x_2(p_1, p_2, y) \equiv y. \tag{2}$$

Price and income elasticities for commodities 1 and 2 are defined by:

$$\begin{cases} \eta_{11} = -\dfrac{p_1}{x_1}\dfrac{\partial x_1}{\partial p_1}, & \eta_{12} = \dfrac{p_2}{x_1}\dfrac{\partial x_1}{\partial p_2}, & \eta_{1y} = \dfrac{y}{x_1}\dfrac{\partial x_1}{\partial y} \\ \eta_{21} = \dfrac{p_1}{x_2}\dfrac{\partial x_2}{\partial p_1}, & \eta_{22} = -\dfrac{p_2}{x_2}\dfrac{\partial x_2}{\partial p_2}, & \eta_{2y} = \dfrac{y}{x_2}\dfrac{\partial x_2}{\partial y} \end{cases} \tag{3}$$

Since both demand functions $x_1(p_1, p_2, y)$ and $x_2(p_1, p_2, y)$ are homogenous of degree zero with respect to p_1, p_2, y, the price and demand elasticities have to satisfy the following relationships:

$$\begin{cases} -\eta_{11} + \eta_{12} + \eta_{1y} = 0 \\ \eta_{21} - \eta_{22} + \eta_{2y} = 0 \end{cases} \tag{4}$$

Price elasticities measure the degree of easiness at which demand for particular commodities may be substituted by other commodities. It will be assumed that, for commodity 1, the price elasticity η_{11} is very small, the commodity 1 being a representative of necessities, while the price elasticity η_{22} for commodity 2 is rather large. However, since we will be concerned with the situation where the per capita income y (in wage-units) is increasing over time, we shall use alternative measures β_1, β_2 to be defined by:

$$\beta_1 = \eta_{11}/\eta_{1y}, \quad \beta_2 = \eta_{22}/\eta_{2y} \tag{5}$$

It will be assumed that commodity 1 has a very small β_1 and commodity 2 has a rather large β_2.

Similar concepts concerning supply conditions may be derived. Again for the sake of simplicity, we assume that there are only two kinds of factors of production, labour and capital. Labour represents those factors of production that are related to the input of human resources, while capital represents physical factors of production. Furthermore, labour is assumed to represent variable factors of production, while capital is assumed to be fixed, in the sense that the level of capital inputs cannot be changed in the short run, but is adjusted only through the processes of investment. In what follows, the quantities of capital being accumulated in the two sectors producing commodities 1 and 2 are assumed to be fixed throughout the time period in question.

Let us assume that the production processes of two sectors may be summarised by the following production functions:

$$X_j = F_j(N_j, K_j) \quad j = 1, 2, \tag{6}$$

where X_j denotes the amount of commodity j being produced, and N_j, K_j denote respectively the quantities of labour and capital employed in the sector where commodity j is produced. It will be assumed that both production functions $F_j(N_j, K_j)$ exhibit standard neo-classical properties; namely, $F_j(N_j, K_j)$ is a linear and homogeneous function with respect to N_j, K_j, and the marginal rate of substitution between N_j and K_j is diminishing.

Therefore, we write as follows:

$$X_j = f_j(n_j)K_j, \quad j = 1, 2, \tag{7}$$

where $n_j = N_j/K_j$ is the labour-capital ratio in the jth sector, and $f_j(n_j) = F_j(n_j, 1)$.

We first consider the case where producers in both sectors are faced with perfectly competitive markets for their products. Each producer then tries to maximise profits to be defined by:

$$p_j X_j - N_j, \tag{8}$$

where p_j is the market price of commodity j measured in wage-units.

Maximising (8) with respect to N_j, we obtain the following condition

$$p_j = 1/f_j'(n_j), \quad j = 1, 2. \tag{9}$$

The supply elasticity σ_j for commodity j represents the percentage rate of increase in the production of commodity j when the market price p_j of commodity j has been increased by 1 per cent:

$$\sigma_j = \frac{p_j}{X_j} \frac{\partial X_j}{\partial p_j}. \tag{10}$$

In the case of perfectly competitive markets, supply elasticities may be calculated from (7) and (9). Logarithmically differentiate (7) and (9) to obtain:

$$\frac{dX_j}{X_j} = \frac{n_j f_j'(n_j) dn_j}{f_j(n_j) n_j} = s_{Nj} \frac{dn_j}{n_j}, \tag{11}$$

$$\frac{dp_j}{p_j} = -\frac{n_j f_j''(n_j)}{f_j'(n_j)} \frac{dn_j}{n_j} = \frac{s_{Kj}}{\sigma_{Sj}} \frac{dn_j}{n_j}, \tag{12}$$

where s_{Nj} and s_{Kj} denote the relative share of labour and capital in the jth sector, respectively:

$$s_{Nj} = \frac{n_j f_j'(n_j)}{f_j(n_j)}, \quad s_{Kj} = \frac{f_j(n_j) - n_j f_j'(n_j)}{f_j(n_j)}, \tag{13}$$

and σ_{Sj} is the elasticity of substitution between labour and capital in the jth sector:

$$\sigma_{Sj} = \frac{f_j(n_j) - n_j f_j'(n_j)}{f_j(n_j)} \frac{f_j'(n_j)}{-n_j f_j''(n_j)} \tag{14}$$

We have

$$s_{Nj} + s_{Kj} = 1. \quad (15)$$

Dividing (11) by (12), we obtain the following formula for supply elasticities σ_j:

$$\sigma_j = \frac{s_{Nj}}{s_{Kj}} \sigma_{Sj}, \quad j = 1, 2. \quad (16)$$

If all the factors of production in the jth sector are fixed, the relative share of labour s_{Nj} will be zero, and the supply elasticity for commodity j will be zero:

$$\sigma_j = 0.$$

Namely, when all factors of production are fixed, an increase in the market price will not have an effect upon the quantity of the commodity to be produced. On the other hand, if all the factors of production in the production of commodity j are variable, the relative share of capital will be zero, and the supply elasticity for commodity j becomes infinity:

$$\sigma_j = +\infty.$$

In general, we may say that the higher the degree of fixity in the production of commodity j, the lower will be the magnitude of the supply elasticity for commodity j.

Since we will be concerned with the situation where the per capita income y is increasing, we introduce the following measure:

$$\gamma_j = \frac{\sigma_j}{\eta_{jy}}, \quad j = 1, 2. \quad (17)$$

It will be assumed that commodity 1 is a representative of necessities in the sense that

$$\beta_1 + \gamma_1 \text{ is small,} \quad (18)$$

while, for commodity 2,

$$\beta_2 + \gamma_2 \text{ is fairly large.} \quad (19)$$

We have assumed that both product markets are perfectly competitive. In the general case where product markets are not necessarily perfectly competitive, the above consideration may be slightly modified. Namely, the marginality condition (9) may be replaced by the following:

$$\left(1-\frac{1}{\eta_j}\right)p_j = \frac{1}{f_j'(n_j)}, \quad j = 1, 2, \tag{20}$$

where η_j is the price elasticity for commodity j (to be derived from the expected demand schedule). If we assume that the price elasticity for commodity j remains approximately constant, the various elasticity concepts introduced above may be applied to the present case.

III EQUILIBRIUM CONDITIONS

The demand and supply conditions discussed above may now be put together to obtain a set of equilibrium conditions for the determination of market prices. Namely, we have

$$\begin{cases} x_1(p_1, p_2, y) = f_1(n_1)K_1 \\ x_2(p_1, p_2, y) = f_2(n_2)K_2, \end{cases} \tag{21}$$

where K_1 and K_2 are respectively the quantities of real capital in sectors 1 and 2.

The equilibrium conditions are assumed to be satisfied at each moment of time t. The variables p_1, p_2, y, n_2 have values changing over time t. It is possible to derive the relationships between various rates of changes concerning relevant variables. In order to facilitate the exposition, we introduce the following notation for the rates of change over time:

$$\hat{p}_1 = \frac{1}{p_1}\frac{dp_1}{dt}, \quad \hat{p}_2 = \frac{1}{p_2}\frac{dp_2}{dt}, \quad \hat{y} = \frac{1}{y}\frac{dy}{dt}, \text{ etc.} \tag{22}$$

Then logarithmically differentiating the equilibrium conditions (21), we obtain the following set of relationships between various rates of change:

$$\begin{cases} -\eta_{11}\hat{p}_1 + \eta_{12}\hat{p}_2 + \eta_{1y}\hat{y} = \sigma_1\hat{p}_1 \\ \eta_{21}\hat{p}_1 - \eta_{22}\hat{p}_2 + \eta_{2y}\hat{y} = \sigma_2\hat{p}_2 \end{cases} \tag{23}$$

or, substituting the relationships (4),

$$\begin{cases} -\eta_{11}\hat{p}_1 + (\eta_{11} - \eta_{1y})\hat{p}_2 + \eta_{1y}\hat{y} = \sigma_1\hat{p}_1 \\ (\eta_{22} - \eta_{2y})\hat{p}_2 - \eta_{22}\hat{p}_2 + \eta_{2y}\hat{y} = \sigma_2\hat{p}_2. \end{cases} \tag{24}$$

Dividing the equations (24) by η_{1y} and η_{2y}, we obtain

$$\begin{cases} -\beta_1\hat{p}_1 + (\beta_1 - 1)\hat{p}_2 + \hat{y} = \gamma_1\hat{p}_1 \\ (\beta_2 - 1)\hat{p}_1 - \beta_2\hat{p}_2 + \hat{y} = \gamma_2\hat{p}_2, \end{cases} \tag{25}$$

or

$$\begin{cases} (\beta_1 + \gamma_1)\hat{p}_1 + (1 - \beta_1)\hat{p}_2 = \hat{y} \\ (1 - \beta_2)\hat{p}_1 + (\beta_2 + \gamma_2)\hat{p}_2 = \hat{y}. \end{cases} \tag{26}$$

The system of linear equations (26) may be solved with respect to $\hat{p}_1$ and $\hat{p}_2$, to obtain

$$\begin{cases} \hat{p}_1 = \dfrac{1}{\Delta}(\gamma_2 + \beta_1 + \beta_2 - 1)\hat{y} \\ \hat{p}_2 = \dfrac{1}{\Delta}(\gamma_1 + \beta_1 + \beta_2 - 1)\hat{y}, \end{cases} \tag{27}$$

where Δ is the determinant of (26):

$$\Delta = \begin{vmatrix} \beta_1 + \gamma_1 & 1 - \beta_1 \\ 1 - \beta_2 & \beta_2 + \gamma_2 \end{vmatrix} = \beta_1\gamma_2 + \beta_2\gamma_1 + \gamma_1\gamma_2 + \beta_1 + \beta_2 - 1. \tag{28}$$

The formulae (27) for $\hat{p}_1$ and $\hat{p}_2$ may be further simplified:

$$\begin{cases} \hat{p}_1 = \dfrac{\dfrac{1}{\gamma_1} + \dfrac{\beta_1 + \beta_2 - 1}{\gamma_1\gamma_2}}{\dfrac{\beta_1}{\gamma_1} + \dfrac{\beta_2}{\gamma_2} + 1 + \dfrac{\beta_1 + \beta_2 - 1}{\gamma_1\gamma_2}}\hat{y} \\ \hat{p}_2 = \dfrac{\dfrac{1}{\gamma_2} + \dfrac{\beta_1 + \beta_2 - 1}{\gamma_1\gamma_2}}{\dfrac{\beta_1}{\gamma_1} + \dfrac{\beta_2}{\gamma_2} + 1 + \dfrac{\beta_1 + \beta_2 - 1}{\gamma_1\gamma_2}}\hat{y}. \end{cases} \tag{29}$$

From the formulae (29), one can easily see that the rate of price increase for commodity 1 is larger than that for commodity 2 if, and only if, the supply elasticity for commodity 1 is smaller than that for commodity 2. Furthermore, the rate of price increase p_1 for commodity 1 is larger than the rate of increase in per capita income y, if, and only if, the following condition is satisfied:

$$\beta_1 + \gamma_1 + \beta_2\frac{\gamma_1}{\gamma_2} < 1. \tag{30}$$

It may be noted that, if the demand functions are derived from the maximisation of a utility function, then

$$\beta_1 + \beta_2 > 1. \tag{31}$$

The formulae obtained above show that the relative magnitude of rates of price increase is closely related with the magnitude of relative elasticities $\beta_1, \beta_2, \gamma_1, \gamma_2$.

IV MINIMUM INCOME AND SOCIAL INSTABILITY

The discussion developed in the previous section may be applied to derive the relationships between the rates of increase in the minimum income and average income. First, we should like to define the concept of the minimum income in terms of a representative utility schedule. Let $u = u(X_1, X_2)$ be the utility function of a representative economic unit, and let us assume that a certain level of utility, u_{min}, has been designated as the socially agreed minimum level of living standard. When market prices of two commodities are given by p_1 and p_2, the minimum level of income which is required to maintain the minimum level of living standard, u_{min}, will be denoted by $y_{min} = y_{min}(p_1, p_2)$. The minimum level of income, y_{min}, may be formally defined as follows:

$$y_{min} = y_{min}(p_1, p_2) = \min\{y = p_1 X_1 + p_2 X_2 : u(X_1, X_2) = u_{min}\}. \tag{32}$$

The minimum income y_{min} may be characterised by the following conditions:

$$y_{min} = p_1 X_1^0 + p_2 X_2^0, \tag{33}$$

$$\begin{cases} u_{min} = u(X_1^0, X_2^0), \\ \dfrac{\partial u/\partial X_1}{p_1} = \dfrac{\partial u/\partial X_2}{p_2}. \end{cases} \tag{34}$$

Logarithmically differentiate (33) to obtain

$$\hat{y}_{min} = (s_1^0 \hat{X}_1^0 + s_2^0 \hat{X}_2^0) + (s_1^0 \hat{p}_1^0 + s_2^0 \hat{p}_2^0), \tag{35}$$

where s_1^0 and s_2^0 are respectively the relative shares of expenditure on commodities 1 and 2, at the minimum level of income:

$$\begin{cases} s_1^0 = p_1 X_1^0 / y_{min}, \quad s_2^0 = p_2 X_2^0 / y_{min}, \\ s_1^0 + s_2^0 = 1, \quad 0 < s_1^0, \quad s_2^0 < 1. \end{cases} \tag{36}$$

Differentiating (34), we get

$$\frac{\partial u}{\partial X_1^0}\hat{X}_1^0 + \frac{\partial u}{\partial X_2^0}\hat{X}_2^0 = 0, \tag{37}$$

where the minimum level of living standard u_{min} is assumed to remain constant. From (35) and (37), we obtain

$$p_1\hat{X}_1^0 + p_2\hat{X}_2^0 = 0. \tag{38}$$

The equation (35) now may be written as

$$\hat{y}_{min} = s_1^0\hat{p}_1^0 + s_2^0\hat{p}_2^0. \tag{39}$$

The relationships (29) and (39) are put together to yield the following basic formula:

$$\hat{y}_{min} = \frac{\dfrac{s_1^0}{\gamma_1} + \dfrac{s_2^0}{\gamma_2} + \dfrac{\beta_1+\beta_2-1}{\gamma_1\gamma_2}}{\dfrac{\beta_1}{\gamma_1} + \dfrac{\beta_2}{\gamma_2} + \dfrac{\beta_1+\beta_2-1}{\gamma_1\gamma_2}}\,\hat{y}_{av}, \tag{40}$$

where $\hat{y}_{av}$ is the rate of increase in per capita income $y = y_{av}$.

From the basic formula (40), we can derive the conditions under which the level of minimum income, y_{min}, increases at a rate higher than per capita income y_{av}. Namely, we obtain the following relationships:

$$\hat{y}_{min} > \hat{y}_{av} \quad \text{if, and only if} \quad \frac{s_1^0-\beta_1}{\gamma_1} + \frac{s_2^0-\beta_2}{\gamma_2} > 1. \tag{41}$$

We have assumed that $\beta_1+\gamma_1$ is small, while β_2 is rather large, and s_1^0 may be assumed to be close to one. Hence, under such circumstances, it is generally the case that the following condition is satisfied:

$$\frac{s_1^0-\beta_1}{\gamma_1} + \frac{s_2^0-\beta_2}{\gamma_2} > 1; \tag{42}$$

hence, under fairly general conditions, *the rate of increase in the minimum income*, y_{min}, *is higher than the rate of increase in the average income*, y_{av}.

Let Y_{av} and Y_{min} be respectively the levels of the average income and the minimum income in money terms. Then we have

$$\hat{Y}_{min} > \hat{Y}_{av} \quad \text{if and only if} \quad \hat{y}_{min} > \hat{y}_{av}. \tag{43}$$

The above proposition may be applied to the situation where all quantities are measured in money terms, instead of wage-units.

We have shown above that, when the per capita level of national income is increasing, then the general price level necessarily increases, the rate of price increase is higher for those commodities which are necessities in the sense that both demand and supply elasticities are small, and the minimum level of income required to maintain the socially recognised minimum standard of living is raised. In such cases, it follows that, in a given society, the percentage of those whose income has fallen below the minimum level steadily increases as the processes of inflation continue and the average level of real national income is increased. If the society tries to give income subsidies to those who have fallen below the minimum income line, then it can be shown that the amount of income subsidies required for such an income redistribution scheme steadily increases relative to the magnitude of real national income, whereby the minimum level of income is also steadily increased relative to the average level of income. When such a situation occurs, the allocative mechanism may be said to be *socially unstable*. The above discussion may now be summarised: *if the commodities, which have to be consumed by a relatively large amount at the minimum level of income, have low demand and supply elasticities, then the allocative mechanism through markets, either perfectly competitive or imperfectly competitive, tends to become socially unstable.*

V SOCIAL INSTABILITY OF MARKET ALLOCATION AND SOCIAL OVERHEAD CAPITAL

Social instability of the allocative mechanism through markets is caused by a number of factors such as fixity of factors of production, low elasticities of necessities, and an increase in per capita real income. However, the primary reason for social instability seems to be the arrangement whereby all the factors of production are privately appropriated and put in use according to the profit maximisation criterion. When the allocative mechanism is socially unstable, the scheme to restore an equitable distribution of real income through tax-subsidy arrangements tends to accelerate the divergence between the rate of increase in the minimum income and the rate of increase in the average income, thus resulting in a spiral increase in the amount of transfer income required for such a scheme. An alternative scheme to stabilise the allocative mechanism would be a socialisation or a collectivisation of those factors of production which are responsible to the divergence of these two rates of increases in income levels; namely, some of the factors of production will be classified as social overhead capital, for which the private ownership arrangement is abolished, but instead they are collectively owned and managed by the members of the society and the services derived from them will be distributed according to a certain social criterion.

Since the institution which is in charge of the management of a particular kind of social overhead capital has to follow a set of administrative criteria which are basically different from those governing private corporations, as has been shown in Uzawa [3], the system of implicit prices which results in a socially optimum allocation of both private and social resources would be different from that of market prices. Such a system of implicit prices in particular has a feature of what might be termed a dual price system. Namely, each commodity has two prices, one governing the processes of production and the other being used as an indicator from the viewpoint of consumption. Let such dual prices for each commodity be denoted by p_P and p_C. The production price p_P is used in allocating scarce resources, both private and social, for the production of the commodity in question, while the consumption price p_C will be used as the price to be implicitly charged to consumption activities. If a social overhead capital is not neutral, then these two prices, p_P and p_C, are different, and the institution which is in charge of the management of such an overhead capital necessarily suffers a deficit or enjoys a surplus, when the resulting allocation of scarce resource is optimum and the allocative mechanism is socially stable.

The formulation of social overhead capital, as introduced in Uzawa [3, 4], may be summarised as follows. Each social overhead capital is assumed to be composed of a homogeneous and measurable quantity; let the quantity of a particular type of social overhead capital existing at a given moment of time be given by V. The services derived from social overhead capital may be utilised both for production and consumption activities. Let α and β represent generic notation for consuming and producing units. Then the level of utility enjoyed by consumer α, u_α, depends on the amount of services derived from the overhead capital, X_α, as well as the amount of services from private capital. It also depends upon the extent to which other members of the society are using the same overhead capital due to the phenomenon of congestion. The utility function then may be written as:

$$u_\alpha = U_\alpha(K_\alpha, X_\alpha, X, V), \tag{44}$$

where K_α is the amount of private capital, X_α is the amount of the services derived from social overhead capital, both used by consumer α, and X is the total amount of the services from overhead capital being used by all the members of the society:

$$X = \sum_{\alpha} X_{\alpha} + \sum_{\beta} X_{\beta}. \tag{45}$$

The phenomenon of congestion occurs when the utility function satisfies the following property:

$$\frac{\partial U_{\alpha}}{\partial X} < 0. \tag{46}$$

A similar formulation may be made for the producing unit β. Let the amount of commodities produced by producer β be denoted by Q_{β}, then the production function for producer β may be of the form:

$$Q_{\beta} = F_{\beta}(K_{\beta}, X_{\beta}, X, V), \tag{47}$$

where X_{β} stands for the amount of the services derived from overhead capital being used by producer β. Again the phenomenon of congestion occurs when the production function F_{β} satisfies the following condition:

$$\frac{\partial F_{\beta}}{\partial X} < 0. \tag{48}$$

Let the quantity of private capital which exists in the society at a given moment of time be denoted by K; then, the following constraint has to be satisfied:

$$\sum_{\alpha} K_{\alpha} + \sum_{\beta} K_{\beta} = K, \tag{49}$$

while the quantity of social overhead capital V appears directly in each individual unit's utility function and production. In general, it may be assumed that

$$\frac{\partial U_{\alpha}}{\partial V} > 0, \quad \frac{\partial F_{\beta}}{\partial V} > 0. \tag{50}$$

It may be noted that, for Samuelsonian public goods, the following conditions have to be satisfied:

$$\begin{cases} \dfrac{\partial U_{\alpha}}{\partial X_{\alpha}} \equiv 0, & \dfrac{\partial F_{\beta}}{\partial X_{\beta}} \equiv 0, \\ \dfrac{\partial U_{\alpha}}{\partial X} \equiv 0, & \dfrac{\partial F_{\beta}}{\partial X} \equiv 0. \end{cases} \tag{51}$$

The concept of marginal social costs then is defined by:

$$\theta = \sum_{\alpha} \frac{-\partial U_\alpha/\partial V}{\partial U_\alpha/\partial K_\alpha} + \sum_{\beta} \frac{\partial F_\beta}{\partial V} \tag{52}$$

while that of marginal social products, r, may be defined by:

$$r = \sum_{\alpha} \frac{\partial U_\alpha/\partial V}{\partial U_\alpha/\partial K_\alpha} + \sum_{\beta} \frac{\partial F_\beta}{\partial V} \tag{53}$$

An intertemporally optimum allocation of scarce resources, including both private and social capital, may be obtained in terms of the following institutional arrangements.

Each social overhead capital is administered by an independent public institution which charges the fees corresponding to the magnitude of marginal social costs θ to those economic units using the services derived from overhead capital. The society gives current subsidies corresponding to the difference $rV - \theta X$ (if rV exceeds θX, the amount of subsidies is $rV - \theta X$; if rV is less then θX, the public institution in charge of overhead capital has to pay surcharges corresponding to $\theta X - rV$). The magnitude of investment to be made in the construction of overhead capital is also determined at the level at which the marginal efficiency of investment in that type of overhead capital is equal to the social rate of discount, implying that an interest subsidy is given to the extent to which the market rate of interest exceeds the social rate of discount. Then it can be shown that, if private capital is allocated in a perfectly competitive market, the resulting time pattern of resource allocation is optimum in terms of an intertemporal social preference criterion.

REFERENCES

[1] Samuelson, P. A., 'The Pure Theory of Public Expenditures', *Review of Economics and Statistics*, 36 (1954), 387–9.

[2] ——, 'Diagramatic Exposition of a Pure Theory of Public Expenditures', *Review of Economics and Statistics*, 37, 350–6.

[3] Uzawa, H., 'Sur la théorie économique du capital collectif social', *Cahiers du seminaire d' économétrie* (1974), 101–22.

[4] ——, 'Optimum Investment in Social Overhead Capital', in *Economic Analysis of Environmental Problems*, E. S. Miller (ed) (1975), pp. 9–26.

[5] ——, 'On the Economics of Social Overhead Capital', unpublished (1972).

Discussion of 'Social Stability in Public Collective Consumption' by Professor H. Uzawa

Professor Modigliani introduced the discussion by pointing out that the paper consisted of two quite distinguishable parts. The first part purported to demonstrate 'the social instability of the allocative mechanism of a . . . competitive market economy . . . which may be resolved' by nationalising certain scarce resources. The second part set forth a generalisation of the traditional Samuelsonian analysis of public goods and social overhead capital. He was very well impressed by the second part, though it was largely a summary of work developed elsewhere. But with respect to the highly original first part, he felt Uzawa's case lacked empirical relevance. For the condition required for the Uzawa instability to arise was that both per capita income and prices *measured in wage units* should tend to rise in time, and that furthermore the prices of necessities should rise even faster. But a rise of prices in wage units was equivalent to a fall in real wages. Thus, for Uzawa's instability to arise, economic development would have to be accompanied by a steady decline in real wages in general, and an even faster decline in the real wages of the poorer segments of the working class. It was because of this assumed process of growing immiserisation that the maintenance of an acceptable distribution of welfare would require an unstable, explosive rise in transfer payments, avoidable only through the nationalisation of the relevant means of production.

In reality, as was well known, the essential feature of economic development had been the spectacular *rise* of real wages. Professor Modigliani said he was not aware of any systematic empirical evidence suggesting that the purchasing power of wages in terms of necessities had done worse than in terms of other commodities. If anything, the opposite seemed to be true. Similarly, income per capita expressed in wage units – i.e. in terms of hours of labour per man – had most likely tended to *fall* in time. Indeed, income so measured might be expected to be proportional (or roughly proportional) to the number of hours worked per man (at least as long as the wealth income ratio was roughly constant and technological progress was Harrod Neutral), and these hours had clearly tended to decline very conspicuously with economic progress.

The reason that in Uzawa's model both per capita income and prices in wage units rose instead, seemed to be that he was abstracting from the most important features of economic development, namely (i) technological progress leading to rising income through rising productivity, and (ii) the process of accumulation resulting from the rise in income. This process had tended to maintain the capital per 'equivalent' worker, ensuring that the increase in productivity was translated into higher real wages (or lower prices in wage units).

In Uzawa's model, the rise in income resulted instead, apparently, from the application of more labour per man to the existing stock of equipment. Decreasing returns then ensured that a rise in per capita output would be accompanied by a declining marginal product of labour and real wage – though this fall in real wages did not occur with realistic imperfectly competitive market structures.

In short, the process described by Professor Uzawa's model was not that typical of recent economic development, but was more akin to the process of cyclical expansion (which by its very nature was a reversible one). This model did not seem to provide an adequate basis to draw inferences about the social instability inherent in the development of a competitive market economy.

Mr Matthews argued that any appraisal of Professor Uzawa's analysis should recognise the alternative time-scales which could be considered. The mechanisms described in the paper could explain the disruptive effects of increasing income transfers to the poor in a cyclical recession. However, if the analysis was seeking to describe a general law of capitalist development in the long run it must explicitly consider technical progress in the production of all commodities in addition to income and price elasticities of demand. However, *Mr Boltho's* view was that price elasticities of demand were crucial to the outcome in the short run, whereas income elasticities of demand were more important in the long run. *Professor Frey* pointed out that the introduction of Harrod-Neutral technical progress into the analysis would change wage rates and per capita incomes equally and thus leave the results of the analysis unaffected.

Several speakers commented on Professor Uzawa's proposition that the price of commodities which were economic necessities would rise faster than the price of all commodities. In support of this conclusion *Professor Bös* cited Austrian evidence that the cost of living index for old age pensioners had risen faster than the general index. *Sir Leo Pliatzky*'s recollection of the figures for the United Kingdom was that the cost of living index for pensioners had not risen more rapidly than the general index. He drew attention to the arrangement whereby social security payments in the United Kingdom had been indexed against inflation. An amendment proposed by the Labour administration of 1974–79 allowed long-term benefits such as old age pensions to be indexed against wage or price inflation whichever was the greater. Such a provision could generate a differential effect in favour of pensioners of the kind analysed in the paper. However, as the new Conservative administration had announced its intention to cancel this amendment, such an effect was unlikely to emerge in the United Kingdom. *Mr Matthews* argued that pensioners were not representatives of all low-income earners. Relative to the younger poor they purchased less manufactured durables, the production of which was subject to rapid technical progress which reduced relative unit costs and prices. *Mr Boltho* referred to OECD studies of the 1960s and early 1980s which did not show any systematic difference between the inflation rates experienced by different income classes. He did not dispute the evidence cited by Professor Bös which referred to different socio-economic classes. *Professor Modigliani*'s recollection of the figures for the United States was that there had been no differential inflation across income classes, at least until the early 1970s. The reason for this had been the impact of exceptional productivity improvements in the agricultural sector on the relative price of food. *Mr Matthews* reported that in the United Kingdom productivity growth in the post-war period had been greater in agriculture than in any sector of manufacturing industry. *Dr Hoch* argued that evidence on inflation rates across income classes was misleading if the possibilities of substitution between commodities open to rich and poor households were not also taken into account. Food and fuel bulked large in the budgets of the poor who could not easily substitute other commodities for them as their relative prices increased. However, rich households could more easily substitute for relatively expensive services of which they consumed proportionately more. There was thus a differential impact between rich and poor which price data alone did not reveal.

Questions were raised about the assumption of the paper that for commodities representing necessities the values of β and γ (respectively the quotient of the price elasticity of demand and the income elasticity of demand, and of the price elasticity of supply and the income elasticity of demand) were small relative to the values for the commodity representing luxuries. *Professors Bös* and *Modigliani* argued that this assumption would be incorrect if the price and income elasticities of demand of the necessity were both very small, as could be the case. Professor Modigliani saw no grounds for the assumption that the price elasticity of supply of the necessity was small, especially in the long run when the elasticity of substitution between factors in the production of necessities could be expected to increase.

Several speakers did not accept Professor Uzawa's conclusion on the inherent instability of a competitive market system in which income was transferred to the poor. *Professor Bös* suggested that a secular increase in minimum income relative to average income would induce changes in elasticities which might ensure a convergence to a stable equilibrium. *Sir Leo Pliatzky*'s view was that in the United Kingdom increases in social security payments and other public expenditures had stabilised income and employment in the post-war period, and had thus avoided severe slumps of the kind experienced in the 1930s. *Professor Frey* was sceptical of Professor Uzawa's conclusion that the socialisation of resources would confer stability. Evidence on the existence of a political business cycle suggested that the political system itself generated instability. A model in which political behaviour was endogenous was required for a full analysis of the stability of a mixed economy.

Professor Sandmo suggested that for long-run analysis it would be more interesting to have labour supply determined by utility-maximising behaviour by consumers. This would make the real wage enter more explicitly into demand functions and thus make them more complicated. In particular conditions (4) of the paper would no longer hold. Such a modification would also allow distinctions to be made between consumer goods according to their degree of complementarity with leisure. This distinction could be interesting for the case discussed earlier of old age pensioners for whom the opportunity cost of time might reasonably be assumed low. *Mr Kaser* suggested that Professor Uzawa's definition of minimum income in terms of utility allowed the possibility of substitution between necessities to maintain a given utility level. Indeed the composition of the minimum income basket could be expected to change in the long run under the so-called 'Gerschenkron effect' whereby the output of relatively scarce products expands relative to the output of more abundant commodities during the process of income growth. If such changes and substitutions did take place the elasticity properties of particular commodities would be less important. *Professor Bös* wondered whether the definition of prices and incomes in terms of wage units was crucial to the results presented. He drew attention to the importance of the policy question analysed in the paper. Income transfers and the socialisation of resources were important alternatives for a policy against poverty. The advantage of transfer payments was that they could be selectively given to the poor, whereas adjustments in the prices of the outputs of nationalised industries, for example, were indiscriminate. *Professor Pajestka* suggested that governments of mixed economies might respond to the sort of problems analysed in the paper by reducing their concern for the poor.

Professor Uzawa did not disagree with many of the points made by Professor Modigliani in his introduction to the discussion. He insisted that a major purpose of his paper had been to extend the traditional Samuelsonian analysis of social overhead capital and public goods. The traditional analysis did not consider the redistributional activities of the state, nor, in particular, did it envisage the instability that could emerge within specific redistributional systems. In order to analyse this instability and the role of social capital, he had deliberately selected a very simple model which abstracted from technical progress, capital accumulation and economic behaviour in other parts of the system. He did not accept the criticisms that had been made of his use of wage-units to measure income and prices, for his results could be derived in terms of money income and nominal prices.

3 The Public Choice Approach to the Explanation of Collective Consumption

Bruno S. Frey

UNIVERSITY OF ZÜRICH

This paper is about a major development in public sector economics that directly bears on collective consumption and its financing, and which is based on the economic theory of politics, otherwise known as Public Choice. The discussion puts particular emphasis on the research results reached in the last two or three years with respect to quantification of the hypotheses derived (in particular 'politico-economic models'). These research results are relatively little known, but serve well to illustrate the new approach. The paper will attempt to show the consequences of using the Public Choice approach. The author believes that this constitutes a major change of view, with three areas of economics – positive economic theory, forecasting and economic policy – being particularly affected.

The first part of this paper contrasts the traditional and the Public Choice views of the public sector. Section II discusses three basic variants of the politico-economic model and presents some empirical research results that have been achieved in testing them. The next section (III) points up some possible and worthwhile extensions of politico-economic models, and the concluding section deals with their consequences for public sector economics, and for collective consumption and its financing in particular.

I VIEWS OF THE PUBLIC SECTOR

1 THE TRADITIONAL APPROACH

Economic analysis of the public sector has traditionally been dominated by two approaches. The first approach is that of a *positive theory* of the public sector which attempts to explain public expenditures by means of *socio-economic factors* such as per capital income, degree of urbanisation and population density, using multiple cross-section regressions. This approach has been championed by fiscal economists (especially Fabricant, 1952; for a survey of the large number of empirical studies see Pryor, 1968; Bahl, 1969 and Wilensky, 1970); it has mostly been applied to local communities and has been able to account for a considerable share (over 70 per cent) of the variance in public outlays. It is based on purely *ad hoc* assumptions; i.e. the political process and the behaviour of decision-makers that leads to the observed expenditure levels is not considered.[1] This approach does not provide a refutable theory about the public sector but is rather an example of 'measurement without theory'. For this reason it has (with a few exceptions) been given up recently, and thus need not be considered further here.

The second approach, which has been widely accepted in economics as a basis for economic policy, is that of a *normative theory* of the public sector based on the assumption that governments *maximise a social welfare function*, subject to the constraints imposed by the economic system. The normative approach has been formalised in:

(1) The theory of quantitative economic policy (Tinbergen, 1956; Theil, 1968), and, subsequently, in the theory of optimal control (e.g. Chow, 1973), which derive how the government should optimally use its policy instruments (among them public expenditures and their financing) to maximise social welfare.
(2) The theory of optimal taxation (see e.g. Diamond and Mirrlees, 1971), which determines the minimal social loss brought about by tax distortions given an exogenously determined tax collection.

[1] Political scientists (e.g. Casstevens and Press, 1963; Dawson and Robinson, 1963; Fry and Winter, 1970) concerned about the seeming absence of 'political' influences on public expenditures in this approach have made a strong effort to introduce determinants such as the amount of party competition, the size of political participation, or the distribution of power between the legislative and executive branches. On the whole these attempts have failed. For an account and criticism of this 'comparative policy analysis', see Frey and Pommerehne (1978).

The normative theory, however, gives a basically mistaken view of the public sector for two reasons:

(1) Government and the rest of the public sector are not exogenous to the politico-economic system as assumed, but rather *endogenous*. In particular, government is held responsible for the state of the economy by the population (voters and interest groups).

(2) Government has in general *little incentive* to undertake the policies suggested by maximising the social welfare function, assuming that such a function existed.[2] (The ideology pursued may be believed to represent the common good, but this may deviate from the social welfare function.) Government is no 'benevolent dictator' but rather acts according to its own interests, of which the most important one is to survive, i.e. to stay in power.

Thus the basic assumptions of the normative theory of the public sector are highly questionable, and there are good grounds for considering a different approach.

2 THE PUBLIC CHOICE VIEW

The economic theory of politics attempts to overcome the basic problems connected with traditional public sector analysis. Here the public sector is taken to be a part of a more extended social system which includes both political and economic subsectors. Government behaviour is endogenous, and is analysed with the help of modern economic theory.

The basic unit of analysis is the individual who responds systematically to positive and negative incentives. This economic model of behaviour corresponds closely to the socio-psychological model of human beings (see Stroebe and Frey, 1979 for a more extended discussion). It has proved useful to assume that individuals are neither saints nor villains, but that they are primarily interested in their own utility.

The behaviour of *all* actors and in *all* situations (i.e. in the marketplace or in politics) is explained by the same model: the individual utility function is maximised subject to various constraints imposed

[2] As has been well known since Arrow (1951), and has been expanded by Plott (1967), Kramer (1973), Fishburn (1973) and others, there exists in general no social welfare function based on individual preferences.

from outside such as earning capacity (budget constraint), time or existing institutions.

On the one side, the individual's behaviour leads to a *demand* for the output of the political sector. Individuals have various means available to them for making their wishes known in the political sector, including the use of exit (switching their vote from the government to an opposition party, for example) and voice (protest with a party or on the streets). Using the individual utility function for deriving the demand for public services makes it possible to take into account that it may be more profitable for an individual to invest her/his effort and resources in the political process rather than in productive market activity in order to reach his/her goals. It explains, for example, under what circumstances it pays to establish or join an interest group in order to get government transfers.

On the other side, the *supply* of public sector output is the result of *utility*-maximising individuals acting as politicians, government officials and civil servants.

For the purpose of analysis it is often useful to take existing institutions (such as interest groups on the demand side, and parties, government and bureaucracy on the supply side) as given in order to concentrate on their interaction. The utility-maximising approach does not require us always to go all the way down to the level of the individual; it suffices that the institutions 'acting' be analysable in terms of the behaviour of individuals.

In the Public Choice context, collective consumption and its financing is explained by a general theory of the politico-economic process which includes all types of government activity. The basic motivations and constraints leading to non-budgetery activity (such as the promulgation of laws and statutes) are the same as those leading to budgetary choices regarding exhaustive (consumption and investment) and transfer expenditures. Public expenditures and their financing through taxes and other means are analysed jointly, quite in contrast to optimum taxation literature which takes one of the two sides of the fiscal account – expenditures for which a certain tax sum must be collected – as exogenously given (see Buchanan, 1976).

Public Choice has developed very rapidly in recent years; for general surveys see Mueller (1976, 1979) or Frey (1978). Non-specialists are often only aware of the pathbreaking contribution of Downs (1957), but his theory of party competition covers only a small part of the whole field and constitutes a rather special case. Public sector economics should also take into account the recent quantitative analyses that have been done using econometric methods. As these deal with the interaction of the economic and political sectors, they are able to capture the determinants of collective consumption and its financing. This part of modern political economy is known as politico-economic modelling:

II POLITICO-ECONOMIC MODELS – VARIANTS AND EMPIRICAL RESULTS

In the simplest case, the interdependence between the economic and the political sectors of society can be studied by considering the behaviour of two decision-makers with respect to public services: the voters, demanding; and the government, supplying.

1 VARIANTS

Three variants of this basic politico-economic model may be distinguished according to the institutional assumptions made about the degree of independence held by the public sector on the supply side of the political process.

1.1 Median voter model

In a system of simple majority voting (and single peaked preferences for individuals), the voter in the median position throws the decisive vote. In particular he/she decides what that combination of collective expenditures and taxes is to be that is to give her/him the greatest net benefit. The supply side (government) is assumed to fulfil the median voter's demands completely.

Empirical estimates of income and tax price elasticities can be derived by regressing first public expenditure (broken down into its various components) and then taxes, both times on income, the tax burden of the median voter, and other explanatory variables such as the population's age distribution. Median voter models have been applied on the basis of cross-section analysis in a great many studies, such as for explaining school expenditures in US communities (e.g. Barr and Davis, 1966; Barlow, 1970; Bergstrom and Goodman, 1973) or expenditures of various sorts in Swiss cities (Pommerehne, 1978). The model can also be used to assess the importance of voters' 'illusion' (i.e. incomplete or biased information) about public expenditures and taxes. Thus it has been shown that the more complicated the tax system, the less voters realise what their tax burden actually is – and the higher therefore are public outlays (Wagner, 1976; Pommerehne and Schneider, 1978).

The central assumption of the median voter model is that government supplies exactly what the median voter demands, i.e. it has no discretionary power or goals of its own. The model is therefore only applicable in those very specific cases in which direct voting exclusively dominates the political process, and propositions are amended until they agree with the median voter's wishes. It is often inappropriately applied in research (see also Romer and Rosenthal, 1978), as for example when it is used to explain the development of public expenditures in representative democracies such as the United States, England and FR Germany (see e.g. Peltzman, 1979; Meltzer and Richard, 1979).

1.2 Party competition

The second variant of the politico-economic model focuses on the outcome of the competition of parties for votes in order to come to power. A voter casts her/his vote for that party which best corresponds to his/her preferences. The programmes advanced by the parties in this quest for votes are put into practice because there is continuous need to win and retain votes, and thus continuous competition.

In the case of two parties that have to maximise votes in order to win, the median voter is again decisive. With more than two parties the outcome is largely undetermined because of the many coalition possibilities.

The model of party competition has rarely been directly empirically tested (but see Kaspar, 1971); it has more often been the case that only some partial and indirect consequences have been considered. One of the main reasons for this is that the assumption of continuous electoral competition and of only two parties – with not even additional potential competitors – does not reflect the actual situation existent in most countries (see Rae, 1971).

1.3 Monopoly government

The third variant of the politico-economic model concentrates on the government's behaviour and considers voters only to the extent that they influence this behaviour. Elections are assumed to take place discontinuously, and voters to forget much of what government has promised and done in the past. Government is taken as having a prominent position as compared to the opposition party(s) because it controls the economic policy instruments, has much greater influence on the mass media, and is continually in the public's eye. It therefore does not have to respond directly to the oppostion's policy but can to a large extent behave as if it were in a monopoly position. In contrast to party competition models, politicians and parties do not go into politics solely in order to gain power but to put their programmes into practice. Government has discretionary power which it can use to further its own goals, but such a monopoly government cannot do whatever it wants. It is subject to constraints, exactly the same as a monopolist on a market is subject to the constraint of a falling demand curve. In a democracy, the most important constraint the government faces is the need to be re-elected. Even a dictator has to retain a minimum level of support in order to survive as otherwise the costs of holding down the populace become too heavy, leaving her/him and the ruling élite no 'rent' from the dictatorship.

The three variants of the politico-economic model here considered are closely related; they may, in fact, be looked upon as a continuum. If a monopoly government is subject to a strongly binding re-election constraint, it must pursue a vote-maximising policy in order to stay in power, i.e. it must behave in the same way as it would under a system of perfect party competition. And, as already mentioned, the party competition model leads to the same median outcome as simple majority voting when there are only two parties.

2 EMPIRICAL RESULTS

The politico-economic model variant with the best prospects for the future seems to be that of monopoly government with both utility-maximising voters and government politicians actively engaged in the political process. The theoretical model sketched above has been empirically analysed with the help of multiple regressions (OLS and TSLS estimates) for several representative democracies and various post-war periods, usually on the basis of quarterly data.[3]

A politico-economic model of this variant is composed of two basic sets of equations:

(1) The voters' *evaluation function* (shown by the lower loop in Figure

[3] The general model has also been econometrically tested for Switzerland, a country with strong elements of direct democracy in the form of referenda and initiatives, but where the government also has discretionary power. See Schneider, Pommerehne and Frey (1978).

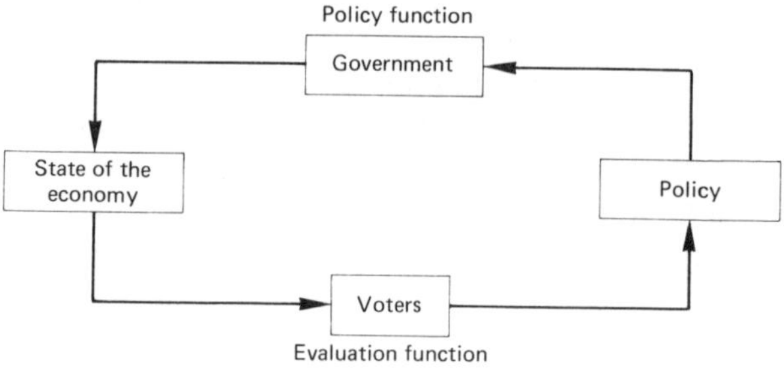

FIG. 3.1 Basic interactions in a politico-economic model with monopoly government

3.1) gives the relationship transmitting economic impulses to the political sector and determining the standing of the government with the voters. It shows the political reaction of the population when the state of the economy changes. This reaction can be measured either by election results (taking place every third or fourth year) or by political popularity surveys (usually done monthly by survey research institutes such as Gallop).

(2) The policy function (upper loop in Figure 3.1) describes the government's use of the economic policy instruments at its disposal (in particular public expenditures and taxes) in order to influence the state of the economy in a direction it considers to be favourable to itself.

The two basic functions will now be discussed in turn.

2.1 Evaluation function

Voters have little incentive to become informed about political matters because each one knows that he/she has extremely little influence upon the outcome (see Downs, 1957). They minimise their exertions when voting by simply attributing the state of the economy to government activity. When they are satisfied with economic conditions, they tend to support the government; when they are dissatisfied, they tend to switch to the opposition party (or parties). The most important elements defining economic conditions from the point of view of the voters are unemployment, inflation and growth of real income. Decreases in unemployment and inflation and increases in growth are expected to raise the government's vote or popularity share. There are, of course, a great many other factors besides these economic factors that have an impact on the government's standing with the voters. They are however either of a long-run nature (such as the composition of the voting population according to age and occupation), and thus may be captured by the constant term; or they are stochastic (such as internal scandals or foreign policy influences) and are captured by the error term in the regression.

Empirical studies done so far have shown superior results for popularity functions over vote functions, because there are many more observations for a given time period. A typical popularity function is that for the United States over the period 1953 (second quarter) to 1976 (third quarter), i.e. covering the presidencies of Eisenhower, Kennedy, Johnson, Nixon and Ford:

Popularity of the President (%) =

−1.58*	Rate of inflation (%)	Economic determinants
(−2.89)		
−4.07*	Rate of unemployment (%)	
(−6.44)		
+0.52*	Growth rate of real disposable income (%)	
(2.19)		
+86.1*	Eisenhower (first term)	Popularity level specific to each president
(24.6)		
+82.9*	Eisenhower (second term)	
(19.0)		
+108.6*	Kennedy	
(23.7)		
+99.7*	Johnson	
(23.9)		
+86.2*	Nixon	
(21.3)		
+97.5*	Ford	
(11.1)		

+0.46* (2.91)	Eisenhowever (first and second terms)	Popularity depreciation specific to presidents /presidential teams
−2.06* (−9.91)	Kennedy and Johnson	
−0.26 (−0.86)	Nixon (first term)	
−5.24* (−6.31)	Watergate scandal	

$\overline{R}^2 = 0.87$, Durbin–Waton = 1.61. *t*-values in parentheses.
Coefficients that are statistically significant at the 95% level are indicated by an asterisk.
(Source: Frey and Schneider, 1979a).

The popularity function shown above is composed of three sets of determinants:

(1) Economic influences. According to this estimate, an increase in the rate of inflation of 1 percentage point tends to decrease the president's popularity by 1.58 percentage points (with a *t*-value of −2.89); an increase in the rate of unemployment of one percentage point reduces presidential popularity by 4.07 percentage points; and a 1 percentage point increase in real income growth increases presidential popularity by 0.52 percentage points. These economic variables all have a statistically significant impact on popularity according to the *t*-test.

(2) The second set of determinants measures each president's specific popularity with the voters independent of all other influences (i.e. the constant term of the regression is broken up and is attributed to the various presidents). It may be seen that Kennedy, Johnson and Ford enjoyed the highest levels of support (108.6, 99.7 and 97.5 respectively).

(3) The third set of determinants measures the 'autonomous' popularity loss or depreciation presidents are subject to during their term, independent of economic conditions. The estimates indicate that presidents Kennedy and Johnson (taken jointly) experienced a marked loss in popularity (see the statistically significant coefficient of −2.06), but that Eisenhower actually became more and more popular. Nixon did not experience a popularity loss over his first term (the coefficient −0.26 is statistically insignificant), but his popularity fell drastically during the Watergate scandal (1973–74).

In the context of politico-economic models the voters' evaluation of the government's performance, based on the state of the economy, is of very great interest because it serves as one of the two basic links between the economy and the polity. Table 3.1 shows the partial impact on government popularity of the three economic variables of inflation, unemployment and real growth in seven countries and over various time periods. This table only serves to give a general impression; because of differences in the variables included in the popularity function, the underlying data, estimation procedures, etc., the coefficients are not strictly comparable.[4]

TABLE 3.1 THE PARTIAL EFFECT OF THREE ECONOMIC VARIABLES ON GOVERNMENT POPULARITY IN SEVEN WESTERN DEMOCRACIES IN POST-WAR PERIODS

	Partial coefficients of economic variables		
Country and period	*Rate of inflation* %	*Rate of unemployment* %	*Growth rate of real disposable income* %
FR Germany 1957–75	−1.5**	−1.7**	0.6*
France 1968–77	−0.81**	−1.26**	—
United Kingdom 1959–74	−0.6**	−6.0**	0.8**
Sweden 1967–73	−0.9**	−5.2**	0.3*
Austria 1960–77	−0.6*	−1.4**	—
United States President 1953–76	−1.6**	−4.1**	0.5**
Australia 1960–77	−0.9**	−2.4**	0.1

* and ** indicate statistical significance at the 90% and 95% levels of significance respectively. The estimates for the United Kingdom and Austria refer to the popularity lead of the government relative to the major opposition party. For definitions of the variables, sources of data, statistical procedures and full estimation results, see the original papers.

Sources: Germany, United Kingdom, United States: various papers by Frey and Schneider, see e.g. 1978a, 1978b, 1979a.
France: Lafay, 1978.
Sweden: Kirchgassner, 1976, Table 4.9.
Austria: Breuss, 1979, p. 51.
Australia: Schneider and Pommerehne, 1979, Table 5.

[4] The coefficients of the economic variables in popularity functions are also quite sensitive to changes in the time periods covered, which may be due to shifts in voters' evaluations and/or to econometric estimation problems.

It can be seen from Table 3.1 that both inflation and unemployment generally have a statistically significant impact on government popularity in western democracies. A 1 percentage point increase in unemployment has a marginally greater impact on popularity than an equivalent increase in the rate of inflation. The growth of real income does not have a significant effect in some of the countries. It thus may be concluded that economic conditions do have an influence on how the voters evaluate the government's performance in representative democracies. The same seems to hold true for direct democracies. It can be shown for Switzerland that the better economic conditions are, the more favourably the population tends to vote on the referenda proposed by the government regardless of their specific content (Schneider, Pommerehne and Frey, 1978). The same seems to be true in communist countries. As there are no elections there in the western sense in which voters can evaluate the government's (or party's) performance, the number of changes in cabinet positions can instead be taken as an indicator. It has been shown (Lafay, 1979) that the worse economic conditions in East European communist countries are, the more frequent are changes in cabinet positions.

2.2 Policy function

Various assumptions about the utility function of the government can be made in the monopoly government version of politico-economic models. The probably best known model of this kind analysing political business cycles (Nordhaus, 1975) assumes that the government maximises its utility by reaching the highest possible vote share at the forthcoming election. This assumption, however, would lead to optimal policies that make little sense and that deviate greatly from actual policies (Fair, 1975).[5] Another assumption of the monopoly government model is that governments derive utility from catering to the preferences of their traditional voting base. Left-wing governments are taken to heavily emphasise policies aimed at reaching full employment because this is in the interest of the lower strata of the population that traditionally support socialist parties; following the same reasoning, right-wing governments are taken to pursue policies leading to price stability (Hibbs, 1977). This approach does not clearly distinguish between the government's utility function and constraints imposed on

[5] Such as bringing about a *real* growth in national income of 20 % (!) in the election year in the United States.

the government from outside. This distinction is made however if it is assumed that the government wishes to pursue its own ideological goals, but that it is subject to a re-election constraint and has to take into account budgetary and balance of payment constraints and limitations on its activity imposed by the public bureaucracy as well.

A model along these lines has been empirically tested for the United States, the United Kingdom and Germany (Frey and Schneider, 1978a, 1978b, 1979b). In this model government politicians concentrate on the crucial re-election constraint because they cannot realise their ideological goals if they are not in power.

For simplicity's sake, a government can be taken as differentiating between two states of the world, according to the degree of popularity it enjoys:

(1) When the government considers its popularity higher than what it thinks is necessary to win the forthcoming election, it can allow itself to undertake policies in line with its ideological ideals. A left-wing government will tend to increase public expenditures and taxes in order to raise the state's share in the national income and therewith socialise the economy, and a right-wing government will tend to decrease public expenditures and taxes in order to encourage the private sector.

(2) If, on the other hand, the government's popularity level is so low that it is afraid of losing the next election, it is forced to undertake policies that will increase its re-election prospects. The government politicians are well aware that their popularity and re-election chances heavily depend on economic conditions. They will therefore (regardless of their ideological bias) undertake an expansionary policy (i.e. increasing public expenditures and decreasing taxes) in order to raise employment and real growth. The negative effect of the increased inflation that may result from such an expansionary policy is under normal circumstances viewed as being considerably smaller than the positive political effects derived from rising employment and growth.[6] This is especially so as the increase in inflation is lagged, and its effect on popularity may be felt only *after* the election.

Table 3.2 shows the qualitative estimation results for three policy

[6] Using a popularity function such as that shown in Table 3.1, simulation experiments with econometric models have shown that an economic upswing increases government popularity except when the rate of inflation is very high.

instruments in the three countries mentioned. The results shown in the table may be summarised as follows:

(1) In all three countries, governments undertake expansionary policies when they are afraid of losing the forthcoming election: exhaustive and transfer public expenditures are increased, and taxes are decreased, as compared to the government's general course.[7]

(2) When governments are confident of winning the next election, left-wing governments (Labour in the UK, Social Democrats in FR Germany) tend to increase public expenditures and taxes. Under this condition right-wing governments (Republican presidents in the US, Tories in the UK, Christian Democrats in FR Germany) tend to decrease public expenditures and taxes.

The econometric estimates shown in Table 3.2 thus tend to support the

TABLE 3.2 DETERMINANTS OF PUBLIC EXPENDITURES AND TAXES. UNITED STATES (1953–75), UNITED KINGDOM (1962–74), FR GERMANY (1951–75). QUALITATIVE RESULTS BASED ON ECONOMETRIC ESTIMATES WITH QUARTERLY DATA

Government policy instruments	*Government's expectations concerning the next election* — *Fearful of losing ⇒ popularity-raising policy*			*Confident of winning ⇒ ideological policy* — *Left-wing governments*			*Right-wing governments*		
	US	UK	G	US	UK	G	US	UK	G
Public expenditures									
(a) Exhaustive	+	+	+	?	(+)	+	−	(−)	−
(b) Transfers	+	+	+	?	(+)	+	−	(−)	(−)
Taxes		−	−		(+)	+		(−)	−

A + sign indicates that the respective economic policy instrument is increased; a − sign, that it is decreased, as compared to the general trend. (+) and (−) indicate that the corresponding parameter estimates are not statistically significant at the 95% level. ? indicates inconclusive results.

Source: Frey and Schneider, 1978a, 1978b, 1979b.

[7] It should be noted that the estimation period extends up to 1975; i.e. it does not cover the period of very high inflation that came thereafter.

theoretical hypotheses developed. The empirical estimates also indicate that when governments are afraid that they will not be re-elected, they pursue an expansionary policy all the more vigorously the nearer the forthcoming elections are. This suggests the existence of a 'political business cycle' that is deliberately produced by government in order to further its election chances.

The monopoly variant of politico-economic models performs quite well in explaining collective consumption and taxes of the public sector despite its very simple structure. Some useful extensions will be discussed in the next section.

IV EXTENSIONS OF THE PUBLIC SECTOR

The politico-economic models empirically estimated so far have a very simple structure and disregard many important features of reality. Work is now under way to extend the model in various directions, in particular to introduce:

(i) additional decision-makers in the public sector;
(ii) interactions within the nation's public sector, and with the outside world;
(iii) specific subsectors within the economy.

These aspects will be sketched briefly in order to show the potential for increasing the verisimilitude of politico-economic models and therewith their ability to explain collective consumption and its financing.

1 ADDITIONAL DECISION-MAKERS IN THE PUBLIC SECTOR

Governments are not homogeneous units but are composed of various factions or are – and this is the usual case in representative democracies – *coalitions* of various parties with differing goals and constraints. So far it has proved difficult to construct theories of coalition formation which are non-trivial (see e.g. Taylor and Laver, 1973; DeSwaan, 1973). It seems that the theory which fares best empirically is simply that parties that are close to each other in the ideological spectrum tend to form coalitions with one another.

In most countries of the world the government is not elected directly by the electorate, but rather via *parliament*. Even if the government is elected directly by the populace, the relationship between it and parliament is of great importance (as for example in the case of the US President and Congress).

Considerable progress has been made in introducing the *central bank* as an actor in its own right in the politico-economic system. In the context of explaining collective consumption, this is of great importance as the central bank has an important role to play with regard to its financing. Thus Gordon (1978) has tested whether the supply of money has any systematic relationship to elections; and Parkin and Bade (1978) have looked at whether the institutional arrangements with respect to the central bank's independence *vis à vis* government has any impact on its policy. These studies are, however, empirical, and do not attempt to formulate a theory of central bank behaviour. The central bank is integrated into an overall politico-economic model by Frey and Schneider (1978c) with the hypothesis that the central bank can pursue a policy of its own liking (essentially, to strive for price stability) provided that it does not conflict too strongly with the government's aims. If conflict goes beyond a certain level of intensity, the central bank is forced to support the government's fiscal policy with monetary policy because the bank's 'independence' will otherwise be threatened by governmental measures to bring it in line.

A very important actor within the public sector that must be taken into account in politico-economic models is the *public bureaucracy*. So far no satisfactory theoretical approach has been developed that can be tested econometrically at the macrolevel. Tullock's (1965) and Downs' (1967) analyses only treat the internal structure of hierarchical organisations; Niskanen (1971) employs a special institutional set-up relevant for the United States, but of little relevance elsewhere; and Wildavsky's (1964) incremental hypothesis is too general to capture important aspects of public bureaucracy. Work is presently under way in various places that promises to overcome these shortcomings.

2 INTERACTION AMONG PUBLIC SECTORS

Most democratic countries have a federal constitution with *various levels of government* having at least some degree of independence. The executives at the communal, state and federal levels act differently because they have different priorities. As one goes down to the lower levels the governments have to seek re-election from increasingly narrower sets of voters, and with the possibility of resorting to debt instead of taxes to finance their expenditures rapidly decreasing. The expenditure behaviour of the different federal units is to a great extent determined by the amounts of transfers. In explaining collective consumption and its financing, it would seem to be of great importance to study the behaviour of the different federal units, and to extend the politico-economic models accordingly.

It is equally important to consider the interaction of the national public sector with governments, central banks and public bureaucracies of other *nations*. This applies in particular for business cycle policy. In many countries (such as England, FR Germany, and Switzerland) internal policy is strongly influenced by the balance of payments, of which a considerable part – namely capital movements – remains largely unexplained in traditional economic models. It is clear, however, that a large amount of capital movement and investment is due to political considerations (relative security[8]) as well as to expectations about future government policy (changes in the exchange rate, the extent of intervention in flexible exchange rates, anti-inflation measures, etc.). These aspects can only be dealt with in the context of a model that includes the behaviour of both economic and political decision-makers. Suggestions as to how to construct *international politico-economic models* may be gained from world simulation models developed by political scientists (see e.g. Hooke and Zinner, 1976; Bremer, 1977; Ward and Guetzkow, 1978).

So far no politico-economic models have been constructed that include federal and/or international aspects, but here again work is under way and results may be expected soon.

3 ECONOMIC BRANCHES WITHIN THE PUBLIC SECTOR

Nationalised industries supply a large part of what is collectively consumed. Some of them act as if they were private, but most of them show a behaviour different from that of private enterprises. Economics has an old and extremely well-developed normative theory of collective enterprises, but extremely little is known about their actual behaviour. As long as this is the case collective consumption and its financing cannot be adequately accounted for. It can be expected that nationalised industries will respond quite differently to economic influences such as changes in relative prices (for example, due to the imposition of emission taxes), the main reason being that they are not subject to the tests of the market and because deficits are covered by the public purse. The manager of a public enterprise gains little by cutting the quality and

[8] Private enterprises (as well as government agencies) put heavy emphasis on the expected political stability of a country in which investments are being considered, especially out of fear concerning strikes, worker unrest and possible expropriation.

amount of service in order to reduce the deficit as he/she may then face a violent protest from the consumers, which may put an end to her/his career. There is a long way to go from these micro and partial considerations to a well-developed theory of the behaviour of the public enterprise sector, but it is certainly well worth doing.

The largest single branch of collective consumption (according to national accounting standards) is devoted to military purposes. Despite its huge size, present economic and econometric models treat the military sector as exogenous. A very important factor influencing economic fluctuations and the structure of the economy thus remains unexplained, and economic models are accordingly of limited use for positive analysis, and for forecasting especially. In attempting to integrate the defence sector politico-economic model builders may profit from the work that has been done on arms races. These models go back to Richardson (1960; see also the exposition and extension in Boulding, 1962) and have recently been developed in two further directions (see Lambelet, 1971, 1973; Intriligator, 1975; McGuire, 1977):

(1) The mechanistic reaction pattern of one nation's military expenditures to the threats imposed by the military build-up of other nations has been improved by using a classical utility-maximising framework subject to budget constraints.
(2) The arms race models have been subjected to econometric testing.

The integration of the politico-economic models as sketched above and the arms race models is still to be done (for an interesting attempt see Cusack and Nincic, 1978). The outlook seems to be very promising for theoretically and empirically explaining this very important sector of collective consumption.

V CONSEQUENCES

The Public Choice view of the public sector and in particular of collective consumption and its financing has important consequences for positive economic theory, forecasting and economic policy.

1 POSITIVE ECONOMIC THEORY

The Public Choice view (especially in the form of politico-economic models) allows us to extend traditional purely economic and econometric models to include a public sector whose behaviour is described with the same underlying theoretical concepts (utility-maximising individuals) as are used for explaining market behaviour. This constitutes a welcome addition to economic analysis wherever the public sector plays an important role – and where does it not in modern societies?

2 FORECASTING

Economists often find themselves in an awkward position when they are asked by the government (or central bank) to make macroeconomic forecasts. The future economic situation depends very crucially on what the government itself will do. So what the government is in fact asking is for the economic experts to tell it what it itself is going to do. Lacking a *theory* of government behaviour, economists either resort to purely conditional forecasts which are of little use to the government, or naïvely try to guess what the government will probably do.

Using the Public Choice approach as a basis, a theoretically based forecast of the likely future behaviour of the public sector may be provided that will allow for better forecasting of the whole system, including the market sector.[9]

3 ECONOMIC POLICY

With respect to government advising, the Public Choice view asks for a radically new perspective (see Buchanan, 1977; also Frey, 1979). If the public sector is accepted as being an endogenous part of the politico-economic system, there is little point in telling government what it should do in order to further 'social welfare' (or rather, what the adviser believes that to be). The adviser has to accept that all political decision-makers pursue their own goals, and that their activities are constrained by the interdependence of the politico-economic system. If this system were completely 'closed', its development could not be influenced by the economic advisers at all but would proceed along a path determined by the parameters of the system. Due to incomplete information, the system is, however, partly 'open', i.e. there is room for advising due to the superior knowledge of the economic experts. There are two distinct

[9] For FR Germany, *ex ante* and *ex post* forecasts of the main macroeconomic variables using a politico-economic model of the monopoly government variant have given superior results compared to those of a traditional econometric model (Frey and Schneider, 1979b).

levels at which the economist can offer his/her advice in the hope of being heard and followed:

(1) At the constitutional level, at which the ground rules of the current politico-economic process are determined. Voluntary contracts among individuals and groups exploiting the possibilities for mutually advantageous arrangements can be formed at this level because there is at least partial uncertainty about one's future position in the society. The economic adviser can make suggestions about such arrangements, and can work out the compromises and compensations that may be necessary in order to make contracts and thus co-operation attractive.

(2) At the level of the current politico-economic process, where the decision-makers can and will only take advice that is in their self-interest. The economist may advise the voters about how well the present government pursues its economic policy in order to help them make political decisions (especially at election time) that are sensible from the point of view of the voters' own preferences. The economists may also be called upon by the government to advise it on how to manage the economy in order to fulfil its ideological goals and be re-elected. The opposition parties may ask for advice on economic aspects of the election programme that will improve their chances of winning the voters' approval and therewith being elected to power. In the current political process the economic adviser has no choice but to be 'partisan'; otherwise, her/his advice will not be listened to. Assuming that the ground rules are adequately set at the constitutional level, the pursuit of self-interest and the resulting competition in the political sphere should tend to further everyone's welfare (analogous to the market system under adequate conditions). This is indeed the basic idea of democracy.

REFERENCES

Arrow, Kenneth J. (1951). *Social Choice and Individual Values* (New York: Wiley).

Bahl, R. W. (1969). 'Studies on the Determinants of Public Expenditures: A Review', in Selma J. Mushkin and J. F. Cotton (eds), *Sharing Federal Funds for State and Local Needs* (New York: Praeger), pp. 184–207.

Barlow, Robin (1970). 'Efficiency Aspects of Local School Finance', *Journal of Political Economy*, 78 (Sept./Oct. 1970), 1028–40.

Barr, James L. and Otto A. Davis (1966). 'An Elementary Political and

Economic Theory of the Expenditures of Local Governments', *Southern Economic Journal*, 33 (Oct. 1966), 149–65.

Bergstrom, Theodore C. and Robert P. Goodman (1973). 'Private Demands for Public Goods', *American Economic Review*, 63 (June 1973), 280–96.

Boulding, Kenneth E. (1962). *Conflict and Defense: A General Theory* (New York: Harper and Row).

Bremer, Stuart A. (1977). *Simulated Worlds: A Computer Model of National Decision-Making* (Princeton, New Jersey: Princeton University Press).

Breuss, Fritz (1979). 'Simulation politischer Konjunkturzyklen', *Wirtschaftspolitische Blätter*, 26 (1979), 48–59.

Buchanan, James M. (1976). 'Taxation in Fiscal Exchange', *Journal of Public Economics*, 6 (July/Aug. 1976), 17–30.

—— (1977). *Freedom in Constitutional Contract. Perspectives of a Political Economist* (College Station and London: Texas A. and M. University Press).

Casstevens, T. W. and C. Press (1962/63). 'The Context of Democratic Competition in American State Politics', *American Journal of Sociology*, 68 (1962/63), 536–43.

Chow, Gregory C. (1973). 'Problems of Economic Policy from the Viewpoint of Optimal Control'. *American Economic Review*, 63 (Dec. 1973), 825–37.

Cusack, Thomas and Miroslav Nincic (1978). 'The Political Economy of U.S. Military Spending', Discussion paper, International Institute for Comparative Social Research, Wissenschaftszentrum Berlin.

Dawson, R. T. and J. A. Robinson (1963). 'Interparty Competition, Economic Variables, and the Welfare Policies in the American States', *Journal of Politics*, 25 (1963), 265–89.

DeSwaan, Abram (1973). *Coalition Theories and Cabinet Formations* (Amsterdam: Elsevier).

Diamond, Peter A. and James A. Mirrlees (1971). 'Optimal Taxation and Public Production', *American Economic Review*, 61 (March 1971), 8–27; 61 (June 1971), 261–78.

Downs, Anthony (1957). *An Economic Theory of Democracy* (New York: Harper).

—— (1967). *Inside Bureaucracy* (Boston: Little, Brown).

Fabricant, Salomon (1952). *The Trend of Government Activity in the United States since 1900* (New York: National Bureau of Economic Research).

Fair, Ray C. (1975). 'On Controlling the Economy to Win Elections', Cowles Foundation Discussion Paper No. 397.

Fishburn, Peter (1973). *The Theory of Social Choice* (Princeton, New Jersey: Princeton University Press).

Frey, Bruno S. (1978). *Modern Political Economy* (London: Martin Robertson).

—— (1979). 'Economic Policy by Constitutional Contract', *Kyklos*, 32 (1979), 307–19.

—— and Werner W. Pommerehne (1978). 'Toward a More Theoretical Foundation for Empirical Policy Analysis', *Comparative Political Studies*, 11 (Oct. 1978), 311–36.

—— and Friedrich Schneider (1978a). 'An Empirical Study of Politico-Economic Interaction in the United States', *Review of Economics and Statistics*, 60 (May 1978), 174–83.

—— and —— (1978b). 'A Politico-Economic Model of the United Kingdom', *Economic Journal*, 88 (June 1978), 243–53.

—— and —— (1978c). 'Central Bank Behaviour: A Positive Empirical Analysis', Discussion Paper No. 7803, Institute for Empirical Research in Economics, University of Zürich.

—— and —— (1979a). 'Economic Conditions and Government Popularity in Germany and the United States', in Paul Whiteley (ed.), *Models of Political Economy* (Beverly Hills and London: Sage).

—— and —— (1979b). 'An Econometric Model with an Endogenous Government Sector', *Public Choice* (forthcoming).

Fry, B. R. and R. F. Winters (1970). 'The Politics of Redistribution', *American Political Science Review*, 64 (1970), 508–22.

Gordon, Robert J. (1978). 'Elections and Monetary Accommodation: A Comparative Analysis'. Paper presented at Stanford Conference on Politics of Inflation, Unemployment and Growth, Feb. 28, 1978.

Hibbs, Douglas A. (1977). 'Political Parties and Macroeconomic Policy', *American Political Science Review*, 71 (Dec. 1977), 1467–87.

Hoole, Francis W. and Dina A. Zinnes, eds. (1976). *Quantitative International Politics: An Appraisal* (New York: Praeger).

Intriligator, Michael D. (1975). 'Strategic Considerations in Richardson Models of Arms Races', *Journal of Political Economy*, 83 (April 1975), 339–54.

Kaspar, Hirschel (1971). 'On Political Competition, Economic Policy and Income Maintenance Programs', *Public Choice*, 10 (Spring 1971), 1–19.

Kirchgässner, Gebhard (1976). 'Rationales Wählerverhalten und optimales Regierungsverhalten'. Dissertation, University of Konstanz.

Kramer, Gerald H. (1973). 'On a Class of Equilibrium Conditions for Majority Rule', *Econometrica*, 41 (March 1973), 285–97.

Lafay, Jean-Dominique (1978). 'The Impact of Economic Variables on Political Behavior in France'. Paper presented at First Meeting of the German-American Workshop on the Politics of Inflation, Unemployment and Growth, Stanford, 27 Feb.–1 March 1978.

—— (1979). 'Empirical Analysis of Politico-Economic Interaction in the East European Countries.' Paper presented at Annual Meeting of the Public Choice Society, Charleston, 17–19 March 1979.

Lambelet, John C. (1971). 'A Dynamic Model of the Arms Race in the Middle East, 1953–1965', *General Systems*, 16 (1971), 145–67.

—— (1973). 'Towards a Dynamic Two-Theater Model of the East-West Arms Race', *Journal of Peace Science*, 1 (1973), 1–38.

McGuire, Martin (1977). 'A Quantitative Study of the Strategic Arms Race in the Missile Age', *Review of Economics and Statistics*, 59 (Aug. 1977), 328–39.

Meltzer, Alan H. and Scott F. Richard (1979). 'A Rational Theory of the Size of Government.' Paper presented at the Sixth Interlaken Seminar on Analysis and Ideology, 5–9 June 1979.

Mueller, Dennis C. (1976). 'Public Choice: A Survey', *Journal of Economic Literature*, 14 (June 1976), 395–433.

—— (1979). *Public Choice* (Cambridge: Cambridge University Press).

Niskanen, William A. (1971). *Bureaucracy and Representative Government* (Chicago and New York: Aldine–Atherton).

Nordhaus, William D. (1975). 'The Political Business Cycle', *Review of Economic Studies*, 42 (April 1975), 169–90.

Parkin, Michael and Robin Bade (1978). 'Central Bank Laws and Monetary Policy.' Paper presented at Fifth Interlaken Seminar on Analysis and Ideology, 16–20 May 1978.

Peltzman, Sam (1979). 'The Growth of Government.' Working Paper No. 001, Center for the Study of the Economy and the State, University of Chicago.

Plott, Charles R. (1967). 'A Notion of Equilibrium and its Possibility under Majority Rule', *American Economic Review*, 57 (1967), 787–806.

Pommerehne, Werner W. (1978). 'Institutional Approaches to Public Expenditure. Empirical Evidence from Swiss Municipalities', *Journal of Public Economics*, 9 (April 1978), 255–80.

—— and Friedrich Schneider (1978). 'Fiscal Illusion, Political Institutions, and Local Public Spending', *Kyklos*, 31 (1978), Fasc. 3, 381–408.

Pryor, Frederic L. (1968). *Public Expenditures in Communist and Capitalist Nations* (London: Allen and Unwin).

Rae, Douglas W. (1971). 'An Estimate of the Decisiveness of Election Outcomes', in Bernhardt Lieberman (ed.), *Social Choice* (New York: Gordon and Breach), pp. 379–92.

Richardson, Lewis F. (1960). *Arms and Insecurity* (Chicago: Quadrangle Books).

Romer, Thomas and Howard Rosenthal (1978). 'The Elusive Median Voter.' Mimeo, Graduate School of Industrial Administration, Carnegie-Mellon University, Pittsburgh.

Schneider, Friedrich and Werner W. Pommerehne (1979). 'Politico-Economic Interaction in Australia: Some Empirical Evidence.' Mimeo, University of Zürich.

——, —— and Bruno S. Frey (1978). 'Politico-Economic Interdependence in a Direct Democracy: The Case of Switzerland.' Mimeo, University of Zürich.

Stroebe, Wolfgang and Bruno S. Frey (1979). 'In Defense of Economic Man: Towards an Integration of Economics and Psychology.' Discussion paper, Department of Psychology, University of Marburg.

Taylor, Michael and Michael Laver (1973). 'Government Coalitions in Western Europe', *European Journal of Political Research*, 1 (1973), 205–48.

Theil, Henry (1968). *Optimal Decision Rules for Government and Industry* (Amsterdam: North Holland).

Tinbergen, Jan (1956). *Economic Policy: Principles and Design* (Amsterdam: North Holland).

Tullock, Gordon (1965). *The Politics of Bureaucracy* (Washington, DC: Public Affairs Press).

Wagner, Richard E. (1976). 'Revenue Structure, Fiscal Illusion, and Budgetary Choice', *Public Choice*, 25 (Spring 1976), 45–62.

Ward, Michael D. and Harold Guetzkow (1978). 'Integrated Global Modeling: Economic Engineering or Social Science.' Mimeo, Gordon Scott Fulcher Chair of Decision-making, Dept. of Political Science, Northwestern University.

Wildavsky, Aaron (1964). *The Politics of the Budgetary Process* (Boston: Little, Brown).

Wilensky, G. (1970). 'Determinants of Local Government Expenditures', in J. Crecine (ed.), *Financing the Metropolis: Public Policy in Urban Economics* (Beverly Hills and London: Sage), pp. 197–218.

Discussion of 'The Public Choice Approach to Collective Consumption' by Professor B. S. Frey

Professor Khachaturov observed that the paper did not present a definition of collective consumption which recognised the importance of alternative methods of finance. Without disputing the importance of the influences on the decisions of voters and governments analysed in the paper, he introduced the discussion by drawing attention to additional specific factors which in his view were not sufficiently considered. These were: broader economic objectives such as national and regional economic development; the influence on government decisions of industrial and financial monopolies and of workers' organisations; prevailing moral laws and principles concerning the well-being of the whole society; and issues such as foreign policy which were outside the area of collective consumption. His general view was that Professor Frey's paper was rather more an exercise in psychology than in economics. *Mr Kaser* suggested the use of the term 'kleptocracy' to describe a system of government inspired by personal power and interests. *Professor Hoch* agreed with the emphasis of the paper on the endogenous nature of government behaviour. However, he objected to the method of analysis used in which the interest of the state was explained in terms of the autonomous preferences of self-interested, utility-maximising, individuals. In his view the individual interests of people working in public institutions must be separated from social and institutional interests. Also the concern shown by all governments for the welfare of society as a whole made the assumption of self-interest inappropriate. *Professor Klein* suggested that the analysis of the paper be extended to include the concern of voters with the legitimacy and authority of government, which could be distinguished from the specific benefits of particular policies. In his view such an extension should include an analysis of the concessions that governments must make to groups whose co-operation is essential for the maintenance of authority. *Professor Bacskai* agreed with Dr Hoch's point on the primacy of institutional factors. He argued that the struggle between government departments for funds can produce a system of competitive relationships resembling that of a market. He questioned the general applicability of the model of central bank behaviour suggested in the paper, in view of the diversity of both the economic problems confronting different societies and the alternative policy instruments available. Thus, for example, external constraints on domestic policy differed between economies, and various instruments were available for the correction of external imbalance including deflation and currency devaluation.

Professor Sandmo did not see a conflict between an optimising model designed for prescriptive purposes and a politico-economic model such as that presented by Professor Frey, designed for the task of explanation, for which an assumption of optimising behaviour might even be useful. In particular, he pointed to similarities between Professor Frey's discussion of government as a monopolist and concepts in the theory of optimal taxation. *Mr Matthews* was concerned that a non-tautological interpretation of the assumption of utility maximisation had not been explicitly given in the paper. He argued that empirically refutable predictions could not be derived from an assumption which amounted to the proposition that individuals have reasons for what they do.

Professor Klein and *Mr Boltho* took the view that the analysis presented provided a useful explanation of the timing of short-run changes in policy over the cycle, but did not see that it gave an understanding of the long-run growth of collective consumption, nor of the observed differences in the level of collective consumption in different countries.

Professor Onitiri urged the conference to turn from considerations of national self-interest, and to discuss the problems of collective consumption from an international point of view. *Sir Leo Pliatzky* argued that such a discussion would be unrealistic because nation states were reluctant to organise international grants on a basis and scale in any way comparable with those adopted within states. Evidence of this was the sharp contrast between the willingness of the United Kingdom government to transfer large sums to Northern Ireland and the unwillingness of the European Economic Community to adjust the distribution of transfers between member states. On a world level the problem could be seen in the difficulty of establishing untied aid programmes. *Professor Pajestka* did not see that practical difficulties of this kind should prevent a discussion of the theory and principles of international grants. *Mr Matthews* suggested that a full discussion of international grants would be conceptually difficult because of the absence of an international granting agency, and that it would make the area of discussion of the conference unmanageably large.

In reply to the discussion, *Professor Frey* pointed to the simple nature of his model and conceded that it was vulnerable to the criticism that the influence of pressure groups had been ignored and that, in its present form, it provided an explanation of the timing of policies rather than their substance. However, he insisted that his model was not confined to an assumption of self-interested behaviour but also admitted the possibility of moral and ideological motives. He insisted that the assumption of utility maximisation was not intended as a tautology but as a hypothesis about behaviour from which refutable predictions about observable events could be derived. However, his view was that the prominence given to this assumption in general economic analysis was as much a matter of the expectations of editors of American academic journals as a matter of its explanatory power. He was less optimistic than Professor Sandmo about the compatibility of the approaches of public choice theory and optimising theory. His overall view was that the analysis of government behaviour provided by the model of public choice was a significant advance on that incorporated in otherwise sophisticated and complex econometric models of macroeconomic policy. In his view it was ludicrous to construct macroeconomic models of 150 equations on the assumption that government behaviour was exogenous.

4 Collective Consumption in Socialist Countries: A Theoretical Approach

Maksymilian Pohorille

CENTRAL SCHOOL OF PLANNING AND STATISTICS WARSAW

I THE DEFINITION OF COLLECTIVE CONSUMPTION

In spite of the considerably growing interest in problems of collective consumption in both socialist and capitalist countries, there is no unanimous definition of that category. Moreover, it is extremely difficult to devise a definition that is equally suitable to different socio-economic systems. In order to avoid unnecessary argument about terminology I accept the suggestion of Professor Matthews, as responsible for the programme of this conference, that collective consumption should be defined to include: (i) pure collective consumption (e.g. expenditure on environment, on justice, on defence) and (ii) distribution of free or substantially subsidised goods and services (such as medical care, education, culture and science), but not transfers of money (such as pensions). What distinguishes collective consumption defined as above is the way goods are distributed and not the manner of consumption.[1]

[1] In my book *Spożycie zbiorowe i świadczenia społeczne* (*Collective Consumption and Social Grants*) I distinguish between 'social consumption' including free and subsidised goods and 'collective' or 'group consumption' of households, taking the form of the utilisation of collective facilities in order to satisfy the personal needs of members of a given community. In English literature see Pohorille and Omelczuk, 'Collective Consumption and Social Transfers', *Eastern European Economics*, no. 2 (1978).

Thus the so-defined collective consumption includes on one hand some goods which are individually consumed (e.g. free medicine for old age pensioners in Poland) and, on the other hand, it does not cover services which are indeed collectively consumed but are sold at normal prices (e.g. passenger transport). The simplest thing would be to say that the objective of collective consumption 'concerns the steps taken by the Government to meet those needs of the population which they cannot, or prefer not to, satisfy themselves individually, in the open market'.[2] This definition is clear enough. The explanation as to *why* the population cannot or does not prefer to satisfy some needs on the open market is much more complex.

Collective consumption embraces goods, mainly services, offered to the population free of charge or below production costs. In such a case the cost must be fully or partially covered by funds obtained from general taxation.

The reason why 'pure collective consumption' should be financed by taxation is quite obvious. The services and goods included in pure collective consumption are indivisible; they are provided by the state free of charge because it cannot charge a price for their use. In the case of general administration, including justice, police, fire protection, flood control and the like, defence, international affairs, the society as an organised collectivity is to be regarded as the consumer. Goods meeting local community needs, such as communal establishments, parks, street lighting, are also indivisible.

There are some cases where the free distribution of goods is justified from the purely economic point of view. In some cases charging a price leads to an uneconomic restriction of the consumption without reducing real costs; for instance, the marginal costs of the use of highways, bridges, tunnels, canals and the like represent no additional cost. In such cases the only reasonable thing to do is to finance this consumption by taxation. The same applies in those cases in which taxation reduces considerably the cost of collecting money through buying and selling goods.[3]

Another form of collective consumption, including goods and services provided free of charge or subsidised by the state, are social

[2] E. S. Kirschen, *Economic Policy in Our Time* (Amsterdam, 1964), VI, p. 13.

[3] Beckwith attaches great importance to this and similar kinds of consumption. In his opinion the share of 'free goods' in the GNP will grow to 50% in the USA or even to 70% in advanced socialist countries. See B. P. Beckwith, *Free Goods: The Theory of Free or Communist Distribution* (Palo Alto, 1976).

benefits in kind. Thus collective consumption covers three different groups of goods and services. In what follows I shall be mainly concerned with social benefits in kind, since they form the component of collective consumption which has provoked many controversies.

II THE SUBSIDISATION OF CONSUMPTION

The problem of subsidising consumption in socialist countries is highly complicated. In all socialist countries the price policy is to debit higher grade goods with higher rates of turnover tax than lower grade goods. In Poland and in some other countries a wide range of foodstuffs are subsidised. Thus the ratios between the shares of different social groups in terms of the production costs of the consumed goods in the consumption fund are different from the corresponding ratios between their nominal incomes.[4] However, the inclusion of all producers' subsidies in the collective consumption fund would not, in my opinion, be justifiable. First, if subsidies to producers are to be treated as elements in the collective consumption fund, then this fund should be reduced by surpluses above the average profit attained on other market goods. This calculation would be very complex; what is more, when the entire production is socialised, it would be rather meaningless.

Secondly, the fact of some prices not covering production costs is connected with the price and wages policy. This, true enough, fulfils certain social aims, but it is not directly linked with the financing of the 'social care' operations of the state. There are no serious economic arguments against the elimination of the losses incurred on many articles – given an immediate assurance of appropriate compensation in the form of a rise in nominal wages. The present situation in this field is a result of the historical development of the prices and wages systems in individual countries, and should not be regarded as a matter of general principle. I am thus of the opinion that in considering the problem of collective consumption it is not the fact of state subsidies that is important in itself, but their character and purpose. In collective consumption I include here only 'socio-cultural' goods, that is to say those connected with health protection, social care, rest, sports, tourism.

[4] According to my estimates, in 1971–72 the influence of the price policy on the reduction of the ratio of consumption in the highest income group to the consumption in the lowest income group varies between the limits of 10–15 % of the highest incomes.

Within this field there may also be certain living-standard goods such as, for example, housing services, workers' canteens.

Social policy always has to consider the alternatives: money grants or benefits in kind. It seems best to solve this dilemma in favour of the solution which is most effective. Collective consumption should cover goods and services with significant external advantages. In other words, subsidies should go to those goods and services which meet important social requirements but which may not always be fully appreciated by consumers. This applies, most notably, to medical treatment, education and culture. We may take the view that in order to ensure medical treatment, education for children and cultural services it is enough to raise people's money incomes. There is no certainty, however, that even persons who have the material resources to use these services will be inclined to spend the necessary proportion of their incomes on them. They may be insufficiently informed and, therefore, may underestimate the benefits to themselves of consuming certain goods or they may not care enough for the welfare of their children.

If we assume that this is their private affair, any further discussion of this subject becomes superfluous. But if we take into account the external economies in consumption, it does not seem best to leave the matter exclusively to market mechanisms. Moreover, there are cases in which it is impossible to achieve an optimum increase in consumption by subsidies, or even by free distribution, alone. Elementary education, protective vaccination, treatment of contagious diseases, for example, are not merely free but are also compulsory.

III EXTERNALITIES IN CONSUMPTION

Consumption cannot be considered as a simple sum of individual actions the purpose of which is to meet the personal needs of individuals. Consumption becomes a subject of interest to economists principally because it is one element in the whole process of social reproduction, including production, distribution, exchange and consumption, and because it is integrated with other elements in the process. Consequently, when investigating the externalities of personal consumption we are interested not only, and not so much, in what influence the consumption of various individuals has on the satisfaction of other individuals, but also in the significance and role of consumption in the whole process of reproduction.

When we look at the problem of externalities in consumption from this point of view, we find that these externalities arise in the sphere of consumption much more frequently and more universally than in any other area. This is only natural because consumption determines the conditions in which the labour force is reproduced, and hence also the whole process of economic development. We may thus clearly see the importance not only of such specific types of consumption as education and health but also of rest, leisure and housing conditions. Furthermore, the claim that the most advantageous conditions of reproduction of the labour force are ensured is not in itself sufficient in an advanced socialist society; favourable conditions for a free development of personality are also important. In investigating the external effects of consumption we must also analyse its role in the expanded reproduction of the whole life of society and in the evolution of a new way of life *Lebensweise*. Thus the external effects of consumption are an integral component of the consumer pattern. This concept emphasises the economic and social structure of consumption and points to the possibility, and even the necessity, for planned and rational development of consumption under conditions of socialism.

Most external economies in consumption cannot easily be measured, so it is difficult to include them in the calculation of prices. Let me take an example. From the point of view of reproduction, the achievement of defined demographic objectives is of great importance – the ensuring of an appropriate birth rate, the creation of conditions favourable to the strengthening of the family, and the upbringing of the young generation. The achievement of these objectives is linked with the consumption of certain defined goods – housing, creches, nurseries, products for infants and children, and the like. It would be impossible in this case to apply the principle that 'third parties' who benefit indirectly by the services should pay for this. The beneficiary here is society as a whole, and only society is able to assess the benefits, directions and volume of the desired consumption of goods serving its determined objectives.

In such cases, to determine the desirable size of subsidy we do not begin by calculating the external benefits of the consumption of given goods and services; we establish the optimum volume of production which will ensure the achievement of certain defined social goals, and then, on this basis, calculate the amount of subsidy necessary to reduce the market price to a level that makes the given goods and services accessible in the desired volume.

The amount of the subsidy has to be determined by an associated act of social evaluation, that is by comparison of the anticipated effects with the required outlays. This, however, is not a cost/benefit analysis *sensu stricto*, because inputs and outputs are not uniform and cannot be calculated in the same units. What really matters is public approval or disapproval of the degree to which the various groups of goods and services are to be subsidised.

When analysis of the whole pattern of consumption is attempted, and not exclusively of the role of individual goods and services, then research becomes concerned with externalities to a lesser degree than with the social effects of consumption. Individual evaluation of the utility of an article which has beneficial social effects need not always fall below its macroeconomic importance. Consequently, it is not always necessary to subsidise such goods in order to ensure a socially desirable level of consumption. This leads to specific practical conclusions. We have shown, for instance, that it is desirable to encourage the consumption of cultural services. Does this mean that theatres, cinemas, operas should all be subsidised to the same degree? It does not, of course. Cinemas may function on the profit principle, while the opera may not.

What matters is not only the support of specific goods and services, but also the necessity to meet, and in some cases to create, a specific level of demand by various social groups. Thus the sweeping statement that cinemas are sufficiently popular and do not require subsidies is not enough. The question to be considered is whether the cinema is available to all. It may then turn out that touring cinemas, serving the rural population, should be subsidised.

Social groups which have not had ready access to cultural goods in the past should be particularly privileged, with cheap tickets distributed through the trade unions and similar devices. When establishing the principles on which the subsidy system is to be based, we must compare the social assessment of the usefulness of the given goods with the corresponding assessment by different groups of consumers.

IV THE AMOUNT OF SUBSIDY

If the amount of benefit reflects the difference between the social and individual assessment of an article or service, is there any justification for covering the whole cost of this difference?

Many economists have various reservations regarding free distribution of 'public goods'. Consumers, they say, voice their demands for free goods so long as marginal utility is greater than zero. In taking decisions on investments designed to produce 'public goods', authorities are guided by the principle that the last 'doses' of investment should produce equal advantages in the different applications; that is that the marginal productivity of inputs in schools, hospitals and the like should be equal. Here two types of danger emerge: (i) if the investment relates to an artificially enlarged demand, it will be excessive in comparison with investment in other fields and thus will reduce the degree to which other needs can be met; (ii) if limited investment means are distributed rationally, there will not be enough to satisfy the demands fully and there will be a gap between supply and demand.

In practice experience shows that the second rather than the first case is typical. It is difficult to find a country where the public health service is developed excessively, while the complaint is frequently made that medical services are poor in quantity and low in quality. Criticism of the shortcomings of public health services argues that zero prices make an efficient utilisation of the resources difficult. This statement is only partially justified. There is no evidence that limitation of demand by means of prices is better, in such services as education and health care, than rationing of the services by non-economic measures, such as the judgements of medical bodies or competitive examinations. Although not without certain defects, this last method of meeting demands in the sphere of medical care and education is socially more just.

It should be emphasised, however, that – from a purely economic point of view – there are no serious arguments supporting the thesis that social benefits in kind should be fully covered by subsidy. On the other hand, for a number of important political and social reasons, it seems inadvisable to expand the scope of fees for services in such fields as health care and education.

First, the need to receive medical treatment differs very substantially from all other needs. The cost connected with medical treatment may be considerable. At the same time the patient's ability to earn a living is greatly reduced. Thus free medical treatment has long been connected with the concept of general social security. This concept recognises the need for public institutions which safeguard the individual against various forms of risks, and particularly against loss of ability to earn a living and against the lack of means to pay for medical treatment. Some people argue that a system of private insurance may form a very effective substitute for a public health service. The question then arises: should this system be voluntary or compulsory? If it is voluntary then it does not give real social security to all. And if the fee used to finance this system is made universal and compulsory, it becomes a tax.

Secondly, the introduction of some system of payment for education and medical aid would require a highly complicated system of price differentiation that would give everybody equal opportunity to attend school and to obtain medical treatment. Thirdly, free medical treatment and education are among the oldest claims of the working class. Thus a return to even small fees for services in this sphere would be politically very unpopular.

V BENEFITS IN KIND

There are two different approaches to the problem of benefits in kind. In the first approach all needs are divided into elementary needs and requirements of a higher order. Some economists think that, with growing affluence, society will subsidise an increasingly wider range of goods and services that will meet the basic needs of all its members. In accordance with this way of thinking we should similarly distinguish basic and other needs in the traditional spheres of collective consumption. Hospitalisation would be free while a fee would be charged for sanatoria; primary and secondary education would be ensured free of charge to all, while there would be a charge for higher education.

Reasoning based on the concept of the external effects of consumption leads to completely different conclusions. A social minimum may be ensured by providing an appropriate income to each consumer unit. We have no reason to fear that part of this money income will not be used for meeting elementary needs. This is determined by the very definition of elementary needs as being those that must be met before all others. Goods with external benefits (health, education and the like) are an exception. Here, as I have already shown, a divergence may arise between the social and individual assessments of the utility of individual goods and services.

We may thus formulate the following conclusion: the problem of ensuring for all members of society conditions that will enable them to meet their basic needs may best be solved through a money income policy, which should reflect the level of a social minimum standard. It is, however, expedient to subsidise consumption which has important social effects. A more emphatic formulation of this idea may be that there is no need to distribute bread gratuitously but there is need for free education for all, or even theatre tickets for certain groups of the population.

VI THE DISTRIBUTIONAL EFFECTS OF COLLECTIVE CONSUMPTION

Until recently the axiom was that collective consumption serves to equalise real incomes of the population. Opinion concerning this has radically changed as a result of statistical research designed to verify that hypothesis. The results of those enquiries in Poland have demonstrated that considerable differences still persist between the volume of social benefits in kind received by different socio-economic groups.[5]

Collective consumption represents a horizontal redistribution of incomes: that is a secondary distribution as between the consumers of the free or subsidised goods and services. But the results are often inconsistent with the general objectives of social benefits: people from higher income groups benefit more, in an absolute sense, from state subsidies than people from lower income groups. This is an effect of (i) the existing inequalities of the social infrastructure which result from environmental and other factors (for example the lack of kindergartens in the rural areas in Poland, which implies that there are considerable differences between the benefits of this kind enjoyed by the urban population as contrasted with the rural population); (ii) the dependence of demand for certain services on factors which are not directly related to income and prices (concern about health depends to a large measure on the level of education; the demand for organised holidays depends on established habits); (iii) the need to cover a part of the cost of a service which is not wholly free (for example holidays, boarding houses, nurseries, and the like).

Some economists argue that the wide variety of functions that collective consumption is supposed to fulfil limits the possibility of using it as a means of equalising the living conditions of the population.[6] This is undoubtedly so. I do not think, however, that we can take it as axiomatic that different kinds of services subsidised by the state fulfil their functions correctly only if they serve to equalise incomes. On the other hand it would be difficult to agree with the idea that collective consumption increases income differentials. It seems right and proper, therefore, to strive to distribute the 'social goods' – those included in collective consumption – in such a way as to ensure at least a neutral redistribution. This objective may be achieved partly through dif-

[5] M. Pohorille, 'Social Welfare Distribution and Social Equality', *Oeconomica Polona*, no. 3 (1979).

[6] J. Morecka, 'Społeczny fundusz spożycia a problemy równości', *Ekonomista*, no. 2 (1971).

ferentiated prices and partly by the distribution of some social benefits in kind to low income groups only.

Of basic importance is the further development, expansion and appropriate localisation of investments in social infrastructure. The issue at stake is not only to improve the pattern of consumption or to encourage specific trends of consumption, but also to meet to some extent the different needs of various social groups.

What is most remarkable, however, in the arguments against a system of social benefits integrated with collective consumption, is the narrow and uni-dimensional concept of equality that reduces it to the equalisation of real incomes. As we have already noted, social benefits do not fulfil that function, and what is more, it is doubtful whether they will (hence the limited requirement that the system of social benefits be 'neutral', i.e. that it ensures at least an approximately equal 'social dividend'). But, this is not the same as stating that social benefits in kind are not an important element of an egalitarian system. The fact that they form in a socialist society an integral part of a system of relations which, taken as a whole, ensures social security, the right to free education and recreation, mother and child care, is evidence enough to support the view that collective consumption embodies the idea of social equality not only in theory but also in practice. For even if it does not lead to levelling of incomes it still contributes to the elimination of many conditions inherited from the past which were the cause of still persisting inequalities. It is directed against 'strategic' inequalities – those that tend to reproduce themselves and are the cause of many other differences in the social standing of people. One has to recognise that the existing differences in incomes are not simply the product of the defective functioning of social institutions superimposed upon some 'natural' state of affairs which could allegedly ensure full economic equality. They are the consequence of the entire process of reproduction at the present stage of socialist society. The application of the same standard – labour input – to determine the distribution of income does not give everybody an equal chance because, personal abilities being unequal, working skills are also unequal.

At the present stage of development it is especially important to enforce resolutely the principle of distribution according to work and to ensure equal opportunity to all. The link between equal opportunity and equal standards is not automatic. In order to establish equal opportunity for all, and especially to ensure equal opportunity for the younger generation, it is necessary to provide additional economic and non-economic resources in various spheres of social relations. These resources are partly represented by the grants for collective consumption and money grants, and partly by the functioning of the whole socio-economic system, including the system of professional promotion.

Equal opportunity at the start does not necessarily lead to an equal final outcome, because people do not have equal ability to take advantage of available opportunities. Only further progress in socialist relations of production can lead to the elimination of the still existing economic inequalities. This is not to say that the functioning of institutions has no effect on the historical process of social transformation. Socialist justice has to be organised.[7] This is the principal objective of social policy and of the efforts to relate it more closely to the economic policy of the socialist state.

VII THE ROLES OF COLLECTIVE CONSUMPTION IN DIFFERENT PERIODS

Generally speaking one can distinguish, it seems, three basic periods during which social grants, and therefore also collective consumption, have played different roles and shown different tendencies to develop. During the first period, immediately after the revolution, the strong pressures for plebeian egalitarianism resulted in a rapid increase in social benefits in kind. An additional argument in favour of this increase was the low consumption level of the whole population, which made difficult any differentiation of wages on a large scale.

During the second period some setback to the increase of benefits in kind appeared, and special emphasis was put on raising the level of remuneration for work. During this period social benefits mitigated, to a certain extent, the conflict between the desire for a rapid increase in the living standard of the lowest income group and the need to maintain a certain spread of wage rates for the purpose of stimulating the productivity of labour. Neutral redistribution does not change income disparities; it only changes the ratios between incomes. Social funds are, on the one hand, a factor diminishing the ratio between high and low incomes, but on the other hand, they permit a bolder use of economic incentives in the form of differentiation of wages.

During the third period the tendency towards equalising wages prevailed. Social benefits in kind became a factor that differentiated the

[7] J. Pajestka, 'Realizacja sprawiedliwości społecznej na obecnym etapie budownictwa socjalistycznego', *Ekonomista*, No. 6 (1971).

share of individual members of society in the general consumption fund, but this reflected needs rather than the quality of work.

During each of these periods the main emphasis in social transfers was different. During the first period rapid and spontaneous increase in social transfers led to the inclusion of a number of services for the population in the system of collective consumption, such as housing, communications, vacations, which resulted in making their further development difficult.

Identification of services consumed collectively with collective consumption (social benefits in kind) may have, in the long run, similar consequences to their underfinancing, that is to say a slowing down in development of the services concerned. Unquestionably, a general availability of social benefits is one of the long-term objectives of the social policy of the socialist state; but at a certain stage of development it is preferable to have them concentrated in certain limited sectors. It is thus essential to examine the areas of collective consumption in which differential charges should be introduced in order to enable different income groups to make use of services with positive social effects. Thus the subsidy of consumption would be related both to the subject and to the object. Medical care would remain totally free, without any distinction between basic and additional services; on the other hand, a system of fees would be charged for the use of holiday centres, creches, kindergartens, boarding houses and similar services with charges related to incomes. Introduction of graduated charges for certain forms of collective consumption could contribute to a rapid expansion of the social infrastructure and help to meet the growing needs of all groups of population.

In this third period social benefits gradually assumed the most general character, with free social health services covering all citizens, and with plans for kindergartens for all children. The division into these three periods does not correspond fully to the present practical experience of all socialist countries. It merely points to some general tendencies in the development of collective consumption. The most essential point here is not so much the actual practice of each country as the changing role of transfers at different stages in the development of a socialist society.

VIII THE FUTURE OF COLLECTIVE CONSUMPTION

Adolf Wagner predicted long ago that in an advanced society government expenditures will grow faster than national income. It appears that

Wagner's forecast is true, but it is much too general. It covers the consequences of very different processes – the growth of the economic role of the state, the substantial expenditures on armaments, and the increased significance of public services in the reproduction of the labour force.

What about the collective consumption itself? Will its share in GNP necessarily grow? I have argued that the main reason for subsidising certain goods and services is their external or social effect. So one might suppose that in the future, when consumers will internalise the social set of values, the need to subsidise consumption will not be so acute. On the other hand, however, certain elements of collective consumption will gain in importance. First, expenditure on the environment will unquestionably greatly increase. Secondly, one may predict a rapid growth of government-financed research. Third, the state will be providing more medical care free of charge. Last but not least, the state will participate more and more in the costs of bringing up the young generation. The system of family allowances is a key measure in reducing inequalities of real income per head. It is to be expected that family allowances will increase and that they will assume the form of money grants and of benefits in kind, such as free meals for children, free textbooks for students, more places in summer camps for children and young people, more places in boarding houses, products for babies and small children, subsidised by the state. A growing importance, therefore, of collective consumption may be regarded as a general rule in an advanced socialist society.

Discussion of 'Collective Consumption in Socialist Countries: A Theoretical Approach' by Professor M. Pohorille

Professor Hanusch opened the discussion by noting the similarities between Professor Pohorille's points on the nature of individual preferences and the rationale of collective consumption, and those to be found in the writings of prominent North American and European economists. He did not see that Professor Pohorille's points gave any new insights into these questions. He invited Professor Pohorille to expand on the following conceptual points which in his view were insufficiently developed in the paper: the distinction between high- and low-grade goods in the context of redistribution policy; the concept of socialist reproduction as an objective of policy; the concept of organic social welfare; and the nature of the optimal mix of allocative and redistributional policies. He questioned the following specific proposals which he saw in the argument of the paper: that access to cinemas should be equally available to all; that medical care but not kindergartens should be provided without fees. Professor Hanusch took Professor Pohorille's report of the perverse redistributional effects of collective consumption in Poland as evidence, additional to that provided by his own study, of the limits of a policy for the redistribution of benefits in kind. He did not agree with the conclusion of the paper that the need to subsidise consumption would diminish in the future as consumers of advanced societies began to assimilate social values.

Professor Khachaturov referred to the problem of the definition of collective consumption and in particular to the treatment of transfer payments which may take a positive form, for example food subsidies, or a negative form as tax exemptions. *Sir Leo Pliatzky* suggested the well-understood definition of 'general government expenditure' accepted by the OECD and the United Nations which would include subsidies but not tax exemptions.

Several speakers commented on common practical problems of collective consumption which were apparent in capitalist and socialist economies. *Professor Manz* referred to the distinction apparent in some socialist countries between collective consumption as a means of satisfying material wants, and as a means of fulfilling the social and cultural needs of the population. He also explained the difficulty of securing a balance between the provision of benefits in cash and those in kind. *Professor Onitiri* wondered whether in socialist countries there was a negative relationship between productivity and the ratio of collective consumption to national income, or whether the ability to direct the allocation of resources implied by a high ratio had led to a full utilisation of capacity and to the elimination of waste. *Professor Boulding* argued that a system of exchange relationships between commodities was a common underlying feature of all societies and that serious damage could result from a use of public grants which distorted the relationships of this system. An example of this had been the adverse effects on conservation of the use of distortionary grants in energy markets.

Mr Boltho pointed to what in his view was the important and surprising evidence cited by Professors Hanusch and Pohorille for western and socialist economies on the ineffectiveness of collective consumption as a tool for redistribution. However, he did not accept that the distribution of benefits from collective consumption had been more favourable to the rich than the distribution of primary income, and thus doubted whether the distribution of income had been worsened in relative terms by the provision of collective consumption.

There was much less agreement on the theoretical approach by which the problems identified might be resolved. *Professor Pajestka* contrasted the individualistic analysis of collective consumption developed by western economists with that adopted in socialist countries which depended on the concept of long-run social rationality. *Mr Matthews* questioned the usefulness of analyses based on either individualistic or organic concepts of social welfare and argued for an approach which recognised the complexity of motives involved in policy on collective consumption. He detected, in contributions from both western and socialist writers, the misguided attitude that the problems of collective consumption were resolvable without great difficulty. *Professor Bacskai* argued for an historical approach which, in the case of Hungary, was able to show that the growth of collective provision was not entirely a result of policy of the general kind being discussed. He cited the history of low wages in Hungary which explained the growth of food subsidies, and the capacity shortages in consumer goods industries in the immediate post-war period which was compensated by an expansion of collective services. The growth of food subsidies had created a major problem of inefficiency in the production of foodstuff. *Professor Pajestka* acknowledged that in socialist countries the provision of collective consumption had given rise to a conflict between economic efficiency and social objectives.

In reply to the discussion, *Professor Pohorille* did not accept the identification of his analysis of collective consumption with that made by western economists. The similarity in the terms used was, he insisted, merely a result of his attempt to make the argument of the paper more accessible to colleagues in the west. There had been an essential difference in the philosophy of social action. The western approach was an individualistic one, whereas the socialist concept was based on the notion of social needs and public interest. It was his view that the idea of collective consumption had been strictly connected with workers' movements and that developments in socialist countries had had an important influence on the growth of public expenditures and collective consumption in western economies. He argued that a market system based on the principle of consumer sovereignty failed to satisfy basic needs and resulted in inequality and waste in the use of resources. The growth of public control over production was a proof that without the application of corrective tools the market mechanism could not solve the problem of resource allocation. He explained that the terms 'low' and 'high'-grade goods were used to distinguish between goods satisfying basic needs and those satisfying other needs. The thesis concerning cinemas, hospitals and kindergartens had been misinterpreted. He stressed that before decisions about subsidies were made a social assessment of the usefulness of 'merit goods' must be compared with the corresponding individual assessments by different groups of consumers. He agreed with Mr Boltho that collective consumption did not worsen the distribution of income in relative terms. The most important thing however was that collective consumption contributed to the reduction of 'strategic inequalities'. It was not stated in the paper that collective consumption would diminish in the future but it was pointed out that its structure would change. In reply to Mr Matthews he enumerated the following problems of collective consumption in Poland which had not been easy to solve: how to abolish or scale down historically determined price subsidies; the relationship between wages and transfers and the problem of incentives; and the issue of benefits in kind versus money grants.

5 The Optimum Supply of Public Goods in a Mixed Economy

Agnar Sandmo

NORWEGIAN SCHOOL OF ECONOMICS AND BUSINESS ADMINISTRATION

I INTRODUCTION AND OVERVIEW

In any economic system decisions about the production and distribution of consumption goods are made partly through the mechanism of the market, partly by governmental bodies, possibly deriving their authority from some collective choice process. The balance between the market and the government in determining the use of resources for consumption varies a great deal from one economic system to another and depends of course to a high degree on historical and ideological differences which it would be presumptuous for an economist to try to explore at all adequately. My task in the following is fortunately a much simpler one. Starting from the point of view of welfare economics I wish to discuss the scope and limits of the market mechanism as a system for the allocation of resources and derive some guidelines for collective decisions in the field of public goods and taxation. A main concern of the paper is to show how the 'ideal' solution has to be modified to allow for the fact that a government in a mixed economy only controls the actions of private agents imperfectly; the best it can hope for, therefore, is a second-best solution.

The core of modern welfare theory is two theorems about the equivalence between competitive equilibria and Pareto-optimal allocations. A competitive equilibrium is characterised by consumers maximising utility and firms maximising profits at given prices, these prices being such that supply equals demand in all markets.[1] A Pareto-

[1] This definition could be generalised to allow for markets in which equilibrium demand falls short of supply with the prices in question being zero.

optimal allocation has the property that there is no reallocation of resources which will improve the situation for one or more consumers – in terms of their own preferences – without making some other consumers worse off. A natural interpretation of this optimality criterion is that it provides a benchmark for *no waste of resources* for the economy as a whole.

The two main theorems of welfare economics can now be stated. Under certain conditions it can be shown that:

(1) A competitive equilibrium is a Pareto optimum.
(2) Any Pareto optimum can be sustained as a competitive equilibrium.

While the interpretation of theorem 1 is straightforward, theorem 2 may require an explanation. Implicit in the conditions for a Pareto optimum lies a set of dual variables which can be interpreted as shadow prices. The solution can therefore be sustained as a competitive equilibrium if a set of equivalent market prices can be found which also satisfy the individual budget constraints of consumers. But this requires the government or the social planner to control the distribution of income, so that the selection of a particular Pareto optimum becomes equivalent – in a competitive economy – to the selection of a particular distribution of income. This selection must of course be based on ethical judgements, by which individual preferences are weighed together by means of a social welfare function. If this social welfare function contains only the individual utility functions as arguments and is increasing in these, an allocation yielding maximal social welfare must necessarily be Pareto optimal. The two theorems therefore acquire a somewhat broader significance than a narrow interpretation in terms of efficiency might perhaps indicate.

In a world satisfying the conditions required by the two theorems there would be no scope for collective consumption. All decisions about the allocation of consumption goods could be left to competitive markets, while the role of the public sector would be limited to that of a redistributor of incomes. In other words, marginal cost pricing by all firms – as required by the competitive assumption – could be combined with a policy of income transfers to achieve a social optimum.

The conditions required for the theorems to hold are essentially (a) convexity of indifference maps and production sets and (b) existence of markets for all goods.[2] The most important departure from

[2] This could be weakened slightly, since theorem 1 does not require assumption (a). See Arrow (1970) for further discussion.

assumption (a) would be the presence of significant economies of scale; this is obviously an important point but will not be discussed further here. Departures from assumption (b) have been widely discussed in the literature under the general heading of market failure. The discussion following will be oriented towards market failure as an argument for collective consumption.

The classic case of market failure is the presence of externalities.[3] Externalities are often defined to be present if an individual's utility function depends on quantities consumed by other consumers. It is important to realise, however, that with this definition the presence of externalities does not necessarily imply market failure. In addition there must be a lack of markets, for otherwise it would be perfectly possible to have markets in externalities, and we could have a generalised concept of competitive equilibrium with all the usual efficiency properties.[4] But there are a number of problems with such markets. First, in cases where there are only a few agents involved in the externality, although a market might develop, there would be little reason to believe that it would be a competitive one. Second, in cases involving many agents transaction costs become very important and may well prevent agents from realising the possibilities of gains from trade. There is also another problem, which has been given a lot of attention in the theoretical literature, *viz.* that of incentives. If my neighbour buys clean air for himself, I automatically benefit; hence I do not have any obvious economic incentive to reveal my preferences truthfully in the market. This so-called free rider problem is particularly serious in the most extreme case of externalities – the pure public goods. It is in such cases that market failure provides the strongest argument for collective decisions about consumption. Without further guidelines for collective decision-making, however, this conclusion is not very helpful. The extension of welfare economics to cover the case of public goods does provide such guidelines, although perhaps mostly on the level of general theoretical principles. The classic statement of this theory is in Samuelson (1954, 1969), and we give an exposition of his model in Section II below. We also show how important real-world phenomena can be analysed as a mixture of the pure private and public goods categories.

Market failure is frequently interpreted to mean not only the non-

[3] For the purposes of this paper the discussion is limited to consumption externalities, but this should of course not be taken to mean that production externalities are of less theoretical interest or practical importance.

[4] See Arrow (1970) for a formal discussion of this point.

existence of markets but also impediments to the efficient working of markets. One such impediment is the presence of distortionary taxation. But, as we shall argue in Section III, this particular imperfection may be an unavoidable one in a realistic analysis of policy choices. For various reasons 'perfect' policy instruments are simply not available. The optimality conditions for the allocation of resources to public goods therefore have to be modified to take account of the need to raise revenue by means of distortionary taxation and of the distributional impact of taxation and public expenditure.

These complications do of course tend to make the implementation of the optimality rules even more difficult than in the ideal case of a fully controlled economy. In section IV we discuss some alternative methods of implementation with particular attention to the role of markets for private goods as a source of information about preferences for public goods. Section V contains some concluding comments and reflections.

II OPTIMAL ALLOCATION IN THE FULLY CONTROLLED ECONOMY

Following Samuelson (1954) we assume that there are two types of goods in the economy. *Private goods* are what we ordinarily think of as consumer goods – food, clothing, etc. For such goods there is an additivity relationship between individual and aggregate consumption. Let x_j be the total consumption of private good j, and let x_j^i be individual i's consumption. Then we have

$$\sum_{i=1}^{I} x_j^i = x_j \qquad j = 0, 1, \ldots, J. \tag{1}$$

For *public goods* there is no clear distinction between individual and total consumption; examples of such cases are national defence, clean air, nature preserves, etc. Such goods are available in equal amounts to all 'consumers', and an increased enjoyment of them on the part of one individual does not appreciably influence other individuals' consumption possibilities. As a polar case we have Samuelson's analytical definition of a public good which simply postulates equality between individual and aggregate consumption. Letting z_k and z_k^i be, respectively, total and individual consumption of collective good k, we have that

$$z_k^i = z_k \qquad i = 1, \ldots, I. \quad k = 1, \ldots, K. \tag{2}$$

Polar cases are not always easy to interpret in practical terms, and for application of the theory it will be necessary also to consider intermediate cases. We first develop the essential parts of the theory for the polar case and then consider modifications.

On the consumption side of the economy we assume that each consumer is endowed with a preference ordering over (1 + J + K)-dimensional vectors of private and public goods. Under rather weak additional assumptions this preference ordering can be represented by a utility function,

$$u^i = u^i(x_0^i, \ldots, x_j^i, z_1^i, \ldots, z_k^i) \qquad \text{for all } i = 1, \ldots, I. \tag{3}$$

This is assumed to be continuous, differentiable and strictly quasi-concave.

For the purposes of this paper the production side of the economy will be simplified as much as possible. Thus, we assume that the production possibilities for the economy as a whole can be summarised by a transformation function

$$F(x_0, \ldots, x_j, z_1, \ldots, z_K) = 0, \tag{4}$$

which is assumed to be continuous, differentiable and convex. In fact, underlying the assumption of an aggregate production constraint for the economy as a whole must be an assumption that production takes place under conditions of constant returns to scale, implying that the convexity assumption is satisfied. In the model developed in the next section an even stronger assumption will be adopted.

The model allows a flexible interpretation of the commodity concept. The amount of labour provided by an individual could be thought of as a negative number, since leisure presumably is a desirable good. In a similar way one could establish the convention that outputs are to be measured positively and inputs negatively on the production side. As regards public goods, 'bads' like noise and water pollution may be assumed to enter both the utility functions and the production constraint with a negative sign. This interpretation allows us to state assumptions and results in a very general form, so that the need for specifying the exact nature of the commodities in question only arises in the context of specific applications.

These are the structural assumptions of the model. We now turn to the analysis of optimal allocations. Equation (4) already gives us a set of feasible production programmes for the economy; indeed, the programmes satisfying equation (4) are not only feasible, but also productively efficient. This means that one cannot, given any one of these allocations, increase the output of one commodity without decreasing the output of one or more other commodities.[5] On the weak assumption that increased output can always be put to some socially valuable use, productive efficiency is obviously a desirable feature of allocation of resources. The conceptually more difficult part of the optimality analysis lies in relating the choice among production programmes to the preferences in the economy.

The social optimality criterion to be used here is the Bergson–Samuelson social welfare function, in which social welfare is taken to be an increasing function of individual utilities:

$$W = W(u^1, \ldots, u^I). \tag{5}$$

It is beyond the scope of this paper to give a full justification for this approach to welfare economics and economic planning. Its most important implication is that a feasible allocation which gives the maximum value of some W function is also a Pareto optimum. For if it were not, we would be able to increase some u^i, holding the others constant, and so increase W – a contradiction. But the welfare function goes beyond the concept of Pareto optimality and provides a framework for the evaluation of alternative allocations which cannot be ranked by the Pareto criterion.

In the fully controlled economy there are no other constraints on social planning than those set by technology and the nature of the commodities. We can therefore formulate the problem of the best use of society's resources as the maximisation of the social welfare function (5) subject to the constraints (1), (2) and (4). The solution to this problem in terms of the first-order conditions is well known and can be written down directly as:

$$\frac{u^i_j}{u^i_0} = \frac{F_j}{F_0} \qquad \begin{matrix} i = 1, \ldots, I \\ j = 1, \ldots, J \end{matrix} \tag{6}$$

$$\sum_{i=1}^{I} \frac{u^i_k}{u^i_0} = \frac{F_k}{F_0} \qquad k = 1, \ldots, K \tag{7}$$

$$W_i u^i_0 = \text{the same for all i.} \tag{8}$$

Subscripts denote partial derivatives.

The set of conditions (6) are the well-known marginal conditions for

[5] Similarly, of course, one cannot decrease the input of one factor of production without having to increase the input of one or more other factors.

efficiency in the allocation of private goods: the marginal rate of substitution between any pair of goods should be the same for all consumers and equal to their marginal rate of transformation.[6] The second set of conditions are the Samuelson conditions for public goods allocation; at the margin the sum of the marginal rates of substitution between each public good and any one private good should be equal to the marginal rate of transformation. Finally, conditions (8) say that the social marginal utility of consumption or income should be the same for all consumers.[7]

Before turning to a discussion of the possibilities of achieving such an optimum in a mixed or partially controlled economy, it may be useful to consider briefly how to modify the sharp distinction drawn between pure private and pure public goods. In particular, it is easy to think of examples that seem to belong to both categories simultaneously. Car-use is on the one hand a private good, on the other hand the resulting air pollution and congestion also make aggregate car-use a private 'bad' from the individual consumer's point of view. Thus, it would seem natural to formalise this case by including in consumer h's utility function both his individual car-use, x_j^h, and the total car-use in the economy, x_j. It is fairly easy to see that we must then have:

$$\frac{\partial u^h}{\partial x_j^h} \Big/ \frac{\partial u^h}{\partial x_0^h} + \sum_i \frac{\partial u^i}{\partial x_j} \Big/ \frac{\partial u^i}{\partial x_0^i} = \frac{F_j}{F_0} \qquad (9)$$

for all h. This condition is in fact a mixture of conditions (6) and (7). The first term on the left is individual h's 'private' marginal rate of substitution between car-use and the commodity serving as unit of account, and this should still, at the optimum, be the same for all consumers. But the private marginal rate of substitution should no longer be equal to the marginal rate of transformation; the two should differ by an amount representing the consumers' marginal evaluation of car-use as a collective 'bad'.

Enough has been said about this point to make it clear that we do not

[6] It should be emphasised that by stating these conditions in the context of an aggregate production constraint for the economy as a whole, we are assuming that production is always allocated efficiently between production units, the marginal cost of production for each commodity being the same in all units.

[7] In the formulation of conditions (6)–(8) we have chosen commodity 0 as our 'unit of account'. This choice has been made for notational convenience and has no further significance. In particular, the reader may easily check that (6) and (8) together imply that the social marginal utility of consumption is equal across individuals for *all* goods.

lose much, as far as the basic analytical structure is concerned, by concentrating attention on the polar cases; mixed cases can always be treated as intermediate between those two extremes.

III TAXATION AND PUBLIC EXPENDITURE WITH COMPETITIVE MARKETS

We assume now that we are in a fully employed economy with competitive markets for all private goods. The supply of public goods is controlled by the government and will be determined on the basis of some form of cost-benefit analysis. The public sector's use of resources must be financed by taxation, so that expenditure on public goods must equal net tax revenue. Our basic concern is with the interaction between the tax system and the rules for optimal allocation of resources to public goods.

We first need a few more concepts. In a competitive economy each consumer maximises his utility function (3) subject to his budget constraint:

$$\sum_{j=0}^{J} P_j x_j^i = a^i \quad i = 1, \ldots, I. \tag{10}$$

Here P_j is the consumer price of commodity j, and a^i is any lump-sum transfer (positive or negative) received from the government. Letting λ^i be the Lagrange multiplier associated with the constraint, the optimality conditions are:

$$u_j^i - \lambda^i P_j = 0 \quad \begin{array}{l} i = 1, \ldots, I \\ j = 0, \ldots, J. \end{array} \tag{11}$$

Selecting commodity 0 as the numéraire ($P_0 = 1$), we can eliminate λ^i and write:

$$\frac{u_j^i}{u_0^i} = P_j \quad \begin{array}{l} i = 1, \ldots, I \\ j = 1, \ldots, J. \end{array} \tag{12}$$

Together with the budget constraint these conditions determine the consumers' demand functions $x_j^i(P, a^i, z)$ – P and z being vectors – as functions of prices, lump-sum income and the supply of public goods. Substituting the demand functions back into the utility function gives us the indirect utility function:

$$v^i = v^i(P, a^i, z). \tag{13}$$

It can easily be shown that:

$$\frac{\partial v^i}{\partial P_j} \equiv v^i_j = -\lambda^i x^i_j \quad \begin{matrix} i = 1, \ldots, I \\ j = 1, \ldots, J \end{matrix} \tag{14a}$$

$$\frac{\partial v^i}{\partial a^i} \equiv v^i_a = \lambda^i \quad i = 1, \ldots, I \tag{14b}$$

$$\frac{\partial v^i}{\partial z_k} = v^i_k = u^i_k \quad \begin{matrix} i = 1, \ldots, I \\ k = 1, \ldots, K. \end{matrix} \tag{14c}$$

We shall now simplify the treatment of the production side a bit further. We assume that unit production costs are constant and equal to p_j for private goods and p_k for public goods. Equation (4) can then be rewritten as:

$$\sum_{j=0}^{J} p_j x_j + \sum_{k=1}^{K} p_k z_k = 0. \tag{15}$$

Obviously, in a competitive economy p_j and p_k will be the equilibrium producer prices. Here too we shall normalise by setting $p_0 = 1$.[8]

The government's budget constraint requires that:

$$\sum_{k=1}^{K} p_k z_k + \sum_{i=1}^{I} a^i - \sum_{j=1}^{J} t_j x_j = 0 \tag{6}$$

where $t_j = p_j - p_j$ are commodity taxes levied on private goods. Note that our price normalisation assumption implies that commodity 0 is not taxed; as shown for example in Sandmo (1976) this does not, however, imply any real constraint on the government's use of its policy instruments.

We can now write the social welfare function as

$$W = W(v^1, \ldots, v^I) \tag{17}$$

and formulate the policy objective as the maximisation of (17) subject to (16). The Lagrangian becomes:

$$L = W(v^1, \ldots, v^I) - \mu \left[\sum_{k=1}^{K} p_k z_k + \sum_{i=1}^{I} a^i - \sum_{j=1}^{J} (p_j - p_j) x_j \right], \tag{18}$$

and the first-order maximum conditions are found by setting the partial

[8] The assumption of constant producer prices is obviously a strong one. However, it could fairly easily be relaxed to an assumption of constant returns to scale, the important point being zero profit for distribution to the consumers. For further discussion see Sandmo (1976).

derivatives of this equal to zero. Differentiating and utilising (14) we obtain:[9]

$$\frac{\partial L}{\partial z_k} = \sum_{i=1}^{I} W_i v_k^i - \mu\left[p_k - \sum_{j=1}^{J} t_j \frac{\partial x_j}{\partial z_k}\right] = 0. \quad k = 1, \ldots, K \tag{19}$$

$$\frac{\partial L}{\partial a^i} = W_i \lambda^i - \mu = 0 \quad i = 1, \ldots, I \tag{20}$$

$$\frac{\partial L}{\partial P_r} = -\sum_{i=1}^{I} W_i \lambda^i x_r^i - \mu\left[-x_r - \sum_{j=1}^{J} t_j \frac{\partial x_j}{\partial P_r}\right] = 0. \quad r = 1, \ldots, J. \tag{21}$$

In principle, these conditions determine the optimal supply of public goods, optimal interpersonal transfers and optimal commodity taxes, i.e. the optimal deviations of consumer prices from marginal costs. However, it is easy to see that if lump-sum transfers can be chosen optimally so that (20) holds, then the last set of conditions (21) are redundant. Substituting from (20), the first two terms between the equality signs cancel out, and we are left with the condition:

$$\sum_{j=1}^{J} t_j \frac{\partial x_j}{\partial P_r} = 0, \quad \text{for all } r = 1, \ldots, J \tag{21'}$$

and this is satisfied by $t_j = 0$ for all j. Hence we may conclude that if lump-sum transfers are available, consumer prices should be set equal to marginal costs, reflecting only efficiency considerations. Moreover, with all $t_j = 0$, we may use (19) and (20) to derive:

$$\sum_{i=1}^{I} (v_k^i/\lambda^i) = p_k, \quad k = 1, \ldots, K, \tag{22}$$

which is just another form of the Samuelson conditions – equality between the sum of the marginal rates of substitution and the marginal cost in terms of the *numéraire* good. Hence we may also conclude that when lump-sum transfers are available, they alone should be used to achieve an optimal distribution of income; *at this optimum* the rules for determining the supply of public goods should be based on efficiency considerations only.[10]

[9] Note that since we are taking producer prices to be constant, we may take consumer prices rather than taxes as the policy instruments of the government.

[10] On the other hand, it might be misleading to say that the rules (22) are 'independent of the distribution of income', since the preference for public goods at the optimum naturally reflects the distribution of income between individuals.

There are various ways of interpreting and elaborating on these conditions. For the purposes of the present paper at least it is natural to see them as rules for ideal cost benefit analysis. They show the conditions that will have to hold in an efficient allocation of resources, and since the market cannot be expected to establish such an allocation, they provide guidelines for economic planners on the proper cost-benefit tests to apply in their calculations.

However, the assumption of ideal lump-sum transfers is very strong, and it is probably a bad one from the point of view of a realistic description of policy instruments. Any tax constitution has to be written in terms of a set of rules relating the individual's tax liability to some observable characteristics, and it seems extremely difficult to do so without bringing in characteristics which are wholly or partly under the individual's control. The tax system then becomes distortionary; the lump-sum intentions have been transformed into realities closely resembling those of commodity taxation. It would therefore seem to be a better procedure to assume that the theoretical ideal of lump-sum transfers is simply not available and to try to make the best out of an inevitably distortionary system of commodity taxation. This is the approach taken in the literature on second-best optimal taxation theory and the one we shall use below.[11]

It may be helpful to introduce some simplifying notation. We define

$$\pi^i_k = \frac{v^i_k}{\lambda^i}, \qquad \gamma^i = W_i \lambda^i, \tag{23}$$

with π^i_k being consumer i's marginal rate of substitution between public good k and the numéraire – or, equivalently, his marginal willingness to pay – and γ^i being his social marginal utility of income. When lump-sum transfers are not available, conditions (20) drop out and we are left with (19) and (21) which we now rewrite as:

$$\sum_{i=1}^{I} \gamma^i \pi^i_k - \mu\left[p_k - \sum_{j=1}^{J} t_j \frac{\partial x_j}{\partial z_k}\right] = 0. \quad k = 1, \ldots, K \tag{24}$$

$$\sum_{i=1}^{I} \gamma^i x^i_r - \mu\left[x_r + \sum_{j=1}^{J} t_j \frac{\partial x_j}{\partial P_r}\right] = 0. \quad r = 1, \ldots, J \tag{25}$$

From the form that these conditions take we can at once draw some

[11] This theory goes back to Ramsey (1927) and was revived in the early seventies in articles by Baumol and Bradford (1970) and Diamond and Mirrlees (1971). For more recent surveys see Sandmo (1976) and Bradford and Rosen (1976).

important conclusions. In a second-best optimum the rules for public goods allocation can no longer neglect their distributional impact. Moreover, these rules also have to take account of the effect of changes in tax revenue through the effects of public goods supplies on the demand for private goods. Finally, conditions (25) give us a set of rules for optimal commodity taxation, which is no longer redundant, and we first turn to a discussion of these.

Conditions (25) may be elaborated upon in a number of ways. To get an intuitive feeling for what is involved it is useful to consider the case of demand independence, i.e. $\partial x_j/\partial P_r = 0$ for all $j \neq r$. (Note that this does not exclude cross-effects between good r and the untaxed numéraire.) We then get a modified version of the well-known inverse elasticity formula:

$$\frac{t_r}{P_r} = \frac{1}{\mu} \cdot \frac{\sum_{i=1}^{I} (\gamma^i - \mu) x_r^i}{\sum_{i=1}^{I} x_r^i} \cdot \frac{1}{\frac{\partial x_r}{\partial P_r} \cdot \frac{P_r}{x_r}}. \quad r = 1, \ldots, J. \tag{26}$$

To interpret this condition we note first that μ is readily interpreted as the marginal value of an exogeneous income receipt by the public sector; $\gamma^i - \mu$, therefore, is the net social value of the transfer of one unit of the numéraire from the public sector to individual i. In formula (26) the weighted average of these values, the amounts consumed of commodity r serving as weights, represents the influence of distributional concerns in the determination of the tax rate. If consumption is concentrated among individuals with high marginal social utilities of income, this calls for a low rate of tax or even a subsidy, which if consumption is mainly by low γ^i-individuals, the rate of tax should, *ceteris paribus*, be high.[12]

Efficiency considerations enter through the inverse elasticity term. The higher the numerical value of the price elasticity, the lower should the tax rate be. The economics behind this result is evidently that it is the deviations of the quantities from the first-best optimum that one really worries about, while the price distortions themselves should only be seen as instruments for controlling the quantity deviations.

This special case gives the flavour of the optimal tax results embedded in the model. We leave a more general characterisation for the Appendix and turn instead to a discussion of conditions (24).

[12] This holds on the assumption that the commodity in question has a negative price elasticity, i.e. that it is not a Giffen good. The modification required for the latter case is obvious.

There are several differences to note between (24) and the corresponding conditions (22) for the first-best case. As for the benefits, we see that the first term on the left-hand side of (24) is no longer a simple sum of marginal rates of substitution; instead, these are weighted by each individual's social marginal utility of income. Thus, if the public good in question happens to be valued especially highly by individuals with high social marginal utilities of income, this 'blows up' the benefit measure compared to the simple unweighted sum. Second, the marginal cost of production, p_k, should be adjusted by the factor μ, the marginal utility of income in the public sector. So also should the third and last term, which shows the effect on tax revenue of a change in the supply of the public good. The significance of this term is not obvious and requires some further comment.

It may to some extent be a matter of taste whether this term should be interpreted as a modification of the measure of benefits or of costs. We choose the latter alternative here; however, it should be noted that Atkinson and Stern (1974) prefer to see it as a part of the benefit term. On the cost interpretation we see that whether the tax revenue effect should be counted as an addition to or subtraction from the cost of production depends on whether tax revenue is decreased or increased by increased supply of the public good, i.e. roughly, on whether the public good and the taxed private goods are substitutes or complements.

To focus on the revenue effect may in itself be somewhat misleading. The price increases following from taxation lead to reductions of private demand away from the optimum; this involves a cost in terms of efficiency. These quantity distortions can however be counteracted by the effects on demand of increases in public goods supply; if these lead to increases in the demand for private goods, the efficiency loss from distortionary taxation is reduced and the social cost of public goods supply is thereby diminished. If, on the other hand, the public good is a substitute for private goods, the distortionary effect is strengthened and the opportunity cost of public goods is increased.[13]

This effect would vanish if it were the case that consumers' utility functions could be written as separable between private and public goods, so that all marginal rates of substitution between private goods were independent of public goods supply. However, this is not only a very special assumption; it also seems particularly unattractive. Public goods like roads, harbours and national parks can certainly not be expected to be neutral with respect to private goods demand; rather, in a

[13] This interpretation agrees with that of Hagen (1979).

large number of cases we would expect there to be strong relationships of complementarity or substitutability. And as we shall see in Section IV, this interdependence provides a fruitful approach to benefit measurement via private goods markets.

There remains the problem of the appropriate value of μ. In the first-best case that is not a problem since the marginal value of resources is the same everywhere; see conditions (20). In a second-best world that is no longer true. However, to go any further than this and try to relate the value of μ to some average of the γ^i's becomes very difficult. The problem has been discussed by Atkinson and Stern (1974) for the simpler case where all individuals are equal; even with that simplification the analysis of this problem becomes very difficult and does not yield unambiguous answers.

We have seen that both the form of the efficiency part of the conditions for optimal public goods supply as well as the 'distributional' parts depend crucially on the nature of the tax instruments available to the government. If lump-sum taxes are available these should be used to establish an optimal distribution of income, and public goods should be supplied according to pure efficiency criteria. When only distortionary taxes can be used, cost-benefit calculations become more complicated:

(1) Marginal rates of substitution have to be weighted by social marginal utilities of income in order to capture the distributional impact of public goods.
(2) The cost of production of public goods has to be corrected by a term showing the effects of the public good on private demands in price-distorted markets.
(3) Allowance has to be made for the fact that the marginal utility of income is no longer the same in all uses.

This discussion has emphasised the increasing complexity of cost-benefit calculations in moving from a first-best to a second-best situation. However, the first-best is not without its complications either. We turn now to a brief discussion of some aspects of the estimation of benefits.

IV THE ESTIMATION OF BENEFITS AND THE ROLE OF THE MARKET

The question of the revelation and estimation of benefits has probably received more attention than any other aspect of the theory of public goods.[14] The problem involved was clearly stated in the original paper by Samuelson (1954). In the context of a critical review of the benefit theory of taxation he pointed out that if the cost of a public good were to be distributed among individuals in proportion to their stated marginal willingness to pay, then each individual would have an incentive to *understate* his true preferences. The problem of incentive distortions goes beyond this specific context, however. If for example the individual believed that there would be no positive association between his declared marginal willingness to pay and his tax liability, he would have an incentive to *overstate* his willingness to pay. Much current research is concerned with finding procedures that can overcome this conflict between individual and collective rationality. Here we shall only be concerned with one aspect of this work, *viz.* the extent to which preferences for public goods can be assumed to be revealed in the markets for private goods.

The basic idea is a simple one and forms the basis for much applied work on cost-benefit analysis. Suppose that there is an identifiable complementarity relationship between the public good (say, a road) and some private good (car-use). By estimating consumers' revealed willingness to pay for the private good one can indirectly estimate their implied willingness to pay for the public good. This line of reasoning would seem to be equally valid in the case of substitutes; we now proceed to a more formal discussion of its theoretical foundations.

One approach is via the 'new theory of consumption' in which the individual or the household is seen as producing final goods, over which preferences are defined, using private goods as inputs into objectively given and observable household production functions. To apply this theory to public goods it is only necessary to extend the list of inputs to include both private and public goods. Take the simplest case where the quantity produced and consumed of final good j depends on the inputs of one private and one public good, so that we can write

$$y_j^i = f_j(x_j^i, z_j). \tag{27}$$

Note that while preference patterns will differ among individuals, this will be reflected only in differences in private goods inputs among them, while the production functions f_j – and, of course, the availability of public goods – are objectively given and the same for all individuals. In the simplest case where both the private and public good j are specific to

[14] For a valuable short survey of this literature see Chapter 1 of the important book by Green and Laffont (1979).

final good j, the marginal rate of substitution $(\partial f_j/\partial z_j)/(\partial f_j/\partial x_j^i)$ can be assessed once we know the private good input x_j^i and the functional relationship f_j. In Sandmo (1973, 1975) it is shown how this formulation can be generalised to more complex and realistic cases.

A more direct approach to this problem is taken by Bradford and Hildebrandt (1977). They start with the observation that demand functions for private goods depend on the supplies of public goods. By making various special assumptions – in particular constant marginal utility of the numéraire good – they are able to derive an estimate of willingness to pay for the public good as the marginal effect on consumers' surplus for private goods of changes in public goods supply. In their model knowledge of the (inverse) demand functions for private goods plays the same role as knowledge of the 'technological' marginal rates of substitution in the household production model.

The procedure for estimating the benefits from public goods supply suggested by these models would seem to be of considerable importance as a set of guidelines for applied cost-benefit studies, although in practice they will probably be useful only in cases where there exist marked relationships of complementarity or substitutability. It should also be emphasised that this approach does not imply that the incentive problem is 'solved'. But the only way in which an individual can misrepresent his preferences under this procedure is to deliberately distort his demand for private goods compared to what would be individually rational for him, given the actual supply of public goods. Misrepresentation of preferences therefore becomes costly to the individual and correspondingly less attractive.

V CONCLUDING REMARKS

This survey of some central issues in the modern theory of public goods and taxation is necessarily highly incomplete. Yet some important ground has been covered. We have seen how public goods are closely associated with the concept of market failure and how welfare theory can be extended so as to provide rules for optimal allocation of resources to public goods. We have also seen that the precise form of these rules depends on the nature of the tax system. With lump-sum transfers available, public goods supply should at the optimum be decided solely on the basis of efficiency criteria. In the more realistic of distortionary taxation the rules get more complicated; not only must distributional objectives be explicitly taken into account, but the efficiency conditions have to reflect the fact that there are social gains from influencing the structure of private goods demand in price-distorted markets. Finally, we have seen that even though public goods are associated with market failure, markets for private goods have an important role to play as a provider of information about preferences for public goods.

The analysis is obviously not of the kind where all that needs to be done is to estimate the coefficients and determine the numerical values of the variables in the optimal solution. The immediate value of this kind of exercise is rather to provide a framework for thinking about problems of taxation and public expenditure in a logical and systematic manner. Hopefully, the discussion also shows that the 'new public economics', emphasising second-best problems and using a general equilibrium approach, provides a flexible framework for studying policy problems, in which realistic restrictions on the availability of policy instruments can be built in from the start.

On the latter point there is hardly general agreement among researchers working in the field. Thus, Musgrave (1976, p. 3) writes that the optimal taxation approach '[does] not provide an analytical link between the provision for social goods and the determination of the tax structure by which they are financed'. As the discussion in Section III above brings out, this is a misleading statement; our model of public goods and commodity taxes does in fact provide a unified treatment of taxation and expenditure policies. In the same article Musgrave also maintains that the optimal taxation approach depends crucially on an assumption of equal preferences and therefore on neglect of the distributional issues arising in tax policy.[15] While it is undoubtedly true that many contributions to this field have stressed the efficiency aspects, sometimes at the cost of neglecting distribution, this can hardly be said to be an inherent weakness of the theory as such, and the approach taken in the present paper should bring this point out clearly.

It has of course to be admitted that the impact of distributional concerns on optimal taxation and expenditure policies is modelled in a less 'operational' way than efficiency considerations; price elasticities are empirically meaningful concepts in a way that social marginal utilities of income are not. However, this could hardly be otherwise. Distributional policies must be based on ethical judgements; the role of economic analysis is clearly not to say what these judgements should be, but to show how they need to be brought in to modify prescriptions based on pure efficiency criteria.

[15] See Musgrave (1976), pp. 3n., 14, 16.

Appendix

AN ALTERNATIVE CHARACTERISATION OF OPTIMAL TAXATION AND PUBLIC GOODS SUPPLY

The inverse elasticity formula (26), while instructive, is based on very restrictive assumptions. We present here an alternative characterisation which was first suggested by Diamond (1975).

We first introduce the concept of the *net* social marginal utility of income.[16] What is the marginal utility to society of giving one unit of lump-sum income to individual i? One's immediate inclination may be to say that it is simply γ^i. But further reflection shows that it is necessary to take into account the increased taxed revenue that this income generates, evaluated at the marginal utility of income in the public sector, μ. The net social marginal utility of income therefore becomes:

$$\alpha^i = \gamma^i + \mu \sum_{j=1}^{J} t_j \frac{\partial x_j^i}{\partial a^i}. \quad i = 1, \ldots, I. \tag{A1}$$

In the model of Section III there is of course no lump-sum income; the a^is are used here simply to characterise the properties of demand functions.

We shall also make use of the Slutsky equations:

$$\frac{\partial x_j^i}{\partial P_r} = -x_r^i \frac{\partial x_j^i}{\partial a^i} + s_{jr}^i, \qquad \begin{array}{l} i = 1, \ldots, I \\ j, r = 0, \ldots, J \end{array} \tag{A2}$$

where the last term is the substitution effect. This has the symmetry property that $s_{jr}^i = s_{rj}^i$.

Substituting from the Slutsky equations into the optimal tax conditions (25) and using (A1) and the symmetry condition, we obtain:

$$\frac{\sum_{i=1}^{I} (\alpha^i - \mu) x_r^i}{\sum_{i=1}^{I} x_r^i} = \mu . \frac{\sum_{j=1}^{J} \sum_{i=1}^{I} t_j s_{rj}^i}{X_r} \qquad r = 1, \ldots, J. \tag{A3}$$

[16] Diamond (1975) refers to this concept simply as the social marginal utility of income while he calls our γ^i the social marginal utility of consumption.

The left-hand side is the distributional measure that also occurred in the inverse elasticity formula, except for the fact that α^i has been substituted for γ^i. This distributional characteristic of commodity r should be proportional to the relative percentage change in compensated demand – weighted by the tax rates – following from a small overall price change at the optimum. This condition is a generalisation of the well-known Ramsey rule for the one-consumer economy; see for example Sandmo (1976).

Analogously, we may define the net social value of providing one more unit of public good k to consumer i as:

$$\beta^i_k = \gamma^i \pi^i_k + \mu \sum_{j=1}^{J} t_j \frac{\partial x^i_j}{\partial z_k} \quad \begin{array}{l} i = 1, \ldots, I \\ k = 1, \ldots, K \end{array} \tag{A4}$$

and conditions (24) can then be rewritten as:

$$\sum_{i=1}^{I} \beta^i_k = \mu p_k \quad k = 1, \ldots, K. \tag{A5}$$

It seems to be purely a matter of taste whether one feels that (24) or (A5) provides the more meaningful support for economic intuition.

REFERENCES

Arrow, K. J. (1970). 'Political and Economic Evaluation of Social Effects and Externalities' in J. Margolis (ed.), *The Analysis of Public Output* (New York: National Bureau of Economic Research, Columbia University Press).

Atkinson, A. B. and N. H. Stern (1974). 'Pigou, Taxation and Public Goods', *Review of Economic Studies*, 41, 119–28.

Baumol, W. J. and D. F. Bradford (1970). 'Optimal Departures from Marginal Cost Pricing', *American Economic Review*, 60, 265–83.

Bradford, D. F. and H. S. Rosen (1976). 'The Optimal Taxation of Commodities and Income', *American Economic Review*, 66, (May), 94–101.

Bradford, D. F. and G. C. Hildebrandt (1977). 'Observable Preferences for Public Goods', *Journal of Public Economics*, 8, 111–31.

Diamond, P. A. (1975). 'A Many-Person Ramsey Tax Rule', *Journal of Public Economics*, 4, 335–42.

Diamond, P. A. and J. A. Mirrlees (1951). 'Optimal Taxation and Public Production I-II', *American Economic Review*, 61, 8–27, 261–78.

Green, J. R. and J.-J. Laffont (1979). *Incentives in Public Decision-Making* (Amsterdam: North-Holland).

Hagen, K. P. (1979). 'Optimal Pricing in Public Firms in an Imperfect Market Economy', *Scandinavian Journal of Economics* (forthcoming).

Musgrave, R. A. (1976). 'ET, OT and SBT', *Journal of Public Economics*, 6, 3–16.

Ramsey, F. P. (1927). 'A Contribution to the Theory of Taxation', *Economic Journal*, 37, 47–61.

Samuelson, P. A. (1954). 'The Pure Theory of Public Expenditure', *Review of Economics and Statistics*, 36, 387–9.
Samuelson, P. A. (1969). 'Pure Theory of Public Expenditure and Taxation' in J. Margolis and H. Guitton (eds), *Public Economics* (London: Macmillan).
Sandmo, A. (1973, 1975). 'Public Goods and the Technology of Consumption' and 'A Correction', *Review of Economic Studies*, 40, 517–28, and 42, 167–68.
Sandmo, A. (1976). 'Optimal Taxation: An Introduction to the Literature', *Journal of Public Economics*, 6, 37–54.

Discussion of 'The Optimal Supply of Public Goods in a Mixed Economy' by Professor A. Sandmo

As a basis for discussion, *Professor Bös* suggested two alternatives to the general equilibrium analysis of public goods described in the paper in which a benevolent politician was depicted as maximising a social welfare function, the arguments of which were individual utilities. These were the model of the prisoners' dilemma or some other game theoretic model based on an assumption that individual preferences for public goods are not revealed; and the models of the new political economy in which politicians were depicted as offering alternative tax and public expenditure packages to voters at elections. His view was that the game theoretic approach might be more useful for those cases in which it was difficult to estimate individual preferences for public goods, and that a politico-economic model might provide useful alternative predictions of the mix between public expenditure and taxation. In a review of the specific assumptions and results of Professor Sandmo's model, he pointed to the additive utilitarian and Rawlsian formulations of the social welfare function as particular specifications of the general formulation presented in the paper. He noted that direct taxes and the distributional effects of public expenditures had not been considered, and that there was no analysis of the interaction between allocation and distribution on the expenditure side of the model. In relation to the indirect tax instruments which were considered, he emphasised that the distributional term of equation (26) of the paper was in part no more than a correction for adverse distributional effects arising from the structure of indirect taxation in the allocative term of that equation. He explained that these effects arose from the optimising condition that, *ceteris paribus*, goods with a low price elasticity of demand (normally assumed to bulk large in the expenditure of low-income classes) attract high rates of indirect taxation. *Dr Hoch* pointed out that this condition would not obtain in a system in which the objective was to influence the pattern of consumption, for in this case high rates of indirect taxation would be most efficiently levied on goods with a high price elasticity of demand.

Professor Hanusch argued that the alternative analyses being discussed did not offer a solution to the problem of non-revelation of preferences. *Professor Frey* suggested the following methods, not so far discussed, by which preferences for public goods might be estimated: opinion surveys; cardinal utility analysis; referenda and voting analysis; inference from studies of transport costs, studies of mobility and property prices; and applications of politico-economic models incorporating popularity and vote functions. He admitted that some of these methods were quite consistent with those described in Professor Sandmo's paper.

Mr Matthews and *Professor Modigliani* found it difficult to see how survey questions could be framed so as to elicit the required information on marginal valuations. But against this *Mr Kaser* reported successful studies by Behrend and Zupanov of individual preferences for policies on income maintenance, and by Sande and Van Eyck of the cardinal ranking of policies by Dutch politicians. Misgivings were also expressed about the method of imputation from market valuations. *Mr Matthews* pointed to the difficulty of drawing general conclusions from specific studies of the kind being suggested. He cited studies using property values as measures of environmental amenity in which individuals with a relatively high tolerance of noise had been found to be living close to long-established airports. The result was that property values were not significantly different from what they otherwise would have been. *Professor Modigliani* argued that the usefulness of the method of imputation from market values was confined to the limited case of complementary goods. His general reaction to Professor Frey's suggestions was that all of them were technically impressive but none of them valid.

A number of criticisms were made of the general equilibrium model of the competitive economy described in the paper. *Dr Hoch* referred to the existence of monopoly and non-constant returns to scale which the model assumed to be absent. He objected to both the general assumption of substitutability between all commodities, which in his view ignored basic needs such as security and nutrition, and to the lack of any analysis of the formation of individual preferences. In particular he objected to the assumption that preferences were independent of prices and income. *Professor Pohorille* argued that, as consumer preferences in capitalist economies had been manipulated by business interests and the media, the analysis should focus on the causes of such distortions and how they might be removed in the social interest, rather than on individual preferences as such. Only in this way could equality of opportunity and individual development be promoted. However, without disputing the importance of factors influencing tastes, *Mr Matthews* did not agree that the concept of autonomous individual preference was empty.

In reply to the discussion, *Professor Sandmo* argued that for the purpose of normative analysis the model described in his paper seemed more appropriate than those suggested by Professor Bös. He conceded that the game theoretic approach would be more useful for the purpose of explanation. He did not accept Professor Bös's point on the omission of the distributional effects of public goods. His view was that the paper made it clear that in the second-best case in which distortionary taxes were levied there was an interaction between distributional and allocative effects which required an adjustment to individuals' willingness to pay for public goods by the use of distributional weights. He also pointed to the need in this case to take account of the supply of public goods on the demand for private goods. He explained the difficulty of incorporating progressive direct taxes into the analysis and pointed out that results similar to those presented obtained when linear direct taxes were introduced. He admitted that the case of increasing returns to scale posed a problem for the analysis. On the question of the autonomy of individual preferences, Professor Sandmo did not dispute some of the points made by Professor Pohorille about the formation of tastes, but expressed his difficulty with the notion of an autonomous social interest against which the expressed preferences of individuals might be judged.

6 The Desirable Scope and Scale of Grants in Kind in Socialist Countries: as illustrated by the case of Hungary

Robert Hoch

HUNGARIAN ACADEMY OF SCIENCES, BUDAPEST

I THE PROBLEMS

One of the central issues of economic and social policy in socialist countries is what should be the rate of growth and the distribution of the increase of social grants. Such a rate of growth and change of distribution is sought in the expansion of the grants economy as will best contribute to the development of the nation, and within it to that of the economy. Among other things, it facilitates the rapid growth of the economy; it reduces social tensions; it accelerates the creation of healthy and improved living conditions for the population. The objectives themselves are varied and multidimensional and may even be mutually inconsistent. Various quantitative and qualitative factors and their interrelations must be analysed in the course of deciding the increases of grants in kind which will achieve the intended purposes most satisfactorily. Important tools in this analysis include mathematical modelling and mathematical programming. But these are no substitute for economic analysis. In this paper I propose to discuss the problems of planning-choices and decision-making in this field.

There are vigorous arguments about the amount of increase and the sectoral distribution of social grants in kind in Hungary. It is obvious that the patterns of development that are regarded as optimal by different economists and different economic politicians with very much the same viewpoint depend on their ideas regarding social objectives and their orders of preference for a cross-section of objectives and their timing.

Optimising models are applied in national planning in general; but consistency models are of primary importance. One must emphasise the value of such models also in connection with the planning of the grants economy. The variety of the grants themselves and of the purposes served by them, the multifarious interrelations of these grants with other components of the social system and of the economy make the assurance of external and internal consistency indispensable from the point of view of the grants economy. Without this, the provision made for the development could become ineffective. Measures taken to achieve different purposes may frustrate or neutralise the effects of each other. The requirement of consistency means not only that the sum of the parts adds up to the whole but also that a uniform preference system is applied throughout the model, thus clarifying the types of grants preferred and determining the minimum development of the non-preferred types of grants and their lowest limit.[1] A number of preference systems suitable for different purposes may be worked out and may serve as possible alternative plans for decision-makers.

In this paper I shall first review – on the basis of simple statistical data – the growth of grants in kind in Hungary. In the following, longer, and I hope more interesting, part of the paper I shall try to describe the main economic and non-economic problems that have arisen in the planning of grants in kind and the conceptual differences of opinion involved.

II THE SCOPE OF GRANTS IN KIND

Grants in kind include first of all those goods which are provided for all the population free of charge. These constitute the main forms of grants in kind, and include first of all medical care and education. Those goods of which only a small part of the cost is borne by the purchaser also

[1] The consistency model known in the literature and practice of the long-term planning of the standard of living as the Alpha Model, which is suitable for this task, was elaborated by János Kovács. See 'The simplified model MEB alpha of the consistency check of Hungarian standard of living planning', *Szigma*, No 2 (1972).

count as grants in kind (medicines sold in pharmacies, certain types of medical equipment, subsidised theatre and concert tickets, the depreciation of state-owned flats to the extent that they are not covered by rents and so on). In the case of certain grants, it is only above a certain level of income, and then depending on the level of income, that the customer must make a contribution to the cost on a progressive basis (nurseries, kindergartens, higher education and the like).

The total of grants in kind in Hungary and their ratio to the total income of the population are shown in Tables 6.1 and 6.2.

In a certain sense goods whose prices are subsidised for social reasons (these are important both in range and volume) are also reckoned to be among grants in kind, though they are not included in the figures in Tables 6.1 and 6.2. They include basic foods, articles of children's wear, school supplies, books, transport (especially public transport in cities), and various kinds of services. Nor do the statistical data cover the amounts of the grants which are given by an enterprise to its employees.[2]

In socialist countries an important proportion of all consumer goods is withdrawn from the sphere of market distribution[3] – in whole or in part – in order that the constraints of purchasing power shall not (or shall only slightly) restrict the consumption of these goods. In other words, the income elasticity is modified through low prices so that consumers shall prefer these goods to others within the limits imposed by their purchasing power. By these means (combined with other policy instruments) the consumption pattern of the whole population and

[2] Items of extra-market consumption such as the armed forces, public administration, public consumption (roads, bridges, street lighting) and environmental maintenance are not included in grants in kind.

[3] 'If social supply is not determined by the technical criteria of products, the difference between commodity vs. non-commodity can only be tracked back to *ideological aspects of the economy*. Established social norms are compulsory for the socialist organisation of the economy. As a general rule *social supply* includes social care for the aged and for children, culture and education as well as health services. In a socialist society this is put into practice by two co-existing systems of distribution: distribution according to work and distribution according to needs. Distribution according to needs refers to needs which from the point of view of the members of society are basic requirements but are ethical requirements from the point of society as a whole.' B. Csikós-Nagy, *Socialist Price Theory and Price Policy* (Akadémiai Kiadó, Budapest, 1975), p. 62.

Actually the volume and the growth of grants in kind is not determined by the technological criteria. Technically all the essential items of grants in kind could be handled by the market system. On the other hand, those items for which individual consumption is technically quite impossible are not included among grants in kind (defence, public lighting and similar services).

TABLE 6.1 THE LEVELS OF GRANTS IN KIND IN HUNGARY 1960–1977[a]

	1960	*1965*	*1966*	*1967*	*1968*	*1969*	*1970*	*1970*	*1971*	*1972*	*1973*	*1974*	*1975*	*1976*	*1977*
Sum total in thousand million fts (current price)	13.5	18.1	19.3	20.3	21.8	23.7	26.2[b]	23.5[b]	25.7	27.8	30.1	32.3	36.0	38.9	43.0
1960 = 100	100	134.3	143.6	151.0	162.0	175.8	195.0[b]	174.4[b]	191.1	206.2	224.7	240.2	267.3	288.9	319.6
The real value of of grants in kind 1960 = 100	100	129.8	.	.	.	.	163.7		171.4	181.2	191.7	202.0	213.8	223.5	233.1
As percentage of total income (current price)	11.4	12.4	12.3	12.1	12.1	12.2	12.4[b]	11.3[b]	11.5	11.7	11.7	11.5	11.7	11.9	12.0

[a] *The Income and the Consumption of the Population 1960–1977*, Central Statistical Office, 1979, pp. 8, 17, 18.
[b] There was an important change in the system of the per costs accounting of medicines in 1970. Without changing the system of supply the item 'Medicines' represents a considerably lower sum in the new set-up than before. The change has an effect on the item 'Health grants' and on the total sum of grants in kind as well.

TABLE 6.2 THE SCALE OF GRANTS IN KIND AS PERCENTAGE[a]

	1960	*1965*	*1970*	*1970*	*1975*	*1976*	*1977*
Health care	28.1	28.1	27.9	30.2	28.8	28.7	28.2
Nurseries	1.8	2.0	1.9	2.1	1.9	2.0	2.1
State subsidy on medicines, therapeutic equipment	6.8	9.0	10.3[b]	1.0[b]	1.2	1.1	1.0
Social grants	2.6	2.2	2.4	2.6	3.7	3.8	3.9
Educational grants	33.7	33.2	33.9	37.9	35.9	36.5	35.8
Kindergartens	3.7	3.5	3.7	4.1	4.5	5.2	5.3
Cultural, sports holiday facilities	7.9	6.9	6.9	8.3	13.1	11.8	13.1
Depreciation allowance of state flats	9.3	8.4	6.8	6.8	5.6	5.4	5.2
Canteen subsidies, further items	6.1	6.7	6.2	7.0	5.3	5.5	5.4
Total	100.0	100.0	100.0	100.0	100.0	100.0	100.0

[a] See footnote *a* of Table 6.1
[b] See note *b* of Table 6.1

particular social groups can be modified in such a way that, in the process of satisfying individual needs, the satisfaction of the basic social needs (for example public health, culture) shall get a higher priority compared with those goods which are suitable to be bought as commodities. Additional objectives are: firstly, that in the consumption of those with low incomes, essential needs shall be satisfied more fully (as compared to the level possible if those commodities had to be bought at an unsubsidised price), thus diminishing distortions coming from accepting the consumption patterns of those with higher incomes; secondly, that a considerable part of the costs of bringing up a child shall be borne by the society as a whole.[4]

In addition to the objectives already described, grants in kind serve to diminish inequalities in incomes and in ways of living. The advantage derived from the use of grants is unequal, but not primarily because of

[4] On average, more than 50 per cent of the costs of bringing up a child are covered in Hungary by grants in kind and money allowances.

differences in incomes. Inequalities arise from the fact, for example, that the supply of health institutions is on a lower level in the rural areas than in the cities. Another source of the unequal use made of grants is differences of cultural level (higher education, for instance). These factors in inequality can be cumulative. Grants in kind, nevertheless, bring some equalisation. Within the same type of town or village and within the same social stratum, the levelling effect of grants in kind is powerful, because the distribution of some at least of the grants is less unequal than the distribution of money incomes. The distribution of a number of other grants is automatically equal (for example, those to children in the first eight grades of elementary schools, or the subsidies to the price of bread).

The distribution of grants in kind as between social strata also shows that it is not the differences of income that cause inequalities but essentially the types of towns and villages and the cultural level (half of all workers, and specially of unskilled workers, live in villages). In this respect, with the exception of the intellectuals–intellectual work involves a higher cultural standard, and the great proportion of this stratum live in a city – grants in kind have an effect in equalising incomes. There is a negative correlation between personal incomes and grants in kind. The reason for this – in addition to what has been said above – is that pensioners have the highest demand for the services of the health service, and while free social insurance is available to all members of the population, their scope is more restricted in the case of self-employed than in the case of workers (see Table 6.3). In subsequent sections of this paper I shall proceed to clarify some of the basic relationships which play an important part in the planning of grants in kind.

TABLE 6.3 INCOME PROPORTIONS BETWEEN THE SOCIAL STRATA IN HUNGARY IN 1971[a]

	Workers = 100				
	Workers	*Intellectuals*	*Peasants*	*Self-employed*	*Pensioners*
1 Personal income	100.0	133.6	103.4	115.3	74.8
2 Grants in kind	100.0	142.5	76.1	85.5	109.4

[a] *The Income and the Consumption of the Population 1960–1977* (CSO, Budapest, 1973), p. 32.

III GRANTS VERSUS EARNINGS

Money allowances and grants in kind form a single organic unity. This is not only because it is common to both of them that they are not earned, although there are some very important forms of monetary grants, such as sickness benefits and pensions, which are closely related to earnings. They form a unity first of all because any given social political purpose can usually be served efficiently only by a combination of money grants and grants in kind; they can substitute for each other only to a very limited extent. For example, we intend to cut down gradually but definitely the factors causing differences in the opportunities open to new entrants into employment that exist even today, after the radical changes of our social revolution. The means of achieving this objective are both the system of money grants (family allowances, scholarships and the like) and the system of grants in kind (health, care of children, the educational system, price subsidies for particular foods, the provision of cheap clothes for children's wear, school appliances, children's furniture, and so on) as well as the appropriate expansion of both these systems. And in the same way, the scheme for provision for the aged includes both the improvement of the pension system and the improvement of services (naturally, pensioners make far more use of the free health services than in proportion to their numbers) and of the network of homes for the aged, of which there is not yet sufficient development in Hungary. In the case of some very important grants it is largely a question of organisation and accounting whether it is treated as a money grant or a grant in kind in the accounts, though the essence of the grant remains the same. For example, health provision can be made directly free of charge or the medical-hospital account can be repaid by an insurance scheme.

It can be seen that the combined handling of grants and money incomes and their comparison is justified. The ratio of earnings to grants in Hungary is shown in Table 6.4.

One of the main and permanent dilemmas of income distribution in socialist countries is the relation between grants and earnings: their contradictions and their unity. The achievements of, or progress towards, our basic social aims – security, social equality, honesty, and healthy and civilised life – postulate the rapid growth of grants. A rapid increase of earnings, and in particular of real earnings, is necessary for economic development; and this is the basic condition of improved welfare. The growth of productivity is inhibited by the exaggerated restraint on the increase of real earnings. Conversely, any restriction of

TABLE 6.4 THE RATIOS OF EARNINGS TO MONEY GRANTS AND GRANTS IN KIND IN 1960–77 IN HUNGARY[a]

	1960	*1965*	*1966*	*1967*	*1968*	*1969*	*1970*	*1970*	*1971*	*1972*	*1973*	*1974*	*1975*	*1976*	*1977*
Grants as percentage of earnings (current price)	22.8	27.2	28.4	28.4	28.9	29.4	30.6[b]	29.6[b]	30.7	32.1	33.9	35.6	37.9	40.2	40.5
Real value of grants per capita 1960 = 100	100.0	135.6	n.a.	n.a.	n.a.	n.a.	192.7	n.a.	203.9	219.5	241.5	265.9	291.0	310.7	327.1
Grants in kind as percentage of money grants (current prices)	161.3	143.9	131.3	125.6	123.1	122.4	119[b]	100[b]	99.7	95.4	87.9	80.4	76.0	72.0	72.0

[a] *The Income and Consumption of the Population*, 1960–77 (CSO, Budapest, 1979), pp. 8, 9, 16, 17.
[b] See Table 6.1, note *b*.

the increase of grants delays progress towards our social goals.

The crucial task of income policy and income planning is to find the right balance between the increase of earnings and the increase of grants. This is difficult even if the economy is growing fast, with surplus resources, making possible considerable increases of both earnings and grants to appropriate extents. But the task becomes extraordinarily difficult in periods when the growth of the available GDP slows down, and surplus resources are limited. In such cases opposing views and ambitions tend to emerge; in practice the increase of earnings is usually preferred to that of grants. But it would not be difficult to develop a theory to justify the conclusion that the continuation of the present trend of the ratio of earnings to grants is not desirable in the longer term.[5]

The advocates of this proposition start from the fear that after a while only the smaller part of the total of income will be available to serve as incentive. In practice, this trend can be restrained but it cannot be reversed. This function can be served by an income of a greater real amount growing appropriately in its purchasing power but becoming smaller in relation to the total of resources. That is to say, even today the situation is that the ambition to obtain superior rather than inferior goods provides an incentive; this will be even more true in the future. But there is, at the same time, another view[6] which holds that one should not care about economic growth, and the material incentives producing this; that our policy of distribution should serve almost exclusively the idea of equality.

Can we use the models designed for the theory of welfare to determine the appropriate ratio of earnings to grants? Welfare economics allows one to draw curves, the poles of which are extreme inequality (associated with the highest possible economic growth) and perfect equality (maximum total utility for society), and – seemingly – their optimum points can be indicated. But these graphs do not help either theoretically or practically in the solution of the issue in question.

This theoretical model does not provide any help in practice because the optimum ratio of the distribution of total income between earnings and grants cannot be calculated. But what is more important, this model does not help theoretically either. First of all, it oversimplifies the actual

[5] László Lengyel, 'Some Main Questions of the Policy of the Distribution of Income and Social Grants', *Penzugyi Szemle*, No. 6 (1968).

[6] Hegedus-Markus, 'Alternatives and the Choice of Values in the Long-term Planning of Distribution and Consumption', *Közgazdasagi Szemle*, No. 9 (1969).

problem. It is not true that the more differentiated the incomes, the more rapid the growth. Material incentives may involve differentiation in incomes, but always in defined relationships, as between professions, jobs, activities. In other relationships, it is the levelling of incomes which is the condition of efficient material incentives.

Secondly, on the basis of my researches I do not find acceptable the theory regarding the maximisation of individual utilities and their aggregation into a social total utility. This theory is one of the theoretical pillars of welfare economics in general and also of the model concerned. I have developed my ideas relating to this in English in my book, entitled *Consumption and Price.*[7]

Thus it is not the conflict between maximum growth and maximum benefit, in static terms, that must actually be removed. Thirdly, and this is what I consider most important, there is not a simple conflict between the conditions of rapid growth and the means of achieving the social objectives, including the reduction of inequalities; they are in each case the precondition of the other.

On the one hand, grants also contribute greatly to economic growth. Witness the importance of public health and of education, for example, in the fixing of minimum wages. Last but not least, the surplus resources that make possible the increase of grants are created by the economic growth that is in turn generated by effective material incentives.

In determining the desirable ratio of earnings to grants our ultimate strategic objective is to reduce all differences in income and more generally in the living standards of families which are not the result of differences in the work done by the earning family members but due, for example, to differences of family size and the like, and to make the differences of earnings reflect more truly the differences arising from the work performed. An important function of the grants in kind is to reduce differences between living standards even in comparison with the differences between incomes arising from work performed.

IV GRANTS IN KIND VERSUS MONEY INCOMES

An important problem in the planning of the extent of grants in kind is what its ratio should be to money incomes; that is to say, to the combined total of money incomes and the total of money grants; or in

[7] Sijthoff and Noordhoff, Alphen aan Den Rijn, Akadémiai Kiadó (Budapest, 1979).

other words, the ratio of extra market consumption to commodity consumption. During the 1950s the proportion of grants in kind in the total income increased; but subsequently this ratio (see Table 6.1) has shown little change, and has diminished as a proportion of total grants (see Table 6.4).

The problems regarding this relationship are familiar:

(1) The greater part of the grants in kind represent the output of non-profit institutions; the market does not determine their output; profitability is slight and cannot be used as the means to stimulate the activity and output.
(2) Purchasing power does not restrict demand and thus considerable shortages may arise even with a significant expansion of supply.
(3) Consumers cannot exercise choice between the free goods and purchasable goods, nor as to the amounts of different goods provided free of charge.
(4) People regard their purchasing power as being represented by their money incomes and increased income in cash is usually preferred to increase of grants in kind.

These are reasons why there has been pressure from some Hungarian economists and sociologists to change the ratio between money incomes and grants in kind in favour of the former; and reduce the scale and scope of the latter. There is at present an attempt, visible even in government policy, to change certain grants in kind into money grants. This latter means in the first place that subsidised prices are to be converted into money grants, and in some cases into earnings. In the past decade it has been the practice to compensate price rises of such basic goods as meat, milk, fuel oil, and the like by simultaneous rises in wages, pensions, family allowances, and the like. For the population as a whole these rises have been overcompensated. These policies are also reflected in the considerably more rapid growth of money grants as compared with grants in kind in the period concerned. But this is not the main cause of this change in their relative proportions. The cause has been the vigorous development of the system of money grants on the one hand, combined with a much less satisfactory development, in many respects, of the network of institutions providing social grants.

The problem of social grants versus money incomes is a real one. I do not myself agree with the general policy of restricting social grants in a broader sense. I do not agree because the actual disadvantages are represented by the loss of the benefits which can be got through social grants and through social grants alone. Moreover, these disadvantages from the point of view of a given objective often make themselves felt in an exaggerated or distorted form.

May I describe the dilemmas?

1 THE PROBLEM OF PROVIDING INCENTIVES FOR EFFICIENT ECONOMIC OPERATION AND APPROPRIATE OUTPUT DECISIONS IN NON-PROFIT-MAKING INSTITUTIONS

In practice it is possible that in these institutions, in comparison with profit-making institutions, there may be some waste, since the possibility of providing incentives is restricted from the beginning, and the possible directions of stimulation are also uncertain. What can be set against this? First of all, profitability is, at most, of secondary importance in the sphere of social grants. The relationship of output and input is not an overriding criterion in appraising the social efficiency of medical care, education and similar services, nor even in the appraisal of their economic efficiency. Secondly, the concept of profitability is wholly different in this sphere from that appropriate, for example, in the sphere of the production of material goods. While in the latter it is of primary importance that a given output be achieved with a minimum input, in estimating profitability in the sphere of grants in kind it is of primary importance to achieve the maximum possible output from a given input, though the significance of using the available resources rationally exists equally in these institutions. But the achievement of the basic functions may be precluded by too vigorous stimulation. Take, for example, the capacity of hospitals: the need of their expansion is obviously determined by the average number of days spent in hospital by any one patient. If we make it an objective to increase the 'velocity of circulation', patients may be sent home before they are well enough. Alternatively, if we make it our objective to minimise the cost to be calculated for one patient per day, they may be kept in hospital longer than is necessary. The problem of profitability of this activity has to be solved, in the first place, by the determination of the *strategy of development*. Thus, for example, the hospital wards that deal with rehabilitation and the whole system of after-care at home must be rapidly improved so as to prevent after-care patients occupying the beds in hospital wards that are supplied with expensive equipment and require highly qualified medical staff. Thirdly, in this group of activities the definition, and, largely as a consequence, the measure of output is problematic from the beginning. Planning and performance estimate output, in total, by the input of these institutions. It is obvious enough that the output so expressed is not the actual performance. The aggregated indicators are supplemented by physical indicators such as the number of patients per physician, the number of students per teacher, and so on. This says something about output. But output at the national level includes the state of health of the population; the trends of morbidity and mortality; the cultural level of the population; the levels and composition of professional skills, and similar things. A diminution of the number of patients for which one physician is responsible or a diminution of the number of students for one teacher may be necessary in many cases for the improvement of these more basic standards.

2 PURCHASING POWER SHALL NOT RESTRICT NECESSARY CONSUMPTION

Extra-market consumption is very often associated with shortages. The simple objective is to remove the satisfaction of needs essential to the balanced development of a society from the constraints of purchasing power. The inevitable price, and a virtually inescapable feature of the system, is that we renounce price as a means of restricting demand. If it is our objective that children of families with lower incomes shall not be excluded from education, the population as a whole will take advantage of the educational and cultural system to a greater extent than it would do if it had to buy these services as commodities; thus we cannot complain that the demands are too great. In this case the only way to overcome shortages is the rapid expansion of the system of institutions. The greatest shortage in the organisations providing grants in kind in Hungary is in that concerned with medical care. The shortages of supply of flats are more urgent, but their costs are recorded only in part among the grants in kind. The basic cause of the shortage is that at the end of the 1940s, and at the beginning of the 1950s, free medical care was granted to all workers and employees, the number of whom increased rapidly throughout the 1950s; at the beginning of the 1960s it was extended to all engaged in agriculture as well (reorganisation of agriculture was carried out early in the 1960s); today it has become a right of every citizen. The capacity of the health service has not kept up with this sudden increase of legitimate claims and rising demands. (This fact cannot be deduced from the statistical data of the volume of health grants.) Long-term planning, as a consequence, regards the improvement of the health service as one of the key problems for the standard of living. More generally, the basic and often the only means of satisfying demands in these activities is likely to be an increase of capacity, bearing in mind that shortages at one level may lead to shortages at a higher level.

3 THE CONSUMER DOES NOT HAVE FREEDOM TO CHOOSE BETWEEN DIFFERENT GOODS AND GROUPS OF GOODS

Money incomes, together with quasi-money-incomes in the form of consumption of self-subsistence production, are often described as personal disposable incomes while grants in kind are described as specifically designated incomes. The term itself makes it clear that these latter kinds of income cannot be converted. Social grants function in just this way. But this is almost a tautology.

The fact that the consumer cannot convert grants in kind into other goods can be described as a criticism of the essential validity of the system only if one starts from a theoretical basis which assumes the market mechanism to be perfect, and what is more represents the sole perfect form of the allocation of resources, and which regards choice made within the market as the maximisation of utility. Grants in kind are the antithesis of all of this. Added to this is the fact that the problem of grants in kind is an issue in a political system in which the one-party system exists, so that decisions about allocation are paternalistic and consumer demand is not the final arbiter.

Theoretical issues of enormous importance and lively disputes about them are involved here. In this paper dealing with many other questions, I cannot present my considered opinions regarding them. I propose only to summarise my views.

Firstly, the market mechanism is an indispensable means for the allocation and reallocation of production resources today. We need to strengthen this mechanism in Hungary. But a long-term perspective of the development of the economy even in the sphere of commodities and for its achievement are necessary to the efficient operation of the market. Moreover, an appropriate combination of the commodity relationship and the relationships outside the market (in the case here at issue between commodity consumption and extra-market consumption) is necessary for the socially and economically efficient operation of the economy as a whole.

Secondly, I have already indicated that I am not in favour of the theory of the maximisation of utility. But I attach great importance to the satisfaction of the consumers' demands, desires, ambitions both in the sphere of commodities and in the sphere of grants in kind. The demands of consumers do in fact influence more or less directly the supply in the field of commodities. For grants in kind the effect of supply is more important in determining demand and consumption. From the point of view of the subject of this paper it is only a question of detail whether this effect is regarded as a result of the nature of the product or whether it is described as an undesirable interference.

Can consumers' desires and demands prevail, and do they prevail, in the sphere of grants in kind? Yes, they can and do. A greatly oversimplified, and thus very inadequate picture of the economic mechanism of a planned economy and of the political mechanism of the one-party system is often to be encountered. This picture may be outlined more or less as follows. A central brains trust thinks out a concept independently of everything and everybody – in our case for the scope and scale of grants in kind – and then forces this policy upon the country without any kind of control. The reality is completely different. It is undeniable that the mechanism for discovering consumers' desires is different in the sphere of grants in kind from that in commodity consumption; that the role of the central decisions is greater. Nonetheless the actual policies are formed on the basis of thorough surveys and vigorous arguments. The views of the public reach the persons framing the policies and decisions through a variety of formal and informal channels. Public opinion research institutions and sociological surveys play an important role in providing information. The various political organisations – for example the trade unions, the press, the TV and radio – not only convey but also *represent* public opinion, in which naturally there are conflicts of ambitions and interests; these affect decisions considerably. The policy for the plan is worked out in detail on committees composed of representatives of different institutions, practical experts in the field concerned, such as physicians or teachers and research workers. This in itself ensures that different views and different interests will be brought before these committees. The problem is very often not that the policy that results does not reflect the desires of the population but the reverse. For in many cases decisions in conflict with long-term planning objectives are made under the pressure of actual public opinion. The essence of this conflict is not that the concepts of the brains trust are opposed to the demands of the population. It is rather that planners have to bear in mind not just what are the demands to be reconciled statistically but at the same time the total composition of demands in the course of the planning period and how particular demands can be limited.

4 PEOPLE PREFER AN INCREASE OF MONEY INCOME TO ONE OF GRANTS IN KIND

This argument needs to be completed as follows. People react very quickly when the increase of grants in kind falls behind the general needs. Reaction is even more evident when a grant in kind is reduced, or even if it is changed, for instance into a money grant. The reason is not simply that they insist on their actual rights of the past, though this is not unimportant. The point is that a proportion of all families suffers actual loss by a change of grants in kind into money incomes, even with favourable compensation, and there are additional families which feel as if they have suffered a loss even though they have received compensation for it. Thus, though families do not reckon grants in kind in their incomes, nevertheless if such grants are reduced they feel conscious of a reduction in real income.

In the analysis of the relationship between grants in kind and money incomes and the study of the advantages and disadvantages of each the following view has emerged – a view that is widely held but not by any means universally accepted. The scale of grants in kind cannot be greatly expanded during the next few decades. It is unquestionable that justification can be found for raising the present scale. For example, free meals for children at school and the supply of free school equipment should if possible be considerably expanded. But within the given economic resources the expansion of such scales could only be achieved by a severe limitation on the increase of money incomes. Any increase of the volume of grants in kind has to come from an improvement of the efficiency of the activities which provide the goods or services involved in these grants during the next decade and a half. As a result of this, it may be reasonable to hope that, after a long period of stagnation, the ratio of grants in kind to the total of income may increase. But there is a very strong trend of government policy in the direction of changing the various grants in kind, mainly in the form of price subsidies, into money incomes. This has the effect of restricting the growth of grants in kind in a broader sense.

V SOCIAL INFRASTRUCTURE VERSUS CONSUMPTION

The development of the social infrastructure is a different dimension of the problem of grants in kind as compared with the subjects dealt with above.[8] The activities making available the most essential grants in kind are parts of the social infrastructure.[9] These grants in kind are treated

[8] R. Hoch, 'Choices in Planning for Social Infrastructure and Consumption', *Acta Oeconomica*, 15, (1975), 3–4, 329–41.

[9] There are important grants in kind (various types of subsidies) which have nothing to do with the infrastructure of a society while the whole or the greater part of the output of certain sectors of the infrastructure (for example housing) does not represent a grant in kind.

for purposes of the plan and in statistical returns as specifically designated incomes and as representing extra-market consumption.

A necessary but imperfect means for overall planning and the measurement of outputs is to take the resulting flows into account. The general level of the supply of these grants for the population as a whole and its necessary increase depend on the state and growth of the system of infrastructure; the equality or inequalities of the distribution of grants are to a considerable extent determined by the regional distribution of the infrastructure.

An approach to the problems involved from this point of view brings to the surface the problem of choice between planning decisions in a fresh aspect. Grants in kind to provide infrastructure form not a flow but a stock: development involves investment. The problem of choice is between the stock and the flow.

Development of the social infrastructure is a very important means of modifying living standards and the pattern of life in a desirable direction. It follows from this that it is right to give priority to the development of infrastructure. The need for this is increased by the fact that a very backward infrastructure has been inherited both from the more distant and more recent past, particularly in certain regions of Hungary. Although in the later 1960s and during the 1970s the state of the infrastructure has improved considerably,[10] the more rapid growth has reflected principally the completion of the fifteen-year housing

[10] A series of calculations have been made in the National Planning Office to find the effects of the change of the share of infrastructure on material consumption. The method of investigation has been the following: resources available for expansion of the total consumption over the fifteen-year period are taken as given; but these resources can be transferred between material and infrastructural consumption. Two extreme versions of the transfer were calculated. In the objective function of the first version (No. 1) the maximum growth of infrastructure consumption was calculated, and the limit was the level of material consumption achieved before the planning period. The function of the other version (No. 5) maximises the increase of material consumption and the limit is the level of infrastructural consumption achieved before the planning period. The intervening versions (Nos 2–4) that may be considered more realistic from the point of view of planning include possible growths of both the two factors. The conclusion is unambiguous: 'The "price" of the increase of infrastructural consumption is relatively high: one unit increase of infra-structural consumption results in more than one unit decrease in material consumption.'

The computations are presented in a book entitled *National Economic Models in Long-term Planning*, (p. 153 and Table 6), edited by Mária Augusztinovics (Közgazdasági és Jogi Könyvkiadó, Budapest, 1979).

programme. The delays in the completion of grants in kind for infrastructure purposes have not been reduced to the extent that is desirable. The problems concerning the desirable development of infrastructure are, in part at least, the following:

(1) Any increase of the share of infrastructure reduces the rate of growth of GDP and of consumption, at least in the short term; in the long term it is just the inadequacy of infrastructure which creates an obstacle to growth.
(2) The problem becomes serious if for other reasons, such as an unfavourable trend in the world market, economic growth slows down. In these circumstances a rapid development of the social infrastructure may reduce the growth of GDP to the extent that the required productive investments cannot be covered and the increase of real income may be reduced to a level below the acceptable minimum.
(3) The time-dimensions of the increase of the stock and of the flow are different. The growth-rate of the income of the population can be increased proportionately with the acceleration of the increase of GDP. Conversely, the construction of the capacity of the infrastructural activities that give embodiment to grants in kind requires a longer period; thus in comparison with any improvement in economic conditions, supply can be improved only after a considerable lag in most of the activities providing grants in kind.

We have thus arrived at the following conclusion (though this conclusion is not universally accepted). The priority for social infrastructure should be maintained. But in the circumstances of slower economic growth a more rigid selection and a more severe priority system are required for the establishment of the objectives in developing infrastructure. Moreover, since a priority needs to be given to housing construction during the coming years and a considerable proportion of infrastructural investment goes to housing construction, any more rapid development of infrastructural activities providing grants in kind can in practice be realised only in the later years of the fifteen-year planning period. That is to say, in addition to 'cross-sectional' priorities 'time priorities' must also be determined.

VI THE SCALE OF GRANTS IN KIND

I have already indicated my views regarding the planning of the scope of grants in kind and about the traditional theory of choice and attempts to impose the model of utility maximisation on the complicated process of choice among goods. For similar reasons I cannot accept the theory of utility maximisation for the explanation of personal choice. The many-sided impulses, the many-sided motives determining the decisions of the consumer must not be forced into one Procrustean bed. There are significant contradictions between the different impulses of the individual consumer. Simultaneously he wants to increase his total consumption and reach a state of equilibrium in it, and at the same time he wants to move out of this state. I myself would interpret the state of equilibrium of the consumer, at least in relation to independent goods, as being that he brings the *intensity of his unsatisfied needs* close to the same level by deciding about the structure of his expenditure and about the pattern of his commodity consumption. This kind of interpretation of the equilibrium is not identical with any optimisation concept. The derivative of the horizontal line is zero at every point and does not have a maximum point.

Moreover, it is not exclusively a subject for economic research to discover what kinds of factors determine the intensity of needs.

I have introduced the problem of the scale of individual preference because, naturally with important differences, it illustrates several similarities with the scale of preference at the national level and with the problems of choice in planning. Social purposes are many-sided and these purposes are contradictory with each other. At the same time the important motivation in decisions is to bring the intensity of the unsatisfied needs approximately to the same level. But a philosophy of behaviourism cannot be adopted in any research into the choices made in planning; the exploration of the motivations of decisions is a basic task. In the decisions made in planning the endeavour to achieve a state of equilibrium is of national importance, and this means that in the choices and decisions the desire to avoid, if possible, any increased inability to satisfy some important demand, and to avoid intensifying social, and ultimately political, tensions must play an important role. The determination of the scope of grants in kind has been handled accordingly in comparison with money incomes, and with special regard to money grants and to earnings. I shall approach the determination of the scale of grants in kind, in short, with this in mind.

Decisions affecting any change in the scale of grants in kind are first of all determined by the development of the scope of grants in kind. We have already seen, however, that scale has an important reaction on scope as well. The difficulty of the decision of scale always arises from the fact that a decision has to be made within defined limits. In the process of planning grants in kind, the sectoral proposals for the development of the different types of grants are prepared, such as the health service, or education. But if the sectoral proposals do not take account of the available resources and of the policies regarding the overall development of grants in kind the sum of the proposals will be a large multiple of the amount of GDP available in the planning period. It can be realised from this that the determination of the scale of grants in kind is the subject of passionate disputes. Arguments about the merits of proposals can only be advanced within these limitations. One of the important tasks of long-term planning is to ensure mutual consistency in the above terms as affecting the scale of grants in kind, often by compromises reached in the course of such disputes. The establishment of a scale of preferences within a family is not by any means a perfectly harmonious process.

I come next to choice within the total of planning and propose to illustrate it with some examples. Planners are agreed that medical care, education and culture have a priority in the development of grants in kind. But these do not cover the whole spectrum. Some grants, such as compensation for canteen meals, do not rate high. There are disputes, again, about the expansion of kindergartens and nurseries. The latter is especially at issue. There is a general consensus regarding the development of kindergartens, that the needs should be satisfied 100 per cent. This level has already been approached in several geographical regions and towns. There are strong social, psychological and health arguments to support the opinion that children should be brought up exclusively by the mother, or at least in the family up to the age of two years, though there are controversies about the precise age-limit. We do not want to provide capacity in nurseries even for a majority of children up to the age of three years. The argument on the other side is that we need a high level of employment of women since there is a general shortage of labour. There are thus disputes as to whether children should be put in nurseries under the age of two years, if that is to be regarded as the critical age. Otherwise, the implications of this decision must be accepted in regard to the labour force of the economy and to the special type of money grant which is called the child-care allowance.

Similar decisions of ranking are necessary within the separate types of grant. Within the given frameworks even the types of preferred grants cannot be developed completely. But in the case of the different grants, differences of opinion to be reconciled are not the same, or not completely the same. In the case of the health service the overcoming of shortages and strains is the primary requisite. Thus the construction of hospitals has a priority as compared with the development of the system of out-patient clinics. That is to say, a policy for the health service is being realised in which ambulatory treatment is to be provided internally by the newly constructed hospitals. In determining the priorities for education, the reduction of differences that help to perpetuate social inequalities is held to be of primary importance. That is why we have preferred to build district schools and dormitories and to speed up closure of the schools for children living on remote farms. The same aim is dominant in the development of the system of primary and secondary schools in Budapest. The resources are in the first stage being concentrated on reducing the sometimes very considerable differences in the material conditions of the different schools of Budapest.

VII CONCLUSIONS

The trends in the extent and growth of grants in kind designed to affect the standards of life are determined by the objectives regarding change of the structure of society. The necessary instruments for the achievement of these objectives include grants in kind, among other measures. The determination of their scope and scale appears in the planning process as a problem of choice within limits imposed by such overriding constraints as GDP and income per head and their rapid or slow growth. Earnings and grants, commodity consumption and extra-market consumption, a stock of social infrastructure and a flow of consumption have all to be regarded as alternatives between which the best choice must be made for achieving the nation's various social and economic objectives. A consistent 'cross-sectional' and 'time' preference system must be applied throughout all decisions regarding the growth of the different grants in kind.

All plans, including plans for grants in kind, must be based on assumptions and forecasts of future trends. The longer the planning period the greater is the freedom of action but the less is the confidence in the forecasts. As a consequence several alternative versions of plans have to be prepared, and the plans themselves must be checked from time to time and the necessary modifications of the course must be effected by the process of overlapping planning.

Discussion of 'The Desirable and Suitable Scope and Scale of Grants in Kind in Socialist Countries, as Illustrated by the Case of Hungary' by Dr R. Hoch

Professor Maillet suggested a discussion of the following points raised by Dr Hoch's paper: the determination of a correct ratio between public grants and wage earnings, and between grants in kind and grants in cash; 'intensity of unsatisfied need' as a criterion for policy as opposed to the criterion of optimisation; the prospects for the growth of ratio of collective consumption to national income in Hungary in view of the evidence in Table 6.1 of the constancy of the ratio over the past period; the effect of collective consumption on the distribution of income in Hungary in view of the evidence in Table 6.3 of the paper of a redistribution towards intellectuals; the claim on the need to give priority to expenditure on infrastructure; the problem of the possible inconsistency of the priorities of citizens expressed through the different channels described in the paper; and the extent to which the identified problems of collective consumption were specific to socialist countries. Professor Maillet did not agree with what he took to be Dr Hoch's argument on the secondary importance of efficiency criteria to policy on grants, although his general view was that many elements of Dr Hoch's formulation of the issues and problems in this area would be readily accepted by western economists.

Dr Jurković argued that grants and national economic efficiency were not competitive in the sense that a certain level of social consumption was a necessary precondition for the efficient working of a wage system. *Professor Klein* and *Sir Leo Pliatzky* noted the similarity of the conflict described between wages and collective consumption in Hungary to that experienced in the United Kingdom. They pointed to the policy of the social contract introduced by the Labour administration of 1974–79 in an attempt to resolve this conflict in the United Kingdom.

Several speakers commented on the issue of benefits in kind versus benefits in cash. *Professor Pohorille* argued firstly, on a point of definition, that a reimbursement of expenditures on public services such as medical care should not be counted as a cash grant as it did not represent income which could be freely spent; and second, that benefits in kind were required in areas such as health and education in which the principle of free consumer choice did not apply. His view was that in areas such as medical care where there was an information problem, competent professionals would be better judges than consumers. *Professor Manz* took the view that an extensive system of grants in kind assisted personality formation and ensured equality of treatment between individuals and families. He reported that in the German Democratic Republic grants in kind formed 24 per cent of the real income of an average worker's family with two children, which was the highest percentage of any country in the world. *Professor Sir Austin Robinson* was concerned that cash grants and benefits in kind were being discussed as mutually exclusive instruments and suggested that it might be more useful to see them as substitutes and to discuss the different purposes to which they might be assigned. *Professor Urquidi* suggested that the observable trend towards grants in cash rather than grants in kind was a result of a growing inequality of income in socialist countries which the authorities had sought to alleviate by cash transfers.

There was then a discussion of the question of user charges and fees for collective services. *Professors Pohorille* and *Klein* pointed to the inefficiency of a fee system in which the providers of services sought to maximise revenue from fees. On the other hand, *Professor Bacskai* argued that under conditions of excess demand, generated in a system without fees, access to services such as health would depend on the payment of illegal fees and bribes, or on the exercise of personal influence, or on the time available for waiting in queues. In the case of education he was concerned that free provision would result in an overexpansion of facilities, and thus in the emergence of an overqualified and potentially unemployable section of the labour force. He thus saw a case for a selective use of fees in the provision of health care and education. *Professor Pohorille* agreed with Professor Bacskai that disequilibrium between demand and supply in the field of medical services had created difficult problems, but he did not agree that the use of fees would solve the problems. He was also opposed to the use of fees in the provision of education on the grounds that a desirable reorientation of education towards the needs of individuals would be made more difficult.

Professor Maillet suggested that the meaning of the term 'intensity of unsatisfied need' was close to that of the term 'utility'. However, *Professor Klein* interpreted these terms as expressions of an underlying difference between individualistic and paternalistic values.

Mr Matthews asked whether Dr Hoch's comments on the future change in the ratio of grants to national income in Hungary implied that it was a positive function of the level of real income, as there did not seem to be evidence for such a relationship in western economies. *Professor Sir Austin Robinson* thought it more reasonable to expect that the relationship between this ratio and the level of real income would be negative because the main purpose of the grants economy was to combat poverty which would be eliminated by rising real income. *Sir Leo Pliatzky* argued that the ratio might be more a function of the rate of growth of real income than of the level of income, at least when per capita income was above the level of subsistence. The reason for this was that a high growth rate acted as an offset to the unwillingness of workers to accept increases in the social wage as a substitute for increases in the private wage. *Professor Klein* drew attention to the importance of the geographical aspect of income distribution and cited studies of health care which showed that equality of income between regions did not ensure equality of access to health services.

Dr Hoch did not attempt to reply to all the points raised in discussion. He agreed with Professor Maillet that there were many similarities between the experience of socialist and capitalist economies in this area, but pointed to what he saw as two major differences: the integration of national economic planning and planning on grants in socialist countries in which all resources were publicly owned; and the lack of a presumption in socialist economies in favour of markets. He conceded that the determination of a correct ratio between grants and wages was extremely difficult, and referred to studies of the relationship between wages and productivity which were used for this purpose in Hungary. He did not agree with the arguments advanced for the use of fees in the provision of health care, nor did he accept Professor Maillet's view of the equivalence of 'need' and 'utility'. Dr Hoch described the rapid growth of benefits in kind in Hingary during the 1950s and the subsequent growth of cash benefits to pensioners and families which made for greater equality. In his view the rate of growth of real income and not its level was the main determinant of the ratio of grants to national income. In view of the present slow-down in the growth rate of income, he did not anticipate an increase in the ratio of grants in kind to national income in the immediate future in Hungary. He did, however, expect greater buoyancy in spending on cash grants and on infrastructure investment. In reply to Professor Maillet's point on efficiency, Dr Hoch drew a distinction between economic efficiency narrowly defined and social efficiency, and argued that the latter was relevant to policy on grants although difficult to measure. In support of this point he referred to the difficulty of measuring the output of health services and of relating such measures as were available to inputs.

Part Two
Trends in Practice

7 Course and Causes of Collective Consumption Trends in the West

Andrea Boltho

UNIVERSITY OF OXFORD

I INTRODUCTION

This paper looks at trends in collective consumption in fifteen developed OECD countries over the years 1950–76.* The introduction defines the concept of collective consumption which is adopted. The first section looks at trends through time and at the intercountry variability of the shares of collective consumption in GDP. The second section presents some tentative explanations for the rapid rise in these shares throughout the OECD area over the period under examination, while the conclusions summarise the findings and very briefly look at future prospects.

The definition of collective consumption used here may in some respects differ from that adopted by other participants in this conference. Very broadly, it covers the direct and indirect supply of what have been called 'merit' goods (or better, services) (Musgrave, 1959), while it excludes 'pure public goods' (like defence or the judiciary). The reasons for this are partly statistical (data on non-defence public goods expenditure are not always easily forthcoming), and partly analytical (defence expenditure responds to different motivations to those of other

* The author's greatest debt is to many of his former colleagues in the OECD's Economics and Statistics Department (in particular M. Emerson, F. Galimbezti, M. Keating, S. Marris, E. Merigo), none of whom is even aware that this paper has been written, let alone responsible for anything specific said in it, but all of whom have, at one time or another, contributed to some of the ideas here formulated.

functions of government, while expenditure on 'merit' goods may be considered as a relatively integrated whole).

The definition of 'merit' goods is perhaps somewhat broader than the one used traditionally – it includes not only the usual functions (education, health and housing), but also a form of 'merit' want which could be called 'security' (individual as opposed to collective), and which is broadly satisfied by income maintenance expenditures. Such a definition may not make for national accounting purity, since it lumps together consumption and transfers,[1] but it can probably be defended on more general grounds. The supply of 'merit' goods by the state has usually been justified for two major reasons – an externality argument (e.g. a more educated population makes for a more pleasant society), and a 'paternalistic' argument (e.g. individuals, if left free, may not choose to consume what the state would regard as a sufficiently high volume of a particular service). Income maintenance expenditures can be seen as fulfilling both these requirements. On the externalities side, government involvement in providing 'security' can be defended on similar lines to the supply of education – a society in which the old and the unemployed receive some guaranteed minimum income is probably a more agreeable society to live in.[2] And the paternalistic argument is also of relevance to social insurance. Individuals, if left to the market, may find themselves choosing a lower level of future security than that provided by the state, either because they may implicitly be risk-takers or because they may suffer (in Pigou's words) from 'defective telescopic faculty'.

Two further reasons can be advanced to defend the inclusion of 'security' in the category of merit goods – the first one involving the similarity of the transfer mechanism between income maintenance and other social welfare expenditures, the second one bringing in the similarity of purpose for which the state provides several of these 'merit' goods. On the payments side, all the four forms of 'merit' wants so far listed involve, *inter alia*, a transfer from the economically active

[1] In fact, even the supply of the more traditional 'merit' goods involves cutting across national accounting definitions. Expenditure on education, health and housing can include, depending on country and function, elements of direct government consumption, transfer payments, subsidies, capital formation and foregone tax revenues. The latter three are not considered in this paper.

[2] It would probably be agreed that one major reason for the lack of social strife over the last few years despite unprecedentedly high rates of unemployment must have been the much greater generosity of unemployment compensation payments.

population to, respectively, the young (in the case of education), the poor (in the case of housing), the ill (in the case of health) and to the young, poor and ill, as well as to the old (in the case of income maintenance). On the aims side, it can be argued that, over and above externality and paternalistic motivations, governments have in the post-war period increasingly used their expenditures to influence income distribution patterns and relieve poverty. It is clear that in this sense, the various 'merit' services so far listed can, and have been, considered as complementary instruments in trying to achieve a broadly similar aim – improvements in the position of lower income receivers via higher money transfers, better and easier access to health or housing and longer run ameliorations in education and, therefore, in earning opportunities.

In so far as possible, therefore, what follows will look at these four major functions of government expenditure. Statistical problems inevitably arise, however, since consistent time-series are seldom available for all four categories and for a sufficient number of countries in easily accessible form. The OECD has assembled data on three major functions (education, income maintenance and health) (OECD, 1976a, b, 1977), and these will be used, but they cover only selected years in the early 1960s and mid-1970s. Inevitably, therefore, some approximations will have to be resorted to when looking at a longer time-span. The most frequently used proxy, for which consistent time-series spanning a quarter of a century could be assembled, will be the sum of public non-defence consumption and transfers to households, data for which appear in the standardised OECD national accounts publications. Very roughly, for the sample of countries here looked at, this approximation overstates the supply of the four 'merit' services singled out above by perhaps 30 per cent.

II COURSE

A first impression of the development of collective consumption, as proxied by non-defence government current expenditure and transfers to households, is provided in Figure 7.1 which shows the (unweighted) average share of this flow in current price GDP for the fifteen OECD (and twelve European) countries here considered, from 1950 to 1976. It will be apparent that this share has increased very rapidly (and at an accelerating rate) over the period, more than doubling from some 15 per

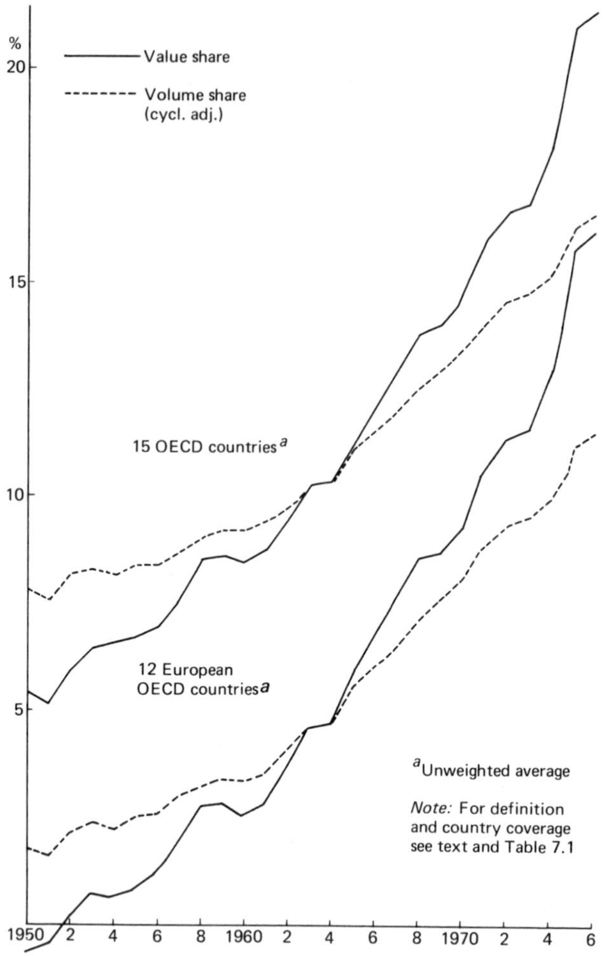

FIG. 7.1 Share of government current non-defence expenditure and transfers to households in GDP (Percentages)

cent in 1950–51 to 31 per cent in 1975–76.[3] The share also exhibits a fairly marked counter-cyclical pattern, tending to rise in recession years like 1958 or 1974–75 and falling, or remaining stable, in periods of rapid growth like 1954–55, 1959–60, 1965, 1969 and 1973.

To avoid the distorting effects of cyclical fluctuations and, possibly, of the recent acceleration in inflation, the broken lines in Figure 7.1 present the same series recalculated in volume terms and cyclically adjusted. In the absence of detailed figures on both values and prices for each function of expenditure, deflation was carried out by using as proxies the public consumption deflator for non-defence consumption expenditure and the private consumption deflator for transfers to households. On the basis of the evidence available on sectoral price indices, it would seem that this procedure underestimates somewhat the probable course of the 'real' deflators – price rises for total government consumption have been less pronounced than for civil consumption alone, in view of the less labour-intensive nature of defence expenditures, and price rises for medical services, an item of private expenditure largely financed by transfers to households, have been more rapid than for other goods and services purchased by consumers. On the other hand, it is likely that the use of conventional deflators underestimates the growth in the 'real' value of the services which governments have been providing, in view of the zero productivity growth assumption for government services usually followed in national accounting practice.

Cyclical adjustment was carried out by introducing in place of the actual output data, trend GDP figures obtained with the help of OECD estimates of potential output (OECD, 1973) (with all the risks inherent in such calculations, particularly for the last few years). Because of data limitations, the cyclical adjustment is confined to smoothing out the denominator of the expenditure/income ratio, while leaving the numerator unchanged. This is reasonable for current spending on the traditional 'merit' goods, which should be little influenced by cyclical fluctuations, but is obviously less so for counter-cyclical unemployment compensation payments. The rise in the ratio in the last two to three years may thus still be subject to some upward cyclical bias (the more so if the trend growth of GDP has been underestimated). Yet, even if full allowance could be made for all these various possible sources of

[3] Reweighting the shares using output weights leads to somewhat lower absolute levels and changes through time (the share rises from 13 to 27 per cent), because of the greater weight of the United States and Japan, but does not fundamentally alter the picture.

distortion, it is unlikely that this would greatly change the picture presented here.

As it stands, this picture suggests that even after adjustment for inflation and cyclical fluctuations, expenditure has risen extremely rapidly. Of the 16 percentage points increase recorded by the value share, relative price shifts account for some 5 percentage points and the end-period economic slowdown for perhaps 1½, leading to a cyclically adjusted volume share rise of 9½ percentage points (of which the bulk, or 6½ points, occurred in the second half of the period under examination). For the narrower definition of collective consumption adopted here, this could correspond to an increase of 7 to 7½ percentage points.[4]

These trends which would, in all likelihood, turn out to be more pronounced if some allowance could be made for increased productivity in the public sector, provide some *prima facie* confirmation for the existence of Wagner's law (for an exposition of this see Pryor (1968)) of a rising share of public expenditure as income grows.[5] They also stand in contrast to the more sluggish developments of the pre-war period, as can be seen in Table 7.1 and Figure 7.2, which present an ill-assorted and not always strictly comparable set of data from, generally, 1880 to 1973 (the choice of periods avoids not only the recent recession but also the 1930s, distorted by both depression and rearmament). Because of data availability the comparisons are usually limited to public consumption flows (at times including defence or even investment expenditures).

Intercountry divergences for the postwar period are shown in Table 7.2. Virtually all countries record a statistically significant acceleration,[6] in the rise of both value and volume shares. At one extreme are several North European countries (the Netherlands, Sweden, Norway and Denmark) which show increases in (volume, cyclically adjusted) shares going from 13 to 18 percentage points.[7] At the other extreme lies Japan

[4] Deflation and cyclical adjustment could not be carried out for the individual functions. In current prices, the second half of the period witnessed a 6½ percentage points rise in the share of collective consumption *strictu sensu*, with income maintenance expenditures rising by 2¾ points, health by 2, education by 1½ and housing by ¼.

[5] As usual, however, cross-section regressions of the expenditure shares on per capita income levels fail to produce any statistically significant results, in line with earlier findings for both total expenditure and subfunctions reported in Pryor (1968), Musgrave (1969) and Lall (1969).

[6] As measured by the coefficient of a t^2 term in equations of the form $E/Y = a + bt + ct^2$, where E/Y represents the expenditure shares in GDP.

[7] Belgium does too, but its figures are not strictly comparable to those of the other countries because Belgian national accounts make an (inevitably arbitrary) allowance for productivity increases in the public sector.

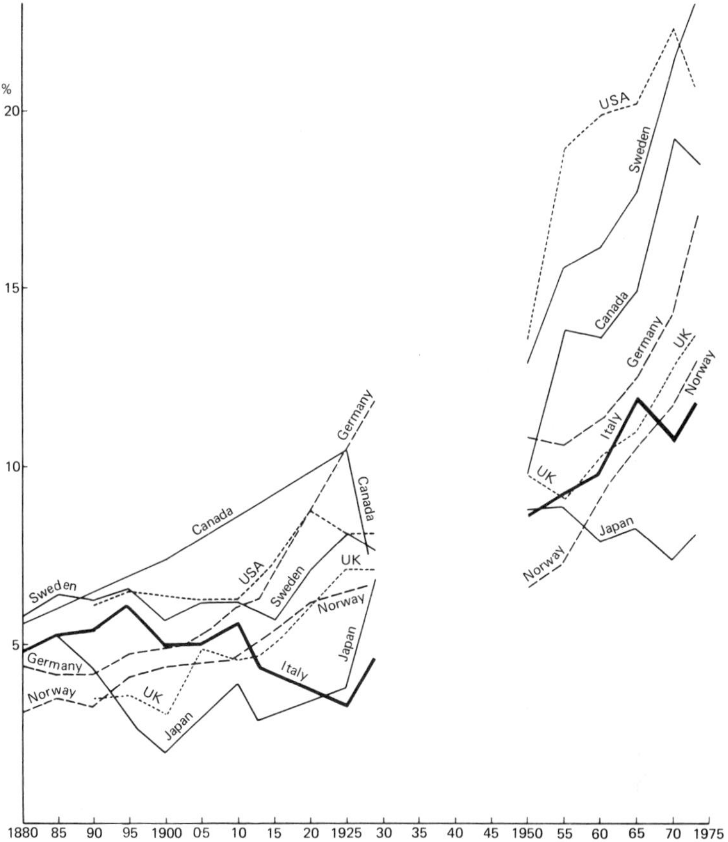

FIG. 7.2 Share of government consumption in GDP in selected OECD countries and periods (Percentages)

TABLE 7.1 PRE- AND POST-WAR SHARES OF GOVERNMENT CONSUMPTION IN GNP IN SELECTED COUNTRIES
Indices: 1929 = 100

	1880	*1905*	*1929*	*1950*	*1973*
Canada	75	99[a]	100[b]	131	247
Germany	37	45	100	92	144
Italy	104	109	100	187	257
Japan	77[c]	57[d]	100	129	121
Norway	46	69[d]	100	99	194
Sweden	76	82	100	170	303
United Kingdom	49[e]	69	100	138	193
United States	75[e]	78	100	167	254

[a] 1900 [b] 1928 [c] 1885 [d] 1910 [e] 1890

Definitions and pre-war sources:

Canada Total public consumption/GNP. S. Kuznets, *Modern Economic Growth* (New Haven, 1966).

Germany Non-defence public consumption/NY. W. G. Hoffmann, *Das Wachstum der Deutscher Wirtschaft seit der Mitte des 19. Jahrhunderts* (Berlin, 1965).

Italy Non-defence public consumption/GNP. G. Fuà, *Lo sviluppo economico in Italia*, Vol. III (Milan, 1969); B. R. Mitchell, *European Historical Statistics, 1750–1970* (London, 1975).

Japan Non-defence public consumption/GNP. K. Ohkawa, M. Shinohara and *M. Umemura (eds.)*, *Estimates of Long Term Economic Statistics of Japan since 1868*, Vols 1 and 7 (Tokyo, 1974).

Norway Non-defence public consumption/GDP. Statistik Sentralbyra. *Langtidslinjer i Norsk Økonomi, 1865–1960* (Oslo, 1966).

Sweden Total public consumption/GDP. Ö. Johansson, *The Gross Domestic Product of Sweden and its Composition, 1861–1955* (Stockholm, 1967).

UK Non-defence public consumption/GNP. (OECD, 1977).

US Total public expenditure on goods and services/GNP. Department of Commerce, *Long Term Economic Growth, 1860–1970* (Washington, 1973).

which, in volume terms, actually shows a sizeable fall. In between come countries like Germany, France and, particularly, Austria, which had already achieved a relatively high ratio at the outset of the period and in which increases go from 7 to barely half a percentage point. More generally, however, there seems to be only weak evidence for a convergence of shares. The standard deviations of both value and volume shares rise through the period (though the coefficients of variation remain stable). Testing for a 'catching-up' hypothesis (i.e. the tendency for low share countries to experience more rapid growth) is not very conclusive. Regressing the change in share over the period on the initial share of collective consumption yields a statistically significant

TABLE 7.2 TRENDS IN THE SHARE OF GOVERNMENT NON-DEFENCE CONSUMPTION EXPENDITURE AND TRANSFERS TO HOUSEHOLDS IN SELECTED OECD COUNTRIES

Percentages

	Shares 1950–51	*Current price* 1975–76	*Change in share: In value terms*	1950–51 *to* 1975–76 *In cyclic. adj. volume terms*[a]
Austria	18.9	29.6	10.7	0.4
Belgium	16.7	33.3	16.6	13.2
Denmark	14.8	37.0	22.2	13.4
Finland	13.9	26.9	13.0	6.6
France	20.2	32.3	12.1	6.0
Germany (FR)	21.1	34.2	13.1	6.9
Ireland	17.9	32.8	14.9	11.1
Italy	15.8	31.2	15.5	8.6
Netherlands	14.9	41.5	26.6	17.9
Norway	11.9[b]	30.1	18.2	14.1
Sweden	15.3	38.9	23.7	16.9
United Kingdom	15.4	28.5	13.0	7.1
Total Europe[c]	16.4	33.0	16.7	10.2
Canada	11.5	28.5	16.9	12.0
Japan	10.6	17.6	7.0	−4.3
United States	10.4	24.6	14.1	10.4
Total OECD[c]	15.3	31.1	15.9	9.4

[a] For explanation, see text [b] 1951–52 [c] Unweighted averages
Sources: OECD, *National Accounts of OECD Countries* (various issues), supplemented by a variety of national sources.

negative coefficient, but only when the extreme Japanese observation is dropped from the sample.

In a less mechanical sense it could, however, be argued that some form of convergence has taken place. The generalised growth of welfare expenditures has meant that, at present, in virtually all OECD countries the total population is covered by some form of national health plan, national pension system and national unemployment insurance, as well as being subject to compulsory education, usually until the age of sixteen, and having much greater access to higher education (with enrolment ratios three times higher than they were in the 1950s). Though the level of benefits and the quality of services supplied still vary substantially across and within countries, the growth of expenditure on these 'merit' services seems to have broadly fulfilled the United Nations' implicit demand that they be considered as basic human rights.[8]

III CAUSES

Increases in the shares of public non-defence consumption in GDP of some 7 percentage points over this period, and of transfers to households of some 8½ percentage points, clearly represent rather major shifts in the allocation of resources and funds in the economies of the western world – shifts a good deal more pronounced than those, for instance, in favour of capital formation and paralleled only by the increases in the shares of foreign trade flows in total output. One would, therefore, expect that this subject had been extensively researched and that numerous hypotheses and explanations were available, which could throw light on the reasons for this rapid growth. Yet in fact, the literature on the causes (as opposed to the consequences) of the phenomenon looks scanty. The available theoretical approaches on (total) public expenditure growth seem, *prima facie*, to have limited empirical relevance, while most empirical research has provided for some 'proximate' but hardly underlying causes for the growth in public outlays. Nor can much guidance come from official statements of aims and policies, which have usually been far too vague and imprecise, or from officially published medium-term projections which, more often than not, have been subject to substantial revisions in the light of actual events.

This paper does not pretend to be able to fill an apparent gap in the literature and 'explain' the fairly unprecedented developments outlined in the previous section. More modestly, it tries to bring together some of the arguments and approaches which have been voiced in the past and assess their relevance.

At what can be called the 'proximate' level, a number of plausible explanations have been put forward. The best known one is, of course, the rising cost hypothesis, formally put forward by Baumol (1967), and which, as was seen above, importantly contributes to the swelling of current price expenditure flows.[9] Looking from now onwards at the

[8] The 1948 United Nations Universal Declaration of Human Rights states that: 'Everyone has the right to education . . . to security in the case of unemployment, sickness, disability, widowhood, old age, or other lack of livelihood in circumstances beyond his control'; quoted in Pryor (1968).

[9] This is due not so much to a divergence in the wage and salary developments of private and public employees (the available evidence suggests that between the early 1960s and the early 1970s at least, differentials have remained roughly constant (OECD, 1978), but to the more labour-intensive nature of, in particular, education and health expenditures.

shorter period from the early 1960s to the mid-1970s for which somewhat more detailed figures on the various functions are available, relative price changes can explain 2 percentage points of the (cyclically adjusted) 6 percentage points change in the combined shares of education, health, housing and income maintenance expenditures in GDP. To this can be added the impact of a second 'inevitable' effect stemming from demographic changes which have influenced education, health and social insurance expenditures. On the basis of some simplified assumptions, the OECD has estimated that population changes have contributed 1 percentage point to the growth of such expenditure – almost entirely because of the rising weight of the old-age population (OECD, 1978). And, following this line of reasoning, one may also wish to allow for two further expenditure-swelling effects over which policy-makers may have had little short-run control: the progressive ageing of the pension systems established from the late 1940s onwards which, by their nature, found themselves spending larger sums of money as entitlements matured, and, possibly, the nature of some of the technical progress in the health sector which may well have added to the demand for public funds. Quantifying these two effects is wellnigh impossible, but an arbitrary estimate of half a percentage point may not be an unreasonable guess.

Close to two-thirds of the total change in the GDP share of collective consumption could thus be explained by recourse to 'inevitable' factors (such as relative price shifts, demographic trends, the maturing of pension systems or the introduction of expensive technological innovations in the health industry). The remainder would then be made up by shifts from private to public provision of certain services (particularly marked in the case of health expenditures), by the extension of higher education to a larger percentage of the student population and of social insurance to virtually the whole eligible population.

Yet, in many ways, this remains a superficial explanation. Not only is it unable to throw light on why policies did expand access to some services or increase the share of the public sector in others. But even in the area of 'inevitable' expenditure increases, it glosses over the fact that any decision, even if it is only to maintain the supply of given services at a particular level, involves a discretionary policy action, the more consciously taken, probably, the more it adds to public expenditure flows.

One is thus driven to the search for some more general and underlying forces at work which, in virtually all the OECD countries here surveyed, have encouraged governments to expand the volume scale of their welfare operations. Economists have, *inter alia*, suggested two broad such sets of forces:

(1) One school has stressed the importance of pressure groups of various forms which try to maximise their utility – be this vote-maximising politicians, budget-maximising bureaucrats or sectoral groups (like teachers, the medical profession, etc.) pursuing their own interests.
(2) A second school has looked at more macroeconomic forces, laying stress either on the income elasticity of demand for certain forms of public intervention (e.g. Wagner's law), or on sudden changes in the (tolerable) taxable capacity of the population (broadly the thesis associated with the names of Peacock and Wiseman (1967)).

The strict version of theories that make governments function as quasi-markets has been criticised in the literature (Buchanan, 1954; Steiner, 1974) and would, particularly in the European context, seem fairly unrealistic. In most OECD countries the bulk of public expenditure is controlled by central rather than local authorities,[10] and elections are almost invariably fought on a few very broad national issues. The idea of politicians buying votes by selling schools or hospitals may possibly apply to some local government elections in the United States; it would seem to have much less relevance in the vote-catching behaviour of national political figures both there and in Europe. This is not to say that economics does not play a role in political behaviour and in elections – far from it. But the economic issues and debates which have tended to dominate the political scene in most countries in the post-war period have been concerned with inflation, employment and, possibly, the balance of payments, while the changes in public expenditures which have taken place close to elections have usually taken the form of variations in government investment made for cyclical reasons. Politico-economic models can provide insight in this area of formulation of demand management policies and short-run fluctuations (Frey and Schneider, 1978); so far at least, they do not seem to have provided an explanation for longer run trend developments.

A second strand of thought stresses somewhat more informal political, bureaucratic or trade union pressures, since it is plausible to

[10] Even in fairly decentralised systems like Canada, Germany, Switzerland or the United States, local governments seldom control more than 40 per cent of total public expenditure. In other countries this percentage falls to barely 10 or 20 per cent (Commission of the European Communities, 1977).

assume that particular public expenditure decisions are taken, at least partly, under the influence of various lobbies. One would find it difficult, however, to account for the extraordinary growth in the share of public expenditure generally, and welfare expenditure in particular, by looking solely at this variable. After all, politicians wishing to be popular thanks to large expenditure programmes, bureaucrats attempting to increase the size of their 'empires' and pressure groups trying to obtain from the state advantages for their members, have been a reality of political life all through this century and, probably, since organised society has existed. Other forces must also have been at work in explaining why they should have been so much more successful over the last quarter-century than ever before.

Turning to more economic arguments, neither of the two 'laws of public expenditure' mentioned earlier would, on the surface, seem to be able to offer much to an explanation of the trends here examined. Wagner's assertion of a rising share of public expenditure was based mainly on his prediction of greater government involvement in the fields of law and order, defence and industry rather than in the supply of 'merit' goods, while the absence of disturbing events like major wars or major depressions in the time-span here considered would not, *prima facie*, have allowed a change in the 'tolerable' taxable capacity of society.[11]

Yet, if one adopted a more liberal interpretation of both Wagner's law and of the Peacock–Wiseman hypothesis, then recent developments could begin to receive some form of explanation. Wagner's law could be reinterpreted so as to suggest that with income growth it is not only the demand for economic but also for welfare services which grows, while the 'disturbance' necessary for the Peacock–Wiseman formulation to work could have been the unprecedentedly rapid rate of growth of per capita incomes. Both these could contribute to an expansion of public welfare services – demand would be fuelled by high income elasticities for health, education but also security, in our increasingly risk-averse societies, and supply would be made possible by the high elasticity of tax revenues with respect to output. Statistical evidence on either of these is

[11] Nor is there much evidence for a modified version of the Peacock–Wiseman hypothesis in the form of a cyclical 'ratchet' effect, i.e. a tendency for expenditures to increase in recessions and remain at the new higher level in the subsequent boom. Slow-downs, at least until recently, have been far too modest and short for this effect to have been much in evidence, and what discretionary counter-cyclical variation there has been in expenditures has frequently taken the form of changes in investment rather than in consumption or transfer flows.

not always easily forthcoming – estimates of the income elasticity of demand for public services (as opposed to 'expenditure' elasticities with respect to GDP), are made difficult by multicollinearity between income and relative price developments (for time-series data), and by multicollinearity between income levels and relative price levels (for cross-section data). Estimates of tax elasticities, on the other hand, face the problem of frequent discretionary changes in rates, brackets and allowances. But both *a priori* reasoning and the scattered evidence available would suggest that all these various elasticities are likely to have been high over the period in question.[12]

These two factors, however, make only for *potential* increase in public expenditure. Nothing prevented governments from granting tax cuts rather than increasing spending and letting the market decide on the 'optimum' supply of medical, educational, housing or social insurance services. What transformed potential into *actual* increases was, in all likelihood, the presence of a further extremely important factor, already stressed by Prior in his work on public expenditure[13] – the extent of social pressures. The spreading of universal suffrage, the achievement of full employment, the strengthening of trade union movements, the gradual expansion of social-democratic ideas and parties were all elements which, in a high growth environment, made for increasing demands for welfare systems, for income redistribution and for poverty relief.

There is a parallel here with the post-war demands for a more active demand management policy. Just as at the macroeconomic level governments strived to minimise cyclical disturbances and maximise

[12] For what they are worth, regressions of per capita (current price) collective consumption expenditure, as here defined, on per capita incomes yield 'income elasticities' of 1.13 in the early 1960s and 1.24 in the mid-1970s. Values greater than one are found for similar regressions for the education and income maintenance functions by the OECD (1976a, b). On the tax side, a study by Hansen for the 1955–65 years showed that for seven developed market economies the total tax elasticity with respect to GNP was invariably above one (Hansen, 1969). Somewhat more qualitative evidence on the elasticity of personal income taxes alone supporting this conclusion is provided in a study of the six major OECD economies by Tanzi (1969).

[13] 'The most important factor explaining the variation of public consumption expenditure for health and welfare among nations is the number of years in which the social insurance system has been in operation. . . The origins of the social insurance system are related to a political variable – the relative importance of unionization. It appears likely that both factors are related to a more basic political phenomenon – the political mobilization of workers' (Pryor, 1968).

longer run growth rates, so at the micro level, society seems to have felt that it would be appropriate for individual economic risks (in the form of unemployment, sickness or sudden poverty) to be minimised, and for the progression of incomes over the life-cycle to be smoother and more egalitarian. In other words, the scope of 'fine tuning' was, *de facto*, extended to encompass individuals' income fluctuations.

Other factors were, of course, also at work – the relative decline in defence expenditures (by roughly 1 percentage point of current price GDP), which freed funds for alternative uses; the widely held belief, particularly in the 1960s, that higher expenditure on education made for higher growth; possible international demonstration effects, etc. And the process itself may well have been reinforced by the short lags between revenue and expenditure increases. Whilst initially governments may have reacted to unexpected tax revenues, as time went by they may have planned for expenditure changes in the expectation of rising receipts.

The explanation advanced here thus runs in terms of a high and unprecedented growth rate of the economy, generating, on the one hand, demand for services with a high income elasticity of demand, and on the other high tax revenues to governments. The latter used these revenues (either *ex post* or in anticipation) to supply the demanded services because of the growing, if inchoate, pressures for increased social welfare arising out of a situation of full employment, rising affluence and, therefore, much greater concern for social justice.

Like all vague explanations, this one has the advantage that it can be made to (loosely) fit a great many facts – in particular, in this instance, the experience of most of the OECD countries surveyed here. All of them witnessed an acceleration in growth rates in the post-war period (though this varied from country to country), most of them experienced conditions approximating full employment (at least in the 1960s) and strengthening trade union influence, and most of them elected into power governments in which social-democratic/reformist parties were at least influential and frequently dominant. The accelerating growth explanation would seem to fit the pre- versus post-war experience, as can be seen in Figure 7.2, but can also be applied within the post-war period for those countries whose growth had lagged in the 1950s (Belgium, Denmark and Ireland) and which in the 1960s witnessed an acceleration in their overall growth rates and in the growth of their collective consumption share. Similarly, the influence of social-democratic ideas and governments, particularly pronounced in Northern Europe, can throw some light on the well-above-average rises in welfare expenditures in Sweden, Norway and Denmark. To this can be added, *inter alia*, the significant rises recorded by expenditure shares in countries like the United Kingdom, after the coming into power of a Labour administration in the mid-1960s, or Italy, after the formation of a centre-left government in 1962 and the great strengthening of trade union influence in the early 1970s.[14]

Yet there are exceptions even to this loose-ended and vague hypothesis. A European exception seems to be provided by Austria, a country in which post-war growth was some two-and-a-half times higher than that of the pre-war period, which enjoyed virtual full employment conditions from the early 1960s onwards and had a strong social democratic party almost continuously in power (alone or in coalition). Despite these apparently favourable pre-conditions, there was virtually no growth in the 'volume' share of collective consumption. Partly this may have been due to the high share already reached by Austria at the outset. But, partly, it is also due to a very high relative price effect for government consumption (by far the highest in this sample of countries), an effect which may owe more to some statistical quirk than to any underlying reasons.

A probably more interesting exception is provided by Japan. Here too one sees a very rapidly growing country, whose tax elasticity to GNP was high (Ishi, 1968; Pechman and Kaizuka, 1976) and whose initial welfare expenditure-output ratio was, together with that of the United States, the lowest in the sample. But in Japan, far from the (volume)

[14] Very rough and ready attempts to 'prove' all this econometrically have, predictably perhaps, failed. Cross-section regressions of the change in shares on initial shares, per capita incomes, growth rates of output, accelerations in output growth from the pre-war period, trade union membership, rates of unemployment or number of years of social-democratic/reformist rule (with reformist and coalition governments being assigned a 50 per cent weight), tend to result in non-significant and/or wrong sign coefficients. Mild improvements are obtained when some of the extreme observations are dropped from the sample. Thus, as already reported, the initial share becomes statistically significant if Japan is excluded, incomes per capita when the 'odd' low-income Irish figure is dropped and the extent of social-democratic rule when Austria is excluded. (A somewhat more elaborate 'leftist parties' variable performs much better, however, in a recent paper by Cameron (1978) explaining the change in current price total public expenditure over the 1960–75 period.) Multiple regression results are even more disappointing – the 'best' equation is one which (excluding all the three countries already mentioned as well as the extreme Dutch observation) links changes in shares to initial shares and the presence of social-democratic governments. Even in this instance, the first variable is, barely, non-significant. In any case, fitting the sample to the theory is hardly recommendable practice!

share of collective consumption rising, it actually fell almost uninterruptedly throughout the period. Some explanations may be forthcoming for the below average *level* of public involvement in this area – Japan is a country with a somewhat more equal income distribution and relative absence of poverty than most (Sawyer, 1976); it has also traditionally laid more stress on group/enterprise rather than state supply of welfare services, as witnessed by the continued, albeit diminishing, importance of the extended family, or by firms' provision of various types of social insurance, including forms of life employment.

But it is much more difficult to see why, in conditions of greater affluence and rising government revenues (as well as in the presence of a strong bureaucracy and corrupt politicians), the shift from the private to the public sector which occurred elsewhere should not have materialised. Rapid growth of outlays in absolute terms, even though the share fell, may have helped and the continuing improvement in many important social indicators[15] to levels well above those of most other OECD countries must also have diminished pressures for government involvement. But probably most important of all was the lack of the socio-political pre-conditions mentioned earlier. Trade unions never really achieved national, as opposed to within-firm, influence, social-democratic/reformist parties remained in opposition virtually throughout the post-war period and the population, however imperfectly, seems to have expressed a collective preference for the supply of private goods. Indeed, the Japanese example would seem to provide further justification for the earlier stress on conditioning social forces as the major driving element in channelling the rising government revenues made possible by high growth into the supply of 'merit' goods.

IV CONCLUSIONS

As was once said when talking about marginal, as opposed to discrete, changes in public spending:

> For the marginal decision a well-developed, highly articulated, and largely uncontroversial set of theories exists and awaits practical implementation. But with respect to the nature of the public interest, theorists are primitives in the sophisticated world of public decision makers. (Steiner, 1974, p. 242)

[15] For example, infant mortality, life expectancy, length of studies, equality of income distribution.

This paper does not claim to have improved on this state of affairs. The forces making for increased collective consumption in our market economies seem to be too varied and numerous for a consistent theory to be set forth to account for them all. The paper's aim has been the more modest one of surveying the existing statistical evidence and putting forward some tentative, and necessarily rather vague, explanations for what has happened.

After providing a definition of the 'merit' goods whose trends are investigated, the paper has shown that the GDP share of public expenditure devoted to these services has risen very rapidly, with some tendency for acceleration, in fifteen OECD countries in the post-war period. Relative price effects have played a non-negligible role in this rise, but even in 'volume' terms (however difficult it is to define the volume of public services), the rise has been substantial almost everywhere.

This rise has been mainly due to the interaction of three factors – a high income elasticity of demand for these services at the high income levels recorded in the post-war period: a high tax revenue elasticity to GDP providing governments with funds in conditions of rapid income growth; and a high degree of social consciousness as a rich and fully employed society expressed progressively more concern about its own security as well as equality of income, of opportunity and of access to basic necessities like health services and housing. Rapid growth is clearly an element that runs through all these three explanations – it is because of rapid growth that demand for these services increases, it is because of rapid growth that more resources are made available to the state, at little or no apparent sacrifice to individuals, it is because of rapid growth that full employment and reasonable private affluence are achieved and that society can turn to preoccupations of distribution through time and space. While in the past the 'shocks' which had changed the share of public expenditure in income had been the rather unfortunate ones of wars and depressions, on this occasion it was the much more welcome one of an acceleration in the growth rate of the economy.

Where do we go from here? In one sense it could be argued that the job is as yet unfinished. Reviewing past experience in poverty relief, in income distribution and in other social indicators, the OECD concluded that:

> Society . . . has more or less succeeded in fulfilling what might be called its 'democratic' objectives – the extension of coverage to as large a share of the relevant population as possible. Only slow

> progress, however, has been made towards fulfilling its more 'egalitarian' aims involving selective help to the economically vulnerable and socially disadvantaged. Indeed in so far as the effort to achieve generalised coverage has restricted the increase of benefits, these two objectives may even have been in conflict. (OECD, 1978)

Hence it could be argued that the scope for further increases in expenditure is there, the more so as the slower growth world into which we seem to have been ushered for the foreseeable future, will no doubt throw up new demands and requirements for social welfare expenditures.

Yet, on the other hand, if it was rapid growth which created the preconditions for rising collective consumption, slow growth may well destroy them. Ideas about what is a 'tolerable' level of taxation can be (and are already being) revised. Pressures against too great state involvement are reappearing. Not too much stress should, of course, be laid on what may turn out to be only ephemeral movements,[16] but it is possible that the growing sense of social responsibility for individual welfare which drove the share of public expenditure upwards may (perhaps only temporarily) be moderated by a climate of lower income growth and retrenchment on more private values.

It is unlikely that society will turn its back on its achievements, but it is probable that it will try to halt the growth of supply of some of the 'merit' goods the state provides, particularly, in the short run, in those areas like health or education in which relative price increases have been very marked, and, in the longer run, in those fields like retirement benefits in which the burden of an ageing population may put significant strains on the financing capacity of the work force.

REFERENCES

W. J. Baumol (1967). 'Macroeconomics of Unbalanced Growth: The Anatomy of Urban Crisis', *American Economic Review*, June.

J. M. Buchanan (1954). 'Individual Choice in Voting and the Market', *Journal of Political Economy*, August.

D. R. Cameron (1978). 'The Expansion of the Public Economy: A Comparative Analysis', *Americal Political Science Review*, December.

[16] Californians have not invented anti-tax movements. France or Denmark, to mention only the best known post-war European examples, have a history of political movements which achieved temporarily a fair degree of success on the basis of anti-taxation tickets but whose impact was, in the longer-run, defused by rising incomes.

Commission of the European Communities (1977). *Report of the Study Group on the Role of Public Finance in European Integration*, ('MacDougall Report'), Brussels.
B. S. Frey and R. Schneider (1978). 'A Politico-Economic Model of the United Kingdom', *Economic Journal*, June.
B. Hansen (1969). *Fiscal Policy in Seven Countries, 1955–65* (Paris).
H. Ishi (1968). 'The Income Elasticity of the Tax Yield in Japan', *Hitotsubashi Journal of Economics*, June.
S. Lall (1969). 'A Note on Government Expenditure in Developing Countries', *Economic Journal*, June.
R. A. Musgrave (1959). *The Theory of Public Finance* (New York).
R. A. Musgrave (1969). *Fiscal Systems* (New Haven).
OECD (1973). 'The Measurement of Domestic Cyclical Fluctuations', *Economic Outlook – Occasional Studies*, July.
OECD (1976a). *Public Expenditure on Education* (Paris).
OECD (1976b). *Public Expenditure on Income Maintenance Programmes* (Paris).
OECD (1977). *Public Expenditure on Health* (Paris).
OECD (1978). *Public Expenditure Trends* (Paris).
A. T. Peacock and J. Wiseman (1967). *The Growth of Public Expenditure in the United Kingdom* (revised edition) (London).
J. A. Pechman and K. Kaizuka (1976). 'Taxation', in H. Patrick and H. Rosovsky (eds.) *Asia's New Giant* (Washington DC: The Brookings Institution).
F. L. Pryor (1968). *Public Expenditure in Communist and Capitalist Nations* (London).
M. Sawyer (1976). 'Income Distribution in OECD Countries', *OECD Economic Outlook – Occasional Studies*, July.
P. O. Steiner (1974). 'Public Expenditure Budgeting', in A. S. Blinder, R. M. Solow and others, *The Economics of Public Finance* (Washington DC: The Brookings Institution).
V. Tanzi (1969). *The Individual Income Tax and Economic Growth* (Baltimore).

Discussion of 'Course and Cause of Collective Consumption Trends in the West' by Mr A. Boltho

In his introduction to the discussion *Professor Bacskai* suggested that the analysis of the paper might be extended to include the impact of differences in the share of government consumption in national income on domestic savings and on international competitiveness, and the impact of public grants on motivation, productivity and economic efficiency. He wondered whether the low ratio of collective consumption to national income in Japan explained the competitiveness of the Japanese economy. *Professor Tsuru* pointed out that the growth rate of collective consumption in Japan had been high notwithstanding its low share in national income.

Several speakers were unhappy with the author's definition of collective consumption and in particular with his treatment of expenditures on defence. *Professor Maillet* argued that the definition of collective consumption should be extended to include subsidies the financing implications of which were no different from direct expenditures on goods and services. He cited the example of the 50 per cent subsidy to the Paris Metro. *Professor Bacskai*'s argument for the inclusion of subsidies was that they were an important instrument in policy for the support of real income. He argued against the exclusion of defence from the definition of collective consumption because of the consumption involved both by society as a whole and by those serving in armed forces. *Professor Sir Austin Robinson*'s argument for inclusion was that the impact of increased defence expenditures on taxation and thus on wage bargaining was no different from that of other expenditures included in the definition. Professors Robinson and *Modigliani* questioned the usefulness of Table 7.1 in which defence expenditures were included for some countries but not others. Professor Modigliani called for a separation of government expenditures on transfers and expenditures on goods and services which recognised that the former were concerned with the distribution objective whereas the latter were designed to promote efficiency. He also argued for a separation of expenditures on public goods such as defence and expenditures on other goods and services such as education which were not public goods but which did confer external benefits. *Professor Tsuru* wondered whether the exceptional position of Japan shown in Table 7.1 could be explained by the high growth rate of income experienced in Japan and by the convention whereby current expenditures on sewage, road and other public works in Japan were counted as investment expenditures.

A number of speakers pointed to possible causes of the observed growth of the share of government consumption in national income which they felt had either been ignored or insufficiently stressed in the paper. *Professor Bacskai* drew attention to what in his view were the following important factors: demographic changes; the extension of the schooling period; the impact of increases in female participation rates on government expenditure concerned with the family; the requirements of demand management and counter-cyclical policies; and the automatic increases in expenditure generated by statutory entitlements to certain benefits. *Professor Pohorille* did not see that the growth of real income, whose importance was stressed in the conclusion of the paper, could explain the observed growth of the share of government consumption in total income. In his view an important cause had been an acceleration in the pace of scientific and technological change which had increased the demand for skilled labour and thus the demand for government investment in human captial. *Professor Bös* felt that both the median voter model and the Baumol model, incorporating a productivity differential between public and private sectors, might add something to the explanation offered. Moreover he pointed out some misunderstandings of Wagner's theory by Boltho. *Professor Sandmo* offered the following additional explanations: relative factor price movements unfavourable to the government sector arising from the labour-intensive nature of government services which inhibited improvements in productivity; an imbalance of pressure arising from the spread of taxation across all citizens on the one hand and the activities of well-organised groups pressing for expenditure increases on the other; and the automatic effect of high rates of inflation and progressive taxation on tax revenues, and thus on the finance available for public expenditure. *Sir Leo Pliatzky* emphasised the great shift of mood in the United Kingdom during and immediately after the Second World War. His view that the 1945 general election was an exceptional event in that citizens voted for a different society. The vision was one in which the unemployment of the pre-war period was to be abolished by a greater reliance on government intervention in market arrangements. He pointed to the influence of the Keynesian revolution on thinking within government, and to the consequences for economic management and expenditure of the commitment to full employment thus established. *Professor Maillet* suggested that there might be a link between the level of public expenditure and the degree of decentralisation in government. *Professor Klein* argued for a separation between explanations of the general upward trend in the share of public consumption observable in all countries and explanations of divergencies between countries in respect of the share. He saw broad sociological factors as being important in the former and more specific institutional factors in the latter.

There was a short discussion of the relationship between public expenditure and economic stability. *Professors Pohorille* and *Khachaturov* pointed to the possible destabilising and inflationary effects of a rapid growth of public expenditure. Professor Pohorille pointed out that there had been a radical change of opinion concerning collective consumption in the west. Welfare transfers had traditionally been regarded as built-in stabilisers, but nowadays the opinion was that public expenditures had destabilising and inflationary effects. But *Professor Klein* argued that the economic instability and high levels of public expenditure observable in recent times were best interpreted as joint results of the exercise of power by organised labour, and not, as is the current orthodoxy, as effect and cause.

Professor Hanusch asked for information on the price deflators used, and wondered whether the results of the analysis would have been altered by the choice of different deflators for government expenditures. *Professor Bös* was surprised at the evidence in Table 7.2 of the constancy of the share of collective consumption in Austria. The figures, which he accepted as accurate, were counter to his expectation of a rising share.

Mr Boltho's general reaction to the discussion was that a close reading of his paper would provide satisfactory answers to some of the points and questions raised. In particular he insisted that his treatment of defence expenditures in Table 7.1 was consistent with the purpose of the table which was to demonstrate the trend of government consumption share over a long time-span for each individual country. In his view it was clear from the text that it was the purpose of Table 7.2 to provide comparable data to demonstrate intercountry divergencies in the share in the post-war period. Mr Boltho defended both his exclusion of defence expenditures and his aggregation of the expenditures on transfers and goods and services on the grounds that the total thus defined was the most appropriate measure of expenditure on social welfare, the analysis of which was the subject of his paper. He did however concede that armed forces could serve in a limited role as instructors of the civilian workforce. In reply to Professor Bacskai, he suggested that changes in female participation rates had been influenced by the growth of income which was incorporated in his analysis. His view was that there was some positive evidence on the displacement of savings by public expenditure, but that any reduction in savings thus caused would be offset by other factors such as inflation-induced saving. In reply to Professor Pohorille, he argued that a growth in income would lead to a rise in the government expenditure share in a system in which the tax structure was progressive and in which the income elasticity of demand for government services was greater than one. Mr Boltho argued that the existence of pressure groups did not provide an explanation of the increase in the share of government consumption because they had been equally active in periods in which the share had not grown rapidly. He took the view that the other explanations suggested by Professors Pohorille, Sandmo and Klein were to be found in one form or another in his paper. His reply to Professor Maillet was that there was no evidence he knew of a connection between decentralisation and the level of government expenditure. Mr Boltho's view of the relationship between government expenditure and economic stability was that the evidence on the adverse effects of unemployment benefits on the level of unemployment was often suspect, and that the evidence on more generalised disincentive effects was either non-existent or controversial. However, he did see tax-push inflation as a serious consequence of a rapid growth of government expenditure, which could undermine economic growth. His reply to Professor Hanusch was that the overall public consumption price index had been used to deflate non-defence public consumption, and the overall private consumption index to deflate public transfers to households. He argued that the construction of more satisfactory sectoral deflators was made difficult by the problem of estimating the productivity of government employees. Such deflators, had they been used, would have affected his results principally by increasing the estimates of the growth of the volume of public consumption expenditures relative to the growth of real expenditures on transfers.

8 Problems of Developing Collective Consumption in Socialist Countries

E. Kapustin

ACADEMY OF SCIENCE OF THE USSR

I DIFFICULTIES OF DEFINITION

In economic literature, including that of the Soviet Union, there is unfortunately no common and precise definition of 'collective consumption' or, in other words, 'joint satisfaction of requirements'.

Some authors use the term to denote those forms of consumption for which a collective nature is determined by the fact that the character of the good makes impossible its use for individual or home consumption. For example, the use of public structures such as theatres or sports arenas, means of public transportation and communication, and the products of social expenditure on the modernisation of cities and villages, environmental protection and the like can be collective only.

Other authors extend the concept to make it embrace all state expenditure for social needs, including, among other things, administration, defence and science. It goes without saying that administration in the broad sense serves the whole of society. Though it is engaged in the task of meeting the personal material or cultural requirements of members of socialist society, it performs the task not directly but indirectly through the production and distribution of the social product.

In some economic research the joint satisfaction of requirements covers all social expenditure involved in meeting the requirements of the population through 'public consumption funds'. Here the criterion for the classification is not the form of consumption itself but the source that covers the expenditure involved in the consumption concerned. In this particular case collective consumption includes, therefore, not only free education, free medical attention, and the care of children in creches free of charge or cheaply, but also all pensions and all kinds of allowances paid from the state budget or from the incomes of enterprises. In relation to consumption, however, pensions and allowances paid in terms of money play a role similar to earnings and other incomes. This is a form of income and not in any sense of consumption. When such incomes are spent, consumption can be either collective or individual. It must also be borne in mind that social maintenance forms a large part in public consumption expenditure. Thus, for example, social maintenance and social insurance account for more than 38 per cent of all payments and allowances which Soviet people receive from public consumption funds.

Such differences of definition of what is meant by 'collective consumption' or 'joint satisfaction of requirements' not only complicates scientific analysis of this important problem but also impedes the provision of appropriate statistics.

II THE ESSENTIAL DISTINCTION BETWEEN PUBLIC AND PERSONAL CONSUMPTION

It seems to me that in the first place the notion of public consumption and that of personal consumption should be clearly differentiated. Public consumption should include all expenditure for public needs, and above all expenditure on administration and defence, on the development of science, on improvement in working conditions, and on labour protection. Personal consumption, in its turn, should include all expenditure for the satisfaction of the physical and spiritual (cultural) needs of man as an individual and of his family as a whole.

This differentiation between public and personal consumption is very important. Unlike collective (joint) personal consumption, joint public consumption represents expenditure of the national income and manpower resources to meet nation-wide and social needs that do not form part of people's personal consumption, that is, expenditure involved in national administration, nation-wide research work, defence, and the like. In actual fact, these represent in another sense pure outlays of consumption of a social rather than individual character. Marx called this sector of consumption 'general outlays of management which have nothing to do with production' and believed that this part of the national product 'will immediately shrink a great deal in comparison with what it is in contemporary society and will diminish still more as new society develops'.[1]

It should be noted that, as regards its functions and influence on people's personal consumption, public consumption is very heterogenous. While expenditures made by a socialist society for administration, science, labour protection and similar purposes have in the final analysis, though not directly, an influence on the well-being of all members of the society and this is their particular function, things are different when defence spending is considered. The growth of such spending leads not to a greater consumption by people but on the contrary reduces it. Under socialism this spending is imposed by external conditions and the task is to create the conditions for reducing it as far as possible. This is the primary aim of the USSR, of other socialist states and of the progressive public of all countries in the struggle for world-wide relaxation of international tension, for détente and arms reduction.

Since administration costs do not directly serve the satisfaction of man's physical and cultural requirements, society is interested in reducing the costs as far as possible through raising the efficiency of the entire machinery of government. For example, the greatest possible reduction of administration costs is a principal aim of the measures taken by the governments of socialist countries to improve administration at all levels and to introduce mechanisation and automation of the work of administrative staff. This can be seen from a comparison of administration costs and the growth of social production in the Soviet Union. Between 1965 and 1977 the share of administration costs in the USSR budget fell from 1.3 per cent to 0.9 per cent, and by 1977 the proportion was reduced to a quarter of what it had been in 1940. It should be also remembered that the national economy and the entire society requiring management have greatly grown in scale while their internal relations have become much more complex. During the same period 1965–77 the gross national product of the USSR grew more than 2.2 times and between 1940 and 1977 it increased more than 12 times.

[1] K. Marx and F. Engels, *Collected Works*, vol. 19, p. 17.

The changes in total administration costs in the USSR are shown below:

Administration Costs in the USSR[2]

	1940	1965	1970	1975	1976	1977	1978[3]	1979[4]
USSR billion roubles	0.7	1.3	1.7	2.0	2.1	2.2	2.3	2.3

During this period the share of administration costs in the expenditures of the state budget has dropped progressively to reach the 0.9 per cent of recent years.

The USSR Ministries and Departments, and the Councils of Ministers of Union Republics have taken various steps to improve the organisational structure of economic management, by introducing automated control systems and reducing expenditure on staff. During the first three years of the current five-year plan the reduction of managerial costs has yielded an economy of 3.1 billion roubles which became available for economic and cultural development. In 1979 further efforts were being taken to improve industrial management, to eliminate unnecessary managerial units in associations and industries, and improve management in construction and other sectors. As a result, the 1979 budget makes an economy of 1 billion roubles in managerial costs.

In the second place, distinction needs to be made between personal individual and personal collective, or joint, consumption. Individual personal consumption should include both the consumption of an individual and the joint consumption of a family. Some Soviet scholars use different terms to define individual personal consumption and collective personal consumption. For example,[5] such concepts as 'individually organised consumption' and 'socially organised consumption' are employed. Individually organised consumption takes place in one's own house: food at home, individual living quarters, clothes, household articles, personal means of transport. Socially organised consumption takes place in public institutions and

[2] *Economicheskaya gazeta* (*Economic Gazette*), no. 50 (1978).
[3] Detailed plan.
[4] Draft.
[5] See P. S. Mstislavsky, *Public Consumption Under Socialism.*

establishments: meals in canteens, cafes, restaurants, vacations in holiday home centres and sanatoria, creches, kindergartens, hospitals, hotel and hostel accommodation, public service establishments, means of public transport and communication, study at educational establishments, visits to libraries, theatres, cinemas, clubs, stadiums and museums.

We should remember, however, that the dividing lines are relative here. What is unquestionable, in my view, is the total coverage of the satisfaction of needs. But it is arguable whether one should treat allowances provided to people in socialist countries in the form of rent for state-owned apartments as personal satisfaction rather than as collective. Meanwhile, social expenditure for this purpose can be very great indeed; In the USSR, for example, the state covers two-thirds of expenditure on housing and communal services. The rent levels fixed as far back as 1928 continue to be effective and a Soviet worker's family pays no more than 3 per cent of its income for rent and communal services. In recent years our state has spent annually about 5 billion roubles on the maintenance of housing facilities, since the rent does not cover the expenses.

III THE REASONS FOR COLLECTIVE FORMS FOR INDIVIDUAL CONSUMPTION

The adoption of collective forms of organisation to meet individual requirements is to be explained in my view, by two factors: (1) by the actual object of consumption, because certain requirements by their nature completely or normally exclude individual consumption; for instance, the premises of a theatre and the services of a theatrical company can obviously be enjoyed only on a collective basis; (2) by the relative economic and social advantage of adopting a collective or an individual form to meet certain requirements; the answer depends partly on the social structure of any particular society, its social orientation, the traditional requirements of its members, and specific features of the economy.

For example, families can be provided with heat or cooling in their homes either through the individual use of air-conditioners or heaters which are their personal property, or by means of collective heating or refrigerating systems (heat and cold can be provided respectively by a central heating system or by public refrigerating plants which supply all apartments or even buildings in a residential area). Food, as is known, can be provided either in the home or through public catering. Which is preferable depends on the economic and social efficiency of the particular form of meeting specific requirements, on public opinion and on the choice of the individual himself.

IV THE DIVIDING LINE BETWEEN INDIVIDUAL AND PERSONAL COLLECTIVE CONSUMPTION

I therefore include in collective personal consumption (or 'joint satisfaction of requirements' or 'collectively organised satisfaction of personal requirements') all consumption of benefits and services carried out in a collective form, whether that determined by the actual object of consumption or by the individual's free choice of the particular form of consumption. In so doing, I take account of economic and social advantage and also to a certain degree of established traditions and customs, and the specific way of life.

The dividing line between individual personal consumption and collective personal consumption under socialism is based, above all, on differences of forms of ownership: individual consumption is based on the personal ownership of consumer goods and on individual or family labour expended on the process of consumption; collective consumption rests on the use of means which under socialism are in public ownership and on the use of directly social labour in the process of consumption.

Collective consumption, or the joint satisfaction of requirements, is effected in socialist countries either on the basis of costing and financing from the state budget or from the incomes of enterprises and organisations. Another way of providing for collective consumption arises from the fact that under socialism the bulk of services are made available to the public through 'public consumption funds' – that is, free of charge or below cost. It is important to have in mind that in this case we are not concerned with commodities. Where services involve payment, whether for individual or collective consumption, the enterprises which provide them operate on the basis of costs.

V THE ADVANTAGES OF COLLECTIVE CONSUMPTION

Though it is only hypothetical the division of consumption between public and personal and of the latter between individual personal consumption against collective personal consumption (or the joint satisfaction of requirements) is of great practical importance. The definition of collective personal consumption is based on specific economic and social features of this sector of people's personal consumption.

When developing collective forms for satisfying requirements, socialist society is guided primarily by the advantages over individual forms of consumption. These are as follows.

Firstly, collective forms of consumption, unlike individual forms, are based on the public ownership of the means of production and the directly social nature of labour. Consequently, any expansion of production to meet these forms of consumption and the accompanying social relations implies nothing more than an expansion of socialist production relations that are typical of the public ownership of the means of production and the directly social nature of labour. At the same time it implies that the public ownership of the means of production will be playing a larger part in satisfying the consumption of the population and especially in the production of services, the share of which in the overall production of commodities and services keeps on growing. As a direct consequence, social labour becomes more significant and mature, gradually taking over the field of consumption which traditionally belonged to personal property and individual personal labour.

Secondly, the development of collective forms of consumption leads, as a rule, to higher efficiency throughout social production, and ultimately to a higher degree of satisfaction of the material and cultural requirements of the nation. With a given volume of total resources for consumption, collective consumption makes it possible to use the resources more effectively and with better results, thus meeting people's requirements more fully. The higher efficiency of collective consumption as compared with individual consumption in meeting the given requirements is accounted for by two factors. The chief is the higher productivity of socialised labour. Engels argued that with public services it would easily be possible to release two-thirds of the workers employed in this kind of work.[6] In the field of consumer goods mass production produces better results than small-scale private production. The latter can compete with mass production only where labour at home is unpaid by society and is very often used wastefully. Such labour inputs are not valued properly either by the worker or his family. But they undoubtedly affect the level of physical and cultural satisfaction of those involved,

[6] K. Marx and F. Engels, *Collected Works* (1955), vol. 2, p. 542.

and there is less time left for the satisfaction of other and especially cultural requirements. There is not enough time for proper rest and leisure, and the care of children by the family may be neglected.

Thirdly, by making use of collective forms to meet requirements socialist society achieves two important economic and social objectives: it creates conditions for increasing each person's leisure time; it makes possible a more effective use of that time for the all-round development of the person concerned.

A socialist society cannot be indifferent to how working people spend their spare time. The whole of society is very much interested in it being used as effectively as possible. Thus more vigorous efforts should be made to ensure that the satisfaction of as many requirements as possible shall take the form of collective consumption. In present conditions the connection between the development of collective forms of consumption and the way working people spend their spare time is multifarious. Thus, the amount of spare time, in the proper sense of the time that a man can spend on his physical or cultural development, depends directly or indirectly on the availability of public transport, public catering and other forms of public services. The more extensive are certain forms of collective consumption, the greater is the time that any worker has to meet his essential requirements, within a given total amount of spare time.

At the same time, the forms and results of the use of spare time depend on the opportunities that society provides for each individual to meet his own requirements as fully as possible, including such things as improvement of one's education, rest and leisure, and the development of one's talents and abilities. These opportunities are provided through collective consumption.

Fourthly, of special importance is the social aspect of collective consumption. The point is that the development of the individual as part of society as a whole is stimulated in the process, thus contributing to the objective of the further improvement of our socialist way of life. The development of collective forms of consumption is one of the major means for the further improvement of the socialist way of life and the development of collective relationships between people. It is also an effective means of combating such elements of individualism as loneliness and social indifference.

If collective forms of consumption accord so closely with the spirit and nature of socialism, it is certainly not because socialism denies individuality. On the contrary, what socialism denies is individualism rather than individuality; the latter receives the fullest and most effective development in a socialist society. When we speak of the gradual intensification of the social homogeneity of a socialist society, we have in mind that the major fundamental aspects of the socialist way of life shall become increasingly characteristic of the way of life of the whole people without exception. At the same time, individual specific elements in the composition of requirements, and in the forms, types and methods of consumption can and must be diversified.

This aspect should be specially emphasised because, despite scientific and technological progress and the steady rise of people's living standards in socialist countries, there still remain factors which weaken ties between the individual and society as a whole. An example of this is the development of mass media, such as radio and television, through which information can be received that is not necessarily in a collective form. The development of general education and cultural standards also contributes occasionally to weakening social and collective ties. For example, literature and the arts very often adopt certain individual forms.

Higher cultural standards lead, and must lead, to a gradual elimination of those ways in which a man spends his spare time which make no contribution to his development as a person and sometimes even impede this development. At the same time, these ways of spending time have involved in some measure relationships between people; thus their reduction or abolition calls for some substitute which will increase rather than diminish the opportunities and needs for contacts between people when they are off duty. Thus it is very important to develop and maintain collective forms of satisfying requirements which will ensure the development and strengthening of various ties within an informal group.

In relation to this social aspect of collective consumption it should be noted that the collective forms of bringing up children in children's institutions affect not only the family budget and the mothers' opportunities for employment in social production but also have a substantial influence on the upbringing of the rising generation. It seems that children in a group who are concerned not only for themselves but also for other members of the group and the group as a whole can be brought up more easily and successfully through collective relationships which substantially complement the individual upbringing in the family.

Special mention should be made of the fact that subsidised collective consumption greatly affects not only the employment of spare time but also the pattern of consumption of material and cultural goods and services. In this case you cannot act as in the case of money income where one's personal tastes are alone taken into account. Provision made for certain types of consumption made available by the state as collective consumption cannot be exchanged for other types of consumption. Thus when society makes resources available it consciously determines the growth of certain requirements and the degree of satisfaction of these requirements. In this way the influence of centralised planning on the amount and structure of people's consumption is increased.

Fifthly, an enormous social role is played by collective consumption in relieving women from the heavy burden of work in the home. This not only saves a great deal of hard work but also is one of the main factors that enables women to take part in social production and as a result promotes their fuller integration, increases family incomes and thus ensures a fuller satisfaction of people's physical and cultural requirements.

Sixthly, it is important to bear in mind that one way in which collective consumption affects social development under socialism is by reducing the differentiation of working people in regard to the level of consumption. This affects in practice not the whole of consumer expenditure but only the expenditure on public education, on health services, on physical culture and the satisfaction of a number of cultural requirements which are provided to people irrespective of employment in socialist production, and to the extent to which the people desire such satisfactions. As a result, the biggest allowances through collective forms of consumption are received by the families with the greatest number of children. These families, as a rule, have the lowest income per member of the family. Medical assistance is needed to the greatest extent by old people, invalids, and that also means by those who, as a rule, have the lowest income. The same applies to allowances for housing and communal services. The collective consumption of all these services profoundly influences the equalisation of the general level of consumption of families which differ in their individual incomes.

When services and material means of education, of medical care, of culture and of certain other things are distributed under socialism they are not linked either directly or indirectly to other criteria. The measure of benefits received in these cases does not depend on length of service, rate of wages or one's employment in social production.

Thus the collective form of consumption, based under socialism on public ownership, the social organisation of production and a high level of mechanisation, makes it possible to use both the consumption fund and the spare time of working people more effectively; it exerts a profound influence on the development of collectivism and the socialist mode of life as a whole; it introduces rational principles into consumption, and on this basis ensures a fuller satisfaction of material and cultural requirements of members of society within the limits of a given consumption fund.

VI THE COMPOSITION OF COLLECTIVE CONSUMPTION

In the light of these advantages of collective forms of satisfying people's personal requirements, a socialist society and in particular the state follow a consistent economic policy to develop further this progressive form of consumption and to improve its composition.

Collective personal consumption covers a wide range of services. They include the following:

(i) the care of children and their upbringing in children's institutions of various types (kindergartens, creches, children's homes, young pioneer camps);
(ii) general education, including evening schools and correspondence courses;
(iii) vocational training, including on-the-job training, vocational schools, secondary technical schools, and institutions of higher learning;
(iv) public catering of various types and forms (restaurants, cafes, canteens, including those at one's place of work);
(v) public transportation and communication, covering only passenger transport and personal communication;
(vi) medical care (health protection) provided by various medical establishments (hospitals, out-patient clinics, maternity hospitals, and various medical consultation centres);
(vii) communal physical culture and sport exercises under communal instructors on communal arenas with the help of communal sports equipment;
(viii) theatrical, concert and sporting performances, motion pictures, shows and entertainments;
(ix) libraries, museums, exhibitions, art and picture galleries;
(x) various kinds of clubs and equipment needed for amateur art activities and folk art;
(xi) certain community services (hotels, laundries, bath houses);
(xii) various facilities for group rest and leisure (holiday home centres, boarding houses, tourist centres and camps);

(xiii) homes for old people and invalids;[7]
(xiv) modernisation of overpopulated areas, roads, and the results of grants for environmental protection.

These are the main forms of joint satisfaction of requirements in socialist countries. In my view, collective forms of consumption should be defined to include also all types irrespective of the source of expenditure covering this consumption. For example, collective consumption should include all instruction and medical services whether free of charge or requiring payment, and the satisfaction of certain cultural requirements. The source of covering such expenditure does not change the joint nature of employment of teachers, physicians, artists, and the use of the corresponding buildings and equipment. This applies, it would seem, to almost all types of collective consumption. Depending on the social system and the functions of the state at a particular stage they can either require payment or be free of charge; that is, they can be provided either from people's personal incomes or at the expense of society as a whole. It can be seen that the essential characteristic of collective consumption does not depend on whether the expenditures are covered by society from the state budget or whether they are borne by certain enterprises and organisations.

VII EXTRAVAGANCE IN USE OF FREE SERVICES

Nonetheless, the analysis of collective consumption from the standpoint of sources covering it does have considerable interest. This is, firstly, because satisfaction of collective requirements at the expense of society gives a powerful impetus to their increase and enables society to profoundly influence the pattern and ways of meeting requirements as a whole. But this process has a negative aspect (negative only at a certain stage of social development); the collective satisfaction of certain requirements free of charge (or on easy terms) in the conditions of a

[7] As regards social expenditure on permanent or temporary disablement benefits, the bulk of these expenditures should not be included in collective consumption, though they are subsidised from the state budget. They are actually paid in terms of money and anyone who receives such benefits is free to spend them either on collective or on personal consumption. However, part of these funds properly belongs to collective consumption, including all the various forms of collective consumption by disabled persons and in particular homes for old people and invalids. Expenditure on their maintenance is properly included in the total of collective consumption.

commodity-money system does not always ensure the most economical and effective use of these resources by consumers. Many regard these benefits as a 'gift of nature', and consequently the impression is created that they cost next to nothing. In actual fact the satisfaction of collective requirements at the expense of society involves society as a whole in tremendous expenditures. When the expenditures provide free collective satisfaction of certain requirements they are not always sufficiently appreciated by members of society. On the other hand, when these same collective requirements are met by spending personal income, the consumer tries to be more economical and careful in using his funds.

In socialist countries, therefore, taking into account not only the tremendous advantage of meeting collective requirements wholly or partially at the expense of society, but also certain disadvantages, the best compromise has to be reached between forms of collective consumption which require payment and those that are free of charge. The study of the organisation of collective consumption from this point of view is of great theoretical and practical importance.

The lack of sufficiently detailed statistics of collective consumption proper makes it necessary to make use of data which analyse only indirectly and inadequately the structure and changes of this form of consumption. Some idea of the progressive growth of collective consumption, especially in such forms as education and medical care, can be derived from statistics of expenditures from the USSR state budget (see Table 8.1).

The patterns of collective consumption in different socialist countries can be seen from the distribution of public consumption funds. Thus, in

TABLE 8.1 STATE BUDGET EXPENDITURE ON HEALTH AND EDUCATION (billion roubles and percentages)

	1940	*1965*	*1970*	*1975*	*1976*	*1977*
USSR State Budget Expenditure on:						
Public education (roubles)	2.4	16.1	23.5	31.0	32.2	33.5
% of all expenses	13.8	15.9	15.2	14.5	14.2	13.8
Specialised training (roubles)	2.0	14.1	19.8	26.2	27.2	28.3
%	11.5	13.9	12.9	12.2	12.0	11.7
Cultural and educational work and arts	0.4	2.0	3.7	4.8	5.0	5.2
%	2.3	2.0	2.4	3.1	2.3	2.1
Health services and physical culture	0.9	6.7	9.3	11.5	11.8	12.5
%	5.2	6.6	6.1	5.3	5.2	5.1

1976 the proportion of public expenditure devoted to medical care and physical culture was 16.5 per cent in Bulgaria, 18.0 per cent in Hungary, 13.1 per cent in the German Democratic Republic, 24.7 per cent in Mongolia, 26.1 per cent in Poland, 14.5 per cent in the Soviet Union, and 17.1 per cent in Czechoslovakia. Expenditure on free education and cultural services accounted for 24.1 per cent of all public consumption funds in Bulgaria, 20.0 per cent in Hungary, 24.5 per cent in the GDR, 25.5 per cent in Mongolia, 24.6 per cent in Poland, 25.3 per cent in the Soviet Union, and 19.3 per cent in Czechoslovakia. Expenditure on the maintenance of housing facilities accounted for 0.2 per cent of public consumption funds in Bulgaria, 2.0 per cent in Hungary, 5.9 per cent in the GDR, 6.0 per cent in Poland, 5.5 per cent in the Soviet Union, and 3.4 per cent in Czechoslovakia.[8]

VIII MEASURING THE SIZE AND TREND OF COLLECTIVE PERSONAL CONSUMPTION

It is practically impossible to state exactly the size and trend of the aggregate fund for collective satisfaction of personal requirements. There are two reasons for this. Firstly, there are neither comprehensive nor sufficiently representative selective studies of the whole range of collective consumption properly defined. Some elements of the collective consumption fund, including their total size and trend, are covered adequately enough by statistics. These include, in particular, education, medical care and public catering. At the same time we have almost no statistics for certain important items.

Secondly, there is a wide difference between our statistics and the statistics of capitalist countries in the methods of measuring the volume of services which make up a large part of collective consumption, thus distorting the general picture and making impossible any comparison of available statistics for different countries. This leads to marked differences in the measurement in money terms of this sector of the collective consumption fund in socialist and capitalist countries. Things are further complicated by the fact that a substantial part of such services as education, medical care and many cultural services are provided free of charge or at subsidised prices.

[8] K. I. Mikulsky, *Public Consumption Funds in the Member-Countries of the Council for Mutual Economic Assistance*. Information Bulletin of the USSR Academy of Sciences, Economic Series, No. 6 (1978), p. 92.

In contrast to western statistics, services in our national income figures are measured only in terms of material expenditure. For international comparison of the role of services in meeting consumers' requirements some economists attempt to estimate and allow for current labour expended on services and the measurement of its product by analogy with the product of labour in material production. A number of uncertain assumptions have to be introduced in this process. But an estimate of this kind indicates in some measure the real economic facts.

There are certain other methods of calculating the full cost of services. One of these takes the form of estimating the total 'cost' of services from data on the consumption of services. The volume of services for which payment is required is estimated from the cost of their provision; the cost of free services is calculated in terms of their social production cost. The total of material expenditure in the whole field of services already included in the national income and the consumption fund is deducted from the total 'cost' of services. The difference between these figures represents an additional 'cost' which must be 'additionally' taken into account not only in the consumption fund and the national income, but also in any calculation of the volume of collective forms of satisfaction of people's personal requirements.[9]

IX THE STATISTICAL EVIDENCE

The statistics of socialist countries indicate accurately the size and trends of some of the most important elements of the collective satisfaction of personal requirements. We have the necessary data on education, health protection, public catering and public transport; data on the chief forms of collective consumption such as education, vocational training and children's institutions are particularly complete.

The achievement of a genuine cultural revolution and the rise of the educational and cultural level of the whole population is one of the essentials of building socialism. All member-countries of the Council for Mutual Economic Assistance (CMEA) have scored signal successes in this field and a similar tendency is visible in all socialist countries. As the economy grows and expands, capital investment in the non-productive

[9] Analysis of the effect of such a method of measurement of services on general economic indices, and in particular on the size of the national income and of consumption funds has shown that the size of the national income as now defined in our statistics would be an increase (in terms of value) of about 12–13 per cent and in the consumption fund by 17–18 per cent.

TABLE 8.2 NUMBER OF CHILDREN'S EXTRA-MURAL INSTITUTIONS OF THE USSR MINISTRY OF PUBLIC EDUCATION AND THE USSR MINISTRY OF RAILWAYS (as of the end of the year)

	1965	*1970*	*1975*	*1976*	*1977*
Palaces, Young Pioneers' and school-children's homes	3409	3865	4403	4501	4587
Young technicians' centres	397	606	1008	1085	1112
Young naturalists' centres	288	338	587	641	675
Excursion and tourist centres	184	169	202	209	216
Children's parks	184	164	155	153	152
Children's railways	33	34	38	37	39

sphere, and especially the needs of public education, become larger. Schools are built rapidly; the network of general education is greatly expanded, to make it possible to provide for young people of all age groups.

One of the remarkable achievements of socialist countries is the establishment of institutions for pre-school education, including kindergartens and creches. The system of pre-school children's institutions has essentially been created anew in these countries. The building of these pre-school children's institutions has made it possible to increase enormously the number of children in them. Thus between 1966 and 1976 the numbers increased 1.5 times in Bulgaria, 1.6 times in Hungary, 1.7 times in the GDR, 3.8 times in Mongolia, 2.0 times in Poland, 2.4 times in Rumania, 2.7 times in the Soviet Union, and 1.9 times in Czechoslovakia.[10] Table 8.2, which gives more detailed data for Soviet pre-school institutions, shows their wide range of structure.

In most of the CMEA member-countries, kindergartens and creches are opened at an increasing pace each year. In the last two or three years the figure has fallen slightly in the GDR and Czechoslovakia because the two countries now have enough pre-school institutions when account is taken of the birth rate.

It should be remembered that the school that provides general education takes the leading place in the whole educational system of any country. At present the system of schools giving general education enables young people in all socialist countries to have school education. Differences in the number of students per thousand of population in different countries are due mainly to differences in the proportion of the

[10] *Statistical Yearbook of CMEA Member-Countries* (1977), p. 436.

population in school-age age-groups. The largest number of students in general education schools is to be expected in those countries in which the birth rate is the highest. This applies, in particular, to Mongolia and Cuba.

Compulsory secondary education has now been introduced in the USSR. In Bulgaria, Hungary and Poland eight-year schooling is compulsory and in the near future the change will be made to universal secondary education. Compulsory nine-year education has been introduced in Czechoslovakia and ten-year schooling has been made compulsory in the GDR.

The data presented in Table 8.3 show a tendency for the rapid growth

TABLE 8.3 NUMBERS OF STUDENTS (000's)[a]

	1950–51	*1960–61*	*1970–71*	*1973–74*
Bulgaria	970	1212	1157	1111
Hungary	1282	1532	1284	1196
German Democratic Republic	2514	2059	2267	2736
Cuba	—	1287	2157	—
Mongolia	68.7	115	240	5282
Poland	3608	5272	5869	5334
Romania	1838	2590	3329	3073
USSR	34636	36051	49010	48812
Czechoslovakia	1736	2227	2077	2018

[a] *Statistical Summary: National Economy of CMEA Member-Countries* (Moscow, 1974), p. 313.

in the number of students in the schools of general education in all CMEA member-countries during the years of building socialism to decline slightly in recent years as a consequence of a drop in the rates of population growth.

To train skilled workers, a system of vocational training has been established in socialist countries. This type of training is growing very rapidly and is an important means of acquiring both general education and skill in a trade. In the USSR, vocational schools will train about 11 million skilled workers during the tenth five-year plan period.[11] Table 8.4 presents additional data on the development of vocational training.

Specialised secondary schools and higher educational establishments have an important place in the whole system of public education in

[11] Baibakov, 'On the State Five-Year Plan of the USSR for National Economic Development for 1976–80', *Pravda*, 28 October 1976.

TABLE 8.4 NUMBERS OF FACTORY AND TRADE SCHOOLS AND THEIR ENROLMENTS[a] (as of the beginning of school year)

	1960–61			1970–71			1976–77		
	Schools	Students		Schools	Students		Schools	Students	
		(000's)	Number per thousand of population		(000's)	Number per thousand of population		(000's)	Number per thousand of population
Bulgaria	236	42.1	5	328	130	15	318	150	17
Hungary	212	125	12	323	223	21	265	158	15
GDR	1146	338	20	1051	406	24	977	433	26
Cuba	—	9.2		215	23.3	3	246	97.8	10
Mongolia	—	—	—	28	10.6	11	32	15.5	10
Poland	3724	363	12	4840	868	27	3803	872	25
Romania	519	127	7	403	282	14	440	119	5
USSR[b]	3684	1064	5	5351	2380	10	6457	3234	12
Czechoslovakia	1806	241	18	2250	349	24	2355	337	22

[a] *Statistical Yearbook of CMEA Member-Countries for 1976*, p. 428.
[b] Data as of 1 January 1961, 1971 and 1977, on schools under the State Committee of the USSR Council of Ministers for Vocational Training.

socialist countries. It is these institutions that train middle-level and highly skilled specialists for all industries in the national economy. This system is quick to react to the needs of social production, the tasks that confront it, and public opinion. As a result, not only the trades involved but also the distribution of training personnel can change within a comparatively short time. The large number of specialised secondary schools is shown by the following figures. In the academic year 1976–77 there were 218 such schools with an enrolment of 126,000 students in Bulgaria, 247 schools and 227,000 students in Hungary, 233 and 161,000 in the GDR, 550 and 175,000 in Cuba, 22 and 15,000 in Mongolia, 6423 and 139,000 in Poland, 933 and 675,000 in Romania, 4303 and 4,623,000 in the USSR, and 588 schools and 307,000 students in Czechoslovakia.[12]

Significant progress has also been made in higher education in socialist countries. This can be seen from the following data. In the academic year 1976–77 there were 29 institutions of higher education with an enrolment of 108,000 students in Bulgaria. Hungary had 56 such establishments and 111,000 students; the GDR 54 and 130,000; Cuba 5 and 106,000; Mongolia 6 and 16,000; Poland 89 and 491,000; Romania 43 and 175,000; the USSR 859 and 4,950,000; Czechoslovakia 36 establishments and 168,000 students. The development of this system is indicated by the number of such students per 10,000 of population. (See Table 8.5.)

Since knowledge initially received ages rapidly, the constant advanced training of all professional people and of specialists in particular, is of

TABLE 8.5 NUMBERS OF STUDENTS IN HIGHER EDUCATION (per 10000 of population)[a]

	1950–51	*1960–61*	*1970–71*	*1973–74*
Bulgaria	46	70	108	125
Hungary	35	45	78	94
German Democratic Republic	17	59	81	86
Cuba	—	27.6	36.7	—
Mongolia	19	73	68	74
Poland	50	56	101	118
Romania	32	39	75	69
USSR	69	111	188	186
Czechoslovakia	55.9	68.7	91.3	93.2

[12] *Statistical Yearbook of CMEA Member-Countries* (1977), p. 411.

great importance. Evening classes and correspondence courses play an important role in training and retraining personnel and enable workers and collective farmers to acquire specialised secondary or higher education by combining work with study. The structure of the entire system of public education and vocational training in the Soviet Union can be seen from the data presented in Table 8.6. It is also of interest to

TABLE 8.6 NUMBERS OF STUDENTS ENGAGED IN DIFFERENT TYPES OF TRAINING IN THE USSR (as of the beginning of the academic year) (000's)

	1940–41	*1965–66*	*1970–71*	*1975–76*	*1976–77*	*1977–78*
Total number of students	47547	71857	79634	92605	93708	94881
of whom:						
in general education schools	35552	48255	49193	47594	46468	45445
in day-time general education schools	34784	43410	45448	42611	41551	40625
in evening general education schools, (including correspondence courses)	768	4845	3745	4983	4917	4820
in vocational technical schools, sectoral vocational schools (under some agency) and factory-training schools	717	1701	2591	3381	3552	3681
in specialised secondary schools	975	3659	4388	4525	4623	46662
in higher educational establishments	812	3861	4581	4854	4950	5037
those studying new trades or improving their skills in enterprises, institutions, organisations and collective farms or engaged in other types of non-political training	9491	14381	18881	32251	34115	36056

[a] *Statistical Summary: National Economy of CMEA Member-Countries* (Moscow, 1974), p. 316.

record the data on the development of such a form of collective consumption as the library service (see Table 8.7).

Of special interest are data on the development of clubs. In 1950 the USSR had a total of 125,400 clubs. Subsequently the figure rose to 135,100 in 1975 and 135,700 in 1977. The functions of all these clubs are divided as follows: 3200 regional centres of culture; 2500 urban centres of culture and clubs; 87,700 rural houses of culture and clubs; 9300 clubs on collective farms; 20,900 trade union clubs; and 2700 clubs belonging to different departments and organisations. Mention should be made of amateur art, a form of collective consumption of culture. In 1977 more than seven million people took part in various amateur art groups. The museum holdings available for the collective consumption of cultural history have been greatly expanded. In 1977 the Soviet Union had 1348 museums which were visited by 139 million people.

It is also interesting to note that the number of visits to theatres in the Soviet Union increased from 84 million in 1940 to 116 million in 1977, and the number of visits to cinemas grew from 900 million in 1940 to 4080 million in 1977.

The same growth in theatre attendance is to be observed in all CMEA

TABLE 8.7 NUMBERS OF PUBLIC LIBRARIES (as of the end of the year)[a]

	1950	*1960*	*1970*	*1973*
Bulgaria	—	4524	6343	6149
Hungary	4333	9773	9215	8660
German Democratic Republic	7385[b]	11987	11694	12747
Cuba[c]	—	—	51	—
Mongolia	22	33	349	351
Poland	4193	7033	8621	8852
Romania[d]	18444	14407	7283	6209
USSR	123077	135721	128034	130377
Czechosolvakia	15131	14554	13553	13250
		Book stocks (million copies)		
Bulgaria	—	13.2	31.4	36.1
Hungary	2.2	11.1	24.7	28.4
German Democratic Republic	—	12.5	20.6	24.7
Mongolia	0.3	0.8	3.9	4.6
Poland	10.4	31.1	56.1	66.8
Romania[e]	11.8	31.9	47.5	51.1
USSR	244	845	1307	1471
Czechoslovakia	11.1	20.8	32.9	38.0

Additional detailed data for the USSR

	1950	*1965*	*1970*	*1975*	*1977*
Total readers using libraries (millions)	23.3	62.7	77.7	94.5	102.2
Average number of books and journals per reader	5.9	12.1	12.7	12.7	12.4
Average number of readers per library (thousands)	0.9	0.9	0.9	0.9	1.0
Average number of books and journals borrowed per reader	19.0	19.1	19.9	20.6	20.9

[a] *Statistical Summary: National Economy of CMEA Member-Countries* (Moscow, 1974), p. 332.

[b] Excluding children's libraries.

[c] The libraries of the National Council of Culture only.

[d] All libraries for 1950–60 are included irrespective of the size of the book stock.

[e] Excluding magazines.

member-countries. This is shown by the number of visits to theatres per thousand people (see Table 8.8).

The increased consumption of services of medical institutions in the USSR is shown in Table 8.9.

TABLE 8.8 NUMBER OF VISITS TO THEATRES PER 1000 OF POPULATION

	1950	*1960*	*1970*	*1973*
Bulgaria	274	747	626	698
Hungary	317	644	541	545
German Democratic Republic	734	935	719	709
Cuba	—	—	791	—
Mongolia	256	734	881	1171
Poland	407	446	405	390
Romania	280	494	408	388
Soviet Union	377	425	458	460
Czechoslovakia	763	935	662	657

TABLE 8.9 MAIN FEATURES OF HEALTH SERVICE (as of the end of the year) (000's)

	1940	*1965*	*1970*	*1975*	*1977*
Numbers of physicians in all branches of medicine	155.3	554.2	668.4	634.1	896.9
Numbers of hospitals	12.8	26.3	26.2	24.3	23.7
Numbers of hospital beds	791	2226	2663	3009	3140

The rapid development of health services is also a characteristic of all other CMEA member-countries. Thus, for example, the number of beds in hospital-type institutions per 10,000 of population has been steadily growing in all CMEA member-countries (see Table 8.10).

The collective forms of medical treatment and recuperation covered by a great deal of data, for example, on the number of people who received medical treatment in sanatoria (see Table 8.11).

In practically all countries of the socialist community capital investment on environmental protection is planned to grow substantially in the current five-year plan period. The Soviet state has allocated 11 billion roubles for this purpose in the tenth five-year plan. In 1976 capital investment in the protection of nature and the rational use of natural resources totalled 1755 million roubles; this included 1385

TABLE 8.10 NUMBERS OF BEDS IN HOSPITAL-TYPE INSTITUTIONS PER 10000 OF POPULATION[a]

	1950	*1960*	*1970*	*1973*
Bulgaria	39.2	62.5	77.2	85.7
Hungary	52.5	67.2	77.6	78.5
German Democratic Republic	102	119	111	109
Cuba	—	—	47.3	—
Mongolia	48.0	81.0	94.3	99.1
Poland	51.1	70.3	74.1	75.0
Romania	42.2	72.5	80.8	87.0
Soviet Union	56	80	109	114
Czechoslovakia	61.7	76.1	79.7	79.4

[a] *Statistical Summary: National Economy of CMEA Member-Countries* (Moscow, 1974), p. 333.

TABLE 8.11 NUMBERS OF PATIENTS RECEIVING MEDICAL TREATMENT IN SANATORIA[a] (000's)

	1950	*1960*	*1970*	*1973*
Bulgaria	—	88.8	165	178
Hungary	7.6	28.0	32.6	35.8
German Democratic Republic	337[b]	329	319	326
Mongolia	2.0	9.7	16.9	17.2
Poland	100	153	318	377
Romania	75.4	226	367	488
Soviet Union	1654	2263	3612	3917
Czechoslovakia	266	397	459	487

[a] *Statistical Summary: National Economy of CMEA Member-Countries* (Moscow, 1974), p. 337.
[b] 1951.

million roubles for the protection and rational use of water resources; in 1978 state capital investment for this purpose is to amount to 2 billion roubles. This investment is earmarked primarily for the construction of engineering facilities for environmental protection and the replacement of certain natural resources, for example, by forest planting.[13]

The development of public transport can be seen from figures of passenger services provided by all types of public transport (see Table 8.12).

The great importance of public catering is indicated by figures showing its ratio to total retail trade turnover. Thus in 1973 public catering accounted for 20.9 per cent of all retail trade in Bulgaria, 14.2 per cent in Hungary, 10.3 per cent in the GDR, 28.8 per cent in Cuba (in 1972), 6.7 per cent in Mongolia, 6.8 per cent in Poland, 14.4 per cent in Romania, 9.4 per cent in the Soviet Union, and 13.5 per cent in Czechoslovakia.[14]

X GENERAL CONCLUSIONS

In framing the plans for long-term socio-economic development, socialist states envisage not only a steady growth in the overall satisfaction of people's material and cultural requirements, but also a

[13] *Voprosy Ekonomiki* (*Economic Problems*), no. 4 (1978), pp. 69–71.
[14] *Statistical Summary: National Economy of CMEA Member-Countries* (1977), p. 245.

TABLE 8.12 PASSENGER SERVICE PROVIDED BY ALL TYPES OF PUBLIC TRANSPORT[a]

(1950 = 100)

	1950	*1960*	*1970*	*1971*	*1972*	*1973*
Bulgaria (1968 = 100)	—	—	122	131	143	154
Hungary	100	257	362	367	383	388
German Democratic Republic	100	152	174	182	193	199
Mongolia	100	885	2000	2200	2500	2700
Poland	100	134	231	243	265	283
Romania	100	142	308	336	366	399
Soviet Union	100	254	563	597	636	669
Czechoslovakia	100	157	194	200	201	214

[a] *Statistical Summary: National Economy of CMEA Member Countries* (1977), p. 218.

necessary increase in expenditure on collective forms of satisfaction of personal requirements. As was said earlier, this is to be explained by a variety of reasons. Firstly, the economic and social productivity of collective satisfaction of personal requirements is much higher than that of the individual expenditure. Secondly, there is an urgent need to adopt collective forms for the collectivist upbringing of members of society and further improvement of the socialist mode of life. Thirdly, this is also the objective demand of scientific and technological progress which provides the requisite conditions at the same time. Scientific and technological progress imposes ever increasing demands on man's all-round development, the level of his general and specialised education, his health, and the extent of the replacement of the physical and mental energy he expends in production. In addition to this, scientific and technological progress provides ever increasing opportunities to change from satisfying requirements in the individual sphere, with individual labour in the home, to the collective sphere, based on labour in social production; this incidentally represents the progress of socialisation not only of production but also of consumption. Fourthly, mention should be made of an interesting feature of the development of collective forms of consumption: the development of any particular thing frequently requires the development of something else to extend it. For example, the development of general education necessarily requires a certain development of secondary and specialised higher education, libraries, mass information and culture. Otherwise the realisation of the potentialities that complete general education creates for young people will be incomplete. Fifthly, the rapid growth of collective forms of consumption is the practical precondition of the further strengthening of the social homogeneity of a socialist society. This process includes equality of treatment in the fields of education, medical care and other forms of collective consumption as between social groups and different regions of the country.

All this in practice necessitates increased priority for the development of the collective forms of satisfaction of personal requirements embodied in the socio-economic development plans of socialist countries.

Discussion of 'Ways and Methods of Developing Collective Consumption in Socialist Countries' by Professor E. Kapustin

Professor Tsuru opened the discussion by inviting Professor Kapustin to expand on the following specific points raised in or by his paper: the desirability of expanding collective personal consumption relative to collective public consumption; the assignment of rent subsidies within the categories of collective consumption defined in the paper; the role of market-oriented institutions and subsidies in the provision of personal collective consumption; and the possible conflict between road improvements which facilitate private transport and public transport services. Professor Tsuru was concerned that the paper did not sufficiently explain the normative goals presented such as 'the socialist mode of life'. He did not see that the system of personal collective consumption described required the socialisation of resources, or that it was compatible with economic efficiency, or that it was superior to a fiscal system as a means of income redistribution.

Dr Hoch described the socialist mode of life as one in which there was no great inequality of incomes and in which existed the social conditions necessary for individual development. However he suggested that a requirement of such a system was the collective organisation of production rather than consumption, and that efficiency was promoted by allowing citizens a choice between alternative modes of consumption. Indeed, he argued that in some cases socially organised private consumption could result in public disorder and hooliganism which was neither socially desirable nor efficient. On the other hand, he did not see that an individual who wished to spend his leisure time alone was thereby anti-social in a wider political sense. *Professor Bacskai* was also not convinced that, for example, the use of crowded public transport facilities necessarily promoted socialist values. He was also unable to see that football, for example, was an activity, more supportive of socialist values than the more solitary pastime of fishing: a popular activity in Eastern Europe which often lacked even the company of fish. However, against these views *Professor Pohorille* argued that the organisation of private consumption had important social and economic effects. The satisfaction of personal needs in a collective manner intensified social contact between individuals, and, in examples such as the sporting games of ancient Rome, formed an important part of the cultural tradition of a society. Without art galleries and museums individuals by themselves would be unable to appreciate fine works of art. Also in some cases cost reductions were possible in a system of personal collective consumption; as was shown by President

Carter's appeal to American citizens to make more use of public transport. But in his view this form of consumption was complementary to private consumption and, unlike Professor Kapustin, he did not see that the concept of the socialist mode of life provided a case for extending the scope of it. *Professor Tsuru* acknowledged the possible social benefits of a system of collective personal consumption but was sceptical of the claim he saw in the paper that such a system ensured social and economic efficiency. He envisaged a trade-off between these objectives and wondered whether Professor Kapustin would be willing to sacrifice economic efficiency for the social advantages of personal collective consumption. In addition, he was not clear how the social efficiency of the system described could be assessed in view of the difficulty of measuring the output of social services.

Professor Onitiri asked for further information on the efficiency of the system of collective consumption described in the paper and on the abuses of it that had been experienced in the USSR. He had in mind the possibility of frivolous and excessive demand in a system of free provision. He also asked about the use of alternative policy instruments for collective consumption, and in particular whether free services had been withdrawn and users compensated by cash payments. *Dr Jašić* wished to know more about decision-making procedures for education at central and local levels, and about the impact of expenditure on education on national productivity in the USSR. *Professor Maillet* asked for an explanation of the large difference between expenditures on education and health reported in Table 8.1. *Mr Boltho* wondered whether it was feasible to express the expenditure information in Table 8.1 as a percentage of some measure of national income, and, if it was, what trend would be shown. On this point, *Mr Kaser* drew attention to the difficulty in this area of using data derived for operational purposes for economic analysis. The aggregate within which Professor Kapustin had cited expenditures on collective consumption was the total budget used for financial planning. His view was that the analytically correct aggregate was some measure of the flow of community income comparable to the GDP measure used in western economies. His general point was that the difficulty of making East-West comparisons in this area was due to the priority given to operational statistics in the East.

Professor Khachaturov took up several points raised in the discussion. He described the policy in the USSR to expand provision in selected areas of collective consumption such as education, health, housing and services for children. His view was that the effectiveness of collective services could not be measured by general statistical techniques, but that in many cases information on productivity could be derived from special studies. He cited examples of those which examined the results of using workers with different skill levels. In connection with Professor Onitiri's question about alternative instruments, he referred to the alternative methods of transportation that were available in socialist and western economies. *Professor Kapustin* replied briefly to the comments made. He insisted that there were real and important distinctions between collective public consumption, collective personal consumption and private consumption. In his view some needs could not be satisfied privately.

Part Three
Organisation and Control

9 Notes on X-Efficiency and Bureaucracy

Harvey Leibenstein
HARVARD UNIVERSITY

I SOME BASIC QUESTIONS AND CONSIDERATIONS

As I write I am very much aware of some of the basic difficulties one faces in attempting to analyse some aspects of the bureaucratic phenomenon. Perusal of the sociological and political science literature does not diminish the difficulties. The general problem, or set of problems, appears to be too amorphous and too large to be handled by traditional economic tools. There is no generally accepted way of abstracting some elements and ignoring others. It seems clear that almost any analysis will leave out aspects that some readers may feel are vitally important. A major handicap is the lack of a central problem focus. There are just too many questions to be asked in any attempt to understand bureaucracy. In this paper we shall limit our attention to the determinants of the internal efficiency of a bureaucratic unit where the services of the unit are given to some degree. More specifically we shall be concerned with what determines the *cost per unit of service* almost to the exclusion of a great many other equally interesting questions. Also we shall focus our attention on the incentives within the bureaucratic unit, and on how these incentives are generated from the outside.

In general, standard economic theory has not been applied to the bureaucratic phenomenon. This is so despite the fact that it is not only governments that operate bureaucracies. The administrative arms of large private enterprises may also be looked upon as bureaucracies. Nevertheless, there are special aspects of government bureaucracies that make them especially inappropriate to handle on the basis of standard microeconomic theory. For one thing, much of standard theory involves the essential postulate of a *simple* and a *measurable* criterion: the maximisation of profits. No similar criterion is readily applicable to the operation of government bureaucracies.

If we look upon cost-benefit analysis as part of micro theory then variants of that type of analysis have been used. Attempts have been made to analyse and calculate cost-efficient options. Under this approach the specific objectives are assumed to be given, and the problem that arises is the determination of cost-efficient allocation of resources to meet the given governmental objective. For example, attempts have sometimes been made to design cost-efficient weapon systems from given components of the system, if some criterion of the desired magnitude of the system is given. In this case the usual substitution theorems of microeconomics are applicable. However, this approach is normative. It misses the basic behavioural characteristics of bureaucracies.

An alternative way of looking at the problem is to examine the essentials of the general equilibrium model and to see whether or not it fits the bureaucracy phenomenon. Basically microeconomic theory is a theory of barter, which leads to an equilibrium that is Pareto optimal. Once equilibrium is reached, no further exchanges that are mutually beneficial to any possible set of agents can take place. It is useful to concentrate on the barter connection. Each agent gives up something and gets something in return. Each feels that what he gets is of greater utility than what he gives up. Let us focus our attention further on the product given up. The very act of focusing on exchange relation eliminates a great many concerns about 'efficiency' that exist in hierarchical organisations. For example, it is quite immaterial how the object given was obtained. It does not matter whether the individual obtained it in some other trade, whether it is an object obtained by inheritance or gift, whether the individual *made* or grew the object in question, or whether or not his (or her) *effort* entered in the creation of the object in question.

Suppose the individual constructed (manufactured) the object, and that he could have worked rapidly and made it in 10 hours, or slowly and completed it in 30 hours. The rate of work, the conditions of work, and the work atmosphere are 'purely private' concerns which are irrelevant to the exchange that takes place. The exchange price is the same irrespective of the pace of the effort. If he takes 30 hours to create the object, then we may calculate that his reward *per hour* is one-third of what it would be than if he took only 10 hours. But if such a *per hour* calculation is made, it is a private calculation and a private concern. Nobody else need care about it.

Once we leave the individual barter phenomenon, and consider what happens when we sever the barter connection, then we can see why many of these private concerns become public concerns. A shift of the individual from making something (which he will exchange) to work in a bureaucracy, creates effort-related considerations beyond the private. The barter connection is broken in the sense that what the individual *does* in the bureaucracy is no longer connected to what he receives in return.

Considerable remoteness from barter exists; layers of intermediaries are inserted into the situation. The bureaucratic employee receives a salary and carries out certain activities subject to a considerable degree of discretion. There is no clear connection between those who contribute to his salary, the taxpayer, direct or indirect services to taxpayers, and what the individual does. His activities are rarely identified as being for the benefit of *particular* taxpayers, and such benefits are never related to particular taxes paid. As a result a great many discretionary elements enter the picture which do not exist in the ordinary barter relation. We can no longer say that some agent is giving up something (taxes) for something he wants in return (government services.)

It is of some interest to see whether or not any aspects of standard microeconomic theory could be applied to the problem of the internal efficiency of bureaucracies. To start with, let us recall how the standard theory determines internal efficiency (or what we shall refer to as X-efficiency). The usual procedure in standard economics is *to assume* the internal efficiency. This usually follows as a corollary of the profit maximisation postulate. If profits are to be maximised, then this implies that for any given output costs must be minimised, and hence internal efficiency is assured. Obviously this approach is not likely to be very helpful if we are to examine the X-inefficiency of bureaucracies. There are some models of bureaucracies which assume the maximisation of some private interest of a chief bureaucrat, which might imply an interest in cost minimisation, but somehow this ignores a great many internal elements of the bureaucratic phenomenon. Hence, we shall not utilise this approach.

A more helpful approach, one which is sometimes used to argue for cost minimisation in competitive markets, is the one that appeals to an evolutionary selection of the fittest type of argument. Under this approach competitive pressure forces out the high-cost firms. Those that survive are the cost minimisers. An additional wrinkle to such an argument is to assume that there are eager entrepreneurs in the wings, so to speak, anxious to enter an industry and displace any firm or set of firms that produce at higher than minimal cost. While the normal idea of the competitive industry, or the idea of anxious entrepreneurs waiting to take over, cannot be applied to the problem of bureaucracies, the more general notion of external pressure on internal behaviour is applicable. In other words, we may view competitive pressures as simply one manifestation of *external pressure on internal performance*. This suggests the question of whether the external pressures that bear on a particular bureaucratic unit result in minimising inefficiency. A related question is whether one could determine differential degrees of efficiency that are the consequences of differential external pressures. In some general sense this will be one approach that we will attempt to use in the bits of analysis that follow.

On the basis of purely general considerations we are likely to come to the conclusion that bureaucratic inefficiency is a matter of degree. It is no different than the problem of the internal efficiency of private monopolistic or non-competitive enterprises. One should expect that many of the considerations that determine the internal efficiency of the latter should have the same bearing on governmental bureaucracies. Unfortunately, there is not a great deal of analysis developed by economists on the internal or the X-inefficiency of enterprises simply as a result of the tradition that we assume cost minimisation both in the case of competitive firms as well as for cases of lapses from competition. Nevertheless, we will attempt to use the X-efficiency theoretical framework to see if we can obtain at least a few conclusions about some of the factors that determine the efficiency of bureaucratic units. At this stage of our knowledge we should expect our results to be extremely limited. Perhaps the most we could hope for is the development of some critical questions suitable for further research.

A normal analytical scheme is to cut down large questions into smaller ones until the point is reached where some of the smaller ones appear to be answerable. It would seem natural in this particular case to separate the objectives of a bureaucratic unit from the efficiency with which it carries out particular objectives. Thus it is possible that the objectives may not make sense but they are carried out efficiently. However, such a separation of ends and means may not be legitimate if those in charge of the bureaucratic unit can also determine, or at least 'interpret', the ends involved. In the procedure to be used in what follows, we will generally assume that such a means/end separation is legitimate, although we should keep in mind the possibility that the interpretation of the ends by the bureaucrats has a bearing on efficiency.

II SOME IMPLICATIONS OF X-EFFICIENCY THEORY FOR A BUREAUCRACY

In this section we consider whether we could derive any implications for bureaucracy from X-efficiency theory. In order to proceed with the argument we will first sketch some of the postulates and characteristics of X-efficiency theory[1] and then attempt to apply them to the bureaucratic phenomenon.

(1) THE SHELTERING HYPOTHESIS

It is generally recognised that standard economic theory works best for competitive markets. This view is not challenged by any of the X-efficiency ideas. Rather, the view to be taken is that economic behaviour in non-competitive markets involves more significant behavioural differences than under pure competition. Furthermore, following certain tendencies recognised by Adam Smith over two centuries ago, we argue that part of economic behaviour involves the search for shelters from competition.

For example, we may visualise a map of the economy in which the X-axis identifies different industries, the Y-axis indicates the amount of GNP generated by each industry, and the Z-axis indicates the degree of shelter from competition of the industry or activity in question. The shelter size may be viewed as the difference between the minimum cost (zero shelter) and the maximum price possible. This idea would have to be reinterpreted for governmental agencies. However, assuming the service involved is determined in advance, we can visualise the size of the bureaucratic shelter as the difference between the actual budget and the budget that would allow the activity to be carried out at minimum cost. Thus we may view what follows as a foray into the economics of sheltered activities. We will return to the shelter notion later in our discussion.

(2) THE X-EFFICIENCY CONCEPT

A sheltered environment by definition permits higher than minimum costs. In standard micro theory efficiency is normally restricted to allocative efficiency. By X-efficiency we have in mind various types of

[1] For a fuller treatment of some of these matters see Leibenstein (1976, 1978, 1979).

non-allocative efficiencies. By X-inefficiency we are concerned with those inefficiencies that occur apart from those attributed to the misallocation of inputs and outputs that result from non-equilibrium market prices. Some types of X-inefficiencies can occur outside a specific economic unit, but for the most part, we will ignore these possibilities. Usually X-inefficiency occurs *within* economic units and may be measured as the deviation between actual cost and minimal cost of output for given purchased inputs. Examples of X-inefficiency are those that result from: (i) the poor utilisation of labour time; (ii) the poor utilisation of equipment; (iii) the poor timing patterns of work; (iv) inappropriate decision rules; (v) the lack of co-operation between unit members; (vi) the inappropriate choice of subobjectives; (vii) poor information processing and clogged information channels; (viii) the inappropriate space utilisation; (ix) the lack of appropriate access to decision-makers; and (x) poor bargaining effectiveness with other units.

(3) A THEORY OF GAMES PAYOFF MATRIX FOR MANAGEMENT-EMPLOYEE OPTIONS

Another introductory matter that we wish to consider is a theory of games approach to the determinants of productivity within an organisation. In standard economics it is assumed that employment contracts are such so that they are similar to ordinary exchange contracts. The employee receives a salary in return for a fixed quantity and quality of work. Herbert Simon has suggested that employment contracts are different, that individuals trade salary for the acceptance of authority. The view to be taken here differs somewhat from Simon's view in the sense that we will argue that within limits, the work aspect involves a significant discretionary element, and the actual amount of work produced will depend on the choice of options open to managers and employees. In any hierarchial organisation we may visualise those at some higher level in the hierarchy representing management, and those at a lower level representing employees. It is not very important for our purposes to change these terms as we shift from private enterprises to governmental bureaucratic units. The set of options on both sides is essentially a continuum, but it is simplest to illustrate it by a 3 by 3 matrix. The choices open to employees are the following:

E1 – co-operate with managers as much as possible;
E2 – co-operate with mates, that is fellow employees at more or less the same effort level;

E3 – maximise self-interest. Here we imply that there are activities which are in the interest of the bureaucracy and others which are primarily in the interest of the employee. Clearly the employee may choose a mix of such activities, or choose those primarily concerned with his own interests.

The management options are as follows:

M1 – maximise the sharing of bureaucratic gains with employees;
M2 – accept the 'mate rate' on the basis of historically established peer group effort standards;
M3 – attempt to use authority to the greatest degree in order to get maximum performance from the viewpoint of management without sharing any perquisites with lower level employees.

The payoff matrix shown in Table 9.1 indicates how the various combinations of options are likely to work out. If we look at the principal diagonal, then we see that there is a co-operative solution for the M1E1 case. Whether or not this solution fits the interests of the principals, i.e. the citizens, is of course another matter. The second possible solution is the peer group standard situation E2M2. The worst solution E3M3 is the one most likely to generate the most conflict and may be viewed as a Prisoner's Dilemma situation.

We shall not consider most aspects of the payoff matrix. The main purpose for introducing it is to indicate the complexity of the motivation problem within the bureaucratic work unit. But a few points should be considered. We want especially to focus our attention on the peer group standard solution, since I would conjecture that in most cases some such solution is likely to result in the long run. We note also that normal self-interest maximising behaviour on all sides can lead to an inferior solution for all concerned.

The co-operative solution has some special characteristics that we must consider. It is optimal only from the viewpoint of the utilities to be obtained by the bureaucratic management and their employees. However, such a co-operative solution in a bureaucracy may go against the interests of the principals, that is, the citizens. Of course if the managers are primarily concerned with citizen interests, then the co-operative solution may be the most desirable one from all viewpoints. The main point is the caution that there exists the possibility of a co-operative solution which is against the interest of the principals.

TABLE 9.1

Bureaucratic Management Options

Employee Options

	Management choices / Employees' choices	M1: Maximise sharing of gains with workers	M2: Accept peer work; Standard-Non-sharing	M3: Get most from employee; Pay least
E1	Co-operate with bureaucratic managers	Optimal Co-operative solutions 20 / 20	9 / 6	Best for Management 30 / 3
E2	Co-operate with mates only	9 / 6	Peer group standards Nash equilibria solutions 7–15 / 7–13	10 / 4
E3	Maximise personal gains	Best for employee 3 / 30	4 / 10	*Worst* Prisoner's Dilemma solution 5 / 5

(4) SOME X-EFFICIENCY THEORY POSTULATES

The basic postulates from which we will attempt to derive implications follow.

(*a*) *Individual effort discretion*

We assume that the relevant unit of analysis is the individual. Normally employment contracts are incomplete. The individual knows his salary, but the work (in some or most respects) is not determined in advance. Hence, some discretion exists. Effort is a major choice variable. We concentrate on three components of effort: activities (A), their pace (P) and the quality (Q) of these activities. Pace is frequently an observable, but quality is not necessarily so. Furthermore, the options from which the activities are chosen may also not be readily observable. Some tradeoffs may exist between A, P and Q.

We assume that an individual chooses an *effort position*. By this we have in mind a set of closely related routines which is a particular interpretation of his job. A specific routine is an APQ bundle. More than one routine may have to exist in order to meet external demands for effort.

(*b*) *Inert areas and routines*

By inert areas we have in mind something akin to inertia. The usual notion is that an effort position within an inert area associated with a certain utility will not result (in the short run) in a movement to a different position, even if that position is associated with a higher utility. Thus shocks may be necessary in order to move individuals out of their effort positions. The inert areas will generally have upper and lower bounds and shocks that result in movements outside of these bounds being required in order to obtain movement out of the inert areas.

(*c*) *General non-maximisation*

We assume that the basic behavioural principle for most individuals is something that might be called selective rationality. That is, the individual selects the degree to which he deviates from maximising behaviour. However, an individual is influenced both by (i) *internal pressures* (an ethic) and (ii) *external pressures* which may move him toward positions which reflect a greater or smaller deviation for maximising behaviour.

The internal pressures are a manifestation of an individual's personality. Usually individuals work out compromises between a desire to avoid responsibility and the demands of conscience.[2] Hence part of our behaviour is (at least in part) in response to an ethic, or to professional standards, to a sense of fairness or to loyalties of some sort – all of these forces may go counter to maximisation in some instances.

Among the external pressures are peer group influences, authority influences, and pressures that come from outside the bureaucratic unit. We assume that this is a general behavioural pattern for most individuals but it does not exclude the possibility of the existence of personalities whose behaviour approximates maximisation.

(*d*) *Agent-principal remoteness*

The employees of a bureaucratic unit are the agents for others. Whether the principals should be defined as the citizens of the country, or whether the principals are senior members of the government responsible for the running of the bureaucracy, is something we do not have to determine for present purposes. Unless otherwise indicated, we will assume that the principals are the citizens. In any event, the agents have some interests that differ from the interest of the principals.

(*e*) *Effort entropy*

We assume that there is a long-run tendency for an individual's effort in pursuit of the aims of the unit to fall to lower levels of effectiveness (up to some point) if external constraints and influences on effort are not maintained.

We now turn to consider some of the implications that are likely to follow from our postulates.

Firstly, it would seem clear that purchased inputs do not determine outputs. That is, the hiring of some set of individuals, and the purchase of equipment, does not by itself determine exactly what gets done within the unit. For a private firm this would suggest that a well-defined production function does not exist. A related way of viewing the matter is to see that even if it is desirable for individuals to work for an

[2] Without this characteristic contracts would hardly be possible.

efficiently operating unit, there is a free rider incentive for each individual not to contribute fully to that effort. In general, all of this follows from the notion of individual effort discretion, and differential interests between agents and principals.

Secondly, it follows immediately from the above that there is no need for costs per unit of service to be minimised. Indeed we should normally expect that cost minimisation will not result.

Thirdly, however, actual effort may turn out to be greater than the minimal effort that would result from following procedural rules, and the risk of facing procedural sanctions. The reason for this is that the variety of pressures external to the individual such as peer group approval, the influence of past history, and the non-maximisation of individual self-interests lead to a higher than minimal performance.

Fourthly, the inert area postulate suggests that historically established effort levels may be difficult to change without some shock element involved.

Finally, the various ideas introduced so far suggest that a balance of pressures mode of analysis may be useful in narrowing down the actual performance level within the range determined by the degree of shelter achieved by the bureaucratic managers. We should note that in this particular formulation, we cannot as readily appeal to some sort of maximisation theory of motivation, since such appeals are less forceful once we have severed the cash or barter nexus. The motivations behind the idea of exchange for mutual gain are no longer fully applicable.

III THE BALANCE OF PRESSURES APPROACH

We will use the word 'pressure' in a very broad sense, and we shall be concerned with both the internal pressure of the individual as well as various types of external pressures; those outside the individual, and those outside the work unit.

There are two broad elements that are likely to determine the degree of X-efficiency: the size of the shelter, which in the short run may depend on the size of the budget, and the nature of the effort choices. However, we do not assume budget maximisation by bureau chiefs.

One of the most difficult elements to determine is the size of the budget. In part this is likely to depend on what the bureau managers want, and the extent to which they can get what they want from others in the larger bureaucracy. We will assume that a bureau chief can carry out certain activities to influence the budget he obtains for his bureau. But he need not wish to maximise the size of the budget. Other considerations may limit or blunt such a desire. For instance, the bureau chief may wish to avoid the confrontations necessary to increase the budget beyond a certain size because such confrontations may also increase the scrutiny that his bureau receives. Part of the sheltered atmosphere may depend on a lack of detailed scrutiny. Other considerations that come to mind are (i) the degree to which a larger budget implies superior performance expectations; or (ii) the degree to which it competes with a public service on the part of bureau managers; (iii) the influence of professional standards; or (iv) competition for limited lobbying resources, some of which can be used for purposes other than budget maximisation. In addition, not all bureau managers are necessarily maximising types. Some may suffer from considerable inertia and be quite happy to let well enough alone. In general we may visualise that the bureau chief, and those closely associated with bureau management, may be concerned with a number of considerations, some of which compete with budget maximisation. In any event, we can assume that they are likely to wish to maintain the current degree of shelter, or to expand it if at all possible. Thus in some way the set of considerations mentioned, and the degree to which the bureau chief is a maximiser, will determine the size of the budget.

However, we should keep it in mind that budget size is not the only element that determines the extent of the shelter. The bureau will usually have some degree of discretion, however limited, in determining the nature of the service it renders to clients, or in the reinterpretation of these services. Hence, the budget and the interpretation of the services will determine what we have referred to as the shelter size.

Let us look briefly at a question of the choice of effort. A systematic way of doing this is in terms of a lexicographic ordering. As an example, consider the case in which this ordering has five levels in a hierarchy. These are (i) a work ethic; (ii) a convention; (iii) habit; (iv) routines determined on the basis of partial calculation; and (v) full calculation (see Figure 9.1). The abscissa in Figure 9.1 represents the switchover costs from one level of the hierarchy to the other. For example, if the choice made according to a work ethic involves too high a 'pressure cost', then there is a shift to a conventional effort level. Note that only the fully calculating choices approximate maximising behaviour.

Another, but related, way of looking at this matter is to assume that the choices are continuous. This is illustrated in Figure 9.2. The ordinate (on a scale from zero to one) indicates the degree to which a decision process approaches fully calculating behaviour. The abscissa indicates

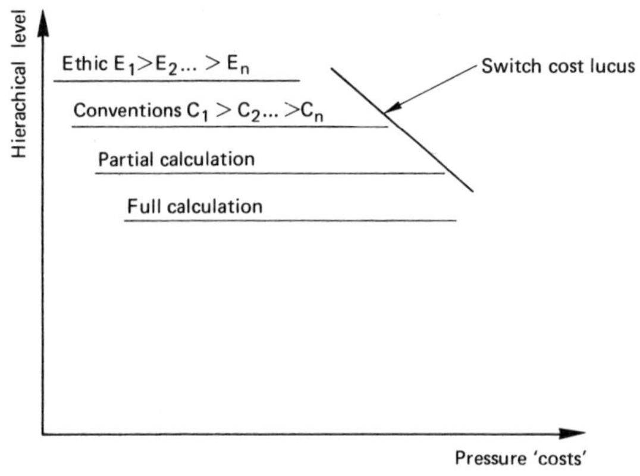

FIG. 9.1

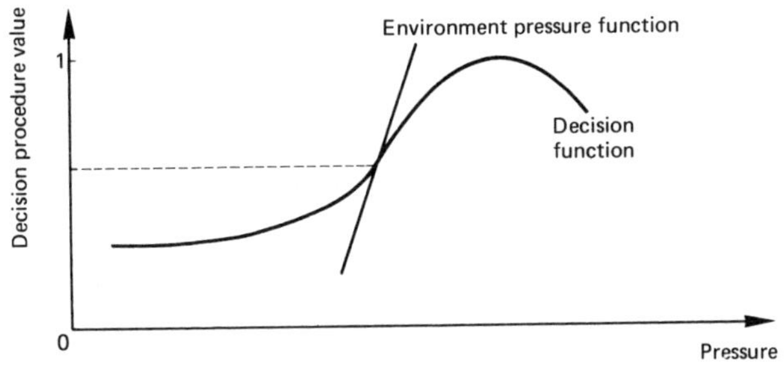

FIG. 9.2

degrees of pressure. The graph indicates that as pressure increases, up to some point, we choose decision procedures that come closer to full calculation. We also show an environmental pressure function, which is in part given by external circumstances, and the intersection between the two curves determines an equilbrium decision procedure.

We observe that the first two levels of the ordering are of a transindividualistic nature. That is to say, they take into account either the feelings of others directly, or the feelings of others in the past, when the work ethic was determined. For the most part such elements as a work ethic or a professional standard involve some sense of internalised pressure which is partially within the individual.

An extremely important type of effort choice is likely to be one that follows some convention. Conventions have been analysed from a number of viewpoints, and it may be useful to consider this matter briefly. One way of doing so would be to look upon the convention as a co-ordination problem from a theory of games perspective. (See the book by Lewis (1969), for an elaboration of this viewpoint.) A simple case is that of the choice of what side of the road to drive an automobile. Both parties can choose either right or left. There is likely to be a very high payoff for those who choose the same side of the road, and a very low payoff for those who choose the opposite side. Once the convention exists (whether it is right or left), there is every reason to stick to the convention. In other words, we may visualise another payoff matrix in which the pro-convention choices have very much higher utilities for all parties than the anti-convention choices.

Another aspect of conventions we should consider is the fact that conventions may continue to have value simply because we care about other people's approval or disapproval of the convention, even if the functional aspects of the convention do not pertain. Thus, some people will not go the wrong way down a one-way street if somebody else is watching, even if there is certainty that no other automobiles are coming the other way. A convention may persist despite the fact that its functional value to a number of individuals may have disappeared. At the same time, because of uncertainty, and free rider considerations, no one may take the initiative to alter the conventional mode of behaviour. It seems likely in many bureaucratic organisations that some form of a convention will determine the nature of individual effort. We may look upon these conventions as themselves imposing pressure from peers (sometimes from authorities) to persist in the convention. This is especially likely to be the case when there is no other guideline for that particular type of behaviour.

There are additional conventions that go beyond the work place. These are clearest in the cases of well-organised professional groups. In fact in such cases non-local professional standards will frequently dominate local conventions. As a consequence these, in a sense, form an important pressure on the nature of work from outside the organisation.

However, it seems quite likely that for most employees in a bureau, such external professional standards are not relevant considerations.

Three other external pressures are likely to be extremely important in determining the nature of effort. These are (i) the budgetary pressure; (ii) client pressure; and (iii) overseer pressure. Obviously, the size of the organisation will depend on the budget provided. We have already touched on the budget determination problem. To some degree costs may determine the budget claim but not all budget claims are met. On the other hand, the budget achieved may by itself determine effort and through determining effort may by itself determine cost. Hence the interaction between budgets determining costs, and costs determining budgets, must be taken into account. We have here a type of demand and supply interaction, or implicit bargaining interactions which determine the budget.

All work in a bureaucratic unit is in some sense for someone – at least in principle. The clearest cases are those for which the work is for clients outside the bureau. For example, bureaux which process drivers' licence applications and issue these licences are in response to the demand of citizens wishing to obtain those licences. Postal savings arrangements, the operation of the post office, and so on, are of a similar nature. In these cases client demand determines the amount of the work involved and to some degree the nature of the work. It is less clear what determines demand when the clients are entirely from within the bureaucracy. However, even such situations may be similar where the nature of the 'product' is fairly clear cut. In any case, we can see that to some degree client pressure would determine the work that is demanded and in its turn the work that is produced.

Almost all bureaucratic organisations have some type of overseeing arrangements. In other words, somebody is usually assigned the job of inspecting either directly or indirectly the operations of various bureaucratic units. For instance, in the US government the Office of Management and the Budget is officially assigned this task. In some cases some overseeing activities may be performed and in others they may actually put on pressure for performance.

In general, we can see that some combination of these external pressures influences the level of internal efficiency. Michel Crozier's classic work on *The Bureaucratic Phenomenon* (1964) starts with an example of a Parisian unit, which renders financial services to citizens, which is highly efficient. The reason for its high degree of internal efficiency seems to be that (i) the services are very well defined. In particular, (ii) clients put on a very high degree of pressure for the provision of the service, and (iii) a traditionally stingy finance department provided a low budget which in its turn put on a high degree of budgetary pressure which kept costs for employees quite low. Because of these pressures the activity in question was carried out efficiently given its scale. The scale of the operation was probably suboptimal. For present purposes it may be easy to see that the absence of such pressures may result in a lax work environment and high costs per unit of service.

IV SUMMARY

An implicit assumption behind the previous section is that the service rendered by the bureau has a positive value. If it has a negative value, then our conclusions have to be reversed. For negative valued services, it is desirable that as little as possible of it be produced for a given budget. In a sense inefficiency is efficiency for negative products. For example, it would be desirable that an oppressive police force be inefficient.

A qualifying remark must be made about the overseeing function. While overseers may put pressure for performance on the bureau, they may also overemphasise accountability and procedural rules. The latter are a drain on effort. As a result it is possible that on balance the overseeing function may reduce performance. However, in what follows we will assume that this is not the case on balance. However, the reader should keep the qualification in mind.

We now turn to summarise our general approach. The degree of X-inefficiency is determined by the range of effort discretion, and by the elements determining effort choice made by all members of the bureaucratic unit. In general the efforts of the bureau chief will be directed towards retaining or expanding the sheltered environment for the bureau. The shelter is facilitated by (i) an adequate or increased budget and/or (ii) the redefinition of the service for the given budget. But there are elements that militate against general budget maximisation, which include the avoidance of confrontations, a public service ethic, and a fear that higher budgets may imply unusually high performance standards, as well as the fact that some budget chiefs may not be maximising personalities.

The balance of pressures that determine X-inefficiency are (i) the size of the budget; (ii) client demand; and (iii) the demands of the overseers. These elements become part of the external pressures on individual bureau members which become part of the determinants of their effort choices. These determine the degree of X-inefficiency of the bureau.

REFERENCES

Because of the pressure of time the body of this paper did not contain adequate references to the literature. The following were of value to the writer and some may be of interest to the reader.

Kenneth J. Arrow, *The Limits of Organization* (Norton, New York, 1974).

Randall Bartlett, *Economic Foundations of Political Power* (Free Press, New Press, New York, 1973).

Michel Crozier, *The Bureaucratic Phenomenon* (University of Chicago Press, 1964).

Anthony Downs, *Inside Bureaucracy* (Little, Brown, Boston, 1967).

Bruno S. Frey, *Modern Political Economy* (Wiley, New York, 1978).

Harvey Leibenstein, *Beyond Economic Man* (Harvard University Press, Cambridge, 1976).

Harvey Leibenstein, 'On the Basic Proposition of X-Efficiency Theory', *American Economic Review* (May 1978), 328–33.

Harvey Leibenstein, 'A Branch of Economics is Missing: Micro-Micro Theory', *Journal of Economic Literature* (June 1979).

David K. Lewis, *Conventions* (Harvard University Press, Cambridge, 1969).

James G. March and Herbert A. Simon, *Organizations* (Wiley, New York, 1958).

William A. Niskanen, *Bureaucracy: Servant or Master*? (Institute of Economic Affairs, London, 1973).

Gordon Tullock, *The Politics of Bureaucracy* (Public Affairs Press, Washington, 1969).

Discussion of 'Notes on X-efficiency and Bureaucracy' by Professor H. Leibenstein

The discussion was introduced by *Dr Stafford* who suggested three areas in which the approach presented might be developed. The first concerned the nature of more specific assumptions than those presented about the motivation of bureaucrats from which specific refutable predictions might be derived. The second concerned what phenomena such predictions might explain. He thought that it would be difficult to derive predictions of unit costs because of the difficulties of measuring bureaucratic output and of accounting for the impact on costs of factors other than those being studied. However, his view was that it should be possible to derive predictions about the nature of the employment contract in bureaucracies and about the reaction of bureaucrats to externally given policy changes. The third area concerned the normative implications, if any, of the analysis. Dr Stafford invited Professor Leibenstein to expand on the following specific points of his argument: the relationship between bureaucratic 'shelter' and the size of the budget; the ill-defined production function of an X-inefficient bureaucracy; and the lexicographic and hierarchical structure of the system of behavioural codes in Figure 9.1. He did not see any reason for a systematic relationship between budget size and the excess of actual costs over minimum attainable costs (the measure of bureaucratic shelter). Professor Leibenstein's argument that the production function only seemed correct to him on the assumption that behaviour patterns within the bureaucracy were unstable. Finally he did not see the sense in which the behavioural codes in Figure 9.1 were related together hierarchically, nor the sense in which the adoption of one code was a precondition for the choice of another.

In order to clarify the concept of the minimum cost of a unit of bureaucratic output, *Professor Bös* suggested a distinction between the institutional and personnel structure of a bureaucracy and the decisions on production made within that structure. He argued that minimum unit cost should be defined for the given decision-making structure, elements of which would be externally determined by, for example, rules on consultation and accessibility imposed on bureaucracies by parliaments. He drew attention to the omission from the matrix of Table 9.1 of the pay-offs E1M2 and E2M1, and to what in his view was the lack of a connection in the paper between the alternative payoffs in the matrix and the level of efficiency of the bureau. On this latter point he argued that the particular result of the Prisoner's Dilemma may not be inefficient from the point of view of the consumers of the service of the bureau, even though it might be the least efficient solution from the point of view of the management and employees of the bureaucracy.

Several speakers expressed the view that Professor Leibenstein's analysis underestimated the forces making for efficiency in bureaux. *Professor Sir Austin Robinson*'s experience was that civil servants in the United Kingdom were less concerned with their own self-interest than the analysis of the paper assumed, and that competition for promotion was an important spur to efficiency. The source of inefficiency of which he had experience in developing countries was the practice of checking and counter-checking everything, which led to overmanning and inefficiency. *Professor Bacskai* thought that the analysis underestimated the pressure on bureaux arising from the coverage of their activities in the media and from the competition between them over the design of major projects such as road-building, which often affected the interests of several government departments. *Sir Leo Pliatzky*'s experience was that many of the features of bureaucratic decision-making described in the paper were to be found at lower levels in government departments. But in his view the picture was very different at the political and higher official levels. He described the Cabinet system of government in the United Kingdom and pointed to the speed with which this system was able to formulate interministerial policy and resolve conflicting objectives, which was the central purpose of government. He contrasted this situation with the difficulty of formulating interagency policy in the central bureaucracy of the United States which did not operate a Cabinet system.

However, other speakers were not convinced that Professor Leibenstein's paper had exaggerated the possibility of inefficient bureaucratic behaviour. *Mr Matthews* suggested that competition for promotion may lead to fawning behaviour designed to satisfy superiors, with highly inefficient results. *Professor Klein*'s view was that a dominant motive in the British Civil Service was the desire to minimise mistakes. His experience was that an assumption of budget maximisation such as was often used in models of bureaucratic behaviour was not appropriate for the United Kingdom. He conceded that it might be more usefully applied to the United States where there was a much more entrepreneurial ethos in government. *Mr Lengyel* identified patterns of routine behaviour as a major cause of bureaucratic inefficiency. He argued that the inability of a code of routine to discriminate between trivial and important issues induced a superficial treatment of the latter and excessive senior supervision over the former. There was thus induced a false sense of perpetual crisis which made an effective response to real crises more difficult. His experience of international bureaucracy was summed up as 'overcontrol and undermanagement'. *Professor Frey* argued that no relevant group or institution had an incentive to control bureaucratic behaviour in the interests of greater efficiency. In his view, interest groups and governments required the active co-operation of bureaucrats. Members of Parliament had no interest in an antagonistic relationship with bureaucrats, and in some western countries (Germany, Switzerland and Austria in particular) bureaucrats occupied a majority of seats in Parliament. The public good characteristic of cost reductions in bureaucracies removed the incentive to act from individual voters. In addition he pointed to the inefficiency of the rigid and protected career structure of public bureaucracies in Germany and Austria. *Professor Modigliani* thought that some of the differences of view expressed on this question derived from the fact that different levels of bureaucratic decision-making were in fact being discussed, whereas the concern of the paper was with lower levels of decision-making within bureaucracies.

There was a short discussion of the related issue of the efficiency of public bureaucracies and private firms. *Mr Matthews* suggested that an important constraint on activity in the public sector which did not limit behaviour of private producers was the requirement of fairness and impartiality between individuals. The application of this required elaborate procedures which might be wrongly interpreted as inefficient. *Sir Leo Pliatzky* took up this point by drawing attention to the resources that must be devoted to the recording of decisions if impartiality were to be observed. He insisted that such activity was not unnecessary and inefficient.

Mr Kaser suggested that numbers employed might be a better indicator of bureaucratic shelter than the size of the budget. However, numbers employed and thus shelter could be reduced by policy. As evidence of this he cited cuts in public expenditure introduced by the new Conservative administration in the United Kingdom and the unrest in the Civil Service they had given rise to. *Professor Klein* pointed to the difficulty of measuring the output to bureaucracies, and to the need for a comprehensive taxonomy of output measures which might prevent the use of contradictory measures. As an example of the latter problem he cited the use by the Department of Health and Social Security in the United Kingdom of measures of applications for social security payment processed per civil servant and of measures of the reciprocal of appeals against decisions on such applications. Different and potentially conflicting measures of output were also used in the health service, one of which was the attainment of consensus between the professional providers of the service.

In reply to Dr Stafford, *Professor Leibenstein* expressed his wish to develop more fully the concept of bureaucratic shelter. His view of the production relationship was that it could not be well-defined if all factors affecting output were not controllable, as was the case in bureaucracies. He did not see any ambiguity in the analysis of behavioural codes. In reply to Professor Bös, he did not accept that existing institutional and personnel structures should be taken as constraints in defining efficiency. He agreed on the importance of linking the outcomes of the matrix with efficiency, but argued that the main purpose of the matrix was to illustrate the complexity of possible outcomes. Professor Leibenstein's response to other points raised was to point out that it was not an implication of his analysis that bureaucratic outcomes were necessarily inefficient, and that his remarks on work effort did not amount to the proposition that bureaucrats did not work hard. His view was that some may work hard and some may not, but that working hard did not mean working efficiently. He found especially useful Professor Frey's comments on incentives, and the distinction that had emerged between the judgement of the citizen and that of the bureaucrat on the efficiency of bureaucratic behaviour.

10 The Financing of Collective Consumption in Yugoslavia

Pero Jurković, Zoran Jăsić and Slobodan Lang

INSTITUTE OF ECONOMICS, ZAGREB

INTRODUCTION

The problems associated with the financing of collective consumption in any country can be analysed from various points of view. In this paper, the problems of the financing of collective consumption in Yugoslavia will be dealt with briefly from three aspects: the volume and the trends in collective consumption; the existing institutional structure of the financing of collective consumption; and finally, from the ideological/theoretical point of view which underlies the existing as well as the future system of financing collective consumption.

I THE VOLUME AND TRENDS OF COLLECTIVE CONSUMPTION

In this paper, collective consumption comprises all financing from the resources obtained from taxes, contributions and other similar receipts. We are, thus, concerned with public and collective goods[1] of different

[1] In Yugoslav terminology 'public goods' ('general social needs' or 'general consumption') are the so-called 'pure public goods', i.e. those goods which require no payment of any kind for their use. On the other hand, by the term 'collective goods' ('collective consumption') we mean all other types of collective goods whose beneficiaries are certain well-defined social groups. However, most collective goods defined in this way are characterised by external effects and their supply should therefore be socially organised. This is the case with such social services as education, health, science, culture and social protection.

types which are at the disposal of all members of the community. By this criterion, collective consumption covers all expenditures required for the functioning of governmental agencies and institutions: national defence, the operation and extension of social services (education, science, culture, health, etc.), social security and social protection; basic communal infrastructure, environmental protection, and, in a wider context, state intervention in the economy.

In 1976, the amount spent in Yugoslavia on financing collective consumption as defined above was 225.492 million dinars which constituted 40.5 per cent of the country's GNP for that year.[2] The structure of social receipts and expenditures was as shown in Table 10.1.

TABLE 10.1

Receipts	%	*Disbursements*	%
Total receipts	100.0	Total expenditures	100.0
1. Taxes and contributions from income of working organisations	11.0	1. Expenditure for commodities, services and investments	51.0
2. Taxes and contributions from personal incomes	39.2	2. For personal incomes	17.7
3. Property taxes and receipts from property ownership	1.1	3. Other outlays and transfers:	31.3
4. Turnover tax	20.9	3.1 Transfers to individuals	23.4
5. Customs duties	11.2		
6. Stamp duties	0.7	3.2 Transfers to economy	7.9
7. Other receipts	15.9		

Source: Statistical Bulletin of SDK, No. 12/1977.

The proportion of collective consumption in the GNP of Yugoslavia is among the highest in the world, while the per capita GNP of about US $1680 in 1976 was at the level reached by OECD countries some twenty years earlier.

Such a large proportion of the social product used for social consumption creates significant difficulties for the Yugoslav economy by diminishing its resources for capital formation, weakening its competitiveness on foreign markets and threatening its economic stability. These difficulties are all the more serious since Yugoslavia is still a country with an extreme need for rapid development.

[2] This figure would be reduced by approximately 10% if the method of calculating the GNP in West European countries were used.

In spite of the already high share of collective consumption in the GNP, there is a tendency towards its further increase. Within collective consumption, there is a particularly dynamic growth in social services (see Table 10.2).

The large increase in collective consumption, and especially the dynamic increases in payments for social services, is due to more or less

TABLE 10.2 THE SHARE OF TOTAL EXPENDITURES FOR SOCIAL SERVICES IN THE GNP OF YUGOSLAVIA
(Percentage measured at current prices)

	1960	*1965*	*1971*	*1976*
Total social services	11.7	12.7	14.7	15.5
education	3.8	4.2	4.6	4.8
science	0.9	1.0	1.0	1.0
arts	0.4	0.4	0.5	0.6
health	4.4	5.0	5.5	5.9
social security	1.0	0.9	1.3	1.4
sports	0.5	0.5	0.8	0.9

Source: Social Services as a Function of Economic Development and the Standard of Living (The Institute of Public Finance, Zagreb, 1978), p. 29.

the same factors that are at work in other countries; they include a general improvement in the standard of living of the population, technical progress which has made social services a prerequisite for economic development, an increasingly important link between the efficiency of certain social services and the capital-labour ratios employed in them. In the Yugoslav case, we have to stress the socialist character of its socio-economic system which values highly the principle of solidarity in meeting collective needs.

As a result of the relatively high expenditures on collective consumption, significant advances have been made in raising the educational, cultural and health standards, as well as in the construction of the overall social infrastructure. In 1976, there were 760 persons for every physician and 167 persons per hospital bed; practically the entire population between the ages of 7–14 was enjoying eight years at elementary school; 39 per cent of those between the ages of 15–18 years were attending some form of secondary education. With a student population of 19 per thousand, Yugoslavia ranks among leading countries in the world; in the same year, there were 270 research institutions with a staff of 7910.

Nonetheless, due to inherited imbalances in regional development, the problem of unequal levels of collective consumption and availability of social services between different republics and autonomous regions remains. This problem persists in spite of considerable resources (around 1 per cent of the GNP) allocated for supplementary financing of collective consumption in less developed regions. If we take average per capita collective consumption in Yugoslavia in 1976 as 100, the breakdown by republics and regions is as follows: Bosnia and Herzegovina 64, Montenegro 81, Croatia 116, Macedonia 68, Slovenia 186, Serbia Proper 109, Kosovo 51 and Vojvodina 104. But since the relative volume of collective consumptions does not depend entirely on the level of economic development, these differences in per capita collective consumption are considerably smaller than the differences in the per capita social products.

It can be seen that in the financing of collective consumption, Yugoslavia is faced by similar problems to those of other (and especially developing) countries. First and foremost is the disparity between increasing demands and limited material resources to satisfy them. Second, under conditions of growing competition between different social needs, there is the problem of optimising the structure of collective consumption. Both problems require a mechanism of optimisation of collective consumption within the limits of restricted material resources and the given socio-economic system.

II THE INSTITUTIONAL STRUCTURE

Under existing constitutional arrangements, the system of financing collective consumption in Yugoslavia can be divided into three subsystems:

(1) the financing of general social needs in socio-political communities (budgetary financing);
(2) the financing of collective needs in the field of social services;
(3) the financing of collective needs in the sphere of material reproduction.

The breakdown of the total social receipts in 1976 between the different forms of financing of collective consumption was as follows:

(1) general social needs, 38.0 per cent;
(2) collective needs in social services, 47.6 per cent;
(3) collective needs in the sphere of material reproduction, 14.4 per cent.

The first subsystem, the financing of general social needs, includes expenditures for the operation of governmental agencies and institutions; expenditures for national defence; supplementary financing of less developed socio-political communities; that part of the financing of social services where beneficiaries are hard to identify and which can therefore not be financed in the usual way through self-managing communities of interest, and similar arrangements.

General social needs are financed through the budgets of socio-political communities. Funds for this purpose are raised through taxes and other similar revenues. In this sense, this subsystem has, at least in the formal sense, retained all the basic characteristics of a classic fiscal system and we shall not analyse it in detail. We should mention, however, that the budget with its atrophied structure of payments and very one-sided structure of budgetary revenues, dominated by indirect taxes, has almost ceased to function as an instrument of economic (and particularly stabilisation) policy. In view of the reduction in the importance of the state in the whole Yugoslav economic system, this should not be considered as a special handicap.

Within the framework of the most recent constitutional reforms,[3] most significant changes have been made in the financing of collective needs, both in respect of social services (education, science, culture and health) and in respect of material reproduction (the financing of certain forms of economic infrastructure and social intervention in the economy). Following this reform, the financing of both categories of collective needs became the responsibility of specially created self-managing communities of interest, organised on the principle of the so-called 'free exchange of labour'.

Having regard to the importance which the concept of free exchange of labour has for the future development of the system for financing collective consumption in Yugoslavia, the remainder of the discussion in this paper will be concerned with an exposition of the essence of this concept, its normative structure and current theoretical thinking with regard to it.

III THE THEORETICAL ISSUES

The concept of free exchange of labour derives from the essential ideas which constitute the basis of the Yugoslav socio-economic system.

[3] See *The Constitution of the Socialist Federal Republic of Yugoslavia* (Official Gazette, Belgrade, 1974).

These are: social ownership of the means of production; self-management as a direct and egalitarian decision-making process within which workers manage all the essential aspects of social reproduction and thus control the conditions and the results of their labour; the free association of labour and pooling of resources; an economic system which includes elements of the market mechanism and planning; and finally, a democratic political system based on the principle of delegation.

Within the framework of the so-defined socio-economic system, the concept of free exchange of labour has an important role. In a self-regulating manner it directly connects two interdependent spheres of social labour – the sphere of material production and the sphere of social services. By free exchange of labour we mean a direct and mutual co-operation between workers in the social services sector (the providers of services) and workers engaged in material production (beneficiaries of services). They co-operate through joint decision-making concerning the conditions, the volume and the manner in which certain collective needs are to be financed and also in joint planning of the development of social services. At the same time workers in the social services have the opportunity to influence the developments in the sphere of material production in such a way that social needs and demands are adequately satisfied. Thus the essence of free exchange of labour is the conscious elimination of middlemen and third parties in the interaction between the different spheres of social labour.[4]

The free exchange of labour is based on the premise that social services have an increasingly important role to play within associated labour. Its role is not only in meeting collective needs and enhancing the quality of life, but in creating certain preconditions for increasing labour productivity in material production as well.

> It is quite clear that social services do not create value in the material sense; but it is also obvious that some of them essentially, often decisively, and in future even more significantly, contribute to the development of productive forces, labour productivity and better results in material production in general. In this sense, the sphere of material production and social services constitutes an integrated whole and a totality of associated labour.[5]

[4] See V. Zeković: 'Free Exchange of Labour in the System of Associated Labour', *Marxist Thought*, no. 2 (Belgrade, 1979), 86.

[5] E. Kardelj, 'Free Association of Labour', *Workers' Press* (Belgrade, 1978), 117.

It follows from what has been said that a portion of the income in the productive sector orginates from the social services sector. Undoubtedly, the contribution of certain social services to the national income is very indirect and hard to measure. Some services are completely unrelated to material production, but contribute to the quality of life and the development of society as a whole. In this sense, their costs must be treated as 'necessary social consumption'.

Since we regard the social services as a part of social productive labour in a wider sense, it is becoming increasingly inappropriate to treat them exclusively as 'consumers' as opposed to 'creators' of income. Considering that social services directly or indirectly influence the performance in material production, they should be enabled to share in the jointly created income. Under conditions of self-management association of labour, it should be regarded as being not only a right but also an obligation of the social services to base their income and their material position on the value they contribute to creating in material production, their contribution to increasing the productivity of social labour and to the development of society as a whole.[6] In this way, an opportunity will be created for the material position of workers in the social services sector to be equated to that of workers in material production.

The free exchange of labour as a system of meeting collective needs has certain characteristics which distinguish it from both the budgetary and the market-determined systems. It is the antithesis of the budgetary system in that it eliminates the state as middleman in this sphere and replaces it with self-management agreements between the providers and the beneficiaries of social services. The existence of free exchange of labour does not however, entirely exclude the role of the state. The function of the state is the legal regulation of those elements on which the free exchange of labour is based. Further, the state must intervene in any situation in which agreements between providers and beneficiaries of social services concerning certain forms of collective consumption do not reflect the wider social interest.

Again, the free exchange of labour differs from the market determined system in the meeting of collective needs since the activity of social services already presents itself as socially necessary labour in the phase of production decisions. In other words, the activity of work organisations in this sector, as expressed in their production programmes, is planned both in volume and quality in terms of the criterion of socially

[6] See 'The Associated Labour Act, Article 92', *Official Gazette of the Socialist Federative Republic of Yugoslavia* (Belgrade, 1976), p. 63.

necessary labour. In this sense, these work organisations are led to carry through those programmes which confirm their labour directly as socially necessary labour. The basic idea behind this principle is not altered by the existence of certain exceptions, for example when the planned costs of marginal producers are absorbed in order to achieve a more even territorial distribution of social services.

The reintroduction of market elements into the free exchange of labour is not acceptable for the very reasons which have led to the placing of social services in the public sector. Among these reasons are that the urgency of collective needs is not always adequately indicated by the volume of effective demand; that there is a time lag between the time when needs are identified and the time when they can be satisfied; the existence of temporal and generational discrepancies between costs and benefits for certain collective needs; the predominantly protective character of outlays in the social services sector; numerous external effects present in the sphere of social services; the role of social services as a foundation for the achievement of social solidarity.

But this does not necessarily imply that all links between the market and the free exchange of labour have been severed. There are at least two reasons why these links must continue to exist under conditions of commodity production. Firstly, the income of the social services sector is created in the sphere of material production, which, in turn, operates under predominantly market conditions; and secondly, decisions reached in the free exchange of labour system are based on valuations which have been established through market relations (input prices, distribution of income parameters, and so on).

We can conclude from the above that the main aims of the free exchange of labour as a mechanism for meeting collective needs are the following: firstly, to ensure an egalitarian socio-economic position for workers in the social services sectors (the providers of services) in relation to other workers in the associated labour system; secondly, to ensure a direct participation of those groups who are beneficiaries of services in the framing of the programmes of the work organisations in the social services sector, and to enable them to influence the way in which funds allocated to this sector are to be used; thirdly, to enable the providers of services to influence the developments in the sphere of material production; fourthly, to ensure that the structural and overall development of social services (and thus the volume of collective consumption) reflects the potentials and the needs of associated labour and of society as a whole. In other words, the socio-political significance of free exchange of labour is its ability to create conditions in which workers (both in the sphere of material production and in social services) can jointly determine the conditions in which they work and dispose of the results of their labour. Using the terminology of Marxist political economy, the free exchange of labour creates the conditions under which surplus of labour is converted into necessary labour.[7] The economic problem takes the form of establishing an optimum level and structure of collective consumption and thereby balancing the development and the activities of the social services with the level of material development of the whole society.

The actual mechanism for the free exchange of labour is based on the following assumptions: self-management communities of interest as the organisational forms of the free exchange of labour; self-management agreements as a means of reaching joint decisions; programmes for satisfying collective needs; contributions as a form of pooling assets; a decision-making system based on the principle of delegation.

Self-management communities of interest are associations of the groups which supply social services and those who benefit from them. The providers and the beneficiaries from social services in a self-management community of interest reach decisions on a basis of equality on the following subjects: the meeting of specific collective needs; the formation of programmes for meeting these needs; the finding of sources of finance and the pooling of funds for these programmes; the criteria for evaluating the performance of existing programmes of services; development plans for various social services and the methods of financing them; and finally any other subject relevant to the satisfactory functioning of the free exchange of labour. Within the framework of self-management communities of interest, the beneficiaries of services meet separately in order to reach agreement among themselves on problems arising from unequal individual capacity to pay or unequal exposure to risks involving differences of demand for certain services (e.g. health). From this point of view, self-management communities of interest are communities of solidarity and common risk.

The mutual relations between the providers and the beneficiaries of services in a self-management community of interest are regulated by self-management agreements. Within self-management communities of interest, the beneficiaries from services have complete power to determine the way in which their funds will be used. On the other hand, the providers of services have the right, through free exchange, to secure a socio-economic position which will put them on a par with workers in

[7] See K. Marx: *Capital, III, Culture* (Zagreb, 1948), p. 782.

other organisations of associated labour. In this sense, all decisions reached in a self-management community of interest must be endorsed by both the 'Chamber of Providers' and the 'Chamber of Beneficiaries'. If agreement cannot be reached between the two chambers on a crucial issue, specially constituted organs or socio-political communities arbitrate as representatives of wider social interests.

Rational decision-making in the process of free exchange of labour pre-supposes different levels of organisation of self-managing communities of interest, as well as a preliminary agreement determining the level at which certain collective needs will be satisfied. Different levels of the organisation of self-managing community of interest in different social services are determined by the optimum internalisation of the effects of decisions and in some cases (for instance in health) by choosing the optimum community of risk.

Self-management communities of interest are constituted either on a territorial or a functional basis or a combination of the two. Self-managing communities of interest are most frequently established at the commune level, and they very rarely cover a wider area. A number of self-management communities of interest can together form larger (regional) communities of interest and establish associations or other organisational bodies at the republic or federal levels.

The actual level at which collective needs are to be satisfied can be determined by law or by self-management agreements and social compacts. Regulation by law is obligatory only in those cases when self-management decision-making proves inadequate for the protection of certain social interests.

One of the most important elements in the free exchange of labour is the programming of collective needs and the planning of the development of the social services. Programming and planning in the free exchange of labour system are essential for the proper identification of collective needs. For that purpose they must include quantitative and qualitative criteria for the evaluation of the execution of the existing programme. The difficulty here is that the methodology of planning in most social services has not defined a satisfactory way of measuring their performance. Plans and programmes for meeting collective needs are made both at the level of the service providers and at the level of the beneficiaries and are co-ordinated with each other in the self-management communities of interest. This results in the programmes of self-managing communities of interest, which are in turn incorporated into the plans of socio-political communities. This procedure of planning has all the characteristics of polycentric-type planning.

A point which needs to be strongly emphasised is the necessity of basing the free exchange of labour on long-term development planning for the social services. This necessity arises from the nature of the financing of collective consumption in which a considerable period of time elapses between the moment when outlays are incurred and the moment when benefits become apparent. In other words, we are dealing with anticipatory financing of social needs, and this has all the characteristics of long-term investment. Some authors go so far as to say that collective planning for the development of the social services in self-management communities of interest constitutes the essence of the free exchange of labour, since they always have in mind the contribution of the social services to material production and the general quality of life.[8]

Collective consumption is financed through pooling funds for the execution of the agreed-upon exchange of labour in communities of interest. The sources of these funds are the incomes of work organisations and personal incomes. The pooling of funds takes the form of contributions that are determined by the volume of the exchange and the prices of the services.

An additional question that arises in connection with the financing of social services is the relative proportion of contributions from the incomes of work organisations and from personal incomes; in other words, which social services ought to be financed from the former and which from the latter source. This is both a question of principle and of the practical results. In principle, costs of social services should be met by those beneficiaries in whose interest it is to maintain these particular needs which arise in the sphere of material production, they should be financed from the incomes of work organisations. Conversely, the provision of services geared to final consumption should come primarily from workers' personal incomes. The principal significance of any answer to this question is that different methods of financing can greatly influence the willingness of workers to devote funds to this purpose and it affects their attitude towards the volume of consumption which is financed in this way. Generally, a preference has been shown for financing consumption through contributions from personal incomes.

At present, about 70 per cent of social service expenditure is financed from workers' personal incomes and 30 per cent on the basis of contributions from the incomes of work organisations, which cannot be considered satisfactory.

[8] See R. Savković, 'The Socio-economic Content of the Free Exchange of Labour', *Marxist Thought*, no. 2 (Belgrade, 1979), 87.

IV SOME CONCLUSIONS

If we exclude the market mechanism from the possible systems of allocating funds to meet collective needs, and concentrate on a comparison between budgetary financing and the free exchange of labour, we can distinguish several factors in favour of the latter, although limited experience and the relative novelty of our system make it impossible to verify our arguments.

Firstly, the providers and the beneficiaries of services become directly involved as equal partners and active agents in the process of satisfying collective needs – from the first moment of identifying a particular need to the moment it has been met. This enables the beneficiaries from services to have their collective consumption needs more adequately covered and to control the efficiency of the manner in which their contributions are being utilised. The providers of services are in the position to secure more adequate valuation of their labour as well as to guide the beneficiaries in their choice of priorities in relation to service utilisation. In this way, the interests of both parties have been taken into account as well as the interests of society as a whole.

Secondly, in contrast to the budget which is based on financial allocations, the free exchange of labour is based on plans and programmes for meeting collective needs where the financial component appears as a derivative of these plans and programmes. In this manner, the real and financial components are better integrated, and this may be of considerable importance from the point of view of making the best use of outlays for collective consumption.

Thirdly, direct contact between providers and beneficiaries of services, and the resulting direct contact between needs and facilities for their satisfaction, leads to a more efficient appraisal of the scope for certain forms of collective consumption. This contributes towards a closer integration of social services into overall development.

Fourthly, the overall decision-making concerning collective consumption is greatly democratised. Most intermediaries and restrictions in this sphere can thus be eliminated. This constitutes a significant step forward in the overall democratisation of society.

In discussing the free exchange of labour certain potential weaknesses of this mechanism for meeting collective needs were pointed out: the possibility of domination by the providers of services; the danger that partial interests may show themselves; the impossibility of using collective consumption as an instrument of economic policy. The possible appearance of weaknesses in the practical application of this mechanism seems to be due mainly to faulty application and its present incompleteness. The possible domination by providers of services is a real threat, especially in cases where demand is partly determined by supply (e.g. in health). Another problem which may arise is neglect of certain insufficiently defined needs representing a wider social interest. This danger can be partly eliminated by including research institutions in the decision-making process. In order to eliminate the threat of these wider interests being subordinated to narrower ones, a continuing supervision and co-ordination of all decisions concerning collective consumption must be maintained and optimum levels for the decision concerning specific forms of consumption must be determined in advance. Finally, in certain situations where wider social interest is dominant, socio-political communities should participate in decision-making on equal terms with the self-managing communities of interest.

There is an additional criticism which does contain a certain element of truth – that in the operation of free exchange of labour, collective consumption cannot be used as in instrument of economic policy. It would seem, however, that attempts at manipulating collective consumption for the purpose of demand management, have always been unsuccessful at least in Yugoslavia, because of the inherent inelasticity of this type of consumption.

Discussion of 'Financing of Collective Consumption in Yugoslavia' by P. Jurković, Z. Jăsić and S. Lang

In order to assist the discussion *Dr Jurković* gave the following additional information on the Yugoslav fiscal system and the system of free exchange of labour. The system was designed to conduce to the Marxist goal of the withering away of the state. The general fiscal system in Yugoslavia comprised three elements: the national budget which financed the provision of public goods such as defence and law and order; the system of the free exchange of labour for the provision of other forms of collective consumption; and fiscal transfers and subsidies from the national government to enterprises. The underlying principle of the free exchange of labour was to establish a complete system of self-management at all levels of society. The state as a separate institution would thus be eliminated, and grants from public to private sectors would not exist. Of all expenditure on collective consumption 60 per cent was allocated through more than 4000 communities of interest which composed the system of free exchange of labour. Communities operated at commune, regional and republic levels. In health care, for example, the chamber of a community of interest comprised mandated delegates from the providers and users of the service in the ratio of one delegate to one hundred users and providers respectively. For each chamber there was an executive body without formal powers of decision-making whose functions included the preparation of analyses and working papers. However, it had been difficult to prevent these bodies gaining decision-making powers. The intention was to restrict such acquisitions as much as possible. A chamber would normally meet five or six times per year to formulate strategic and operational plans for the finance and provision of the service, and to evaluate performance. Decisions were normally settled by bargaining and consensus rather than by voting. A chamber of interest could thus be seen as a quasi-market. In the case of health care, the finance for a community of interest was provided by deductions from wages and by a limited system of fees which typically accounted for between 2 per cent and 4 per cent of total revenue. Redistributions of finance were negotiated between national, regional and local communities to ensure a uniform standard of service for all. In the case of transfers to pensioners and unemployed, finance was organised entirely on a national basis.

Professor Onitiri pointed to similarities between the system of free exchange of labour and the functioning of governing boards of hospitals and schools in western countries. He raised the question of the relationship between market and self-management systems and asked whether a market economy could develop institutions such as those described. He requested more information on the relationship reported between efficiency and the capital-labour ratio in social services. He also wished to explore the links between international economic developments and the internal organisation of collective consumption. Both he and *Sir Leo Pliatzky* asked for information on the impact of increasing oil prices on the Yugoslav economy. *Professor Khachaturov* asked how the salaries of doctors were determined in the system of free exchange of labour and requested information on investment in health and education services.

A number of speakers saw a conflict between the aim of decentralisation and other economic and social objectives. *Professor Pohorille* acknowledged some advantages of decentralisation, but questioned the ability of such a system to provide for national economic and social needs, and for the needs of those not in employment. *Professor Hoch* asked how a decentralised system could ensure equality in standards of service. *Mr Matthews* pointed to the possibility that the total of contributions for an individual might be excessive in view of the fact that any individual would contribute to up to fourteen different communities of interest.

In reply to Professor Onitiri and Sir Leo Pliatzky, *Dr Jurković* reported that the increase in oil prices had had a major impact on the rate of inflation in Yugoslavia which was currently about 15 per cent. There had been no immediate effect on demand and growth because of compensating increases in wages. The annual growth rate of income over the previous five years had been about 7 per cent. In reply to Professor Khachaturov, he reported that in the health service a minimum wage was fixed in advance and additional payments were made according to performance; and that in Yugoslavia total investment was about 30 per cent of gross material product, and investment on social services was about one-third of total investment. He acknowledged that there had been a problem in securing efficiency in the delivery of social services in the system described in which need and not demand was the criterion. *Dr Jăsić* took up the question of co-ordination between national and local objectives in the system of free exchange of labour. He explained the form in which this problem had emerged in the education service. An example was the expansion of economics teaching at the University of Zagreb, decisions on which were the responsibility of a regional community of interest for economics training. Decisions had to be co-ordinated vertically with national requirements for trained manpower and horizontally with other communities of interest concerned with research and development and with unemployment. It was the intention of the next five-year plan to improve both vertical and horizontal co-ordination between communities of interest.

11 The Rise and Fall of Public Expenditure Planning: An essay on the British system of public expenditure planning and control

Sir Leo Pliatzky

FORMERLY PERMANENT SECRETARY, DEPARTMENT OF TRADE

I THE POLITICAL DIMENSION

Decision-making on public expenditure in Britain is a curious amalgam of the political and the technocratic.

Policy-making is collectivised under the system of Cabinet responsibility, though management of programmes and projects is decentralised to Departments. The pressures which give rise to expenditure requirements – whether objective developments such as demographic and industrial change or the espousal of particular causes by pressure groups or people of influence – do not start in Cabinet or Cabinet Committee, but they end there.

In one way or another, the pressures feed up through our system of government by parliamentary democracy, until decisions to spend or not to spend are reached through the process of inter-Departmental and inter-Ministerial government. In one sense there is an exception to this at the time of a General Election. Influence passes out of the hands of the Whitehall machine into the party machinery, and commitments are undertaken in the party manifesto, by-passing the hurdles otherwise erected by the Whitehall process of scrutiny, analysis and advice. Increasingly policies, programmes and priorities, for at least the initial period of a government's life, are determined by these extra-governmental processes coming to a head during the election interregnum. But even then these commitments have to be legitimised by the collective decision-making process of the government once it is in power.

Thus, though the Chancellor of the Exchequer is responsible for the management of the nation's finances, on the expenditure side of financial affairs he is in commission to the Cabinet system. This is a situation not unlike that in a number of countries, especially those Commonwealth countries which have to a greater or lesser extent inherited British political institutions. But it is quite unlike the situation in countries which have a presidential system of government, where decision-making is concentrated in the office of the President – though in the United States there is the countervailing force of Congressional power, not matched in the British Parliamentary system.

On the taxation side, however, the Chancellor of the Exchequer has traditionally been master in his own house to a large extent, and this special situation has been largely preserved – with the important proviso that the holder of the office of Prime Minister, who also has the title of First Lord of the Treasury, tends to take a great interest in taxation policy. Subject to this, the Chancellor of the Exchequer is not in commission to Cabinet on the revenue side in the same way as on the expenditure side. He may, nowadays, go somewhat beyond the tradition of informing Cabinet of his Budget proposals immediately before the Budget itself. Cabinet Ministers generally may be given a somewhat earlier opportunity to air their views on Budget strategy. But for practical purposes they are not put in a position to approve or disapprove the specific tax proposals in the Budget.

There are drawbacks to this separation of powers within Cabinet. Neither individual spending Ministers who sponsor expenditure proposals, nor Cabinet who collectively have the ultimate right of approval over them, have a similar responsibility for raising the money to finance these measures. Treasury Ministers therefore tend to occupy a lonely position in Cabinet on expenditure matters. Much depends on the standing and force of character of the Chancellor of the Exchequer, and also on the Chief Secretary, who is the Treasury Minister with particular responsibility for public expenditure. As much or more depends on the support which they get from the Prime Minister.

II THE TECHNOCRATIC DIMENSION

But these political decisions have to be brought together, related to one another and to the available resources, and translated into specific financial provision through a technocratic system involving the whole Whitehall machine and operated at the centre by the Treasury and to a lesser extent the Civil Service Department – a system so complex and even in some aspects so scholastic that the flavour of high politics evaporates altogether, and public expenditure has generally acquired the reputation, in Whitehall at any rate, of being a dull subject. In the Treasury itself, though there are the old expenditure hands who are dedicated to this field of work, public expenditure control tends to be regarded as an unglamorous and unattractive area of activity as compared with, say, overseas finance or industrial policy – though public expenditure is one thing which the government, through the Treasury, can actually manage and which makes a decisive difference to the economy, whereas overseas financial affairs are determined at least as much by forces outside as within the government's control, and this is as much or more the case with regard to industrial affairs.

What follows is a brief description of the system of public expenditure planning and control in Britain, and of the way in which it has evolved up to 1979. The system as a whole embraces central government, local government, and the nationalised industries, but in the first instance this description concentrates on central government financing.

1 THE ANNUAL BUDGET

Financial provision for cash expenditure on public services is made in Britain, as it must be in practically any country, on a year-to-year basis, through the system of annual budgets. All the government's tax revenues and other current receipts are paid into an Exchequer account, and form what is known as the Consolidated Fund; the larger part of central government current expenditure (not counting national insurance payments) comes out of the Consolidated Fund. Estimates for the services to be financed in this way are put to Parliament shortly before the beginning of the financial year, classified by Votes and broken down into subheads. Legislative authority for the appropriation of money for Votes from the Consolidated Fund is secured by an annual Appropriation Act. Meanwhile there is a system of Votes on Account to make enough money available until the Appropriation Act is passed.

Additional provision for particular services may be made in the course of the financial year by means of Supplementary Estimates. These increases may be offset by reductions in the original provision for services which are found not to require the full amount.

A smaller proportion of central government expenditure, but still a very large amount, does not go through Votes but through the National Loans Fund. This is capital finance which central government raises and passes on to such bodies as local authorities and nationalised industries at full cost – that is, on terms such as to recover the whole amount of principal repayments and interest charges which the government itself must meet, plus a small margin to cover handling charges. These sums appear as part of the Budget arithmetic as a whole in the annual Financial Statement and Budget Report. Popularly known as the Red Book, this document brings together all public spending, whether out of Votes or the National Loans Fund or otherwise, and all the tax revenue and public sector borrowing which go to finance it.

The function of the Red Book is purely presentational; it is not a document requiring Parliamentary approval. Though the tax proposals which it reflects have to be approved through a Finance Act, and Vote expenditures have to be approved in the manner already described, provision for the issue of money from the National Loans Fund in the course of the year is not subject to any corresponding arrangement and does not require specific Parliamentary approval. The total amounts which can be issued from the National Loans Fund over time to, say, the various nationalised industries, are prescribed in the Acts relating to those industries, but within these totals there is no statutory limit on the amount which can be lent in a single year. These loan figures can therefore be varied in the course of a year in a more flexible way than is possible with Vote finance. Apart from that, however, it is arguable that Parliamentary control of Vote expenditure is not particularly more rigorous than of National Loans Fund money, because the approval of Vote Estimates is generally to a large extent a formality.

At one time there was nothing beyond this annual budgetary system. This was still the case when the writer of this paper went to the Treasury in the Principal grade at the beginning of the 1950s and was assigned to successive desks concerned with expenditure control where, at

Estimates time of year, he would scrutinise the proposals from a particular group of Departments for expenditure in the coming financial year, having regard to some extent to expenditure in previous years, but not to any projections going beyond the year immediately ahead, and without any wider frame of reference extending beyond these particular Estimates. Of course the figures recommended by each and every Treasury Principal would be put together at a central point in the Treasury and become part of the Budget arithmetic as a whole, but still only as an exercise relating to a single year.

2 THE BIRTH OF THE SURVEY SYSTEM

However, concern developed about the manner in which this year-by-year approach made it possible for a series of new commitments to be undertaken which might have little or no financial effect in the period immediately ahead, but which could lead to a large increase in total expenditure in future years. In 1959 the Government of the day set up an internal committee to consider this problem under the chairmanship of Lord Plowden. In 1961 the Plowden Report recommended that arrangements should be introduced for making surveys of public expenditure for a period of years ahead, and that all major individual decisions involving future expenditure should be taken against the background of such a survey and in relation to prospective resources. This recommendation was accepted by the government, and the new public expenditure survey system was introduced under the direction of Sir Richard Clarke, who from 1962 to 1966 was a Second Permanent Secretary in the Treasury. He was a mathematician by background, and has also been a financial journalist writing under the pseudonym Otto, the forename by which he was generally known. His own account of the inception and early history of the system is given in his posthumously published book *Public Expenditure, Management and Control.*[1]

Two key features of the system have been that it is constructed in terms of functional programmes, not in terms of spending authorities; and that the programmes are costed in constant prices, not at current prices. As an illustration of the first point, the salient figures for the education programme bring together all the expenditure devoted to the function of educating people, broken down into spending on young children, on primary schools, on secondary schools, on universities and so on – not broken down according to the spending authorities who

[1] (London, Macmillan, 1978.)

provide or disburse the money, that is, the Department of Education and Science, the Department of Education for Scotland, the local authorities or the University Grants Committee.

This functional breakdown is accompanied by a variety of supplementary pieces of analysis which have proliferated over the years – partly to meet the demands of the House of Commons Expenditure Committee. The supplementary data include a breakdown of programmes in terms of spending authorities – central government, local government and public corporations – and a further breakdown in terms of economic category, that is, into current expenditure on goods and services, current expenditure on subsidies and grants, and capital expenditure of various kinds. However, the system as conceived gives primacy to the functional approach as the basis of medium-term resource allocation.

As regards the price basis, if we take the survey carried out in 1979, year one is the financial year 1979–80, and the programme for this year, which of course is going ahead even while the survey is taking place, is costed at 1979 survey prices. These are the actual price levels for school buildings, books, teachers' pay, etc, at a fixed point in time shortly before the start of the 1979–80 year. Projections are worked out of the cost of the programme on given policy assumptions for four future years, and these projected programmes also are costed at 1979 survey prices.

Thus the survey as a whole displays the allocation of resources to the public sector on a functional basis and in real terms over a five-year period. In order to relate this allocation of resources for the public sector to the resources available for the economy as a whole, it has been customary in recent years to carry out the public expenditure survey in conjunction with an assessment of the economic prospects in the medium term on given assumptions about economic growth and other key economic variables.

The process of decision-making on the public expenditure totals, and on the share of the totals for individual programmes, has in the past engaged the attention of Cabinet intermittently over a period of months, and tends to be a difficult business. However, for roughly a decade this arduous gestation period has resulted each year in the publication of the results of the survey in a public expenditure White Paper. Publication has tended to run late but up to 1979 has always taken place in the end.

However, at the end of the survey process, funny money (as constant price arithmetic has been termed by its critics) which is immune to the power of inflation, has to be translated back into ordinary money of the day which has no such immunity. That is to say, once programmes for the financial year ahead have been determined in terms of survey prices, before the financial year begins they have to be recalculated at current prices, allowing for cost inflation since the start of the survey. The programme figures for two years ahead continue to be expressed for the time being in constant prices; their turn to find expression in terms of money of the day will come in another year's time, after another annual survey.

The creation of this system was a great conceptual achievement. To secure its acceptance by Whitehall was a feat of will and organisation.

The system appeared to be admired by foreign observers, especially visitors from the United States which had still to develop its own initiatives aiming at improved budgetary control, and which eventually took the different route of strengthening the apparatus for Congressional oversight. Two American writers, Hugh Heclo and Aaron Wildavsky, in their book *The Private Government of Public Money*,[2] while far from uncritical of many aspects of the British system, especially the subordination of micro-analysis of policies to macro-analysis of the economy, found it a sophisticated system and one well adapted to the talents of the 'private' political administrative community at the centre of British government. (Hence their concept that 'governing public money is a private affair', a term which may be valid as a description of the 'village life' of Whitehall, but which leaves out of account the forces and ideas abroad in society which create both pressures for expenditure and counter-pressures to contain it.)

And yet, in spite of the sophistication of the system, by 1975 there was mounting criticism to the effect that public expenditure was out of control and that this was a major factor in the country's economic ills. An influential report by the Expenditure Committee – itself considerably influenced by a memorandum from Wynne Godley, a former economic adviser in the Treasury who had played his part in the development of the survey system and contributed to its increasing complexity, but by now Director of the Department of Applied Economics at Cambridge and disillusioned with his own former handiwork – was exceptionally critical of the system and appeared to hold its shortcomings responsible for what had happened. The charge was, in effect, not simply that expenditure had escalated year by year above the levels previously planned, but also that decisions on public expenditure had been taken without regard to the means of

[2] (London, Macmillan, 1974.)

financing it, so that the end result was inflation of the money supply.

III WHAT WENT WRONG?

There is no mystery about what had gone wrong on the political plane. The mystery is, rather, how some observers could manage to analyse and interpret this period of history in other than primarily political terms.

The leadership of the Conservative government, which had come to power in 1970, committed to restoring the workings of a market economy, felt themselves obliged to adopt interventionist policies when faced with the collapse of Upper Clyde Shipbuilders and Rolls Royce and the potential domino effects on other enterprises. As unemployment rose towards and beyond the then traumatic figure of a million, recourse was had to tax reliefs – which, however, appeared to be working too slowly – and to reflationary expenditure of both a general and a selective character. Moreover, faced with the relatively new phenomenon of stagflation, that is, escalating price inflation in spite of a stagnant economy, expenditure on price subsidies intended to be counter-inflationary was added to expenditure intended to be contracyclical: even if there had been no change of government, these measures made an excess over previously planned expenditure inevitable.

However, in fact, following the oil crisis, the miners' strike and the reduction of British industry to a three-day working week, there was a General Election and the return to office of a Labour government committed to a latter-day version of the social contract. In return for the co-operation and support of the trade unions, the new government was to introduce industrial and social measures designed to secure an irreversible shift of wealth and power in favour of working people. This entailed a further increase in expenditure to help employment, subsidise rents and prices and raise social beneifts.

This succession of measures during the period of office of first a Conservative and then a Labour government – in the course of which the oil crisis and its after-effects, coupled with domestic industrial disruption, brought a major setback to economic activity – led to a rise in public expenditure greatly in excess of economic growth. Inflation, the public sector borrowing requirement and the balance of payments deficit all shot up.

It is more difficult to judge how far the public expenditure system can be criticised for failing to contain this process or even for facilitating it. Technocratic procedures cannot be expected to prevail over political forces.

Nevertheless it was a weakness of the system that the emphasis was on planning and not on control. There were elaborate procedures for framing forward plans, but not for monitoring their implementation. The first requirement to ensure that plans are adhered to is a political will to secure this. Given this prerequisite, it is possible to frame decision-making procedures so that individual expenditure decisions are taken within the constraints of the approved overall plan. Both of these conditions for keeping *ex post* out-turn of expenditure in real terms within *ex ante* planned limits were in fact secured in the course of 1976, and involved a few crucial procedural changes which are not discussed in detail here.

1 CASH LIMITS

This in itself does not, however, dispose of the further criticism that a commitment to maintain predetermined expenditure programmes in real terms, irrespective of their eventual cost in money terms, reflects an indifference to the monetary dimension of economic management, that at the least it has represented acquiescence in price inflation and at the worst has contributed to it. In this respect also a dramatic turn round took place through the introduction, for a wide range of programmes, of cash limits which, at Budget time, fixed a ceiling in advance on the cash to be made available both through the initial Estimates and through Supplementary Estimates later in the year. Cash limits were also introduced for loan money channelled otherwise than through Votes. Thus the government was calling its shots, so to speak, and declaring in advance the rate of price inflation for which it was prepared to budget.

This turn round in financial control coincided with a turn round in wage and price inflation. For the next two years pay settlements in the public services were in line with the targets set by the government's incomes policy. The out-turn of public expenditure was well within the planned total whether in real terms or in terms of cash.

But by 1979 the attempt at a further round of voluntary income restraint had failed. The assumed rate of inflation and the target for public service pay increases on which the Estimates and cash limits for 1979–80 had been prepared had clearly become unrealistic. Therefore the time had come to resolve what had always been a potential issue since the introduction of cash limits – whether the commitment to put a predetermined limit on cash expenditure should override the predetermined commitment to programmes in real terms, or vice versa.

Before the General Election of May 1979 there were indications from the Labour Administration that the cash limits for the public service wage bill would not be raised by the full amount required to cover the excess of wage increases over the target figure, which implied something of a manpower squeeze; while cash limits for other components of public expenditure would not be raised at all above the previously assumed inflation rate, with the further implication that there would not be enough cash fully to maintain planned programmes in real terms. After the Conservative Party's success in the election, the new government announced its intention both to use cash limits in this way so as to secure a generalised squeeze on programmes in volume terms – but a more severe squeeze, because a greater increase in prices was now in prospect – and to effect more specific policy measures in order to reduce expenditure programmes.

IV PLANNING REDUX?

The new government has found to hand a rehabilitated system of planning and control enabling it to set about reducing public expenditure both in volume terms and in money terms. It is arguable, therefore, that the title of this paper, in order to make itself a little interesting and provocative, is in fact misleading, and that at any rate the final sub-title should be 'Planning Redux'.

Nevertheless, so long as a question mark remains about the future course of inflation, there must be a question mark about the scope for returning to forward planning of public expenditure in terms of volumes reasonably immune to price changes. And so long as doubt persists about the future ability of the world economy, and the United Kingdom economy within it, to achieve sustained economic growth, there must be an even more serious question mark about the underlying assumptions on which the future planning of public expenditure is to be based.

On the other hand, public expenditure now accounts for a high percentage of GDP in the United Kingdom, as it does in the western economies generally, though not in Japan. The proportion varies from one western country to another, and could no doubt be reduced in time by some percentage points in the United Kingdom, but it will still account for a substantial part of all expenditure. The drawbacks of an attempt to revert to its management on a purely year-by-year basis would be formidable, while an unpredictable rate of inflation makes it hardly feasible to construct future expenditure scenarios in simple cash terms. There may therefore be some interesting dilemmas to resolve.

Discussion of 'The Rise and Fall of Public Expenditure Planning' by Sir Leo Pliatzky

As a basis for discussion, *Professor Sir Austin Robinson* gave an interpretation of the interplay between economic, political and bureaucratic factors in the formation of public expenditure policy in the United Kingdom. He pointed to the political nature of the choice between market and public provision of goods and services involved in decisions on the total of public expenditure. He saw the interaction between political and bureaucratic systems as being particularly prominent in two areas. The first concerned decision-making on the allocation of any total between different programmes of public spending, which involved bargaining between different government departments. The second concerned the translation of political manifestos and other conflicting political pressures into internally consistent and workable policies. On this point he cited the example of the manifesto of the new Conservative administration in the United Kingdom which was to reduce public expenditure and the rate of inflation, to improve economic incentives, and to maintain public consumption by improving efficiency within the government. He also pointed to the pressures from constituencies on individual Members of Parliament which underlie the pressures that Members apply on the Civil Service. In his view the important economic issues at stake were as follows: the adverse effects on incentives of high levels of public expenditure and taxation, and of a well-developed system of social insurance against poverty and unemployment; and the conflict in the area of public expenditure between the requirements of counter-cyclical policy and of allocation policy concerned with particular services. His view was that expenditures on capital items should be varied counter-cyclically, and not current expenditures on services such as health and education. Adverse balance of payments effects of public expenditure could be minimised by a choice of public expenditures of low import content, such as housing investment.

Much of the discussion which followed was concerned with the stabilisation aspects of public expenditure policy. *Professor Bacskai* argued that although the effects of public expenditure on the balance of payments could be regulated at the first round by a choice of expenditures of low import content, control was much more difficult at the second and subsequent rounds at which increases in private incomes were induced. *Mr Kaser* wondered whether Professor Bacskai's point implied that public expenditure on goods and services had a smaller impact on the balance of payments than expenditure on transfers which could not be so regulated at the first round. *Professor Maillet* did not see that this was generally so because of the high import content of certain public expenditures. *Professor Modigliani*'s view was that public investment in housing had been a useful method of maintaining demand during periods in which a balance of payments constraint had been effective.

Professor Urquidi disagreed with Professor Robinson's argument on the suitability of capital expenditures for counter-cyclical policy. His view was that in the case of developing economies, public capital expenditure were less effective as an instrument of counter-cyclical policy mainly because of their disequilibrating effects on the balance of payments. But such expenditures were essential for the promotion of economic development. However, *Professor Modigliani* supported Professor Robinson's view with the argument that in periods of depression the rate of public investment should be increased because the opportunity cost of it in terms of the foregone return on private investment would be falling. In addition he argued that the determination of an optimal cyclical path for public expenditure was made very complicated by a change in the basic nature of cyclical policy, which in recent times had been directed towards the management of supply shocks and away from its traditional purpose of counteracting exogenous changes in demand. The interaction of supply shocks had been a cause of inflation. Governments had responded with deflationary policies which had been painful but the only strategy available. As a result rates of public expenditure on unemployment-related services had increased, which in turn had worked against deflationary policies.

Mr Matthews hoped that speakers would go on to discuss the administrative problems of implementing a given policy on public expenditure. In this context he referred to his experience in the United Kingdom Social Science Research Council of the inefficiency arising from sudden changes in policy; from the use of crude price indices for the supplementation of planning budgets to allow for subsequent inflation; and from the conventional budget rule whereby unspent funds in one period could not be carried over to subsequent periods. *Professor Modigliani* argued that although there was no rational basis for the planning of public expenditures in nominal terms, it might be sensible to reduce planned real public expenditure in the face of unanticipated inflation. *Professor Boulding*'s view was that some of the problems described in the paper were not so much the result of external factors but rather a result of the growing sophistication of the planning system itself. In this he saw a reflection of a general trend in economic thought in which sophisticated structures had been applied to irrelevant issues, whereas oversimplified, wholesale structures had been applied to the complex, retail problems of policy. As examples of the latter problem he cited the invention of the correlation coefficient and the success of Keynesian macroeconomics, both of which had induced economists and policy-makers to represent the cloud of reality by oversimplified concepts and straight lines.

Sir Leo Pliatzky insisted that the criticisms of institutions and policies in his paper should not be misinterpreted. He wished the conference to be aware of his commitment to the values represented by the system of government and policy-making he had analysed. He then described the broad political and economic developments in the United Kingdom during the post-war period which were the setting for the specific issues analysed in his paper. He pointed to the disengagement of the United Kingdom from the unsustainable world military and political role which the nation had assumed at the end of the Second World War. The long period of sustained economic growth up to 1973 at an average of 2½ per cent to 3 per cent per annum had resulted in substantial improvements in the standard of living and large changes in social conditions. However, British political leaders made unfavourable comparisons between this growth performance and the higher performance achieved in other countries, such as France. The stop-go cycle of this period was the result of attempts to reconcile the desire for faster growth and full employment with a low inflation rate and a satisfactory balance of payments. By the early 1960s disaffection with these events had given rise to attempts at national economic planning. The important feature of the planning exercises undertaken by Conservative and Labour administrations before 1970 was in his view the discrepancy between the target annual growth rates of national income (4 per cent) and public expenditure (4 per cent, rising to 4½ per cent under the Labour administration of 1966–70), and the historical evidence that the maximum sustainable growth rate of the economy was between 2½ and 3 per cent per annum. He described the policy changes of the Conservative administration of 1970–74 designed to regenerate British industry, and the policy of the social contract of the Labour administration after 1974 under which increases in public consumption were offered in exchange for wage restraint. These strategies resulted in an inflationary growth of public expenditure. The eventual result of this long train of events was, he argued, the increase in the share of general government expenditure in gross domestic product from 39 per cent in 1972/73 to 46½ per cent in 1975/76, over which period gross domestic product had grown at about 0.4 per cent per annum. This shift represented a breakdown of the well-established system of public expenditure control. However, in contrast to other explanations that had been offered, his view was that this outcome was a result of a long history of the political mismanagement of economic policy. Even though the system of control had since been re-established and the share of public expenditure reduced, he was not confident that the system would survive in its present form during a future period of continuous slow growth.

In principle he agreed with Professor Modigliani's point that plans for public expenditure should be formulated in real terms and supplementation given for subsequent inflation. However, he pointed to the danger that an open-ended commitment to supplementation could undermine the control of expenditure programmes which had to be exercised in cash terms.

12 Spending More and Getting Less: Recent Experiences with the Allocation and Control of Public Expenditure in the Netherlands[1]

Th. A. J. Meys

DIRECTOR-GENERAL OF THE BUDGET, NETHERLANDS

I THE GROWTH OF THE PUBLIC SECTOR

In recent decades the size of the public sector, expressed as a percentage of national income, has increased sharply in virtually all developed countries. In terms of both volume and rate of growth the Netherlands has exemplified this trend to a particularly marked extent, as Figure 12.1 clearly demonstrates. Within the overall total of government expenditure, however, differences exist between the countries concerned: in the Netherlands' case the growth in transfer payments has been especially rapid. The size of government spending on goods and services, expressed as a percentage of national income, has been almost stable since the beginning of the sixties.

[1] I am indebted to Messrs Erkens, Kuipers, Verwayen and Zalm, all of the Ministry of Finance. None of these persons is of course responsible for any errors or omissions. The views expressed in this paper do not necessarily reflect official opinion.

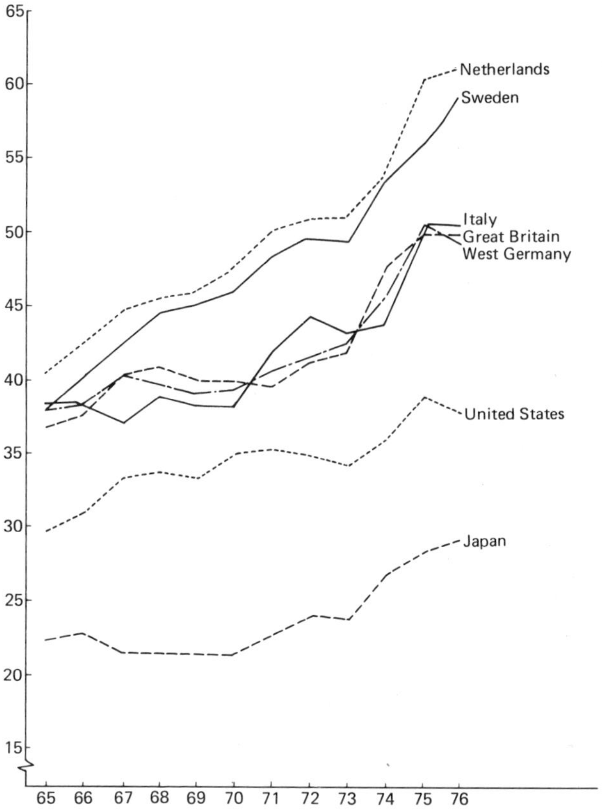

FIG. 12.1 Share of social expenditures in the net national income (market prices)
Source: OECD *National Accounts*

The sharp increase in natural gas revenues since 1970 has certainly facilitated the growth in total expenditure and these revenues now amount to more than 3 per cent of national income. This does not however explain the growth in government expenditure. The explanation is to be found principally in the following factors. First, there is the desire, also felt in other countries, to develop an effective social security system by the introduction of a variety of new or improved benefit schemes. A second factor is the rapid increase in the average level of benefits, notably because of indexation: many benefits are linked in some way to the statutory minimum wage, which in recent years has frequently been raised by a considerable margin as a result of legislative action.

A third factor is the increased use which has been made of benefit schemes, mainly as a result of the worsening employment situation. This has led to increasing demands being made not only on the unemployment benefit scheme itself but also on, for example, the disability benefit scheme.[2]

These elements combined have boosted transfer payments to families from 19 per cent of national income in 1970 to 28 per cent in 1977. Regarding transfer expenditures, the government's function is little more than that of a postbox, since the greater part of the income transfers flow directly back to the private sector. Nonetheless it is clear that the increase in government revenues needed to finance these expenditures exercises virtually the same upward pressure on real labour costs as that needed to finance increased public expenditure on goods and services. Higher taxation and social security contributions both have the effect of raising labour costs (since both are passed on, whether or not by some institutionalised mechanism), while the growth of income transfers as such has only a very slight tendency – if any – to reduce them. This is related to the quite strong emphasis placed in wage negotiations on the growth of real personal disposable incomes: the increases in the 'social wage' (i.e. the improvements taking place in public services), which ought also to be seen as increasing disposable income, in fact have no moderating effect on wage demands. The growth in transfer expenditures thus leads, via the increase in government revenue needed to finance them, to an increase in real labour costs and, consequently, to a threat to employment. At the same time, however, the growth in transfer payments is an important factor in the maintenance

[2] It is important to note that one of the criteria for disability is the impossibility of finding a new job.

and even raising of effective demand, given the fact that the savings ratio of the recipients of social security benefits is low.

The upward pressure on real labour costs which may result both from increased government expenditure on goods and services and from increased transfer expenditures has a detrimental effect on the private sector, industry in particular. Not only does it reduce the capacity to invest, it also accelerates the scrapping of old, relatively labour-intensive capital goods, which are technically far from obsolete, and encourages the search for labour-saving production methods. This, in turn, constitutes a serious danger to the employment situation.

Although the general picture of trends and developments in the Netherlands does not very much differ from that found in other developed countries, the very considerable size and recent growth of transfer payments definitely adds an important constraint to economic and social policies. Furthermore, the relatively 'automatic' features of the transfer payment system imply that an enormous amount of political will must be engendered in order effectively to control expenditures in this domain.

II THE POLITICAL BACKGROUND

The political situation in the Netherlands is such that virtually every government must be based on a coalition of parties: no single party is large enough to gain sufficient parliamentary support on its own. A considerable degree of separation exists between parliament and government: members of cabinet may not be or remain members of parliament. In addition, the parliamentary groups making up the government coalition operate very largely independently of the cabinet they formally support.

Within cabinet, the votes of all ministers are of equal weight. The Prime Minister's opinion is given extra weight only in cases of deadlock, when his vote is decisive. This arrangement does not make the position of the Minister of Finance any easier. As regards ensuring that a sound financial and economic policy is pursued, the Minister of Finance is – in Orwell's phrase – 'more equal' than the others: he has the primary responsibility here, as he has for ensuring the legal and efficient management of central government's funds.

The powers of the Minister of Finance are laid down in the Government Accounting Act of 1976, on the basis of which he assesses both the annual draft budgets submitted to him by his fellow ministers and all other proposals which have financial consequences. The various specialist ministers generally seek to defend and promote the interests of their own departments. Because the cabinet as a whole – with its tradition of one man, one vote – also decides on the main elements of financial and economic policy, they tend to adopt non-interventionist attitudes as regards each other's special fields, avoiding mutual conflicts and trying to ensure that they are not played off one against the other if differences arise between any of them and the Minister of Finance regarding the volume and composition of their respective budgets. This makes control by the Minister of Finance of the volume and growth of public expenditure an extremely complex and laborious process.

The Minister of Finance may try to break out of this impasse in two ways. He can seek to force a decision in cabinet on the expenditure framework as a whole before the cabinet begins dealing with the separate budgets: partly because of the non-interventionist attitudes just mentioned this will still not be easy to achieve. In addition, he can seek to obtain the support, at least on the main issues, of the Prime Minister and perhaps also of the Ministers for Economic and Social Affairs before starting his negotiations – whether bilaterally or in cabinet – with the ministers at the spending departments.

A comparable process generally takes place while parliament is dealing with the budget, as the representatives of a variety of special interests press for a whole range of increases in expenditure. Of importance here is the fact that parliament discusses in detail the separate budgets and must eventually give its approval to each one. The various pressure groups both on the opposition side and – because of the separation between parliament and government – among the government's own supporters, often press for special treatment of particular interests, without indicating the funds needed or the consequences for the overall expenditure picture.

It should perhaps be added here that in this matter some degree of self-discipline has developed in parliament in recent years. In the general financial discussions regarding the next budgetary year it has become customary that the opposition submit an alternative budget, thus promoting a more consistent approach to the budget submitted by the cabinet. It is now also the practice, before the separate draft budgets are dealt with, to discuss the government's general financial policy and the overall picture of expenditures, receipts and deficit. Finally, it has for some time been customary, when any proposal is placed before parliament, to indicate what funds would be needed. Recently, however, there have been frequent departures from this custom, or the estimations of funds needed have been totally in conflict with overall government policy and therefore in fact unrealistic.

The conclusion to be drawn from all this is that strong upward pressures are exercised on public expenditure, in parliament and in cabinet, against which the Minister of Finance – given the constitutional framework and the general political background – can defend himself only with great circumspection. The realisation of more rational decision-making procedures regarding the volume and composition of public expenditure clearly is no simple matter.

III ATTEMPTS AT CONTROLLING EXPENDITURES AT MACRO LEVEL

The problems that have been outlined are not new. Indeed, they are more or less inherent in the Dutch political system. In order nevertheless to achieve as much control as possible over the volume of public expenditure (as well as to some extent its composition) a number of 'instruments' have, in the course of time, been developed.

1 MULTI-YEAR PUBLIC EXPENDITURE ESTIMATES

Since 1969 each annual budget has been accompanied by estimates of public expenditure for the next four years. Unlike the annual budget, these estimates do not constitute any form of authorisation. For the cabinet they are often in the nature of agreements, to the extent that they relate to the lifetime of the government currently in office. The figures are generally based on an extrapolation from existing policy and the working through of policy agreements already reached at cabinet level. In order to give expression to expected increases in real labour costs, thus taking account as accurately as possible of relative changes in wage- and price-sensitive expenditure categories, the estimates of future expenditure are given in relatively constant prices. Price-sensitive expenditures are subject to a price increase of 0 per cent per year, wage-sensitive expenditures to one of 2 per cent.

One of the main functions of the system of public expenditure estimates is the identification of the so called 'camel-nose' effects, familiar from the literature on public finance. Not only does this clarify the time path of expenditures needed for certain activities (something which is important for decision-making in connection with those activities), it also helps avoid over- or underestimation of the necessary funds occurring over a period of years. The estimates also make it possible to bring into the picture policy shifts which will lead to expenditure changes only in the somewhat longer term.

Another important aspect of the multi-year public expenditure estimates is the possibility they open up of gearing the government's revenue and expenditure policy in the medium term to expected macroeconomic trends. It has become the custom in the Netherlands to issue new medium-term forecasts for the economy as a whole and to adjust the figures in the budget estimates accordingly once every two years, and certainly every time a new government takes office. This brings the public expenditure estimates into line with the latest views and information on economic developments (with the result currently that the figures are being adjusted downwards). At the same time an attempt is made, by means of reorderings within the adjusted total, to maximise the macroeconomic impact of the budget (in stimulating growth, reducing unemployment, etc.).

A number of question marks have recently been placed against the system which has so far been used. Experience in recent years with two retrenchment operations has shown that figures based on extrapolation from existing policy and on planned new policy tend to function as minimum expectations in budget negotiations, entailing a marked downward inflexibility in total expenditure. The expenditures shown in the estimates are regarded both by the spending ministries and by groups inside and outside parliament as something to which they have acquired a right. This problem has clearly been exacerbated in the recent past, since worsening economic prospects have repeatedly caused the estimates to be adjusted downwards. In addition to the extreme difficulty of making downward adjustments in the total multi-year estimates for public expenditure, the system also tends to mean that existing policies remain virtually undiscussed and that any reordering on the basis of changed political priorities thus risks being frustated. Attention is transferred to the changes, both positive and negative, which must be made in the expenditure estimates on the basis of new information, while the great majority of existing expenditures escape critical consideration.

2 THE CONTROL OF EXPENDITURE IN RELATION TO MACROECONOMIC DEVELOPMENTS

As has already been remarked, the government's revenue and expenditure policies are, as far as possible, fitted into and aligned with macroeconomic developments and forecasts. A system of norms for the public sector was introduced in the Netherlands in 1961. The norms are referred to as structural budget norms and the system as a whole bears the name, also familiar abroad, of structural budget policy.[3] Of central importance in this approach is the structural level of the budget deficit, which is determined in such a way as to produce as balanced an impact as possible on the national economy. The margin for growth in expenditure consists of the trend rate of growth in government revenue (allowing for the progressive operation of the tax system), the increase – if any – in the acceptable structural level of the budget deficit, and the yield from any new tax measures. The macroeconomic considerations involved in calculating this margin are derived in large part from the forecasts of the Central Planning Bureau.

During the implementation of the budget stringent rules are applied to ensure that the norms for the structural budget deficit are strictly enforced: in principle, any excess over planned total expenditure, to the extent that it does not result from purely nominal changes, must be compensated by means of expenditure cuts. The manner of compensation depends on the cause of the excess. If it results from policy changes by a department the compensation must be made in the first instance by the same department, while if the cause of the excess is exogenous (e.g. higher unemployment, higher number of students) the compensation becomes general, i.e. it is shared out in some way among the departmental totals. Where expenditure excesses occur as a result of higher-than-expected inflation they are normally compensated by the higher tax revenues which also flow from the higher inflation. Only if this still leaves an excess must this be compensated in the expenditure total. The stringent budget rules are thus concerned primarily with controlling the financial deficit. It is perhaps unnecessary to emphasise that the norms for the deficit, embodied in this policy budget, do not tell us much about the desirable volume of public spending. Given the norm for the structural budget deficit, the margin for expenditure can in principle be widened or narrowed as desired by means of fiscal measures.

This relative freedom as regards the volume of public spending was restricted for the first time in 1976 by the introduction of a general budgetary norm. Macroeconomic forecasts had been made which showed that in the medium term the government's objectives as regards unemployment and the financial deficit could be achieved only if the increase in the burden of taxation and social security contributions were

[3] For a full discussion see H. Burger, 'Structural Budget Policy in the Netherlands', *De Economist*, 123, No 3 (1975).

limited. The then government, under Prime Minister Den Uyl, decided on the basis of these forecasts on a 1 per cent norm, i.e. the increase in government revenue[4] would be limited to not more than 1 per cent of national income per year. Calculations showed that, assuming the public sector's share in national income to be 55 per cent and the real rate of growth in national income to be 3.75 per cent per year, the growth of public expenditure still accounted for over 80 per cent of the increase in national income in spite of the 1 per cent norm. The government which took office in 1978 under Prime Minister Van Agt adopted a roughly similar policy, but in view of the worsening economic prospects decided on a further limitation of the increase in the overall tax burden.

Meanwhile, another development ran more or less parallel to the introduction of norms for the tax burden. In the 1960s and early 1970s the acceptable structural budget deficit, having initially been expressed as a fixed absolute amount, was set at a constant percentage of national income. Since it was thought desirable that the budget should have a stimulating effect on the economy, especially at a time when private investment had begun to grow much less rapidly, in the course of the 1970s it was considered acceptable that the financial deficit should exceed the fixed percentage of national income. However, this led to the deficit rising so rapidly that problems were encountered in financing it.

It was against this background that a new budgetary norm was introduced in 1979, when a upper limit was also set for the growth of the actual budget deficit. For 1979 the limit was fixed at 6 per cent of national income. If it is exceeded measures must be taken which have an immediate effect on the size of the financial deficit – this is why the procedure is called the 'emergency brake'. When the Spring Memorandum was presented (this is a report, issued every year in June, on the progress of the current budget), it appeared likely that the 6 per cent limit would indeed be exceeded. Measures were therefore taken – notably a slowing-down of payments by means of cash limits, inspired by the instrument of expenditure control which has been in use for some time in the United Kingdom, and a speeding-up of the collection of taxes – intended to ensure that the limit of 6 per cent would not in fact be exceeded.

It is particularly interesting to compare the system of revenue and deficit norms used in the Netherlands with the United Kingdom's system of cash limits, dealt with by Sir Leo Pliatzky in his paper. The

[4] Taxes, social premiums, and other non-tax revenues such as from domestic sales of natural gas.

most striking difference appears to be that the central element in the Dutch system is the level of the deficit, while in the British system it is the level of expenditure. Since higher-than-expected inflation leads to an increase not only in public expenditure but also in revenue, seen in trend terms, it does not necessarily exercise any downward pressure on the budget balance.

The stress in the Dutch system on the financial balance is an attempt to keep as closely in line as possible with the monetary aims and side constraints while allotting central importance to the question of financing. In this way the budget's other functions are left untouched as far and as long as possible, particularly the programme effects of expenditures, something which is probably not as much the case in the British system as a consequence of cash limits.

The system of cash limits, by allotting a central role to the level of expenditure, seems to imply a rather one-sided stress on the budget as a counter-inflationary instrument. To what extent it is an effective instrument in this respect, I cannot adequately judge for the British situation. For the Netherlands its usefulness, separated from the financial deficit and from the growth in the overall tax burden, would not seem to be such as to make one recommend the British system.

IV CONTROLLING EXPENDITURES: A RECENT CASE

It has already emerged at various points that both the political background and the institutional framework place quite large obstacles in the way of rational decision-making processes in connection with the control of the volume of public expenditure and the determination of its composition. Before discussing some of the instruments in existence or being developed for the control of expenditure at the micro and meso levels, it may be interesting to consider – as an illustration and as a constrast – how the decision-making process operated in practice in connection with the most recent retrenchment scheme. This exercise was based on 'Blueprint 81', the programme of the Van Agt government coalition.

Given the desire to bring down the financial deficit to an acceptable level in the medium term and the need to place further limits on the rise in taxation and social security contributions, the main aim of 'Blueprint 81' was to bring down public expenditure by ten billion guilders as against the original medium-term estimate for 1981. This meant an adjustment of some 5 per cent to the (growing) total of public expenditure for which provision had been made. The work of preparation and decision-making took place over a period of less than six months, with the concrete decision-making concentrated in the last two months.

The first decision related to the distribution of the total cut of ten billion guilders among, on the one hand, the spheres of social security and health care and general salary arrangements for public employees and, on the other hand, the national budget in the narrow sense, consisting mainly of the government's own spending on goods and services. In order to act as effectively as possible on the main reason why public spending as a whole was almost out of control, i.e. the rapid growth in transfer payments (whose causes were briefly discussed in Section I), while at the same time minimising the direct negative effects on employment, it was decided that the two spending categories would bear two-thirds and one-third of the cuts respectively. It will be evident that this justification does not alter the fact that the distribution chosen was ultimately based on political considerations.

When it came to the detailed distribution of the cuts – 6.5. billion guilders for social security and so on and 3.5. billion for the national budget in the narrow sense – three procedures were used. First, a working party consisting of representatives of the ministries most directly concerned – including the Treasury – listed and examined the economies which might be made in the fields of social security, health care and general salary arrangements of public employees.

At the same time a procedure was initiated relating to the national budget in the narrow sense: each specialist minister had to draw up a list of his lowest expenditure priorities (hence the name 'posteriorities exercise' which was given to this operation) amounting to a certain percentage of his total budget. This was then submitted to the Minister of Finance. Finally, retrenchment schemes were developed within the Ministry of Finance: a systematic examination was made of elements in respect of which the public expenditure estimates had provided for volume growth, while at the same time the possibility was examined of scrapping certain elements of existing policy.

The possible economies which emerged from these exercises and procedures were then evaluated at ministerial level. Final cabinet decisions were not taken until after bilateral discussions had taken place between the Minister of Finance and each specialist minister separately, on the basis of an overall proposal formulated by the Minister of Finance. In order to match the detailed economies to the overall cuts required such shortfalls as remained were distributed among the ministries, as is frequently the practice in the last phase of budget negotiations. In order to determine the size of each share use is generally made of such criteria as (i) the volume of total expenditure per department; (ii) the volume of expenditure on material items per department; and (iii) the real growth in expenditure per department provided in the budgetary year concerned.

If we consider the various instruments and the way in which they are used it is clear that each of them has had and can have significant positive effects – provided it is strictly and consistently applied – from the standpoint of the control of the total growth in public expenditure. However, when we move to their application in practice it has to be said that – to keep to very general terms – the introduction of the political dimension and of the dimension of social acceptability means that we still lack adequate methods – or perhaps I should say we lack the willingness – to control the growth in public expenditure in an effective fashion.[5]

In order to achieve a more systematic and satisfactory approach we therefore need to pay greater attention than we have done in the past to other methods: policy analysis, physical performance budgeting, reconsideration of government responsibilities, and perhaps the revision of the system of multi-year public expenditure estimates.

V ATTEMPTS TO IMPROVE THE ALLOCATION OF RESOURCES

The instruments mentioned above, i.e. policy analysis, reconsideration of government functions, physical performance budgeting and multi-year public expenditure estimates are all products of the last decade. The first three are specially designed to improve the allocation of resources. Taken together they have a bearing on the total volume of collective consumption. Multi-year public expenditure estimates, on the other hand, are primarily an instrument for influencing the total volume of the budget, and this has therefore been discussed in Section III of this paper. Nevertheless it can easily be seen that this operation also has a relationship with respect to allocation decisions at micro level: the typical phenomena of 'camel-nose' effects has already been mentioned.

[5] In this respect it is very interesting to see what the new British government is going to make of it. Is there really going to be a 'Battle of the axe'? (*Economist*).

1 THE INSPECTION OF THE MINISTRY OF FINANCE

An instrument of long standing, intended first of all to influence discussions at micro level, but which has played an important role within the Minister of Finance's responsibility to control the total volume of public expenditure, is the Inspection at the Ministry of Finance.

An important aspect of the work of the Inspection is testing effectiveness and efficiency of government measures, both *ex post* and *ex ante*. Within the traditional budgeting process all budget proposals from the various Departments are to be tested by the Inspection with respect to efficiency and effectiveness. The results of this testing procedure subsequently become part of the discussions between the Minister of Finance and his collegues. These very often lead to modifications and adaptations regarding existing as well as new activities.

This procedure, which is always carried out under severe pressures of time (generally taken, less than two months is available) has severe limitations. For one thing, the more fundamental discussions about objectives and priorities do not have a sufficient chance to come to the fore.

The introduction of multi-year public expenditure estimates still aggravated the difficulties for the Inspection, particularly with respect to the testing of measures. As has already been indicated in Section III, the preparation of the budget for next year on the basis of these estimates in fact excludes discussions on existing policies. These and related problems have stimulated the search for alternative methods for improving allocation decisions.

2 RECONSIDERATION OF GOVERNMENT FUNCTIONS

One of these alternatives has been the so-called reconsideration of government functions. In 1975 the possibility of calling into question the existence of and responsibility for specific government tasks was given a structural basis, by establishing a procedure giving explicit responsibility to cabinet. The procedure implies that each minister can propose that government functions be reconsidered, also concerning subjects outside his own responsibility. Decision-making power is given to cabinet as a whole, both with respect to the question whether or not to reconsider as such, and with respect to the conclusions of any analysis carried out. Actual work between the two decisions is carried out by a permanent commission of civil servants.

The answer to the question 'what has been achieved' is: extremely little. Until now only one subject has been taken into (re)consideration.

The subject concerned the construction of two new university hospitals.

The question why this procedure has been so little used has, once again, to do with the non-interventionist attitude of ministers, mentioned earlier. Ministers will not easily be tempted to make proposals to reconsider subjects falling within the competence of colleagues. Also with respect to their own areas of responsibility ministers will be little inclined to make them the subject of discussions in cabinet. This leaves the Minister of Finance as one of the few actors who could initiate such proposals. However, as the procedure requires preliminary discussions with the minister concerned, the risk of important delay is built in. Also, even if cabinet could have agreed to reconsider a particular subject, the Department concerned will generally try to limit either the possibilities for arriving at decisions or the scope of an eventual decision. An additional reason why 'reconsideration' has hardly worked has probably been the fairly large-scale efforts to reduce the budget as a whole (e.g. Blueprint 1981).

3 PHYSICAL PERFORMANCE BUDGETING

Another instrument which should be mentioned with respect to allocation issues is physical performance budgeting. This was introduced with the 1976 Government Accounting Act. By physical performance budgeting an attempt is made to increase insight in outputs and costs of government services. Little can be said about the possible contribution of physical performance budgeting in allocation decisions as relatively little experience exists at this point in time.

4 POLICY ANALYSIS

An important initiative towards improving the basis for resource allocation decisions within central government was taken in 1971, with the establishment of the Commission for the Development of Policy Analysis (COBA).

The use of new techniques, such as systems analysis and cost-benefit analysis, had demonstrated that some of the tools for policy analysis were, at least in principle, available. Several government departments had, in fact, started to use these tools in analyses of their own, often with interesting results, but in such a way that extensions to other fields were hampered rather than encouraged and comparisons were difficult to make. Experience in other countries (for example PPBS in the United States and CRCB in France) had provided an indication of the potential for centrally guided attempts at rationalising allocation decisions, as well as the pitfalls one could encounter in doing so. It was felt that in the Dutch situation a commission, composed of top level civil servants from the various ministries and assisted by a relatively sizeable secretariat, would – in the long run – be the most effective way to guide and stimulate policy analysis. The main tasks of the Commission can be summarised as follows:

(1) To advise the cabinet on the possibilities and limitations of policy analysis, and areas to which analysis could be extended.
(2) To stimulate the implementation of policy analysis within the various ministies and throughout Government.
(3) To co-ordinate the development and extension of policy analysis across ministries.
(4) To develop appropriate methods and techniques for policy analysis.

The Commission is chaired by the Director-General of the Budget, and is assisted by a Secretariat of approximately thirty persons.

During the nearly eight years of its existence COBA has developed three major lines of activity:

(i) development of methodology for policy analysis;
(ii) implementation of policy analysis;
(iii) documentation, information and training in policy analysis. These activities will be briefly surveyed in turn, illustrating how problems are conceived and tackled and – sometimes – resolved.

Developments of methods and techniques

A considerable amount of energy has been devoted to inventorising available techniques for *ex post* and *ex ante* evaluation of policies, refining them where possible, and mapping out when and how to use them. This work is generally carried out by special working parties of COBA in which experts from inside as well as from outside government participate. Thus far, most of the primarily methodological work has focused on techniques of cost-benefit analysis, systematic analysis of objectives and what has been called 'instrument analysis'.[6]

[6] The latter embraces the development of methods for testing relative effectiveness of policy instruments (e.g. subsidies, taxation, information), as well as relative effectiveness and efficiency of particular forms within a single instrument category (e.g. different subsidy structures). So far, work has concentrated on the areas of subsidies and of levies.

Furthermore, attention has been paid to different approaches in planning.

Though useful in itself, this work has suffered to some extent from the risk of being theoretically sound (and within particular economic conceptions at that), but having limited applicability. This can, of course, be countered by strengthening the empirical element, but in actual practice it turns out to be exceedingly difficult to steer a course between dogma and real life. A related problem resides in the pursuit of, on the one hand, sets of commonly agreed definitions, criteria and procedures, so as to further comparability of results and, on the other hand, developing relatively simple and easily understood guidelines with which practitioners in a variety of problem areas can work. These remain serious issues for which, to my knowledge, no easy and simple solution exists. Up to now guidelines have been produced for (aspects of) cost-benefit analysis, analysis of objectives, and analysis of subsidies. Improvements/extensions are presently being made, with results anticipated by early next year. These will also include the subjects of strategic planning and levies.

Implementation of policy analysis

By implementation is meant, first and foremost, the analysis itself, to be discussed first. In addition, some remarks will be made regarding the implementation of results of particular analyses.

Up till recently, COBA has paid relatively little attention to what can properly be called implementation. It is true that the Secretariat has participated in a fair number of studies, but on the whole, its involvement has been limited to an advisory role with respect to methodology. The development work on methods has certainly brought about a great amount of analysis, but the focus has been primarily on testing out preliminary guidelines and only in the second instance on analysing the subject-matter concerned. Indirectly COBA has undoubtedly stimulated the implementation of policy analysis in the Netherlands, as witnessed by the references to its work in government papers and publications, as well as in academic journals, and by the use made in analytical studies of what has sometimes come to be called 'COBA methodology'. It is, of course, impossible to determine to what extent the volume and quality of policy analysis would have been less had COBA not existed. More directly, COBA effects can be traced in departmental work as the structures responsible for departmental studies have – to a large extent – been set up in response to COBA activities. Furthermore, the expansion of policy analysis has certainly benefited from the educational and informational activities carried out under its auspices (discussed below).

Taken together, however, it is clear that the implementation of policy analysis has been an effect, to some extent directly attributable to COBA work, but not a direct concern of the Commission so far. In fact, reviewing its activities over the period of its existence, the Commission, early this year, came to precisely that conclusion. This review also included an assessment of present needs for policy analysis. Balancing these needs against capabilities, and taking into account the structural and methodological basis which had been developed, the Commission has decided to make implementation its explicit concern from now on. The translation into practice of this new orientation will be that the Secretariat will move beyond a strictly advisory function and, jointly with the departments concerned, carry out policy analyses,

It is too early to tell how much can be achieved. What is clear already at this stage, however, is that there is certainly no lack of demand. This raises the interesting question whether this shift towards operational activities could have been made earlier and, more generally, at what point in time and on what basis a change in emphasis from methodology to implementation could be fostered at central level. The important subsequent question is, of course, how one can ensure that the results of any analysis (assuming it is properly conducted) are adequately taken into account in allocation decisions. Experience here is very haphazard and any success story could easily be countered with an equally impressive example of miserable failure. There are, clearly, no hard and fast rules in this matter, but experience and common sense, at the very least, indicate the pitfalls one should try to avoid. At the risk of listing platitudes, I mention some of these below. First there are those bearing on what I would call 'genuineness of demand':

(i) trival problems;
(ii) problems where no solution is wanted;
(iii) problems where the conclusions are already set.

These criteria may seem obvious. However, all too often resources are wasted on problems whose solution will have an exceedingly limited impact on policies broadly conceived, or on problems defined in such a way that their solution is either improbable, or not in time to be of any interest. In fact, the first two criteria cover the well-known bureaucratic devices for diverting attention and/or energy. The third issue is rather more intractable. Nevertheless, in many cases existing commitments towards particular courses of action are sufficiently strong and visible to warrant the prediction that no analysis, no matter how good, will influence decisions. In addition to wasting resources the pressures to use indicators as vindicators for particular viewpoints may risk discrediting policy analysis as a whole. Barring innocence, the three criteria are, I believe, a reasonable test of 'genuineness' of demand for policy analysis, i.e. real interest in the results of any particular exercise. How that interest can be sustained is an even murkier issue. The following criteria are offered as food for thought and certainly not as a conclusive set:

(i) involvement;
(ii) time;
(iii) input-issue ratio.

By involvement is meant the involvement of the parties concerned, the decision-makers on present and future policies in particular; by time the time it takes to complete the analysis; and by input-issue ratio the quantity and quality of resources put in over that required to carry out the analysis, given the scope and complexity of the issue. Clearly, the three are very much related to each other. Involvement is to a large extent dependent on the time it takes to reach a final product, while the time it takes may be much longer than the time required if resources are not on a par with the issue.

Involvement is, I believe, the most important of the three, as well as the most difficult. It is the essential element to ensure that the problem is conceived in a way that – in the end – can be acted upon (by the decision-maker), and to reduce the risk that relevant aspects are overlooked (as perceived by those concerned or affected). It is also an important tonic to the morale of the analysts, as it is generally more satisfactory to be able to believe that one's product will be used rather than stocked in libraries or, even worse, ending up in a drawer before reaching that stage. As the real world is not static, maintaining involvement may assist in adapting the original conception of the issue to changing circumstances, retaining relevance to and possibilities of acting for the decision-maker. The simultaneous involvement of other parties concerned may assist in adapting the decision-maker's conception of the issue to take account of variables he had not originally considered.

Of course there are limits to involvement, as well as its usefulness! On the whole, however, policy analysis has suffered more from too little than too much. Decisions with respect to the location of a liquid natural gas terminal (having established the desirability of importing LNG), in which regional economic considerations at the last moment weighed more heavily than the analysis had anticipated, are only one example from recent Dutch history.

The element of time requires little discussion. Although the parties concerned may remain the same, personalities will change as time passes, and political affiliations and social and economic realities often change as well. Even if this is not the case, or not important to the issue at hand, it is a well-known phenomenon that interest tends to fade with time. A good example of a study which went astray because too little attention was given to the element of time is provided by the COBA-initiated analysis of departmental objectives.

The analysis started in 1972 with a fairly high level of interest and resource commitment from both the Secretariat and several Departments. Particularly in retrospect it is clear that it set out with too high ambitions, a too vaguely defined rationale, and too many uncertainties regarding methodology. Had clear intermediate targets been built in, uncertainties with respect to the direction and results of the exercise could have been reduced during its course, with concomitant reductions in resource waste and maintenance of interest. In fact, the recently decided stock-taking effort, which should be completed in a few months' time, has considerably boosted interest already. The resource issue is, of course, fundamental to most problems (particularly if treated by economists), and of increasing importance as real resources become scarcer. At the same time, I feel, the present economic circumstances are conducive to increasing resources for policy analysis, as more people will want better arguments why to spend money this way rather than the other, or why to spend it at all on any particular subject. For that matter too little attention in the past as well as the present has been given, in my view, to qualitative aspects. What is good for analysing a particular set of issues, may not be adequate to deal with another. Professional interests or, if this is not the same, professional blindness, all too often hamper finding new solutions to old problems. I need only mention the field of energy studies as a case in point.

Documentation, information and training

Since its inception COBA has devoted a great deal of attention to disseminating information about and training in policy analysis. A quarterly journal with literature references, articles and reports on COBA activities distributes some 4000 copies. In addition to COBA, mention should be made of the various reports and periodicals produced by the planning agencies, ministries and university departments of increasingly policy-analytical and policy-relevant nature.

Several times a year courses of different level and duration are organised by the COBA Secretariat. Three-week courses are held for university-graduated civil servants with at least three years work experience with government administration, a one-week course is held for senior administrators, and two-day orientation conferences are organised for top-level civil servants. In the future, seminars on particular topics will be held on an incidental basis. A documentation centre, although still quite small, is now being expanded.

Following the rule that what is once learnt is not easily forgotten, and the equally important rule that in order to be able to appreciate something knowledge of its existence is a prerequisite, 'educational' work has been an important part of COBA activities. With the single difficulty that education about cannot go faster than experience with policy analysis, the programme has, on the whole, been well received and, although its mission is certainly not completed, it has undoubtedly contributed to laying the foundation for the implementation-of-policy-analysis policy.

V CONCLUSIONS

The issues of overall control of the budget and getting the best value for money within the public sector revert to a very large extent to decisions on priorities and allocations at micro level. Accepting that these decisions are partly based on political considerations and partly on analytical grounds, and assuming that the two are not necessarily antithetical, continuing to ask those nagging questions of 'why' and 'how' is probably the most hopeful way for improving the quality of policy decisions.

Some of the tools for getting answers to those questions, employed in isolation or in combination in the Netherlands, have been discussed above. A number of the issues arising in conjunction with their use, particularly the pressures of time, have been illustrated. There may be many ways to Rome, but in budgetary matters it is important to get there in time. The same is true for The Hague and, I trust, for other capitals as well.

On the other hand, it is clear that miracle solutions do not exist. Attempting to improve the quality of budget decisions, attempting to 'spend less, while getting more', implies a lot of hard work over an extended period of time, the results of which will become visible only gradually. If they do just that, I think that a sufficient basis exists to press on and to continue trying.

Discussion of 'Spending More and Getting Less? Some Experience with the Control of the Growth of Public Expenditure in the Netherlands' by Mr Th. A. J. Meys

The discussion was opened by *Professor Manz* who pointed to the very general nature of the policy problem of maintaining levels of employment in the face of rapid technological change which reduced labour requirements. He suggested further discussion of the relationship between the growth of total income and the limits on public expenditure as described in the section of the paper dealing with structural budget policy. Finally, he asked Mr Verwayen to give more information on the extent to which the Commission for the Development of Policy Analysis had been able to control public expenditure in the interests of both stabilisation and allocative policy.

Several speakers wished to question or qualify the conclusion of the paper that the application of formal techniques of analysis would probably lead to better decisions on policy. *Professor Boulding* argued that technocratic procedures such as those described tended to undermine the vital political structure of government. In his view it was for this reason that formal techniques of decision-making had been resisted within governments. He proposed a distinction between technical government and political government in which the governing system was open to a continuous feedback from citizens. Technical government involved attempts to control economic and political events by a strategy of fine-tuning which massively overestimated the capability of governments to determine outcomes. He gave the example of slow growth in the United Kingdom which in his view was neither government induced nor susceptible to improvement by policy. It was rather the result of a playful and inefficient national culture which in the long run may be a factor making for survival. *Sir Leo Pliatzky*'s view was that the application of cost-benefit analysis could lead to enormous waste, an example of which was the Concorde project. This danger was particularly acute when national prestige was defined as a social benefit, as it was in cost-benefit analyses that had been carried out within the French government. In a set of comments addressed also to Sir Leo Pliatzky's paper, *Professor Klein* pointed to two limitations on the application of microeconomic theory. The first arose from the inevitability of political judgements on issues such as equity. The values involved were not susceptible to economic analysis and could not be expressed as prices in the form required by cost-benefit analysis. The second concerned the important symbolic character of services such as health care which provided a general reassurance to the population which could be distinguished from the specific benefits provided to individuals. This factor was also difficult to capture in a formal economic calculus. He argued that the potential contribution that such techniques could make would only be fully realised within an open institutional structure without rules of secrecy in which politicians could not easily ignore or conceal technical advice and in which a broad constituency for rationality could be formed. *Professor Frey* observed that the introduction of formal analysis was not sufficient for the control of public expenditure because bureaucrats and pressure groups were able to manipulate such techniques in their own interests, and to the disadvantage of unorganised interests. The United States provided an example of spending more and getting less in the case of education where the result of higher expenditures had been higher salaries without any improvement in services provided. His view was that such behaviour might explain recent dramatic increases in public expenditure and that it provided a general argument for constitutional reform.

Other speakers did not accept some of these arguments against formal techniques. *Professor Maillet* insisted that it was not the main purpose of such techniques to control public expenditure, in the sense of reducing the level of it, but to reallocate total public expenditure amongst different items in the light of changing social and political priorities. *Professor Sandmo* argued first, that the evidence of increasing public expenditures was not proof that decisions taken had been wrong, and secondly that, in any case, cost-benefit analysis had not been applied in areas such as social security in which expenditure increases had been particularly rapid. On a more general level, *Professor Pohorille* suggested that observable increases in public expenditure had not been the result of economic or bureaucratic inefficiency but had rather been a response to genuine social needs, which had become increasingly difficult to satisfy.

Mr Matthews asked how the system of control in terms of the total budget deficit described in the paper could be used to regulate spending on individual programmes. *Professor Modigliani* asked whether there was evidence for the statement in the paper that both direct and indirect taxes had been shifted from wages. He did not see how it could be assumed that in wage bargaining workers were not subject to tax illusion, but were subject to the illusion that public expenditures on social services did not contribute to real income. *Professor Urquidi* asked for information about the formulation of policy on foreign aid in the Netherlands. *Professor Sandmo*'s view was that relatively less effort should be devoted to *ex ante* cost-benefit analysis and more to *ex post* evaluation. This would bring the public sector more into line with the private sector and promote efficiency. *Professor Modigliani* asked how the 60 per cent share of social expenditures in national income shown in Figure 12.1 could be sustained in terms of the required levels of taxation and savings.

A number of speakers described the arrangements for public expenditure planning in their own countries. *Professor Manz* outlined the system in the German Democratic Republic whereby social service organisations submitted budget proposals to the government which then decided on planning targets and carried out efficiency audits. *Professor Hanusch* referred to the projections of national income and tax revenue which were an ingredient of the system of four-year expenditure planning operated in the Federal Republic of Germany. His view was that this system was weakened by the exclusion from it of information on policy outputs, and of spending by federal states and communities which accounted for two-thirds of the total of public expenditure. *Professor Bös* described the operation of a similar system in Austria, and the political use to which it had been put in restraining parliamentary demands for increases in public expenditure. *Professor Maillet* described two elements of the French planning system: the application of output and budgeting and cost-benefit techniques in areas such as health, education and transport; and the submission from the government to the parliament of both traditional and programme budgets. He reported that the programme form had not been well received in parliament because of the difficulty of assigning expenditures within it to constituencies. *Professor Urquidi* pointed to the problems of budgeting in developing countries, in which the lack of buoyancy in tax revenues led to a reliance on foreign borrowing which was difficult to control and co-ordinate.

In response to the discussion, *Mr Verwayen* gave his assessment of the success of the planning instruments described in the paper. In his view dissatisfaction with the system of medium-term projections had outweighed the advantages of it. A particular problem was that projections of public expenditure had been taken as a minimum with the result that outcomes had become inflated. He reported that the provisions for the reconsideration of government functions had had little effect. Although the activities of the Inspection of the Ministry of Finance had had a considerable effect on the volume of spending of the various departments, its influence on improving effectiveness and efficiency in public spending had probably been limited. It was too early to judge the impact of the system of physical performance budgeting. His reply to

Professor Urquidi's question on foreign aid was that this item was not subjected to formal analysis. He did not dispute the particular points which had been raised against formal techniques. Nevertheless he reported that there was optimism in the Netherlands that their application could yield significant benefits.

13 Modelling the US Federal Spending Process: Overview and Implications

Michael Dempster

SYSTEM AND DECISION SCIENCES, IIASA

and

Aaron Wildavsky

UNIVERSITY OF CALIFORNIA, BERKELEY

If increased economy and efficiency in the expenditure of funds is to be secured, it is thus imperative that the evils should be attacked at their source. The only way by which this can be done is by placing definite responsibility upon some officer of the Government to receive the requests for funds as originally formulated by bureau and departmental chiefs and subjecting them to that scrutiny, revision, and correlation that has been described. In the National Government there can be no question but that the officer upon whom should be placed this responsibility is the President of the United States.

House Select Committee on the Budget
(regarding the 1921 Budget and
Accounting Act)
H. Rept. No. 14, 67th Congress,
1st Sess., at 5.

I INTRODUCTION

The purpose of this paper is to show how inflation is endemic to the budgetary process of the United States Federal Government. To do this we relate models of government expenditure to models of the economy, thus joining in theory what have in practice always been together.

The description we shall give – although presented in summary rather than detail – is based on hard statistical and econometric evidence amassed over more than a decade. We shall attempt to show that, while they are complex, the relevant processes can be modelled reasonably simply. We shall conclude that the forces influencing US Federal expenditures – bureaucratic, political and economic – are too entrenched and powerful to be easily deflected from their current course. Although expenditures decline during restrictive periods, they do not decline by nearly as much as they previously increased; thus each cycle of spending begins from a higher base. For empirical detail the reader is referred to our forthcoming monograph, *The Political Economy of Public Expenditure*.

To make this paper self-contained, this introduction contains very brief descriptions of the process by which fiscal policy and the budget are formed in the name of the President and of the evolution of the broad pattern of Federal expenditure post the Second World War. An interesting observation is that both the necessity and the opportunity for increased spending arose through the exigencies of economic policy-making in the grip of the 'New Economics'.

In the second section we turn to the bureaucratic processes by which the Chief Executive receives 'the requests for funds as originally formulated by bureau and departmental chiefs' and subjects them to 'scrutiny, revision and correlation' before submitting them to Congress as formal requests for appropriations. Our simple, empirically supported models of the formation and co-ordination of budget requests, appropriations and timing of expenditures will be presented in this section. Here we shall encounter the powerful influence of momentum.

Section III outlines, by means of the comparative static analysis of a simple macroeconomic model with an endogenous government sector, the short- and medium-term economic implications of a government reacting – through its wage bill, 'mandatory' transfer payments and attempted fiscal policy – to output, the price level and unemployment. Unlike both the established Keynesian and Monetarist equivalents, the model is capable, depending on recognisably plausible parameter configurations, of generating a wide range of behaviour – including the evil modern phenomenon of 'stagflation'. The message here is that when government involves a sizeable proportion of economic activity, its budget deficit – rather than private consumer and investment credit alone – represents a major intertemporal credit demand, fuelling both growth and inflation. In these circumstances a tight fiscal and monetary policy, which reduces this credit in response to inflation, can have precisely the opposite effect to that desired, namely, simultaneous stagnation and accelerating inflation.

In the final section of the paper we speculate on the *long-term* effects of the resulting growth of the public sector necessitated by short-term political and economic forces.

BRIEF DESCRIPTION OF THE EXECUTIVE FISCAL POLICY AND BUDGET PROCESS[1]

The Budgeting and Accounting Act of 1921 makes the President formally responsible for the initiation of an annual budget through his staff agency, the Office of Management and Budget (OMB, formerly the Bureau of the Budget, BOB). The preparation and execution of the Federal budget for any fiscal year covers at least 31 months. Each spring, attention is given to: (i) the control of (contractual) obligations and outlays (expenditures) during the last half of the fiscal year in progress; (ii) the planning of programmes for the upcoming fiscal year, which will begin the next October; and (iii) the development of preliminary plans and policies for the succeeding fiscal year.

During the time that Congress is considering the budget for the imminent fiscal year (1 October–30 September), the agencies are preparing estimates of their expenditures for the next year. These estimates are compiled by budget officers under the direction of agency and departmental heads. Of necessity, estimates are detailed, but they may incorporate modifications to take account both of the overall Presidental programme and possible Congressional reaction. When complete, they are submitted to OMB. There they are reviewed in the light of Presidential plans by examiners familiar with the respective agencies. Subsequently, hearings allow both agency defence and clarification of estimated requirements. During this part of the process, the Director of OMB confers frequently with the President and

[1] In the preparation of the remainder of this section and the next we have made extensive use of the work of John P. Crecine and his colleagues, Mark Kamlett, David Mowery and Chandler Stolp, under the support of NSF Grant SOC-72-05488. We are grateful for extensive discussions with them and refer the reader to Crecine's work on budgeting processes in the Department of Defence in *Volume IV, Appendices: Commission on the Organization of Government for the Conduct of Foreign Policy*, US Government Printing Office (1975), pp. 63–110, and our forthcoming joint paper with Crecine, 'Some Structural Characteristics of the Federal Budgetary Process'. We also gratefully acknowledge the support of the Center for Advanced Study in the Behavioral Sciences during the academic year 1974–75.

endeavours to keep agency requests within Presidential limits. By December, the Director presents to the President a consolidated account of expected revenues and requested expenditures. Next, under the direction of the President, OMB, the Treasury Department and the Council of Economic Advisors prepare the budget message. In January, the President presents his budget to Congress.

The Congressional budget process has undergone significant changes due to the enactment of the Congressional Budget and Impoundment Act in 1972.[2] Under this Act, Congress also focuses on *overall budget totals* and relates individual appropriation actions to one another within a general set of spending priorities. To aid in this process, the Act established a new committee on the Budget in each House to augment the Appropriations Committees and a new, professionally staffed, Congressional Budget Office (CBO). The Act also provides a tight timetable for the new budget process and shifted the fiscal year from 1 July through 30 June to 1 October through 30 September, in order to give Congress three additional months to complete action on the Federal budget. Note that in the new budget cycle which has been in effect since fiscal 1977 (actual 1975) the timing and nature of the Executive portion of the cycle has not changed substantially.

OMB's role in the Executive budget process has two principal phases: a macro planning or 'target setting' phase, called the *Spring Budget Preview*, and a more detailed *Director's Review* phase in which agency budget submissions are examined in detail. At the Director's Review in the autumn, requests generated for each agency during the planning phase are co-ordinated in light of overall fiscal policy. The principal role of a department is to reconcile the requests of its agencies before submission to OMB for the Director's Review. The Department of Defense has a process for reconciling Service requests similar to that of the Office of Management and Budget.

For at least the past decade, OMB has prepared the necessary forecasts and determined agency appropriation and expenditure targets in the Spring Preview without any *formal* input from the agencies. The Preview exercise results in a set of plans consistent with anticipated fiscal policy which OMB produces almost entirely internally. Although the Budget Office attempts to set aside 2 or 3 per cent of the planned budget total for contingencies (mostly pay raises) during the Preview, the allocations of budgetary resources have been broadly determined at this point. Without changes of total resources available, an increase in any

[2] For a more complete description see, *Preparation and Execution of the Federal Budget*, Office of Management and Budget, November (1976).

one allocation over its target implies a decrease in another. Because agencies tend to interpret these OMB ceilings as essentially minimum guarantees, it is easy to see that after targets have been sent to the agencies any significant increase in a part of the total can result in very painful reallocation decisions for departments and the Office of Management and Budget. Features of the fall Director's Review process are a compression of information and the suppression of detail.

As might be suspected for a department spending from one-half (in the early post-war years) to one-fifth (more recently) of the Federal budget, the Department of Defense has a budget process essentially separate from – but of course co-ordinated with – OMB. In this process the Office of the Secretary of Defense (OSD), in particular the Controller's Office under an Assistant Secretary, plays the role with regard to the Services that is played by OMB with regard to the non-defence agencies and departments.

The method for determining the defence/non-defence split was essentially developed in the decade immediately after the Second World War. Basically the story is one of deducting, from estimates of revenues accrued, breakdowns of 'uncontrollable', or fixed expenditures over which there is little immediate discretion, and controllable domestic expenditures over which there is some spending discretion, to leave the amount available for military expenditure, broadly defined.[3]

Estimation is performed by only a very few people – during the Truman and Eisenhower administrations by the same people over a number of years – during a period of a few weeks. We would therefore expect various aids to calculation to be employed even in the preparation of this simplified aid to Presidential decision-making. However simple-minded such aids appear, they can be made still easier for the men on the run. Although the resulting defence total is subject to appeals by the Department of Defense and the Pentagon, the numbers remain relatively fixed over the Executive budget cycle. They stay stable because the process separates detailed and programmatic responsibility for defence and non-defence expenditures between the Office of the Secretary of Defense and OMB/BOB over the period from the Spring Preview to the October reviews. Because timing is critical to budgeting,

[3] During the Kennedy–Johnson era, for political reasons Defense Secretary McNamara avoided communicating *explicit* military ceilings during the executive portion of the budget cycle. However, it is not clear whether or not *implicit* military totals were used but not reported. See J. P. Crecine, 'Defense Budgeting', Chapter 7 in R. F. Byrne, A. Charnes, W. W. Cooper, O. A. Davis and Dorothy Gifford (eds), *Studies in Budgeting* (North Holland, Amsterdam, 1971).

it is important to recall that these estimates are made eighteen to twenty months in advance of the average timing of actual expenditures in the fiscal year under consideration. Hence we should not be surprised that estimates made in the recent past are more important for their bearing on events occurring during and immediately after their composition than as predictions of an uncertain future. Thus the Presidential review of appeals in December is less one of policy-making than of dispute settling in view of changes in fiscal and economic estimates by the Treasury, OMB/BOB, and the Council of Economic Advisors. Indeed, barring major changes in foreign policy, the broad lines of Presidential policy are fixed during the Spring Preview four to eight quarters in advance of the corresponding outlays. Throughout the ensuing budget cycle to the submission of the President's budget to Congress, adjustments to these broad outlines are relatively marginal in light of changing economic and environmental circumstances, and detailed adjustments are made in light of the policy advocacy process of agencies, Congress and clientele groups in the economy and polity. The whole process is one of continual adjustment and mutual adaptation of the estimates of various interests within the bureaucracy to the final estimates submitted to Congress in the President's budget.

THE POST-WAR INCREASE IN EXPENDITURE

In the decade of the fifties, the budget process appeared to be working reasonably well – revenue and expenditure were kept within hailing distance. Congressmen respected the process; so did the Executive. After all, even in fiscal 1961, the Federal budget was only about $82 billion, representing some 16 per cent of the gross national product, a growth of nearly 40 billions since fiscal 1951, but only a negligible increase in the proportion of the GNP. By fiscal 1979, however, the budget has increased to a whopping $500 billion and an even larger proportion of the GNP to nearly 25 per cent.[4] The late sixties and the seventies really represented different eras in budgeting from the decades that preceded them. What happened?

One thing that did not happen was an absolute increase in military expenditures. These have remained virtually stable in constant dollars since the rundown after the close of the Korean War in 1953 – the period

[4] The percentages for earlier years are for the administrative Federal budget. Percentages for total outlays, comparable to the 1978 (cash consolidated) budget, are 15 % of GNP in fiscal 1951 and 20 % in fiscal 1961. Source: Fiscal 1967 Budget.

of the Vietnam War increasing them only temporarily. Thus, the effect of the Truman–Eisenhower–Nixon–Ford policy of calculating the first approximation to military expenditure as a residual, and the exigencies of the separate structure of military and non-defence calculations within the Executive budget process, have resulted in increments in total military spending which on average have just kept up with cost increases due to wage and price rises. Furthermore, in terms of proportion of GNP – which represents the proportion of national resources diverted to military spending – this has been relatively constant. Although over the post-war period from fiscal 1950 to fiscal 1975 this proportion has varied from 5 to approximately 13 per cent (at the peak of the Korean War) and rose by roughly 3 per cent of GNP during the Vietnam War, it has fluctuated about a level of approximately 8 per cent over the period. To find the substantial increases in government expenditure over the post-war period, we must therefore look elsewhere.

The great increases in public expenditure have come in social and welfare expenditures, from a total of about 8 billions in fiscal 1965 immediately before LBJ's Great Society programmes, to 168 billions in fiscal 1975 – over a fourfold increase in real terms. This is only to say that there was a marked agreement within the country that expenditures on human resources should rise and that this consensus has been reflected in Congressional appropriations and subsequent Federal expenditures.[5]

The 1960s and early 1970s witnessed a series of struggles over the size and scope of government spending, as the political forces behind spending grew far more powerful. Presidents Kennedy and Johnson and Nixon, in spite of initiating increased spending, wanted to *appear* financially responsible. Whether it was Johnson's effort to come in below $100 billion, or Nixon's at no more than $200 billion, they promoted their announced targets publicly. Executive interplay with Congress became a game to shift responsibility to the other branch for cutting or failing to cut expenditures. The size of budgets became as never before part of political strategy. Successive governments, therefore, whatever their announced orientation to spending, have found it imperative to make the deficit look smaller either by making revenues look larger or expenditures lower or both.

Economics (or, at least, economists) came to the rescue. The

[5] See Aaron Wildavsky, 'Co-ordination Without a Co-ordinator', *Speaking Truth to Power: The Art and Craft of Policy Analysis* Chapter 4, (Little, Brown, Boston, 1979).

increasing importance of economics in government has provided doctrinal aid – sometimes on purpose, other times by accident – for higher levels of spending. The consolidated budget, the nature of the forecasting exercise for fiscal policy-making itself and the concept of the full employment surplus – all inventions of economists – simultaneously strove to justify higher spending and to make it appear lower.

By far the most important of the specific devices for increasing government spending mentioned above has been the abandonment of the norm of the balanced budget by President Nixon in the fiscal 1972 budget in favour of a less restrictive one. The idea that Federal budgets *ought* to be balanced was widely accepted in the United States, even after the Keynesian revolution in thought, through the administrations of Democrat Harry Truman and Republican Dwight Eisenhower. Life was simple (outside of wartime) and *cash* control was exercised; expenditures were monies the regular governmental departments paid out and revenues were taxes collected. A deficit, then, meant a cash difference between ordinary revenue and expenditure; what was *ordinary* was sanctified as much by usage and custom as by formal definition. When the government took in as much cash as it paid out, the budget was balanced. Keynesian economic theory was interpreted to mean that a *temporary* Federal deficit could stimulate the economy at a downturn of the business cycle, but the cash loss would be recovered at the subsequent peak as a revenue surplus. In the long run – in theory – no increase in the public debt need be sustained; economic debate centred on the effectiveness and timing of this counter-cyclical policy.

Whereas Presidents Truman and Eisenhower believed in the norm of the balanced budget and acted on their beliefs, Presidents Kennedy, Johnson and Nixon abandoned these beliefs and acted accordingly. The *direct* mechanism for superseding the older norm was called the *full employment deficit*. In a word, this doctrine meant that federal expenditures should rise to the point that would have been justified if the nation's economy had been at full employment. Under the new interpretation of Keynesian theory, the difference between this full employment level and current revenues would be the appropriate Federal deficit to impart exactly the right stimulus to the economy to achieve full employment. A cash surplus under these conditions is most unlikely, especially since Kennedy established the precedent of cutting tax rates to go along with it. The extent of the permissible deficit, however, was rather vague, depending as it did on whatever level of unemployment was considered too high, and whatever calculations were judged to provide an approximation of full employment. The cash-balanced budget was not only regarded as unnecessary and theoretically undesirable, but 'balance' at the full employment level, rather than at a recognisable particular point, was in practice becoming a rather sizeable range. Keynesian thought was now interpreted to mean that the budget should be balanced at expenditures that would provide sufficient stimulation to create full employment at whatever level was designated as being full. Might this blissful full employment state come about? Not never, perhaps, but hardly ever; and yet apparently paradoxically a cash *surplus* – coupled with a tight monetary policy – wreaked havoc on the economy in 1969–70 and again in 1974–75.

From the perspective of theoretical economic management, the new economic concepts no doubt represent improvements, but from the point of view of political management of expenditure, the proposition is doubtful. It is a matter of distinguishing between economic and political rationality. From an economic point of view, for example, it makes substantive sense to index social security contributions so as to mitigate the effects of inflation by recipients. But if one realises that Congressmen love to vote increases, so that protection against inflation is likely to be achieved first, followed by repeated increases, the political economist of social security might have advocated a different approach. In the same way, the political economist of Federal expenditures might have preferred to keep separate accounts for economic purposes rather than compromising an essentially political document – the budget of the United States Federal government – with economic accounting concepts that bias the results in the direction of increased spending. Of course, if one *wants* increased spending, then what has been done is not only correct but creative.

'Playing politics' with the budget is what everyone does, and should do, in a democratic polity. 'Politics' once included the expectation that voters would apply sanctions if unbalanced budgets were regularly submitted. Thus, in the past, significant departures from the norm of a balanced budget placed informal but real limits on the amount of manipulation that could take place in order to get past the next election or to maintain or increase popularity in the short run. This restraint no longer applies. If Presidents wish to avoid the appearance of confrontation between policies of 'guns or butter' (or to spend largesse before election day), their possibilities are multiplied. Who, after all, can say how large the full employment deficit might appropriately be or what the margin of error in the total actually is or what the level of deficit would have to be to know that the *political* impact had become too large? In this way, inflation under the impetus of increased spending has been built into the budgetary process to a much larger degree than was heretofore the case.

Now in the past it has been argued that long-run interests in holding down spending have been sacrificed to short-term interests in gaining the approval of beneficiaries. The norm of the balanced budget, however, limited how much of this could be done at any one time. When President Johnson discovered that almost everyone was interested in new obligational authority, that is, the amount appearing in the budget in a particular year, rather than in future obligations incurred under the corresponding authorisation, another past restraint in the budgetary process was loosened. Present reductions could be traded for future increases. Spending in relation to revenue over the past two decades has in fact been made *less* rather than more accountable, hence less *controllable*.[6]

We must understand that what is or is not considered a controllable expenditure – hence subject to discretion, hence part of the budget that can be changed – is a *subjective* and not an objective definition. The important point is that uncontrollable is not the same as *unchangeable*. It remains true, as it always has been, that budgets are made by people and can be changed by them. It may take a few years (a 10 per cent increase a year amounts to over a 100 per cent in seven years) but if we are interested in the cumulative results of budgetary processes, little is left that human beings cannot change.

II MODELLING THE EXECUTIVE BUDGET PROCESS: INCREMENTALISM, CO-ORDINATION AND THE PROPORTIONAL CUT

Despite the complexities of the Federal budget and expenditure processes the immediate forces behind the growth of the United States Government can be reasonably simply and accurately modelled. In this section we introduce empirically supported:

(1) Micro-models of *appropriation* formation – taking as basic unit major agencies and departments in OMB Divisions and including

[6] For an excellent discussion of controllability see Barry M. Blechman, Edward M. Gramlich and Robert W. Hartman, Budget controllability and planning, Chapter 7 of *Setting National Priorities, The 1976 Budget* (The Brookings Institution, Washington DC, 1976), pp. 190–230.

external economic, social and political influences operating through the Executive, President and Congress.

(2) Models of non-market co-ordinating mechanisms – Office of Management and Budget procedures by which agency *appropriation* requests are fitted within current fiscal constraints.

(3) Distributed lag-spending models – to represent the timing of actual agency and departmental *outlays* from appropriated funds.

In the next section we shall describe a simple macroeconomic model and use it to analyse the effects of Presidential policy-making interacting with bureaucratic and Congressional upwards spending pressures (represented in the models of this section) to generate a public policy-induced economic cycle.

Rather than present detailed econometric estimates,[7] it will suffice here to set out the basic models together with a brief description of their empirical support. We begin with a verbal description of the models developed in our earliest work which investigated the correspondence of simple two-equation models – based on considerations of limited rationality in the face of complexity and uncertainty – to the *appropriate* budgeting behaviour of 116 domestic agencies, large and small, over the period fiscal 1947 to fiscal 1963. The basic model for an individual agency stated that (up to mutually and serially independent disturbances representing non-recurring events specific to respectively the demand and supply of funds):

> Executive requests on behalf of an agency were a proportional mark-up of the previous years appropriation, while the corresponding Congressional appropriation was a simple proportion of the Presidential estimate (request),

usually, of course – but not always[8] – a *mark-down*. Although the incremental behaviour specified by these models of the appropriations

[7] See Otto A. Davis, M. A. H. Dempster and Aaron Wildavsky, 'A theory of the budgetary process', *Amer. Political Sci. Rev.*, 60 (1966), 529–47; 'On the process of budgeting: An empirical study of Congressional appropriation', *Papers in Non-Market Decision Making*, 1 (1966), 63–132; 'On the process of budgeting II: An empirical study of Congressional appropriation', Chapter 9 in R. F. Byrne, A. Charnes, W. W. Cooper, O. A. Davis and Dorothy Gifford (eds), *Studies in Budgeting* (North Holland, Amsterdam, 1971); 'Towards a predictive theory of government expenditure: U.S. domestic appropriations', *British J. Political Sci.*, 4 (1974), 419–52, and our forthcoming monograph.

[8] Outstanding exceptions in the fiscal 1947–63 period were the National Institutes of Health and NASA.

process for an individual agency appeared to be the general rule, a major finding concerned the nature of the exceptions. For many agencies, epochs in which the underlying incremental relationships appeared to change were identified statistically; a subset of these epochs was investigated by documentary analysis and the major influences at work on the corresponding agencies classified. While some of these influences were essentially random and non-recurring, most could be seen to be due to specific political, or general economic or social events. This suggested that, although it is basically incremental, the budget process does respond to the needs of the economy and society, but only after sufficient pressure has built up to cause *abrupt* changes precipitated by events.[9]

Next we attempted to model this extended notion of the nature of the budget process at agency level by incorporating a number of political, economic and social exogenous variables into our earlier model in such a way as to preserve the behavioural interpretation of its coefficients. The explanatory variables for these extended micro models are set out in Table 13.1. The models were estimated over the fiscal 1947–63 period for a representative selection of 53 agencies from our previous 116. Confidence in the validity of an econometric model can only be justified by successful performance in prediction – both *ex post* (after the fact) and *ex ante* in genuine forecasting. We therefore analysed the increase in level of explanation of the budget process obtained by the extended model in terms of some reasonable criteria for evaluating *ex post* prediction over the five-year post-estimation period fiscal 1964–68. We also compared the predictive performances over this period of the extended model and various obvious or naive alternatives for predicting appropriations – current Presidential budget estimate (request), previous appropriation and an autoregressive model for appropriations. The exogenous shocks causing abrupt changes in the incremental dynamics of the budget process for a *single* agency were modelled with some degree of success in prediction (both absolutely and vis-à-vis naive alternatives) by the introduction of a statistically significant *subset* of the exogenous political, social and economic variables. But the Executive side of the process performed poorly for predictive purposes. We set out, therefore, to uncover the cause of the difficulty and to improve our models of Executive action.

It was first necessary to confirm these findings by extending the data

[9] For a discussion of the implications of this effect for the concept of incrementalism, see our 'On Change: Or, there is no magic size for an increment', *Political Studies*, 27 (1979), 371–89.

TABLE 13.1 EXPLANATORY VARIABLES IN THE MICROMODELS EXTENDED TO EXPLAIN EXOGENOUS INFLUENCES

Process		
LV	Leading variable	Either agency request (estimate in President's budget message) x_1 (endogenous), or fiscal appropriation in previous year y_{t-1} (pre-determined).
$(y-x)_{t-1}$		Difference between request and appropriation in the previous fiscal year.
Political		
1. HND	House non-southern Democrats	Non-southern (including western) Democrats hold between 100 and 150 seats in the House of Representatives.
2. NLND	House large non-southern Democrats	Non-southern democrats hold over 150 seats in the House.
3. HDM	House Democratic majority	Democrats hold between 217 and 250 seats in the House.
4. HLDM	House large Democratic majority	Democrats hold over 250 seats in the House.
5. SDM	Senate Democratic majority	Democrats hold 50 or more seats in the Senate.
6. RP	Republican President	—
7. PRE-EL	Pre-election year	Fiscal year of Presidential election (dated one year subsequent to election year).
Administrative		
8. $B.DEF_{-1}$	Budget deficit in previous fiscal year	Previous fiscal year estimated in surplus (0) or deficit (1) by the Council of Economic Advisors, as announced in the current President's budget message in January.
9. PBRR	Projected budget receipts ratio	Estimate of administrative budget receipts for the coming fiscal year divided by the estimate for the previous fiscal year at the time of the six month review in December (Kessel).
Economic		
10. EC.REC	Economic recession	Fiscal year judged a recession year by Council in a *subsequent* budget message.

11. UER	Unemployment rate	5 per cent is 1.00.
12. RNNP	Real Net National Product	Net national product deflated by the private price index per head of adult population (Niskanen). F71 is 1.00.
13. GNPD	GNP Deflator	F58 is 1.00.
14. FPPR	Federal/private price ratio	Ratio of federal government to private price index (Niskanen).
Social		
15. WAR	—	Nation at war (declared or *de facto*).
16. AFO	Armed forces overseas	A two year (t and t + 1) moving average of armed forces overseas *per head* of adult population 10^2 (Niskanen).
17. YPR	Young population ratio	Ratio of young to adult population (Niskanen).
18. ADP	Adult population	F71 is 1.00.

period. Comparison of model performance over two periods resulted in better fits in the longer estimation period (fiscal 1948–67) for the agency equation, and comparable fits over both estimation periods for the Congressional equation. Best specifications in terms of significant exogenous variables changed only marginally between the two periods. Over the second prediction period (fiscal 1968–72), prediction by both equations – and hence prediction of appropriations by the system – improved markedly. This finding held both absolutely, and relative to the naive alternatives. Given good Congressional results, the earlier conclusion that request prediction was the key to good system prediction remained unchanged. When our predictions for requests by Executive agencies worked well, so did our predictions for the budgetary process as a whole.

Though they were not allowed in the earlier behavioural specifications, constant terms entered significantly into the specification of our new micromodels, even after we introduced exogenous variables. To see what was wrong, we suppressed the constant terms, and simultaneously re-entered an intertemporal gaming term, represented by the previous year's cut (or increase) on the agency requests, into both the Executive and Congressional equations. The results were a considerable increase in the number of cases of significance of the interyear gaming term, together with a large increase in explanation of agency appropriations by extended equations containing exogenous variables. We interpreted this as strong evidence for the behavioural specifications of our micro-agency equations in terms of agency 'mark-ups' and Congressional 'mark-downs'.

When, contrary to the behavioural specification, a constant term is significant, the main reason is either that key variables have been omitted or that non-linearities are present. Since the latter explanation was explicitly tested and found wanting, and the introduction of exogenous variables had not significantly improved the fit or predictive power of our agency equations, our findings so far indicated that the omission of behavioural variables was the more likely explanation. Since our Congressional equations performed well, it became all the more imperative for us to re-examine the Executive side of the process.

If, as we surmised, external variables entered our equations mainly through the Congressional side of the process, and internal variables operate mainly through the Executive, the missing factor was likely to be a relationship *among* relevant organisations. It was inappropriate to continue to study individual agency requests in *isolation*. Indeed, as we have seen, not only OMB, but also the major departments such as Defense, Agriculture, Interior, etc., are charged with relating the various requests of their services and agencies to the President's overall interests – especially fiscal policy. We had omitted rules used by central Executive organisations for regulating their internal relationships; to add to explanation and prediction we needed models of inter-agency *co-ordination* within the Executive. Since our new agency models explicitly incorporated major political, economic and social considerations into the budgetary behaviour relating to an individual agency, we were able to perform and classify interagency comparisons of these influences. We found that general services provided by large agencies (including the Public Health Service, together with natural resource agencies) are most susceptible to political influences. On the other hand economic variables were usually found to influence non-controversial appropriations, such as the Commodity Exchange Authority and the Immigration and Naturalisation Service – indirect evidence for the application of fiscal policy considerations within the Executive budget process.

The most fruitful approach to modelling the co-ordinating behaviour required of the Executive process appeared to us to be an effort to create a more sophisticated version of the *fair share* hypothesis – the often-expressed belief among Executive practitioners that agencies should be treated not only by their programmatic merits, but also with regard to their organisational needs, so that all agencies concerned should receive some portion of the distributed goods (increases) or bads (decreases).[10] After all, if agencies were treated in terms of their merits, this would lead to precipitous increases and decreases as political leadership or public fashion changed. Putting oneself in the other's place suggests it is worth being fair – winning less one year to lose less another. Besides, knowledge to ascertain effectiveness may be lacking. Calculations may be conserved, therefore, by treating all agencies equally well or badly. Now we could model the 'fair' co-ordinating relationships between bureaus and departments by which the environmental influences, represented by the exogenous variables, are modified to suit *internal* organisational needs. Preliminary tests of this interagency Executive co-ordinating mechanism – the *proportional cut*, to be described below – were made on the Post Office and the major appropriations categories of the Defense Department. As a result it became clear that certain subagencies and appropriations categories were treated as uncontrollable and exempted from the fair-share treatment, while minor ones were lumped together for the calculation of shares.

Like departments that must bring the total of their agency requests within target figures both before and after the fall Review, the Director of OMB must bring the major agencies and departments within a fiscal total late in the autumn, see Table 13.2. Moreover, we have seen that in spite of the enormous programmatic complexities and vast sums of money involved, very few people deal with the required reconciliations in very short periods of time. To quote an early account by Mosher,[11] 'Some budget offices can make "flash" budget estimates almost overnight within 3 or 4 percent of complete accuracy [of final requests]'. Departmental budgeting officers have a few weeks in September and October; analysts in OMB have a few weeks in October and November, and staff of the Comptroller's Office in the Office of the Secretary of Defense have a similar period at the same time.

Thus in developing a model of the interagency co-ordination process we should be looking for a simplified rule of thumb by which collective resources may be fairly allocated across agencies. Given past discussion of civilian and military executive budget processes, we might expect that the essential mechanism of such an allocation process would be

[10] See Aaron Wildavsky, *The Politics of the Budget Process* (Little, Brown, Boston, 1975).

[11] Mosher, F., *Program Budgeting: Theory and Practice* (Chicago: Public Administration Service, 1954), p. 239.

TABLE 13.2 MAJOR UNITS IN OMB DIVISIONS STUDIED[a]

Funds Appropriated to the President
Agriculture
Commerce
Defence – Military
Army Corps of Engineers
Health, Education and Welfare
Housing and Home Finance Agency (1955–65)
i.e. Housing and Urban Development (1966–73)
Interior
Justice
Labour
Transportation (1967–73)
Treasury
State
Atomic Energy Commission
General Services Administration
National Aeronautics and Space Administration
Veterans Administration
Civil Service Commission
Railroad Retirement Board
Post Office Department (1955–68)/Postal Service (1969–73)
Federal Aviation Administration
All Other (Residual from non-defence total)

[a] The data were kindly provided to us by Professor Crecine in 1975 at the Center for Advanced Study in the Behavioral Sciences. It came originally from OMB sources, Office of Budget Review, and was obtained and analysed in detail by Professor Crecine and his coworkers – Mark Kamlet, David Mowery, John Padgett and Chandler Stolp – under NSF Grant SOC 72-05488.

incremental. Indeed, the emphasis in both processes is on squeezing a sum of agency requests under a projected total – that is to say, in distributing a total cut across *exaggerated* agency requests to result in some increment over previous appropriations for all. Since such a process is bound to be highly political within the bureaucracy, it should not be surprising that a rule of thumb would be used which would minimise conflict through being seen by the participants as 'fair'. Assume that a Department Secretary, assisted by his staff, has identified his policy preferences for his department and would like to implement them. Although problems of the relative influence of his agencies with respect to the President, Congress and their respective clientele arise immediately, it is usual practice[12]

[12] Wildavsky, op.cit., p. 35.

> for a high departmental official to lay the whole budget down in front of the bureau heads in an effort to explain why they cannot get any more than their share despite the fact that their programs are eminently deserving. *Some budget officials are extremely talented at cutting without getting the blame.* (Italics added)

The necessity for a simple 'fair' mechanism was pointed out in *The Politics of the Budgetary Process* more than a decade ago:[13]

> 'Fair share' means not only the base an agency has established but also *the expectation that it will receive some portion of the funds, if any, which are to be increased over or decreased below the base of the various governmental agencies.* 'Fair share', then, reflects a convergence of expectations on roughly how much the agency is to receive in comparison to others. (Italics added)
>
> The absence of . . . an agreement upon fair shares makes the calculation of what the program or agency should get much more difficult. That happens when an agency or problem is new or when rapid shifts of sentiment toward it take place.

However, the recent operationalisation of the notion of 'fair shares' as an incremental non-market mechanism for the allocation of scarce resources within an organisation, is due to Crecine and Fischer following an important, but generally overlooked, contribution of Shubik.[14] In a pioneering study[15] of the Executive budget process within the Department of Defense, Crecine and Fischer proposed that the overall cut to total service requests occasioned at the fall Secretary's Review should be distributed across appropriations categories in proportion to each category's share of the total. This was the abstract interagency allocation rule proposed by Shubik in his single time period game-theoretic analysis of the central organisation competing agencies budget game. Although their analyses are responsible for the 'proportional cut' model, which we shall develop mathematically below, it is interesting to note that both contributions considered this allocation mechanism only a temporary expedient. As Crecine and Fischer say,[16]

[13] Wildavsky, op. cit., p. 17.

[14] Shubik, Martin, 'Budgets in a decentralized organisation with incomplete organisation', Report P-4514, Rand Corporation, Santa Monica, December (1970).

[15] Crecine, J. P. and Gregory Fischer, 'On resource allocation processes in the U.S. Department of Defense', Discussion Paper, University of Michigan, Institute of Public Policy Studies, October (1971).

[16] Crecine and Fischer, op. cit., p. 57.

> Earlier . . . we argued that different budget accounts should be more or less vulnerable to additional cuts. In preliminary tests of the model, however, we made the *simplifying assumption* that additional cuts or restorations are allocated in proportion to planning forecasts . . . Future versions of the model will be based on the *more reasonable* assumption that the various appropriations categories are differently sensitive to additional adjustments beyond the planning stage. (Italics added)

Their 'simplifying assumption' is – as the quotation from *The Politics of the Budgetary Process* suggests – our theory.

The context is calculation: the Executive budget authority must be able to reduce agency bids (mark down their markups, as we have said) in a simple, speedy and perceivably fair manner. We would expect to find, therefore, that cuts are (i) proportional to the requested increase and (ii) applied to the largest agencies or appropriations accounts (with smaller ones aggregated for convenience) that are (iii) controllable without changing legislation. Reductions, if our hypothesis is correct, fall disproportionately on major categories and agencies that are controllable in the short run, such as military personnel, or that limit spending possibilities a few months later, like surveys preparatory to construction. Political pressure for increased spending is countered by pushing back the *detailed* allocation of reductions on the agencies. After all, the President and his OMB know where to expect constant political pressure, especially where Congress is likely to mark up, so it is only natural they should begin by marking down. Budgeting is not a single act, but a series of reactions in which each participant is aware of the tendencies of the other.

We shall shortly set out the proportional cut model formally as a means by which a central planning agency can reconcile individual requests by programme or subagency. For a domestic department, this reconciliation will be done in two stages, by the department and OMB. Even if the rule is in operation at both stages, however, especially when the department must *subsequently* allocate OMB cuts (or increases) amongst its agencies, we might nevertheless expect to apply it effectively just once to improve our estimates of the President's budget requests over our earlier micro-models for individual agencies or departments within OMB's Divisions as listed in Table 13.2.

Let us first set out the general model for the President's budget request, for the ith agency, x_{it}, which is to be applied to an 'uncontrollable' agency or department, i.e. one exempted from the proportional cut, *viz.*

$$x_{it} = (\beta_{i0} + \beta_{i1}z_{1t} + \ldots + \beta_{ik}z_{kt})\,y_{it-1} + \beta_{ik+1}(y-x)_{it-1} + \xi_{it}. \qquad (1)$$

Here the z_{it}s, $i = 1, \ldots, k$, represent observations on the exogenous variables (see Table 13.1) which influence the 'mark-up' or the previous year's appropriation y_{t-1} in the current fiscal year t; the term in $(y-x)_{t-1}$ represents intertemporal gaming behaviour of the agency with respect to Congress; and ξ_{it} is a random disturbance to the relationship representing non-recurring special circumstances.

Alternatively, for the ith OMB major unit – agency or department – subject to the proportional cut, requests d_{it} to the October OMB Director's Review in fiscal year t are given by an equation similar to (1), *viz.*

$$d_{it} = (\alpha_{i0} + \alpha_{i1}z_{1t} + \ldots + \alpha_{ik}z_{kt})\,y_{it-1} + \alpha_{ik+1}(y-x)_{it-1} + \xi_{it}. \qquad (2)$$

Define x_t to be the total non-defence request in the President's budget for the m agencies subject to the proportional cut in fiscal year t and let

$$d_t = \sum_{i=1}^{m} d_{it} \qquad (3)$$

represent the total request for these agencies to the Director's Review. In general we would expect that

$$d_t - x_t \gg 0,$$

i.e. that the sum of agency and department requests normally far exceeds the fiscal target for non-defence units subject to the proportional cut. For the ith agency subject to the proportional cut, the request x_{it} in the President's budget will be given by the proportional cut model in fiscal year t as

$$x_{it} = d_{it} - \frac{d_{it}}{d_t}(d-x)_t \quad i = 1, \ldots, m, \qquad (4)$$

i.e., the approved request for the ith agency is the initial request minus [plus] that proportion of the total cut [increase] required to meet the central organisation's budget target given by the proportion of its initial request in the initial request total.

Rearranging slightly yields

$$x_{it} = \frac{d_{it}}{d_t}x_t \quad i = 1, \ldots, m, \qquad (4a)$$

i.e., the approved budget request for the ith agency is that proportion of the central organisation's budget target given by the proportion of its initial request in the initial request total.

Thus the central organisation – OMB – returns to each agency or department an approved allocation in such a way as to make the total of the individual allocations approved sum to a desired target total (usually an increase over the total in the previous year's budget). The approved allocations can be generated rapidly, so that little attention need be given to the programmes behind individual agency requests, and 'fairly', in order to minimise dissonance from the agency actors in the process, both vis-a-vis each other and with the central organisation.

The proportional cut model works as well in the case of a rapid and 'fair' allocation of a target *surplus* by the central organisation to the agencies as in the more usual case of a cut below requested totals. It is of course incremental; both in that it takes as basic data the initial agency requests, and in that the current budget target is usually incrementally related to the actual budget total in the previous year.

Equations (3) and (4) constitute an application of the basic proportional cut model for the allocation of a single cut by the central organisation to the inflated total of agency budget requests. We are of course interested in applying the model to improve our prediction of annual major OMB unit requests in the President's budget. But first we must report an empirical test of the assumption implicit in this approach to modelling the President's budget request for a major OMB unit subject to the proportional cut, namely, that

> up to changes due to non-recurring events (represented by a random disturbance term) the Budget Director's recommendations are those appearing in the President's budget.

Regressions of President's Budget figures on the Director's mark over the fiscal period 1955–73 for the agencies and departments listed in Table 13.2 support the view that the Director's mark *essentially* embodies Presidential economic and political policy decisions.

Thus the use of the proportional cut model to represent the effect of the fall Director's Review on agency and department submissions, d_{it}, is justified, providing we can ascertain *a priori* which major OMB units are subjected to the proportional cut. This was done by using the actual data, rather than estimates based on our Executive models, to ascertain for which configurations of agencies the proportional cut improved the statistical relationship between OMB unit submissions to the fall review and the corresponding President's budget figures. The results for the *estimation period* (fiscal 1956–68) and the post-unified budget *prediction period* (fiscal 1969–73) and their interpretations are displayed in Table 13.3.

For the agencies listed in Table 13.3 as outside the proportional cut, our original model (1) was estimated and used to generate predictions of requests over the prediction period as before. However, for the remaining major units of Table 13.2, the model of Review request formation (2) was estimated and used together with the proportional cut model (4) relating to the appropriate agencies to generate the President's budget request predictions over the fiscal 1969–73 period.

TABLE 13.3 AGENCIES AND DEPARTMENTS NOT SUBJECTED TO THE PROPORTIONAL CUT AT THE OMB DIRECTORS REVIEW

Fiscal 1956–68		*Fiscal* 1969–73	
Justice	*Premiere Departments* (Justice, State, Treasury)	Justice	
State		State	
Treasury		Treasury	
AEC	*Cold War*	AEC	
NASA	*Space Race*	NASA	
Veterans Administration	*Uncontrollable (Pensions)*	Veterans Administration	
Army Corps of Engineers	*Eisenhower*	Army Corps of Engineers	
		HEW	*Great Society*
		Commerce	*LBJ/Nixon Business interests*

In both cases Congressional appropriation predictions were generated by estimating the model which had proved successful in earlier studies, *viz.*

$$y_{it} = (\gamma_{i0} + \gamma_{i1}z_{1t} + \ldots + \gamma_{ik}z_{kt})x_{it} + \gamma_{ik+1}(y - x)_{it-1} + \eta_{it}. \quad (5)$$

After statistically insignificant coefficients were rejected, the fit and predictive power of these models for the major OMB units listed in Table 13.2 was significantly improved over comparable earlier studies. This was due to the use of the proportional cut models to co-ordinate relevant agency requests. We may conclude that the proportional cut, together with our earlier models for 'uncontrollable' units, is a reasonable representation of OMB's interagency co-ordination function.

Finally, following Galper and Wendell,[17] the distributed lag model

$$z_{it} = \delta_{i0}y_{it} + \delta_{i-1}y_{it-1} + \delta_{i-2}y_{it-2} + \xi_{it}, \quad (6)$$

where z_{it} represents actual *outlays* for fiscal year t, was found to be adequate to represent actual agency and department disbursements from appropriations y_i. These results are consistent with the hypothesis of *fixed* lags in the timing of actual disbursements from given Congressional appropriations for individual agencies.

Moreover, in the estimation of both executive and legislative models for generating *appropriations* few pre-election variables were found to be significant.[18] Thus it would appear that there is little evidence for either classical Keynesian demand tuning by the US Government or a political business cycle induced by *pre-election* spending.[19] Appropriations do not appear to vary either to dampen oscillations in the business cycle – we shall in fact argue that causality runs the other way – or to increase spending to help incumbent Presidents *in pre-election years*. Pre-election spending therefore appears to be restricted to effects of outlay *timing* – of necessarily limited impact.

At the risk of some oversimplification, let us reconsider the Keynesian verities as they have been popularised, for that is the form in which politicians are most likely to be influenced by them. An attractive feature is that there are only two decision rules that matter: save and spend. When there is economic expansion, government lowers spending to reduce demand and when the economy is contracting, the government raises spending to increase demand. So far so good. But government itself, the main actor in this drama, is left out. Curiously, the economy, which is the passive recipient of all this attention, is modelled, but government, the active element, is not. Thus the prime passive assumption – that the economy would respond with an acceptable trade-off between employment and inflation – has been much studied, of

[17] Harvey Galper and Helmut F. Wendell, 'Progress in forecasting the Federal budget', *Proc. Economics & Business Section Amer. Statistical Society* (1968), 86–98.

[18] In Collat's study of corporate and individual tax revenue, a similar conclusion was reached. See Donald S. Collat, *Voting Behaviour and the Formation of Tax Policy*. D. Phil. Thesis, University of Oxford (1978), Chapters 6, 7 and 8.

[19] See, for example, William D. Nordhaus, 'The political business cycle', *Rev. of Economic Studies*, 42 (1975), 169–190; Bruno S. Frey and Friedrich Schneider, 'On the modelling of politico-economic interdependence', *European J. of Political Res.*, 3 (1975), 339–60; and Edward R. Tufte, *Political Control of the Economy*, (Princeton University Press, Princeton, 1978).

course, and lamentably, the *active* assumption – that government could raise and lower spending at will – has remained unexamined. What could we learn by applying our microspending models to different regimes?

The short-run effects we have covered in our modelling have led us to say that we doubt that the flexibility of reason required by a Keynesian government exists. The two-year time-lags in applying overall spending targets to the budgetary process, which should be obvious to any schoolboy who follows the formal charts, but which did not become clear to us until our models revealed the obvious, make short-term adjustment (i) untimely and (ii) perverse. Our concern in the remainder of this section and the next, however, is not the short but the medium term, say five to fifteen years, long enough to experience more than a single set of economic conditions in one or more economic cycles.

At least four separate relational activities between pairs of transactions must be monitored at the same time: expenditures are related to revenues, appropriations are related to outlays, executive and legislative actions are related to each other, and the public sector is related to the private. In considering each pair of related transactions, it is important to understand that efforts to achieve balance within a single relation have effects across them all. For example, changing the relative sizes of the public and private sectors may provide a solution to problems posed by imbalances between expenditures and revenues.

In our original studies[20] three alternative equations were used to describe executive-legislative interaction within the budgetary process. The basic – most frequently found – equation is one (described above) where the Executive proposes and Congress disposes by granting some fixed proportion of the initial bid. Agencies mark up and Congress marks down. Over time a budgetary base is negotiated from which increases are proposed by agencies and reduced by Congress. Both actors fulfil their roles: agencies act as advocates by requesting more and Congress acts as guardian by giving less than was asked for but more than was received the prior year. Congress gets credit for cutting while agencies get more money for spending. This basic rule is most generally in force over the long expansive phase of the economic cycle.

At the beginning of the cycle, with the economy in stagnation, however, government spending spurts ahead in a Keynesian attempt to induce the economy to follow, and a different pattern assumes prominence. Agency requests are less a function of what Congress previously granted and more a reflection of simply the agency's prior

[20] Davis, Dempster, and Wildavsky (1966), (1966), (1971), op. cit.

request. Support for spending is so strong that *internal* desires rather than external forces dominate.

Eventually, to be sure, deficit-spending-induced inflation makes economic – and political – conditions change, bringing with them a desire to *reduce* spending. Enter the third alternative equation, with its gaming terms, in which Congress takes account of past patterns of requests and seeks to counter them. What happens? The rate of increase slows down but does not disappear. Every time period shows an increase in the base from which subsequent calculations are made. However the drastic effects of the resulting even short-term excess of government revenues over expenditures inevitably lead to a sharp reversal of the anti-spending climate (with the effects outlined in the previous paragraph). Thus gaming must disappear to be eventually replaced by the ordinary relationships modelled by our basic equations.

The alternative regimes affect different agencies – for example, agencies within and without the proportional cut mechanism at OMB – differently. In time-series analyses across several economic cycles, such as our early studies, we would therefore expect econometric selection techniques to select non-basic decision rules for agencies whose budget histories were principally determined by the shorter periods at the beginning and end of the government spending cycles when spending rates are rapidly adjusted. These are, respectively, the agencies most able to increase appropriations and outlays in the early expansive phases of a cycle and those most able to resist cuts in increased requests during the downturn when public expenditure must be severely restrained.

Why, to add our refrain to those of many others, does spending nevertheless go up but not down? Everyone knows that programmes develop clientele who combine to resist their dissolution. It is not so obvious that the ideas of progress and equality combine to generate programmes that always increase in size. Progress is translated to mean that no benefit once conferred may be eliminated or reduced. Equality is interpreted to require that no one who is qualified should be rejected even if that means allowing in some people who are not. Hence, when considering welfare reform, the only way out of these constraints is to increase the size of the programme so all will get more. On the other hand, decreases in spending create difficulties for the bureaucracies in governmental agencies. This occurs not only because they are empire builders, or because it hurts to disappoint colleagues and clientele, but because of the need for equity in internal relations within the executive branch. Agencies do not normally control one another, even within the same departments. They lack levers to alter each other's behaviour.

They could, of course, appeal to the President through the OMB but that would be dangerous; OMB might prove hostile to their cause or undependable. So it is far safer to negotiate alliances within the bureaucracy. And whatever the bases of these alliances, they must not be based on merit because no one either knows or is able to agree on that. Certainly this is what we found when we discovered that our isolated agency models were in many cases inadequate. Instead, OMB allocates decreases, from agency asking price, by fair shares.

Should internal dislocations within the bureaucracy threaten to become severe, moreover, the burden of change can be shifted to the future or to the private sector or both. When Lyndon Johnson discovered the appropriation-outlay game, he was able to keep next year's expenditures under his $100 billion target in return for which future obligations were increased. Evoking the private sector is even easier because it requires no explicit decision. When expenditures increase faster than national product, and when substantial proportions are indexed against inflation, the money has to come from somewhere, namely, from a corresponding shrinkage of the private sector.

In sum, there is no mechanism that compels a consideration of the relative merits of public policies or of the public or private sectors. In government, resource allocation has become resource addition. The consequences of this expansion of expenditure for the economic cycle are now becoming clear.

III THE ENDOGENOUS GOVERNMENT: FORGET KEYNES

A touch of recession makes the whole world Keynesian.
Professor Herbert Stein

It's like rearranging deck chairs on the Titanic.
Anon. Congressman

We now turn to a brief analysis of the effects of public spending in generating an economic cycle, using a simple macroeconomic model developed previously.[21] The distinctive feature of this model of

[21] M. A. H. Dempster, 'A crude model of the modern economy', Center for Advanced Study in the Behavioral Sciences, Stanford, California (1975). Revised January (1976); M. A. H. Dempster and Otto A. Davis, 'On macroeconomics: Comparative statics', Center for Advanced Study in the Behavioral Sciences, Stanford, June (1975). Revised January (1976).

momentary macroeconomic equilibrium – in contrast to both its eclectic Keynesian and Monetarist equivalents – is that in comparative static analysis it is capable of generating the range of behaviour exhibited by the US economy, *including stagflation*, in the various regimes of the cycle. Our present purpose is merely to outline the dynamics of the economic cycle resulting from the *mutual* interaction of the economy and polity, from the theoretical – i.e. model – viewpoint. The construction of a full dynamic model reproducing the public policy-induced economic cycle is left to future work.

In recent times, Professor Friedman has revived a sophisticated version of the original quantity theory of money which holds that the only effective policy instrument in the hands of the government is the control of the money supply. Although there has been much debate between the Neo-Keynesian and Monetarist schools of macroeconomic theorists, a popular conclusion is that neither addresses the problems of the modern economy.[22]

Table 13.4 sets out the comparative static version of a model of the macro economy which attempts to synthesise and extend recent eclectic Keynesian and Monetarist views in light of the findings reported in previous sections of this paper. The accompanying Table 13.5 lists the variables and exogenous parameters in this model of short-term macroeconomic equilibrium. The model explicitly attempts to represent at the macro level the productive sector of the economy, the government expenditure process, and the behaviour of the central banking authorities and the private banking sector. Debt financing, open market operations, trade balance and foreign capital transfers influence real activity and inflation through the money and stock markets. The six equations determining real output, investment, employment, profit, the price level, and the interest rate have previously been analysed with respect to both domestic policy parameters and the effects of the global economy as represented in the balance of payments and net foreign capital transfers.[23] The analysis of the productive sector is essentially neo-classical with the exception that the wage rate is allowed to depend

[22] Cf. Walter W. Heller, 'What's right with economics?' Presidential address to the American Economic Association, San Francisco, 29 December 1974.

[23] The reader is referred to Davis and Dempster (1975), op. cit., for details. For a discussion of related research see J. P. Crecine, M. A. H. Dempster and Aaron Wildavsky, 'Budgets, bureaucrats and the Executive: Influences on the size of the public sector', to appear in *Proceedings of the Conference on the Causes and Consequences of Public Sector Growth*, Dorado Beach, Puerto Rico, 1–5 November 1978, P. Aranson and P. Ordeshook (eds).

TABLE 13.4 A MACROECONOMIC MODEL WITH ENDOGENOUS GOVERNMENTAL AND PRODUCTIVE SECTORS

Production

Production function: $Y = f[(1-\delta)K + I, N]$

Definition of profit: $P\Pi = PY - rPI - w(P)N - r(1-\delta)PK$ (1)

Investment equation: $f_K(I, N) = r$ (2)

Employment equation: $Pf_N(I, N) = w(P)$ (3)

Expenditure

National income identity:

$$Y = c(Y - T, W) + I(r, P) + G + X/P + F/P \quad (4)$$

Tax function: $T = t(PY; \tau)/P$

Government expenditure: $G = g(PY, U; \gamma)/P$

Government income identity: $G = T + \Delta$ (5)

Capital and Money Markets

Stock Market index: $S = s(\Pi, Y, r, P; X, F)$

Definition of wealth:

$$W = [(1-\delta)K + I] + \left(\frac{M}{P} + \mu\nu\Delta\right) + \left[(1-\mu)\nu\Delta + \frac{B}{rP}\right]$$

Demand for money:

$$L = \tau(Y, W) + \eta(s)I = l(Y, r, P; X, F)$$

Supply of money:

$$M/P = m(r, P, \nu(1-\mu)\Delta + \frac{B}{rP}, \mu\Delta, \lambda; F, \rho, R) = M(r, P, Y; \lambda, F)/P$$

Money market equilibrium: $M(r, P, Y; \lambda, F)/P = l(Y, r, P; X, F)$ (6)

Source: Davis and Dempster (1975), op. cit.
Subscripts in (2) and (3) denote partial derivatives.

on the price level in order to represent collective bargaining processes. This analysis allows a consideration of output, investment and unemployment in terms of the relative effects of the price level and the rate of interest on capital and labour intensities at (momentary) equilibrium. A by-product is an analysis of the conditions under which the Phillips curve can be expected to hold locally about the current position of the economy.

Although the textbook national income identity supplemented by a tax function representing a progressive tax structure in nominal GNP is retained, the standard government expenditure parameter has been replaced with a government expenditure function based on our findings.

TABLE 13.5 PARAMETERS AND VARIABLES OF THE MACRO-ECONOMIC MODEL

Given:
- K – existing capital stock
- δ – rate of capital depreciation,
- N_0 – work force,
- X – net exports,
- F – net foreign capital transfers,
- τ – gross tax rate,
- γ – level of government activity,
- Δ – real government deficit,
- ν – proportion of new government debt held domestically,
- μ – proportion of new government debt monetized,
- B – existing stock of government bonds,
- λ – open market activity level,
- ρ – rediscount rate,
- R – reserve requirement,

the six equations (1–6) of Table 13.4 determine the six variables:

1. I – real investment,
2. N – employment (or unemployment, $U = N_0 - N$),
3. Y – real GNP,
4. Π – real profit,
5. r – interest rate,
6. P – price level (GNP deflator).

We argue that the lags in fiscal policy are such that, barring a major change in government activity level, government expenditure is better modelled as reacting to *nominal* GNP – which incorporates both real and price effects – and unemployment.

The modelling of the capital markets is radically different from that generally accepted by both Keynesian and Monetarist schools of macroeconomics. Although the implicit treatment of the bond market as moving in parallel with the stock market is retained, the stock market index, reacting to the natural financial and real variables, is introduced explicitly as the principal determinant in the demand for money (including credit) for investment in new capital. This demand has replaced the standard Keynesian speculative demand for money, which here appears on the supply side of the money market equation. The demand for money term in the model of Table 13.4 is, through the stock market, a major link between financial and productive sectors of the economy. The treatment of the supply of money intimately links the response of the money market, and hence the economy, to the marginal responses of taxation and government expenditures to changes in nominal GNP.

The response of the model to changes in the major public policy parameters is capable of exhibiting a wealth of behaviours ranging from the classical to the target behaviour of both the Keynesian and Monetarist schools of macroeconomics. With regard to the controversy between these two Schools, the most important parameters of Table 13.5 are: the gross tax rate τ, the level of government activity parameter γ,[24] the real government deficit Δ, the open market activity parameter λ and the proportion of new government debt monetised μ. The proportion of new government debt held domestically v is probably outside the government's control, and would in any event probably be taken as exogenous. When the US Government has large deficits, it is very important how much of this new debt can be sold to the public as government securities and how much must be sold to the Federal Reserve, debt which will then, eventually at least, find its way into the money supply.

Analysis of the model shows that its behaviour in response to changes in policy parameters can be divided into four regimes determined by the relative sizes of three parameters: the ratios of the marginal responses of real activity and the money market to real output Y, the interest rate r, and the price level P. The marginal response of the money market to changes in these variables is in terms of the excess demand for money; the marginal response of real activity in each case is more complicated. Under a reasonable set of further assumptions the behaviour of the model in the four regimes follows.

The first regime corresponds to the classical economy, while the second regime corresponds in one mode to the extreme Keynesian view of the world and displays in the other mode the unpleasant modern phenomenon of *stagflation*. In this and the remaining two regimes – which are of central interest for the effects of public spending on the economic cycle – the response of investment, unemployment, and profit to government spending will depend on the behaviour of the wage rate with respect to the price level.

The third regime provides a description of the performance of western economies during the early post-war period. In this situation, real GNP, the price level and the interest rate move together in response to policy

[24] Note that by this parameter we model, not the month-to-month demand tuning of theoretical Keynesian macroeconomics, but rather the major changes in Federal Government activity levels induced by wars and such programmes as Johnson's Great Society and NASA's Lunar Landings.

variables. This is the model regime consistent with the classical business cycle; real growth is accompanied by inflation and an increasing interest rate, while real decline is accompanied by a falling of the price level and interest rate. Although an increase in government activity or the money supply occasions growth in real GNP, it is accompanied by an increase in both the price level and the rate of interest. Conversely, the tightening of the money supply decreases the price level and the rate of interest, but only at the expense of a decline in real GNP.

In the fourth regime, the model displays in one mode – when the marginal response of the price level to an increase in real government deficit is negative – the behaviour which has been the target of Keynesian fiscal policy in the post-war period; in the other – that of positive price level response to deficit increments – it again displays the stagflationary response.

We have seen that the response of the model economy to changes in the policy parameters is capable of exhibiting a range of behaviour. Unlike the standard textbook analyses, however, our analysis shows that the effects of domestic policy variables will be radically different depending on the values of the structural parameters. The effects of monetary policy have been seen to depend on the relative magnitudes of the marginal increases in taxation and government spending with respect to nominal GNP – i.e. *net marginal (nominal) government impact*. In the situation that marginal government spending exceeds marginal government taxation with respect to nominal GNP, we may expect the relative share of government expenditure in GNP to grow with the growth of the economy, *however growth is induced.*

We have reported the analysis of the response of the short-term equilibrium represented by the solution of the model to policy parameters one at a time. In practice, of course, they are moved simultaneously – often in opposition to each other. In the model the *marginal* effects of these parameters may be added, but, even if the conditions for the target regimes of both Keynesian and Monetarist Schools are met, the effects of increased government expenditure could be overwhelmed by a tightening of the money supply to produce a decline in real GNP. A similar occurrence with regard to relative *rates* of growth – when money supply expansion was insufficient to fund Korean War defence expenditures – was probably responsible for the 'pause' in the growth of the US economy in 1953–54, see Figure 13.1.[25]

The next such period, in 1957–58, was again the result of fiscal and

[25] Recessionary periods are shown shaded in the graphs of Figure 13.1.

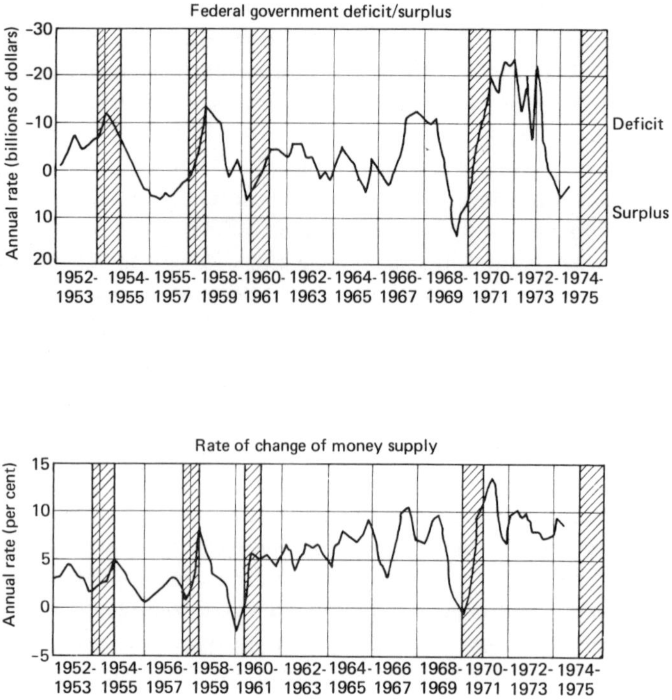

FIG. 13.1 The business cycle induced by public policy, federal deficits and easy money generate inflation, federal surplus and tight money generate recession (Periods of recession are shown shaded)

monetary policy operating in conditions valid for the target regimes of both Keynesian and Monetarist Schools. Eisenhower, in an attempt to reverse the increments in the public debt due to Korea and to Keynesian expansionary policy during the post-Korean War recession, operated a tight fiscal policy throughout the next business cycle boom – actually running a Federal surplus from early 1955 through 1957. In the second half of this period, tight fiscal policy was roughly balanced by counteracting expansionary monetary policy. Early in 1957, however, in order to stop the inflation generated by an overheating economy, money supply growth was reversed – initially to halt growth in the third quarter of 1957 and send the economy into recession in the fourth.

The steady growth and mild inflation over the period 1961–65 (prior to the start of the 1966–70 cycle) was the only period in post-war US economic history in which not only were conditions for the achievement of the *medium-term* target regimes of both Keynesian and Monetarist policies valid, but economic stabilisation was broadly achieved. Nevertheless, under steady bureaucratic and political pressure for expansion throughout the period – Federal government expenditures grew in real terms over the longer term.

The remaining three recessionary periods – 1960–61, 1969–70 and 1974–75 – were consequences of an economic cycle induced by public spending. Now we shall attempt a general description of the two principal phases of such a cycle in terms of appropriate modes of the third and fourth regimes of the short-term macroeconomic model of Table 13.4. Beginning as a response to recessionary conditions – as in 1961 or 1970 – or autonomously through Presidential policy – as in 1966 – both fiscal and monetary policy is strongly expansionary. This early point in the cycle is modelled by regime three of the model in which real GNP, the price level, and the interest rate move upward together, since effective marginal wage escalation due to collective bargaining is small, while net marginal nominal government impact – the excess of government expenditure over receipts at the margin – is strongly positive. The second half of this first phase – still in model regime three – is characterised by increasing inflation, due to the response of the price level to the effects of expansionary fiscal and monetary policy and to accelerating wage claims. In model terms, effective marginal wage escalation is increasing, while net marginal government impact is declining due to the interaction of inflation with the progressive tax structure to raise tax take relative to less rapidly expanding government expenditures – to produce a Federal budget surplus. These stringent fiscal policy measures are reinforced by a contraction of the money supply, cf. Figure 13.1 (1960, 1969 and 1974). By this time, exaggerated claims (justified by inflation) have escalated wages, while the increment of tax take over that of government spending in current dollars has increased. In model terms, these are the conditions for regime four in which the marginal price level response to *expansionary* fiscal or monetary policy is *negative*. If fiscal and monetary controls were to be relaxed at this point in the cycle, real economic expansion and price stabilisation would result.[26] Since, however, both fiscal and monetary policy instruments are strongly restrictive at this point in the cycle in a

[26] In the above model analysis the interaction of domestic policy and international trade and financial considerations has of course been ignored through taking the latter (X, F and v of Table 13.5) as fixed. In this regard see H. Sneesons, 'Inflation in Western economies', CORE Discussion Paper 7819, Université Catholique de Louvain, May (1978).

vain and mistimed attempt to counteract inflation, the result – both in the model and the real world – is *stagflation*, a simultaneous decline in real activity, accompanied by increased interest rates, and continuing inflation.

The current dissatisfaction with economic management is amply justified. Economists have not been of much help to the economy. Standard theories do not work and alternatives are not much better. By the time econometric models are perfected they appear as relics of a bygone era. The main problem, as we conceive it, is that most existing models do not generate a sufficient variety of behaviour.[27] Therefore when a new situation occurs, the result is to discredit existing models, and what is worse, economic analysis. By bringing in a wider variety of considerations – from the presence of the production sector of the economy to the impracticality of manipulating totals of government spending and the necessity of marketing the government debt – the present model generates a wide enough variety of economic behaviours to be appropriate to the historical conditions experienced by real economies in different regimes.

Political and bureaucratic pressures for increased government spending are omnipresent. As inflation accelerates towards the end of the expansionary phase of the cycle, it has become common practice for the Executive to indulge in much rhetoric concerning wage and price guidelines, policies, controls, etc. This is always a vain attempt to stem the wage and price increases which are natural consequences – captured in the model – of the inflation which the Administration has itself induced. As the government initially spends rapidly to rise from a recession, it must market its debt and thus eventually expand the money supply. Wages, which had been near their marginal product, increase as the cost of living goes up. Fearing inflation the government seeks to cut spending and restrict the money supply. At the same time, however, taxes are going up due to inflation, so there is less apparent need to close the gap and spending is, in any event, difficult to reduce. When restrictive action is finally required, it must be all the more severe. Each time the cycle is repeated, the spending level is higher. Currently, government has become so to speak, the nation's largest firm, to which other firms have adjusted so that a substantial reduction in governmental demand has serious economic consequences. Nevertheless,

[27] An exception to this statement is presented by models of constrained economic equilibria, but these have so far failed to handle dynamic considerations satisfactorily and in any event appear to us to rest on a very thin empirical base.

throughout the post-Second World War period, virtually steady growth in the relative size of the public sector has been the *long-term* result.

4 THE LONG RUN: RECALL SCHUMPETER, MISES AND HAYEK

In the previous section we used a momentary, i.e., short term macro-economic model of analyse the medium term public policy induced economic cycle. In this final section of our paper we attempt to identify the longer term effects of the growth of the bureaucratic public sector.

Consider first the behaviour of the empirically based models of the Federal budget/expenditure process set out in Section 2 (equations 1–5). We have seen in Section 2 that the magnitudes of the fundamental Executive markup and Congressional markdown for an agency's appropriation are subject to periodic ratchet adjustments to keep an agency's expenditures on a politically expedient course. The implication is that bureaucratic momentum – in the face of complexity and uncertainty – keeps the budgeting behaviour of the relevant process participants stationary until the organisationally perceived penalties for failure to act exceed the combined costs of search and changeover involved in the adaptation to a new budget path.

For the participants on the Congressional side of the budget process, this pressure for change largely manifests itself at times of partisan changes in the Presidency and the composition of the House and Senate. At these epochs, significant internal political costs are attached to maintaining the *status quo ante*. Partisan forces, together with medium term fiscal policy considerations, are also present as environmental influences on the Executive. But there is an additional necessity for periodic change *inherent* in the use of the proportional cut as a fair Executive allocation/coordination mechanism for agency requests. The proportional cut mechanism has since 1921 doubtless saved considerably the time of Congressional appropriations committees in relieving them from 'exploding the visionary schemes of bureau chiefs for which no administration would be willing to stand responsible'.[28] In conjunction with the other decision rules it has however the unacceptable property that if left to run its course over the years in an era of expanding total expenditure, the largest budget unit would eventually swallow the total. Clearly, periodic adjustment to such a dynamically unbalanced interagency co-ordinating mechanism is a matter of organisational *necessity*. It should therefore not be surprising that the

[28] H. Rept. No. 14, 67th Cong., 1st Sess., at 4.

opportunity will be taken at times of partisan and other environmental change to move agencies across the boundaries of the proportional cut or to otherwise bring its allocative results back on the currently expedient course.

Notice that what we have called the *gaming term* in the equations governing the demand and supply of an agency's appropriations – i.e. the difference between the previous year's appropriation and agency request – has the stabilising effect of distributing periodic major shocks across both sides of the process. However, nothing serves to change permanently the continual pressure for growth embodied in inflated agency requests and only partial Congressional pruning of the resulting increment, represented in the model by the time-varying leading coefficients of the equations. That this phenomenon is another undesirable consequence of the proportional cut allocation mechanism – coupled with the limited review capability of the central budget organisation (OMB) – has been pointed out by Shubik in his game-theoretic analysis of an executive budget process.[29]

Taken together, the properties of the process represented by the models of Section II imply relatively infrequent adjustments of their incremental growth dynamics to partisan changes, Presidential ambitions and the periodic (mistaken or, at least mistimed) anti-inflationary fiscal stringencies which form part of the public policy-induced business cycle. In summary, we have seen that from the short-term point of view the growth of government has been the engine of the growth of economy.[30] When the intertemporal credit represented by a deficit in its operations is too large, inflation results; when this credit is called in, recession – with continuing inflation – is the consequence. This is a government expenditure-induced 'business' cycle. President Carter is at the time of writing keeping silent on the present rapid speed-up in Federal outlays to counter the effects of the current recession. Meanwhile, pre-election Congressional economic policy debate centres on 'necessary' upwards revision of the Federal budget deficit for the fiscal year (1981) beginning on 1 October and the Federal Reserve has

[29] Shubik (1970), op. cit.

[30] It is interesting to note that the *necessity* for this state of affairs was explicitly argued by Alvin H. Hansen in the late 1940s: see Robert L. Heilbroner, *The Worldly Philosophers* (Simon & Schuster, New York, 1961), Chapter 10. Hansen saw underlying population growth – Harrod's 'warranted' growth – as insufficient to allow capitalist industrial economies to continue to expand. But this view ignores the role of technical progress and the possibility of a service – versus a goods-based economy.

completely reversed its tight money policy of the first two quarters. Inflation continues unabated.

Consider next the long run. The perception that competitive markets operate *dynamically* like a Darwinian biological selection environment for firms – supporting the survival of sufficiently adaptive variants and leading to the demise of the remainder – was explicit in the writings of many of the great nineteenth century economic theorists. In the first half of this century the evolutionary approach to competition was clearly set out by Schumpeter, Mises and Hayek.[31] More recently, this view of market processes has been re-emphasised in a number of articles by Nelson and Winter, who have summarised it variously as follows:

> In a stylized Schumpeterian evolutionary system, there is both a carrot and a stick to motivate firms to introduce 'better' production methods or products. Better here has an unambiguous meaning: lower cost of production, or a product that consumers are willing to buy at a price above cost. In either case the criterion boils down to higher monetary profit. Successful innovation leads both to higher profit for the innovator and to profitable investment opportunities. Thus profitable firms grow. In so doing they cut away the market for the noninnovators and reduce their profitability which, in turn, will force these firms to contract. Both the visible profits of the innovators and the losses experienced by the laggers stimulate the latter to try to imitate.[32]
>
> Hayek proposed that the central problem of economic organization was to *respond to change* – change in demands, change in factor supply conditions. He argued that a socialist regime . . . would be slow and cumbersome in response. To get rapid response one needs 'real' markets, real profit incentives. It should be emphasized that his argument was *not* about 'optimality'; it was about effective and speedy *adaptation*. This is not what the theory of modern welfare

[31] See, for example: Joseph A. Schumpeter, *The Theory of Economic Development* (Harvard University Press, Cambridge, 1934), and *Capitalism, Socialism and Democracy* (Harper & Row, New York, 1950); Ludwig von Mises, *Human Action* (Yale University Press, New Haven, 1949); and Friedrich A. von Hayek, *The Road to Serfdom* (Chicago University Press, Chicago, 1944). For an elegantly succinct statement of this dynamic – as opposed to the static neo-classical relative price – role of the market, see Hayek's Chapter 12, 'Competition as a discovery procedure', in *New Studies in Philosophy, Politics, Economics and the History of Ideas* (Routledge & Kegan Paul, London, 1978).

[32] Richard R. Nelson and Sidney G. Winter, 'In search of useful theory of innovation', *Research Policy*, 6 (1977), 36–76, 64.

economics including that concerning public goods is about. Note also that Hayek was not arguing that the competitive market system was ideal in any sense. Rather, he was *implicitly* arguing the demerits of large governmental bureaucracies.[33] (Italics added)

Bureaucratic process innovation is closely related to changes in the nature of government provision of goods and services for short-term consumption, while product innovation in government relates to research, development and construction activities involved in longer term investment in energy production, aerospace, medical and educational technology, etc. As is the tendency in the private sector – but to the considerably greater extent demonstrated by the empirical models of Section IV – bureaucratic *process* innovation is shielded from environmental influences and must result when it does, from internal pressures. On the other hand, while external influences must *eventually* determine innovation and change in the longer term investment activities of government, just as in the market sector, the interaction of the political decision-making process with the slow reacting bureaucratic dynamic must alone tend to reduce adaptability.

How might selection be introduced into the expenditure process? Are there structural changes which, when introduced, would lead to less inflationary outcomes? We have seen that intertemporal opportunity cost considerations, giving up something now for what you get later, are not effective in government over long time periods. More for one agency and programme need not, over time, lead to less for another. The problem, to paraphrase an earlier comment, is how to make allocation over time more like subtraction and less like addition.

The most direct approach to a less inflationary expenditure process would be to prevent spending from exceeding productivity by limiting it to a fixed proportion of Gross National Product, or some other more appropriate measure. Assuming such a limit could or would be enforced (big assumptions that we will not go into here) it would give outside interests a stake in productivity as well as distribution since the latter would depend on the former. Inside the bureaucracy, an expenditure limitation would create a strong disincentive against inflationary measures. For whenever the inflation rate exceeded productivity increases, the effective purchasing power of governmental agencies

[33] Richard R. Nelson and Sidney G. Winter, 'Firm and industry response to changed market conditions: An evolutionary approach', Ins. for Social and Policy Research Working Paper No. 788, Yale University, January (1978), p. 29.

would decline. At the limit, something new would have to displace something old. Fair-shares would be less likely to operate within a context of declining real resources; internal conflict within the Executive would be intensified. Another way of saying this is that collusion would be replaced by competition. Instead of regarding policy evaluation as an external excrescence, ignored when possible and distorted when not, interest in efficiency would grow, as would efforts to uncover weaknesses in other agency's programmes. Log-rolling, whether in the legislature or the Executive, would continue, of course, but in a new competitive context; each coalition would not only augment returns to its members but suggest decreases in returns to others. There would be less internal harmony and more information for outsiders.

Obviously, the stability of spending agencies would be impaired. One way of looking at it is that their bureaucratic instability is our citizen stability. Another point of view, since 'they' are also 'us' acting in a collective capacity, is that agencies *need* a stable environment in which to carry out our desires. If spending patterns are to change so as to smooth out the economic cycle described above, instability has to be allocated like any other good. Perhaps sufficient has been said here, however, to suggest that government spending is not the world's best or most flexible instrument for short-term economic management. Varying the tax is surer and swifter, though of course also subject to political pressures. Were spending totals fixed relative to national product, it would be easier to agree that social issues involving spending thus constrained should be argued on their relative merits. Without worrying about the possibility that avaricious spending would devour the national patrimony, it may be possible to secure stability in spending for socially desirable objects.

Discussion of 'Modelling the US Federal Spending Process: Overview and Implications' by Dr M. A. H. Dempster and Professor A. Wildavsky

Professor Uzawa introduced the discussion by asking for more information on the nature of the models of the budgetary process presented in Section IV of the paper and on the empirical support that had been claimed for them. In his view the central element of the paper was the model presented in Section V in which the process of budget formation was related to macroeconomic behaviour. He was not convinced by some of the equations of the macroeconomic model presented in Table 13.4. In particular the term $(1-\delta)K+I$ in the production function seemed to imply that output today was a function of the capital stock tomorrow.

In order to assist the discussion *Dr Dempster* outlined the large body of work by himself and Professors Wildavsky, Davis and Crecine that was very briefly summarised in Section IV of the paper. Their early work had found that simple rules of marking-up and marking-down were followed in negotiations between individual agencies and the relevant Congressional Appropriations Committees. The product of the mark-up and mark-down coefficients had usually been greater than one which resulted in the growth of agency budgets over time. Shifts in these relationships had been found to occur at times of political change. However, in some cases changes in unemployment and the price level had also been found to be important in explaining such changes. The introduction of exogenous political and economic variables had given a better explanation of Congressional behaviour than of Executive behaviour. The later work of Professor Crecine had suggested the operation of a simple rule within the Executive by which the Office of Management and the Budget co-ordinated bids from different agencies. The following simple rule governing the allocation of funds to agencies was supported empirically: the proportion of the total allocation allotted to an agency equalled the proportion of the total request made by the agency. Some agencies were exempt from this rule if they were in political favour with the President or the Congress. The introduction of unemployment and price variables into models of the government-spending process made possible the closure of conventional macroeconomic models and a development on both Keynesian and monetarist formulations. The principal developments were in the equation for government expenditure; in the employment equation, which allowed for cost-push inflation; and in the equations for the capital and money markets (all shown in Table 13.4 of the paper).

Several speakers commented on the mark-up, mark-down hypothesis. *Professor Sir Austin Robinson* did not see why the agency mark-up should systematically exceed the Congressional mark-down. His experience of budget processes similar to that described was that this was not so. *Mr Boltho* wondered whether such a simple hypothesis could provide a satisfactory explanation of the growth of public spending in the United States over the long run. *Mr Matthews* was concerned that the hypothesis had been defined so broadly, and with so many possible modifications, as to be compatible with all conceivable outcomes. *Sir Leo Pliatzky*'s view was that the paper presented an accurate description of budgetary processes. However, the nature of these processes was already well-understood. He did not see the advantages of formalising such understanding into an algebraic model. *Professor Modigliani* drew a distinction between the casting of arguments in an algebraic language and the empirical testing of propositions about behaviour. By itself the former was no more than a convenience. But the formal testing of propositions using the empirical evidence of a large sample provided evidence on the generality of the proposed explanation which could not be obtained by casual observation. In his view the hypothesis of proportionate cuts had been plausibly demonstrated by this method. However, he felt that it was in need of some modification in that it seemed to allow an escalating series of bids, cuts and counter-bids which had not in fact been observed.

Professor Frey's view was that the work reported in the paper was amongst the most sophisticated that had been done in this area. He was surprised that no evidence had been found for the existence of a political business cycle in the United States. A great deal of positive evidence had been found in other countries. The conclusions of the studies of vote functions by Kramer and Stigler referred to were now out of date. More recent studies had shown that election outcomes were significantly influenced by the level of unemployment, and to a lesser extent by the inflation rate and the level of real income. He suggested that the macroeconomic model of the paper could be developed by making endogenous the behaviour of the Federal Reserve Bank.

The bulk of the remaining discussion concerned the macroeconomic model presented in Section V. *Professor Modigliani* objected to several aspects of the model and to some arguments that had been used to distinguish it from Keynesian and monetarist formulations. He argued that modern Keynesians did not assume that the aggregate price level was fixed. Furthermore, the distinguishing feature of Keynesian economics was a belief in the desirability of stabilisation policy, and not, as seemed to be suggested, a belief in the desirability of high levels of public spending and high budget deficits. Conventional models did include endogenous government expenditures and taxation through the device of counter-cyclical policy rules. He thought that the model did not properly distinguish between stocks and flows. He wondered about the extent to which the results presented depended on a breach of the assumption that demand functions – in particular the demand function for money – were homogeneous of degree zero in the absolute price level. There was strong theoretical and empirical support for this assumption. Also he felt that the movement of the system between the different macroeconomic regimes had been insufficiently explained. In particular he could not see how the model generated the stagflation outcome of the fourth regime. He objected to the formulation whereby the money supply was dependent on public debt. It was only in very extreme cases in which the savings capacity of the system was exhausted that an increase in public debt required an increase in the money supply. The relationship shown in Figure 13.1 between the Federal government deficit and the growth of the money supply was not causal but rather a reflection of the fact that fiscal and monetary variables had been expanded and contracted at the same time. There was evidence that the money supply depended on the level of unemployment, but this relationship was not included in the model presented in the paper. *Mr Matthews* drew attention to the evidence of the McCracken Report that only in the United States was the government deficit correlated with the growth of the money supply. *Professor Boulding* pointed out that since the early 1970s the surpluses of State governments in the United States had fully offset the deficit of the Federal government. *Sir Leo Pliatzky* agreed with Professor Modigliani that a high borrowing requirement did not necessarily produce inflation. Indeed, by pre-empting finance for private investment, it was more likely to result in deflation and unemployment.

Professor Boulding expressed his surprise at the finding that military expenditure in the United States had been determined as a residual. He also wondered whether reorganisations of the institutions of government had had an effect on budgetary processes.

In response to Professor Uzawa's point on the production function, *Dr Dempster* argued that there was no difficulty once it was recognised that the model depicted a single moment of continuous time. This allowed for the instantaneous depreciation of and addition to the capital stock. In reply to Professor Sir Austin Robinson he pointed out that the budgets of some agencies had not grown. The growth of the budgets of other agencies was in part a consequence of inflation and thus did not entirely represent a growth of real activity. He did not believe that the mark-up mark-down hypothesis provided a satisfactory explanation of budget outcomes in the long term. The relevant relationships had not been stable in the long run. Very broad politico-economic changes had influenced the rules determining budget outcomes. A clear example of this was President Johnson's abandonment of the long-established norm of the balanced budget. He agreed with Professor Frey on the need to make endogenous the behaviour of the Federal Reserve Bank, especially as the Bank often acted in concert with the fiscal authorities. He did not agree with Professor Modigliani that there was firm empirical support for the assumption of zero homogeneity in demand functions. Finally, in order to clarify the argument on the different macroeconomic regimes, he gave a brief description of the cyclical behaviour of the system analysed in the paper. At the bottom of the cycle there was a large step increase in public spending which was followed by a monetary expansion. A strong bureaucratic momentum supported the increased rates of public expenditure. A wage-price spiral then developed to the point where the fiscal and monetary authorities were forced to deflate.

Part Four
Conclusion – the Questions at Issue

14 Collective Consumption – an Overview of the Issues

R. C. O. Matthews

UNIVERSITY OF CAMBRIDGE

My main purpose is to place in a common context the various papers contributed to the conference. What follows was written after the papers had been received but before the conference took place. It therefore takes account only of the papers themselves, not of points raised in discussion.

Section I refers to the observed trends in collective consumption. Section II, which comprises the main part of the paper, deals with the various classes of consideration that are relevant to the interpretation of events and to the formulation of policy. Section III briefly deals with the interactions of these considerations.

A preliminary point concerns the distinction between capitalist and socialist countries. I shall use those terms as a shorthand. However, the very concept of collective consumption shows that they are oversimplifications. The existence of collective consumption in capitalist countries implies that those countries do not wholly conform to the textbook norm of capitalism; and the existence of a distinction between marketed goods and collective consumption in socialist countries implies that unequal progress has been made in different sectors of those countries to the full socialist ideal (as spelled out, for example, in Marx's *Critique of the Gotha Programme*). Many of the problems about collective consumption are common to capitalist and socialist countries. However, there are certain problems that are not common.

I THE FACTUAL BACKGROUND: THE RISE IN COLLECTIVE CONSUMPTION

Much of the concern with collective consumption has arisen from the growth in its quantitative importance. The extent of the increase in collective consumption's share in GNP in capitalist countries is documented by Boltho. His data show that the annual rate of increase in the share, measured in percentage points, was substantially higher in the post-war period than previously in all the principal OECD countries except Japan, where the share actually fell in the post-war period. There was not quite such a large difference between post-war and pre-war in the *proportional* rate of increase in the share (that is to say the excess of the growth rate of collective consumption over the growth rate of GNP). However, calculation from Boltho's figures reveals that even on that basis the post-war rate of increase in the share was significantly faster than the pre-war one in all the countries except Japan and (surprisingly) the UK.

These facts have an important bearing on possible explanations. It is not enough to postulate general forces making for an increase in the share, whether these arise from political or bureaucratic processes or from economic considerations about income- and price-elasticities. It is necessary to supplement such general explanations by an explanation of why the share rose particularly rapidly in the post-war period. Possibilities suggested by Boltho are rapid rise in real incomes and the influence of social-democratic political parties. Reference will be made later to hypotheses put forward by other contributors, including the effects of Keynesian fiscal policies, of inflation, and of excess aspirations.

The case of Japan shows that the post-war rise in collective consumption's share in GNP has not been common to all cultures. There are unfortunately statistical obstacles to making comparisons with socialist countries, as Kapustin explains, and comprehensive comparative data for those countries are not available in the conference papers. Hoch shows that in Hungary there has been no significant trend in the share since 1960. In the case of Yugoslavia, however, Jurković, Jašić and Lang show a proportional rise of about the same order as occurred in OECD countries. Perhaps some of the East European participants in the conference will be able to give us their impressions of what the trend in the share has been in the USSR and other socialist countries. It would be interesting to know whether the forces making for a rise in the post-war period have been chiefly confined to capitalist countries in Europe and North America or whether they have operated more widely. The answer could make a difference to our interpretation of the rise in the capitalist countries themselves.

II CLASSES OF CONSIDERATIONS

Any categorisation of considerations is bound to do violence to their interrelatedness. Some attempt may none the less be helpful. The considerations will be divided among four heads.

The first two are susceptible to economic analysis of the traditional kind:

(1) The micro-theory of the optimum allocation of resources to collective consumption in total, and to its constituent parts, assuming the society's objective function to be given.
(2) The relation between collective consumption and macroeconomic trends (especially inflation) and macroeconomic policies. This theme is of concern mainly in capitalist countries.

The third and fourth considerations require an enlargement of perspectives to take account of matters that fall within the domains of political science and organisation theory:

(3) The effect of political processes of trends in collective consumption. Here too there are important differences between countries, but the distinction is not between capitalist and socialist countries as such but between types of political arrangement – the extent to which there is competition between political parties, the mode by which public opinion makes itself felt, and so on.
(4) Problems of organisation and budgeting. These problems are inherent in collective consumption. They arise from the lack of a marketed output and the consequent lack of market signals.

Of the above classes of consideration, the third and fourth – political and organisational arrangements – relate to the means by which decisions are arrived at on the substantive microeconomic and macroeconomic issues referred to under the first and second headings.

Let me take these four classes of consideration in turn.

1 THE MICRO-THEORY OF RESOURCE ALLOCATION

This has been the central contribution of formal economic analysis to decision-making on collective consumption. It is the normative approach referred to by Frey in his introduction.

The first question is why it is sensible to have collective consumption at all. This question receives particular attention at the hands of the contributors from socialist countries. They would not, I think, dispute the standard justifications cited by Boltho, externalities and paternalism, together with correction of income inequality. However they would interpret them widely. Jurković, Jašić and Lang emphasise the role of collective consumption as a platform of social solidarity. This notion is not unknown in non-socialist countries, though it is now rather out of vogue there. It was certainly present in the extension of collective consumption in Britain during the Second World War (perhaps we were a socialist country then). It is related to the equalisation of real incomes and that in turn is related to the notion that certain 'basic' needs should be provided irrespective of the consumer's income. In the same spirit, Boulding refers to collective consumption as an expression of the moral tone of society.

Western economists in writing about externalities have tended to focus on technical considerations on the production side that cause marginal costs to be low or zero or else make the transactions costs of operating a market prohibitive. By contrast, all the contributors from socialist countries regard a different kind of externality as crucial, namely the effects of collective consumption on social structure and on the minds of the people. Kapustin perhaps goes furthest in seeing the goals of society as transcending the present goals of the individuals comprising it. Adopting a broader definition of collective consumption than other contributors, Kapustin sees it as the means of changing people's attitudes and preferences in a direction deemed to be more in their interests by a higher authority. From the formal point of view there is no difficulty in incorporating such a notion of the goals of society into the social objective function that is to be maximised. To do so is somewhat alien to present-day western economics, rooted as that discipline is in the traditions of Benthamite individualism. It would have seemed less alien to Alfred Marshall – as well as to those of his contemporaries who claimed insight into the goals of the Highest Authority.

Turning from these grand matters to the determination of the optimum amount and type of collective consumption, it must be acknowledged that, although this is one of the best-developed branches of economic theory, the application of that theory in practice has been rather disappointing. Sandmo's paper points to a possible reason. He shows that, even apart from difficulties created by imperfect knowledge and by political or administrative constraints, the conclusions are likely to be complicated. This is chiefly because considerations about income distribution cannot be treated in separation from other considerations. The consequence is that the analysis has to be conducted in terms of the theory of the second best. Unfortunately, as Sandmo points out, this means that the conclusions are not as operational as they would be if they could be stated as simple rules of thumb. There is a risk of their not being operational at all. Complicated chains of reasoning are unlikely to survive the rough and tumble of the decision-making process. The question naturally suggests itself whether in this domain economics does not have some great and easily intelligible *half*-truths to offer. In their absence, a cloud of agnosticism may be generated in which any proposal seems about as tenable as any other. I raise this question without attempting to answer it.

2 MACROECONOMIC CONSIDERATIONS

These have been responsible for many of the problems about collective consumption experienced in capitalist countries since the war. In fact more trouble has arisen from this source than from the micro-problems of attaining allocative efficiency and X-efficiency that are inherent in collective consumption. In this sense it would not be true to say that the problems currently experienced with collective consumption arise from its own internal contradictions. However, the micro-problems and the macro-problems are both there and they interact with each other.

Three main points may be singled out under this heading.

(*a*) Dempster and Wildavsky suggest that Keynesian fiscal policy, by blunting the edge of traditional constraints, contributed to an undue rise in collective consumption – another example of intellectually more sophisticated rules being less effective operationally. More particularly, attempts at anti-cyclical measures led to overshooting, as suggested by Pliatzky with reference to the UK in 1970 and 1974. The recent swing away from Keynesianism towards the opposite doctrine that public spending should 'take its share' of cyclical reductions in real GNP has made for large changes in planned expenditures, thereby increasing the difficulty of developing orderly priorities and carrying out programmes efficiently.[1]

(*b*) Stabilisation policy apart, there have been swings of opinion, first in favour of collective consumption (in the days when we shared Galbraith's anxiety about public squalor amidst private affluence), latterly away from it in favour of private consumption. To judge by Hoch's remarks, the latter swing has extended from California to Hungary and to points east. It could be regarded as a (micro) change in objective functions. However, it may alternatively be regarded as an expression of a macro-phenomenon, that of aspirations outstripping capabilities. We want more than we can get, so sometimes we complain about one thing, sometimes about another. This is analogous to wage-wage inflation. The process itself generates inflation and, as Meys points out, ultimately unemployment as well. The gap between aspirations and capabilities has been widened by the check to the growth of real income brought about by the recession, which in turn has been aggravated by it.

(*c*) High and variable rates of inflation complicate any form of budgeting, creating the dilemma referred to by Pliatzky between control and planning. This would be true even if the control of public expenditure were not itself also a weapon against inflation.

I come now to the topics where the discipline of economics is least adequate on its own. These are concerned with the processes by which decisions on collective consumption are actually made and implemented.

3 THE POLITICAL DIMENSION[2]

This is the main subject of Frey's paper and it features largely also in several other contributions. In normative economics of the traditional kind, government is cast for the role of philosopher king. No profound knowledge of political science is required to recognise that this does not accord with reality. One does not need to go all the way with Boulding's

[1] It has sometimes been argued that attempts to implement Keynesian policies led, on balance, to results opposite from those intended, because of time-lags. It would be ironical, but perhaps unlikely, if the new policies turned out, for the same reason, to be stabilising by Keynesian criteria.

[2] I use 'political' in a narrower sense than Pliatzky, confining it to matters directly arising from government's accountability to the public. The interplay of ministers within a government is subsumed under the next heading.

pessimistic suggestion that politicians as such may, by virtue of their career-patterns, be systematically *less* suited to exercise power than most people. Politicians are not philosophers, because they are at least partly self-interested; and they are not kings, because the need to stay in power makes them at least partly accountable to public opinion (how accountable and by what means depending on the kind of regime). In Frey's model, politicians are utility-maximisers, like everyone else, but he does not push this hypothesis to extremes, since his politicians do have distinctive views – presumably not self-interested ones – about public policy, even if they are often not able to give effect to them. Their self-interestedness is not, in his view, a negation of democracy, because voters can choose between them. Very large issues are involved here about the extent to which political decisions can be deemed rational on the one hand and responsive to the popular will on the other.[3] These issues apply to government decisions in general, not just to those relating to collective consumption. As Dempster and Wildavsky emphasise, the realities of political pressures have to be borne in mind in defining the optimum scope of collective consumption and in defining normative rules relating to it. Politico-econometric models of the kind offered by Frey and Dempster and Wildavsky are useful in helping to understand what actually goes on. In the present state of knowledge their usefulness is perhaps chiefly illustrative, spelling out quantitatively the implications of a given model. It may be doubted whether they enable us to discriminate between fundamentally different models of how the system works. Much the same has been found of macroeconometrics generally, and it is not surprising that the problems should be aggravated by the addition of the political dimension, where the theoretical underpinnings are weaker.[4]

4 ORGANISATION AND BUDGETING

The theoretical aspects of problems of organisation and budgeting are dealt with by Leibenstein and are also touched on by Boulding, among

[3] The pure theory of voting and public choice was deliberately not included among the topics of the conference, partly because it is already the subject of a huge literature and partly because much of it pertains to a situation that is not typical of reality, namely decision of referendum on specific issues.

[4] There appears to be some difference between the findings of Frey and of Dempster and Wildavsky on the effect of imminent elections. In Frey's model they pay a large part (along with other manifestations of political insecurity), whereas Dempster and Wildavsky (p. 275) find their effects to be small.

others. The practical aspects in individual countries are dealt with by a number of contributors, including Dempster and Wildavsky, Hoch, Jurković, Jašić and Lang, Meys, and Pliatzky.

It was the original intention of the programme committee that the theoretical aspects of this topic should feature more prominently in the conference agenda than they have turned out to do.[5] I have therefore chosen to say rather more about it here than about the three classes of consideration so far discussed.

The problems concern procedural rationality, to use the terminology of Simon (1978), as opposed to the substantive rationality that is the subject of traditional welfare economics. As Leibenstein correctly points out, they are a very general group of problems. They arise in all contexts – including the internal operations of firms in the private sector – when the market (i.e. competition) does not serve as a monitor. The problems are of several kinds.

In the first place, there are *cognitive* problems. Sources of information must be devised in place of the absent market signals. Moreover, even if all the information exists, there remains a problem of attention: decision-makers simply cannot absorb in the time available all the information that would be relevant (the bounded rationality concept of Simon, 1976). These problems of information and of attention are most acute in large organisations, especially in the largest organisation of all, government.

In the second place, there is a problem of ensuring that the *motivation* of individual administrators is conformable with the goals sought by the sovereign authority.

In the third place, the *goals* of the sovereign authority itself may not be too clear. This does not necessarily imply an intellectual failure by policy-makers. The goals of many types of collective consumption (such as education, personal social services, and even to some extent defence) are by their nature diffuse and not susceptible without distortion to simple formulation. If goals are unclear or manifold, criteria of success or failure will not be plain either.

It is worth noting that there are two different reasons why these problems arise with collective consumption in a way that they do not in an idealised market system. The first is that the services offered for

[5] Leibenstein refers to the difficulty of finding a central focus in this area. It is perhaps significant that another eminent economist, who had originally intended to contribute a paper about it to the conference, had to cry off because he could not produce one that he regarded as satisfactory.

collective consumption are not marketed, so that there is a lack of feedback to the organisation about the provision of those services.[6] The second is that government is an extremely large organisation, hence a complex organisation, and there is therefore no assurance of feedback to individual bureaucrats about the contribution to organisational goals made by the decisions in which they themselves are involved. These reasons are separate. Problems of how to evaluate non-marketed services can affect quite small organisations, for example local authorities or private foundations. Problems arising from organisational size can affect businesses that supply a marketed output. However, both classes of problem occur in conjunction in the provision of non-marketed services by central government, and this is much the most important category of collective consumption quantitatively.

These problems are inherent. It is no good hankering after idealised market solutions. It is precisely because the activities in question are not well handled by markets that they are assigned to collective consumption – in just the same way as decisions are internalised to firms when the market would not handle them efficiently (Coase, 1937). Of course it is a matter for consideration in each case whether the bureaucratic failures that result from placing activities in the sphere of collective consumption may not be even worse than the acknowledged market failures. But a large residue must remain for which the market is a non-starter.

A substitute for the discipline of the market can be supplied by other forms of external pressure. In this spirit Leibenstein proposes, as do Dempster and Wildavsky, that the best way of achieving efficiency in collective consumption is the crude one of imposing a tight budget. However, this is only a qualitative guide. How tight is tight? As a substitute for the market or for the inevitably non-existent omniscient central bureaucrat, the device commonly used to arrive at a rough-and-ready approximation to an optimum is an (implicit) adversary system. The role of each programme manager is to put forward the best case he can for his programme, and the role of the finance ministry (or Congress) is to try to cut him back. This opposition does not need to imply any disagreement on fundamental goals between the actual

[6] It would not be true to say that there is *no* feedback on the provision of collective consumption, comparable to market signals. There is a 'voice', in the form of client pressure (Leibenstein) and in the case of collectively provided goods and services (though not transfers) there may be shortages and queues (Pohorille) and spill-overs to related marketed goods (Sandmo). However, these are imperfect signals.

individuals concerned. It is just a division of labour. Programme managers and finance ministry officials are both servants of government, just as the advocates on the two sides of a law-suit are both officers of the court.

Various conditions have to be satisfied if the adversary system is to work. They relate partly to the formal rules that are laid down and partly to the way discretion is exercised within them. All parties must understand the rules of the game, informal as well as formal, and abide by them. There must be a good understanding, for example, about the permissible limits to 'gaming', including what Williamson *et al.* (1975) call opportunism (the selective presentation or suppression of information). Most important of all, the two sides should be evenly balanced. Pliatzky and Meys give reasons for supposing that in much of the post-war period the dice were loaded against finance ministries, leading to an excessive upward drift in expenditure. As they point out, the reasons for this are largely political. However, there is also an inherent problem that programme managers are bound to be better informed about their programmes than finance ministries are. Hence either the finance ministries are liable to be outsmarted by the programme managers or else, if the finance ministries dig in their heels, they may through lack of information enforce an inefficient allocation of resources between and within programmes.

One way out is to retreat somewhat from the adversary principle and involve finance ministries more intimately in the planning of programmes, as in the operational activities of COBA, described by Meys. The dangers here are largely on the side of motivation: on the one hand specialised finance ministry officials may come to identify too closely with individual programmes ('go native'); on the other hand the programme managers may lose some of their sense of responsibility.

Another much more radical solution is to involve the programme managers in the task of raising their own funds, as described in the very interesting Yugoslav paper. This scheme would appear to be feasible only if the scale of operations is relatively small.

Given the difficulties of the whole business, and given too the importance commonly attached to consensus and the reluctance of programme managers to poke their noses into each other's affairs, it is not surprising that governments – and other agencies in the grants economy – often fall back on incrementalism, that is to say across the board proportional cuts or increases on last year's budget. Nobody wants to be examining everything from first principles all the time. Incrementalism is a way of avoiding that. It is the despair of the radical rationalist and it certainly does not simulate what goes on in the market sector. However, a case can be made for it, as has been done by Downs (1966), provided there are periodical opportunities for more fundamental reappraisal. Such opportunities do occur, for example when governments change or when pressures relating to a particular programme have built up to a critical point. Programmes do not all expand or contract at the same rate over the medium term. Unfortunately it is these periodical reappraisals that are most subject to the attention-constraint. Simplistic slogans can too easily dominate.

It is obvious that the decision-making process in the grants economy is an extremely rough-and-ready one. Moreover some writers, like March and Olsen (1976), view the process as being even less rational than I have described it. In their eyes, the many participants are perpetually groping in a mist of uncertainty about the facts, about causal relationships, about their own personal roles, and about the goals of their bureaus; they are prone to treat their own activities and the conservation of their bureaus as ends rather than as means; and they are subject to haphazard pressures on their time, which distract their attention and affect unpredictably the outcome on each issue. All this has a disturbing ring of truth in some contexts. It leads to conclusions resembling the Tolstoyan interpretation of history. It is, however, perhaps rather less applicable to budgeting than it is to some other government decisions, since budgeting does at least have a regular time-table imposed on it and has a similar structure from year to year.

The foregoing remarks about the organisational aspect have been written with the problems of capitalist countries chiefly in mind, because I am most familiar with them. In principle, however, they apply at least as much to socialist countries. Indeed in so far as the problems arise with any form of centralised economic decision-making, not just with collective consumption, the experience of socialist countries in attempting to resolve them is especially relevant.[7]

[7] A feature of arrangements in many socialist countries is that much of what would normally be classed as collective consumption is provided by the enterprises in which people are employed rather than by the government. The same has always been the case in Japan, and it has become increasingly so in other capitalist countries. The question of the relative merits of employer-provision and government-provision is an important one not much discussed in any of the conference papers.

III INTERACTIONS AND CONCLUSIONS

The interrelations between the above four classes of considerations are close. Political and organisational arrangements are indeed in some respects aspects of the same thing. There is no sharp distinction between politicians and administrators or between the kinds of power they wield. Countries are probably more like each other in their administrative arrangements than they are in their political arrangements, and in that respect the organisational problems are more general. It would be interesting to know whether trends in collective consumption have been systematically related to the quite considerable differences that exist between countries' political institutions – the presidential system, the parliamentary system, the two-party system, the multiparty system with coalitions, the systems prevailing in socialist countries, and so on. Boltho's data suggest a negative reply to this question as far as capitalist countries are concerned, at least regarding the trends in total expenditure.

There is nothing in the least new about the political and organisational problems in the management of collective consumption. They have been present as long as collective consumption has existed. Why then are we so much more conscious of the problems than we used to be? The reasons are to be found largely in its rapid growth: both the process of growth and the high level that has been established by it. The rapid growth itself was the result, probably, of quite deep underlying social and economic forces, rather than of accidents or organisational mishaps.

On the macro side, the high share of collective consumption in GNP gave it a new importance in demand management. The rapid growth, moreover, acquired a momentum of its own; the movement was more difficult to control than it had been when it was around a more stable trend. The result of these forces (and also partly of macroeconomic problems of independent origin) has been the curious combination of quite rapid actual rise with an atmosphere that for a good many years seemed to programme managers to be one of continual cuts. At some stages the need to prevent the growth from getting out of control became paramount and worrying about the cost-effectiveness of the expenditure seemed like straightening one's tie when the house is on fire – another example of an attention-constraint.

On the micro side, rapid growth meant that a view had to be taken on the merits of a plethora of new or expanded programmes while they were still barely under way – programmes that would probably have been difficult to evaluate at the best of times. A stable environment is required for the smooth working of 'village customs' in the government machine, to use the anthropological analogy of Heclo and Wildavsky (1974). Such an environment is present in primitive societies but was absent in the post-war Whitehall that Heclo and Wildavsky were studying.

One area where macro- and micro-problems are particularly intertwined is the time-horizon of planning and budgeting. The old tradition of a one-year horizon makes sense when circumstances and expenditure do not alter much from year to year. It scarcely makes sense otherwise. The tendency to a wedge-effect inherent in rapid growth created the need for multiyear rolling programmes. Macroeconomic instability and inflation threaten to destroy this system and to restore primacy to the annual cash flow. 'Few big businesses . . . would tolerate such a position. Indeed in exacting modern conditions they could scarcely live in a "cash in the year" position' (Vinter, 1978, p. 24).[8] As is well known, one of the chief resulting misallocations of resources is that too large a proportion of year-to-year variations tends to be borne by capital items in programmes.

The increase in the scale of collective consumption may undergo a temporary halt or reversal, but it seems most unlikely that the whole historical upward trend will go permanently into reverse. There is no need to be unduly distressed by the fact that the amount and allocation of resources to collective consumption are not within sight of being optimal, since optimality in this context is a pretty chimerical concept. However, some outcomes are a lot better than others and some procedures are a lot more rational than others. It *is* possible to get stuck in a Prisoner's Dilemma situation which everyone deplores but which no-one is able to alter. The increase in scale both increases the problems and increases the importance of solving them. This is well enough recognised in the macro-context. In the micro-context too, a large proportion of the GNP is involved, and allocative inefficiency or X-inefficiency is capable of having a correspondingly serious effect on economic welfare and on the harmony of society.

REFERENCES (other than conference papers)

Ronald H. Coase, 'The Nature of the Firm', *Economica*, N.S. 4 (November 1937), 386–405.

[8] There do of course exist businesses in the private sector which are subject to short-term variations in their cash flow that are large relative to their reserves. If things go badly, such firms become bankrupt, a course not open to a department of central government.

Anthony Downs, *Inside Bureaucracy* (Boston: Little, Brown, 1966), Chapter XX.

Hugh Heclo and Aaron Wildavsky, *The Private Government of Public Money* (London: Macmillan, 1974).

James G. March and Johan P. Olsen, *Ambiguity and Choice in Organizations* (Bergen: Universitetsforlaget, 1976).

Herbert A. Simon, *Administrative Behaviour* (New York: The Free Press, third edition, 1976).

Herbert A. Simon, 'Rationality as Process and as Product of Thought', *American Economic Review*, 68, 2 (May 1978), 1–16.

Peter Vinter, 'Public Expenditure – the Next Steps on the Road to Reform', *Lloyds Bank Review*, 130 (October 1978), 18–31.

Oliver E. Williamson, Michael L. Wachter and Jeffrey E. Harris, 'Understanding the Employment Relation: the Analysis of Idiosyncratic Exchange', *Bell Journal of Economics*, 6, 1 (Spring 1975), 250–78.

Discussion of 'Collective Consumption–an Overview of the Issues' by Mr R. C. O. Matthews

Professor Boulding introduced the discussion by pointing to the new perspective that the conference had offered on the familiar issue of budget decision-making. An examination of the total structure of grants both within and between governmental and private agencies was an important step towards the development of a more general theory of budget decisions in which all-important determinants could be treated as being endogenous. Behind much of the discussion on specific issues he detected a general concern with the problem of 'stagflation'. The inability of both market and centrally planned economies to achieve full employment and growth without accelerating inflation had created great uncertainty in all countries. The conventional wisdoms of policy seemed no longer to work and the world economy had an uncomfortable feeling of the 1920s and 1930s with adverse dynamic processes that defied both theory and policy. In his view two factors had contributed to this turmoil. The first was the well-recognised danger that counter-cyclical variations in public expenditures were in the event more likely to increase rather than reduce the amplitude of fluctuations. His view was that counter-cyclical policy should be mainly confined to tax variations. The second factor was the dependence of private employment on the difference between the rate of interest and the rate of profit. This had not emerged in recent discussions although it had been recognised by economists more than 50 years ago. When a private employer hired a worker he gave up the certainty of interest on the wage payment for the hope of profit on the capital received in exchange for the wage. When interest exceeded profit, as it did for instance in the USA in 1931 and 1932, anyone who gave employment was either a philanthropist or a fool. In recent times the rise in interest rates and the fall in profits had been the fundamental reason why governments in market economies had implemented inflationary policies; for any attempt to stop inflation without an accompanying reduction in nominal interest rates would have had catastrophic effects on employment. Thus if governments wished to stop inflation and preserve employment they must be prepared to intervene in all financial contracts in order to reduce nominal interest rates.

Professor Modigliani did not accept Professor Boulding's conclusion on the need to cut interest rates. In western economies interest on accumulated savings was the income of the poor who did not own real property. High rates of inflation had certainly reduced the real value of this income, but the answer was to reduce the rate of inflation not the rate of interest for this policy would simply make the poor poorer. *Mr Boltho* regretted that there had not been more discussion in the conference of the favourable and unfavourable effects of collective consumption on income distribution, efficiency, inflation and economic growth, which in his view were the essential considerations for policy on collective consumption.

Mr Kaser offered a wide range of points in reaction to Mr Matthew's paper and to the conference discussion which had preceded it. In his view the papers by Leibenstein, Frey, Dempster, Pliatzky and Jurković, Jăsić and Lang offered interesting comparisions on the behaviour of public good suppliers in different western economies and between western systems and a socialist system (the Yugoslav). The material for a full comparison between the different countries of the socialist group had been much more limited, although the comments by Pohorille, Khachaturov and Hoch on the paper by Jurković, Jăsić and Lang suggested that they saw the new Yugoslav system as being too decentralised to implement national economic and social policies. In his view there was no unified framework of analysis which could be applied to the problems of collective consumption in both developed and underdeveloped economies. The motivations of governments and economic relationships in the latter were quite distinctive and required special analysis. Mr Kaser noted that a comparison of the share of collective consumption in national income between western and socialist economies had not been possible because such data as had been provided for socialist economies (on the ratio of grants in kind to net material product in Hungary in the appendix to Dr Hoch's paper) used different definitions to those of the figures provided by Boltho for fifteen OECD countries (on the ratio of resource and transfer expenditures on non-defence collective consumption to GDP). He drew attention to the volume edited by Cao-Pinna and Shatalin (1979) which provided fully comparable data for five east European and three west European economies on (i) market and non-market consumption by households – 'enlarged consumption' and (ii) non-market consumption disaggregated into expenditures on (a) pure public goods (such as defence, law enforcements and foreign affairs) – 'non-divisible public consumption', and (b) marketable goods such as education and health which are provided through public sectors – 'divisible public consumption'. The definition under (b) was roughly equivalent to Boltho's definition of 'collective consumption'. A comparison of the scale of 'collective consumption' relative to total (market and non-market) consumption was shown by the opposite table from Cao-Pinna and Shatalin.

Country		Total				Per capita		
		Currency unit		*Annual growth rate, %*	*Per cent of enlarged consumption*	*Currency unit*	*Values*	*Annual growth rate, %*
France	1959		9.1		5.0		0.1	
	1965	10^9 F	14.4	9.7	4.6	10^3 F	0.3	17.5
	1969		23.0		5.0		0.5	
Italy	1959		0.4		3.1		8.3	
	1965	10^{12} L	1.3	14.9	4.9	10^3 L	25.6	14.0
	1969		1.8		4.8		30.7	
Switzerland	1960		1.2	12.6	5.2		0.2	
	1969	10^9 FS	3.5		7.0	10^3 FS	0.6	13.0
Hungary	1960		10.1		8.8		1.0	
	1965	10^9 Ft	13.3	5.8	9.5	10^3 Ft	1.3	5.2
	1968		15.8		9.3		1.6	
GDR	1960		9.4		14.7		0.5	
	1965	10^9 M	13.4	3.9	15.0	10^3 M	0.6	5.4
	1969		15.8		15.2		0.8	
Poland	1960		24.3		8.3		0.8	
	1965	10^9 Zlo	34.3	7.7	8.6	10^3 Zlo	1.1	6.4
	1969		47.2		9.2		1.4	
USSR	1960		12.3		10.5		0.6	
	1965	10^9 R	19.5	9.2	12.4	10^3 R	0.8	7.0
	1969		27.1		12.5		1.1	
Czechoslovakia[a]	1960		15.6		12.9		1.1	
	1965	10^9 CR	18.4	5.8	12.5	10^3 CR	1.3	5.6
	1968		24.4		13.2		1.7	

[a] Social benefits in kind included.
Source: Cao-Pinna and Shatalin (1979).

His view on the general question of the definition of collective consumption was that the different objectives or effects of provision required different definitions. Thus an extensive definition was required for an analysis of the macroeconomic effects of collective consumption on income, prices and employment. Narrower and different definitions were required for analyses of effects on social goals and income distribution: for the former expenditures on defence, general administration and, possibly, cash transfers should be excluded; whereas for the latter cash transfers should be included but not expenditures on pure public goods. He supported Professor Frey's arguments on the possibility of estimating the benefits of public goods (made in a comment on Professor Sandmo's paper), and referred to the results of a study on the satisfaction achieved from public goods in eastern and western economies carried out by the European Co-ordination Centre (Pitou, 1979). He was concerned that insufficient attention had been given to the influence of historical and ideological factors on the provision of collective consumption. *Professor Urquidi* insisted that the analysis of collective consumption and grants could and should be extended to include the problems of economic development. An extensive system of grants for human and physical capital formation was in his view a precondition for rapid development. *Mr Boltho* questioned the reliability of the figures cited by Mr Kaser for the ratio of 'divisible public consumption' to total consumption in Switzerland. In relation to the ratios cited for France and Italy, they were very much higher than those he knew of in other sources. *Professor Pohorille* provided additional information on the share of collective consumption in real income in socialist countries. Between 1965 and 1974, the share of social benefits in total real income rose from 29.9 per cent to 33.2 per cent in the Soviet Union and from 19.5 per cent to 23.0 per cent in Poland. The higher share in the Soviet Union was due to the greater involvement of public authorities in the provision of housing. On the question of definitions, *Professor Sir Austin Robinson* was concerned that the definition of collective consumption for use in international comparisons should recognise the insurance characteristics of collective consumption and take account of private insurance in those cases in which it was an alternative to public insurance. In many countries, a large part of public collective consumption provided insurance against misfortunes such as unemployment and ill-health. A comparison between the welfare effects of collective consumption in, for example, the United Kingdom and the United States would be misleading unless the definition allowed in some way for the fact that private health insurance was the form in which protection was arranged in the United States, and, to a much lesser extent, in the United Kingdom.

Several speakers commented on the similarities and differences that had emerged in the discussions of the provision of collective consumption in western and eastern economies. *Dr Manz* argued that collective consumption served different aims in capitalist and socialist economies. In the former the main purpose was to reduce economic inequality, whereas in socialist countries the main task was to promote personality formation and the socialist way of living. *Professor Pohorille* also stressed the differences of approach and objectives. In his view the problem of inflation was an overriding consideration in policy-making on collective consumption in capitalist economies. In socialist economies the concern was with the relationship between grants and wages and the problem of incentives, and with the effect of the organisation of consumption on social life. He regretted that there had not been a fuller discussion and explanation of the 'socialist mode of life'. In *Professor Sandmo's* view there was a wide measure of agreement between western and eastern economists on the necessity for the collective provision of pure public goods, although western theory did not give any precise indication of the required scale of provision. He conceded that there was much less agreement on the scope for the collective provision of private goods. Although western economists were generally hostile to such provision on grounds of ideology and economic efficiency, an allowance was made in the case of 'merit goods', the characteristics of which were often ill-defined. He suggested that an exploration of this concept might reveal another area of common ground between eastern and western perceptions. *Dr Stafford* suggested that common ground in this area might also be discovered in the western economic theory of private clubs. *Professors Khachaturov and Pohorille* argued that Mr Matthews' interpretation of socialist views on the nature of social welfare was incorrect. In socialist countries the well-being of society depended entirely on the welfare of individual citizens: there was no higher authority which transcended individual goals and against which they were to be judged. The wishes of the people were expressed through democratic institutions and were the ultimate criterion for policy on collective consumption in socialist countries. Professor Pohorille's view was that improvements in the pattern of consumption could be best achieved by fuller public discussion rather than by private control. *Professor Uzawa* did not think it was possible to discern the preferences of individuals either by direct observation or by theoretical inference. In his experience of rural communities in Japan, the preferences of individuals were very different from what bureaucrats and economists imagined them to be.

In *Professor Maillet*'s view an important cause of the observable increase in collective consumption in France had been the pressure from organised labour. Trade unions had realised that an increase in collective consumption was the most effective means of redistributing real income towards themselves; particularly as social security contributions fell largely on employers. *Professor Jurković* felt that, with the exception of Mr Matthews' paper, the organisational aspects and problems of collective consumption had been insufficiently stressed in the conference discussion. His view was that the inefficiency of bureaucratic systems was a powerful argument for more decentralised systems of provision in which consumers were directly and extensively involved.

Mr Matthews confined his response to the discussion to points on which there had seemed to be some uncertainty or disagreement. His view on the question of the definition of collective consumption was that there was no single definition which could serve all of the purposes and interests that had emerged in the discussion. He agreed with Mr Kaser's view that different definitions were required for analyses of the macroeconomic, distributional, allocative, and administrative aspects and effects of collective consumption. In his view the conference discussion had provided valuable insights into the importance of objectives other than economic efficiency in the provision of collective consumption. The constraints on a strategy of economic optimisation had been shown to include consensus and fairness, accountability, historical circumstances, and the authority and legitimacy of the political system through which collective consumption was provided. Thus, for example, Professor Bacskai's account of the emergence of unofficial payments in free health systems (in a comment on Dr Hoch's paper) highlighted a conflict between economic efficiency and legitimacy. In response to the comments of Professors Khachaturov and Pohorille he wished to make clear what he saw as the difference between ideas on the nature of social welfare expressed by western and socialist contributors. The impression he had formed from reading the conference papers was that, although there was no country in which individual preferences were never overridden, the areas in which paternalism was practised were more extensive in socialist countries than in western countries. This reflected the existence in socialist systems of certain principles that had been deemed immutable, at least for a given period. It was not his view that such principles were undesirable.

They were, however, out of vogue in western countries although this had not always been the case. Thus, for example, many references to the contribution of economic growth to 'the moral advancement of the people' were to be found in the writings of Alfred Marshall. He agreed with those speakers who had insisted that individual preferences were a product of social conditions and experience. He also agreed with the more general argument that the pattern and organisation of consumption was significant for the structure of society. A helpful expression of this idea was that of the social anthropologist Mary Douglas who had interpreted consumption as the language of social intercourse. In the literature of western economics such social aspects of preferences and consumption had been neglected. His final point on the comparison between western and socialist systems was that the major difference did not seem to relate to the specific problems of implementing programmes of collective consumption. Indeed it had emerged that problems such as the conflict between grants and efficiency and the issue of grants in kind and cash were common to both systems. It was the economic, political and organisational contexts in which such problems emerged and had to be tackled that constituted the major difference. He conceded that his paper had perhaps given insufficient emphasis to macroeconomic factors such as slow growth and inflation which had recently preoccupied thinking about the provision of collective consumption. However, he felt that economists and others had overreacted to the recent slump as they had overreacted to previous recessions. His view was that recent events represented a major cyclical recession, and not a major structural change which made well-established theories redundant. Finally, he referred to the difficulty of evolving a positive theory of organisational, non-market behaviour which could stand beside the theory of market exchange. It was only when such a theory had been developed that normative theoretical conclusions about organisational behaviour and the reform of institutions could be derived.

REFERENCES

V. Cao-Pinna and S.S. Shatalin (eds) (1979), *Consumption Patterns in Eastern and Western Europe: an Economic Comparative Approach* (Pergamon, Oxford).

A. Pitou (ed.) (1979), 'Les Services dans les Pays de l'Est et de l'Ouest', *Revue d'Etudes Comparatives Est-Ouest*, X, No. 1–2 (March–June 1979).

Index

Entries in the Index in bold type under the names of participants in the Conference indicate their Papers or Discussions of their Papers. Entries in italic type indicate Contributions by participants to the Discussions.